Dr. Nyangabyaki Bazaara passed away in August 2003 after a severe bout of malaria. Bazaara, as he was known to friends and colleagues, participated with the other contributors to this volume in the February 2002 meeting in Bellagio, Italy, on 'Decentralization and the Environment'. He drafted an essay for this volume, which he never completed and we are thus unable to include here. We will work with Bazaara's colleagues in Uganda to complete his essay for publication elsewhere.

Bazaara was Director of the Centre for Basic Research in Kampala, Uganda. He was the leader of the Uganda research programme on 'Decentralisation and the Environment' which was part of the Africa-wide comparative-research effort that fed into the Bellagio meeting from which the contributions in this volume were selected. Bazaara's ideas and his spirit can be felt throughout this volume. Bazaara was a thinker and scholar, a musician, patron of the arts, positive-spirited man and a mentor to many. He remains present among us through all those he has touched with his generosity, kindness, enthusiasm and intelligence. This volume is dedicated to his memory.

THE EUROPEAN JOURNAL OF
DEVELOPMENT RESEARCH

Volume 16 Number 1 Spring 2004

Democratic Decentralisation through a Natural Resource Lens

Experiences from Africa, Asia and Latin America

Edited by

Jesse C. Ribot and

Anne M. Larson

A FRANK CASS JOURNAL
Member of the Taylor & Francis Group

THE EUROPEAN JOURNAL OF DEVELOPMENT RESEARCH

Journal of the European Association of Development Research and Training Institutes (EADI)

Articles appearing in this journal are abstracted and indexed in *EconLit*, *CSA Political Science & Government*, *International Political Science Abstracts*, *International Development Abstracts*, *Geographical Abstracts: Human Geography and GEOBASE*, *British Humanities Index*, *Applied Social Sciences Index and Abstracts*, *The International Bibliography of the Social Sciences*, *Sociological Abstracts*, *PAIS* and *Studies on Women Abstracts*.

Manuscripts and editorial correspondence should be sent to **Susanne von Itter**, The European Journal of Development Research, European Association of Development Research and Training Institutes (EADI), Kaiser-Friedrich-Strasse 11, D-53113 Bonn, Germany. Email: ejdr@eadi.org. **Books for review** should be sent to **Morten Bøås**, Fafo – Institute for Applied International Studies, Borggt. 2B, PO Box 2947 Tøyen, 0608 Oslo, Norway.

Subscriptions and advertising inquiries should be sent to *The European Journal of Development Research* at the address given below.

Annual subscription:	Institutions **£170/$265** postage included
Volume 16	Individuals **£48/$68** postage included
	Single issue and back issue prices available from the publisher

Published in March, June, September and December

4 Park Square, Milton Park, Abingdon OX14 4RN, UK
Tel.: + 44 (0)1235 828600; Fax: +44 (0)1235 829000; Email: enquiry@tandf.co.uk
Website: www.tandf.co.uk/journals

Printed in Great Britain by Antony Rowe Ltd., Chippenham, Wiltshire

Contents

The online version of this journal is hosted by Metapress. ***taylorandfrancis.metapress.com***

For details of past and future contents of this and our other journals, please visit our website at *www.tandf.co.uk/journals*

This special issue of *The European Journal of Development Research* is available in book form as *Democratic Decentralisation through a Natural Resource Lens: Experiences from Africa, Asia and Latin America*. ISBN 0 4153 4786 6.

Books Reviewed

EADI gratefully acknowledges the generous support of NORAD which has enabled the Association to distribute copies of the *EJDR* free of charge to institutes in the Third World.

EADI – the European Association of Development Research and Training Institutes – is a Europe-wide network of institutes, researchers, and students of various disciplines in the field of development studies. EADI offers facilities for the international exchange of knowledge and experience in the professional field. The association was founded in 1975 and is an independent and non-profit-making international non-governmental organisation. Its Secretariat is based in Bonn, Germany. Membership presently covers 170 institutional and 200 individual and student members in 28 European countries.

EADI's objectives are:

- to generate and stimulate exchange of information among European scientists and researchers concerned with development issues;
- to promote interdisciplinary studies on specific themes;
- to develop contacts with researchers from other regions of the world.

Members take part in thematic working groups which organise conferences, seminars, research projects and publish their results in the EADI Book Series and the EADI Newsletter. Twice yearly, EADI publishes its academic journal, the *EJDR – The European Journal of Development Research.* Its most prominent activity is a General Conference devoted to a topical theme every three years. EADI is part of ICCDA – Inter-regional Coordinating Committee of Development Associations and an active partner of CIC – Centre for International Cooperation Bonn.

European Association of Development
Research and Training Institutes (EADI)
Kaiser-Friedrich-Strasse 11
53113 Bonn
Tel.: +49 228 26 18 101
Fax: +49 228 26 18 103
Email: postmaster@eadi.org
www.eadi.org

Democratic Decentralisation through a Natural Resource Lens: An Introduction

ANNE M. LARSON and JESSE C. RIBOT

I. INTRODUCTION

Decentralisations have taken place around the world over the past century [*Ribot, 1999*]. Since the mid-1980s, however, decentralisation has become a truly global movement, affecting most developing countries [*UNCDF, 2000: 5–11; World Bank, 2000; Totemeyer, 2000; Dillinger, 1994; Therkildsen, 1993; Fisher, 1991*]. Governments have decentralised for multiple political–economic, social and ideological reasons, and often with the support and pressure of aid agencies [*Ribot, 2002b*]. At least 60 countries now claim to be decentralising some aspect of natural resource management [*Agrawal, 2001*]. The language of decentralisation has changed in this most recent set of reforms [*Ribot, forthcoming*]. Earlier reforms emphasised national cohesion, effective rule and the efficient management of rural subjects [*Buell, 1928; Mair, 1936; Mamdani, 1996*]. In contrast, the most recent decentralisations are introducing a new emancipatory language of democracy, pluralism and rights. Wollenberg, Edmunds and Anderson [*2001*], Anderson, Clement and Crowder [*1998*], Alden Wily [*2000a, b*], Meinzen-Dick and Pradhan [*2000*] and Utting [*1999*]

Anne M. Larson is a Research Associate at the Center for International Forestry Research and Nitlapán Institute for Research and Development, Managua, Nicaragua. Jesse C. Ribot is a Senior Associate at the Institutions and Governance Program, World Resources Institute (WRI), Washington, DC. They are indebted to the Rockefeller Foundation for providing the funds and an inspiring venue for the conference at Bellagio, at which the papers in this volume were first presented. They wish to express their thanks to: the Africa Bureau of USAID for funding much of the background research for the Africa contributions to this project and for supporting many of the Bellagio participants; Jon Anderson at the Africa Bureau of USAID for encouraging critical thinking, policy research and outreach on governance issues at the frontier between environment and democracy; David Kaimowitz at the Center for International Forestry Research (CIFOR) in Bogor, Indonesia, for contributing CIFOR's experience and in-depth research to the Bellagio meeting by generously financing several CIFOR participants, and for supporting the research behind the Latin American cases in this volume; the South Africa office of the Ford Foundation for generously supporting the final stages of this publication; Judy Butler for diligent copy-editing; Catherine Benson for logistical support; and Peter G. Veit at WRI for being supportive of this project throughout. They also acknowledge the key role of the anonymous peer reviewers.

European Journal of Development Research, Vol.16, No.1, Spring 2004, pp.1–25
ISSN 0957-8811 print
DOI:10.1080/0957881041000168870

point out that natural resource management is moving toward more democratic and rights-based premises.[1] Indeed, most countries are labelling their decentralisations 'democratic'.

While a mix of factors and forces shape decentralisation, most decentralisation theorists and policy makers argue that reforms are done for developmentalist reasons. They justify decentralisation reforms on the grounds that the increased efficiency, equity and inclusion that should arise from decentralisation result in better and more sustainable management [*Smoke, 2000; Manor, 1999; Crook and Manor, 1998; Mawhood, 1983; Uphoff and Esman, 1974; UNDP, 1999*]. Some focus on its political and economic advantages, arguing that decentralisation plays important roles in the following: democratisation and people's participation [*Crook and Manor, 1998; Ribot, 1996; Mbassi, 1995: 23; Rothchild, 1994: 1*]; rural development [*Uphoff and Esman, 1974: xx; UNDP, 1999; Helmsing, 2001; Roe, 1995: 833; De Valk, 1990; Ribot, 2002b*]; public service performance [*World Bank, 2000: 107*]; poverty alleviation [*Crook and Sverrisson, 2001: iii*]; relief of fiscal crisis [*Olowu, 2001; Menizen-Dick and Knox, 1999: 5*]; political and macroeconomic stability [*World Bank, 2000: 107; Prud'homme, 2001: 14*]; national unity and state building [*Conyers, 2000: 7; Mamdani, 1996; Bazaara, 2002, 2003; Muhereza 2003*]; and helping to increase the legitimacy of government [*Ribot, 2002a, b*].

Is this tidal wave of decentralisation discourse being legislated into appropriate laws and implemented in practice? What are its effects on the ground? This volume queries the state and effect of this movement through the lens of natural resource decentralisations. The contributions in this special issue use a comparative framework to characterise the degree to which natural resource decentralisations can be said to be taking place and, where possible, to measure their social and environmental consequences. The contributions, except for that of Meynen and Doornbos, which came to our attention later, are a subset of the papers presented at the 'Workshop on Decentralization and the Environment', held in Bellagio, Italy, 18–22 February, 2002.[2] The purpose of this workshop was to consolidate the findings of research on decentralisation and natural resources from around the world.

This volume includes case studies from Africa (Cameroon and South Africa), Asia (Indonesia, Mongolia, China and India) and Latin America (Nicaragua, Brazil and Bolivia), which address the management of water, land, forests or pasture. In addition to the particular theoretical or practical concerns of each author, the comparative framework guiding the case studies focuses attention on 1) the extent to which central governments have decentralised authority over natural resources to local governments or other sub-national entities, 2) the relations between these local-level entities and the population, and 3) the effects of these processes on local peoples and natural resources [*see Ribot, 2001*]. This introductory essay also draws on other cases presented at Bellagio and those available in the broader literature.

Actors, Powers and Accountability: An Analytic Starting Point

By definition, decentralisation involves the transfer of power from the central government to actors and institutions at lower levels in a political–administrative and territorial hierarchy [*Mawhood, 1983; Smith, 1985; Agrawal and Ribot, 1999*]. The mechanism through which theorists believe that efficiency and equity should increase is by public decisions being brought closer and made more open and accountable to local populations [*Oyogi, 2000; Smoke, 2000; Manor, 1999; Mawhood, 1983*].[3] For this to happen, several authors argue that some form of downwardly accountable local representation is necessary [*Ribot, 1995; Smoke, 2000; Agrawal and Ribot, 1999*]. Through broad-based local input and influence, decentralisation brings local knowledge into the decision-making process, which should result in better-targeted policies and reduced information and transaction costs [*World Bank, 1997*]. Other authors argue that local participation in decision making makes people more likely to have a sense of 'ownership' of those decisions [*see Ostrom, 1990; Hirschman, 2003*], such as rules for resource use. Because of this 'ownership' ostensibly they will provide better information and be more engaged in implementing, monitoring and enforcing such rules. In addition, marginalised groups could have greater influence on local policies because of the open nature of decision-making, thus increasing equity. [*Smoke, 2000*; *Carney, 1995; Kaimowitz et al., 1998; Margulis, 1999; Ostrom, 1990.*]

The transfer of power from central to local authorities has taken administrative and political forms. Administrative decentralisation, or deconcentration, of public services – transfers of power to local administrative bodies – aims to help line ministries, such as health, education, public works and environment, to read the preferences of local populations and to better mobilise local resources and labour. Political or democratic decentralisation integrates local populations into decision-making through better representation by creating and empowering representative local governments. Democratic decentralisation is premised on new local institutions 1) being representative of and accountable to local populations and 2) having a secure and autonomous domain of powers to make and implement meaningful decisions [*Ribot, 2002b*].

Deconcentration is a weaker form of decentralisation than is democratic decentralisation since the mechanisms by which deconcentrated decision-makers are responsive and accountable to local populations are weaker [*Ribot, 2002a*]. If efficiency and equity benefits arise from the democratic processes which encourage local authorities to serve the needs and desires of their constituents [*Smoke, 2000; Crook and Sverrisson, 2001*], then democratic decentralisation should be the most effective form of decentralisation. With regard to natural resources, however, democratic decentralisation has proven difficult to find, and the results of existing policies are highly varied.

The actors, powers and accountability framework [*Agrawal and Ribot, 1999*] provides an important tool for analysing the type and extent of decentralisation in a specific country. In particular, it considers 1) the powers, and accompanying resources, actually transferred to lower-level actors to determine whether an autonomous domain of decision making actually exists around issues of local significance; and 2) the local-level entities receiving powers and their relation to the population in order to understand the extent to which these are both representative of and downwardly accountable to local peoples.

This volume, however, illustrates that the type and extent of decentralisation is not the only relevant factor in understanding how local actors will use their new powers or what outcomes these will have for local people and resources. The way in which decentralisation is implemented as well as the economic context associated with each particular natural resource, for example, also affect the kinds of choices that are made by local decision makers. Central governments can also make an important difference through their overall commitment to implementation, local capacity building and social equity for marginal actors. Grass roots and donor pressures for change strongly influence central government commitment or resistance to decentralisation. At the local level, at least four factors affect decision-making: the overall capacity of the decision-making body, local power relations, the incentive structure for resource management, and environmental and social ideology [*Larson, 2003a; see also Larson, 2002*].

Natural Resources: A Lens on Decentralisation Dynamics

The contributions in this volume interrogate decentralisation through the lens of natural resources, which the contributors have found to be a sharp optic for insights into decentralisation writ large – not just into natural resource management and use [*Kaimowitz and Ribot, 2002*]. This optic is particularly powerful since natural resources differ from other sectors in ways that augment and throw into relief decentralisation's potential and risks as a lever for local democratisation and development. Natural resources are at once critical for local livelihoods (subsistence and income generation) and are also the basis of significant wealth for governments and national elites. As such they have historically been a point of struggle between rural people and these elites.

With decentralisation, natural resource transfer is a great opportunity for increasing the relevance of local authorities to local people, yet it is simultaneously a threat to central authorities and elites who fear loss of income or patronage resources. For example, there has been considerable political conflict and resistance associated with the redistribution of power and resources that, by definition, accompanies decentralisation [*see Larson, Ntsebeza, Cousins and Kepe, all this volume; Peluso, 2002; Ribot and Oyono, forthcoming*]. Nevertheless, given their local importance and historical local uses and claims, local knowledge and input are highly relevant to their management – making them good candidates for decentralised management and use. The evidence from these and other essays, however, shows that threats to national-level interests are producing resistance which is fettering the struggle for reform.

Some Central Problems in Decentralisation – or Decentralising Problems?

Several observations concerning decentralisations that involve natural resources emerge from essays in this volume. First, the democratic decentralisation of natural resource management is *barely happening*. All of the case studies in this issue highlight problems with – or central government resistance to – power transfers to local entities and/or problems with the downward accountability of the local entities receiving powers [*see Bazaara, 2002; Kassibo, 2002; Peluso, 2002*]. Second, democratic decentralisation of natural resources appears to be more fully developed where local people and/or local governments have had at least partial success in *mobilising to demand greater authority* [*see Larson, Oyono, Pacheco, Resosudarmo, Meynen and Doornbos, Baviskar, all this volume; see also Kassibo, 2002*]. Third, the essays all demonstrate that the outcomes of these partial, blocked and hybrid decentralisations are *highly varied*, both among and within countries, and the cases begin to explain some of the reasons for those differences [*see Ribot, 2001*].

Greater local participation in decision making or, at the very least, a better understanding of local needs and desires and the incorporation of these into government programs, are key aspects of decentralisation theory [*Ribot, 1996; Crook and Manor, 1998; Agrawal and Ribot, 1999*]. Yet, just as decentralisation in practice is not always what central governments and donors purport it to be, this volume also brings into question the claims of ‘participation’ [*see also Mosse, 2001; Hirschmann, 2003*]. This volume shows that ‘participation’ – whether through elected authorities, co-management, committee-based management, or ‘traditional’ authorities – usually looks like a modern reproduction of indirect rule (that is, a means for managing labour and resources) [*Ribot, 1995, forthcoming*]. It does not reflect the enfranchisement that participation and decentralisation discourses – through empowered downwardly accountable representation – promise. Resosudarmo [*2002*] has astutely labelled some of these new co-management arrangements ‘co-administration’: a form of deconcentration where elected local authorities are used by central government and donors as local administrators to implement outside agendas.[4] Participatory processes, however, can also be positive, particularly as an instrument for identifying and including poor and marginalised people in decision-making [*Mansuri and Rao, 2003; Edmunds and Wollenberg, 2003*]. Participatory methods, then, can be important tools for enhancing the inclusiveness of democratic processes. Given their limits and proneness to abuse, though, participatory methods should not be used in ways that compete with or substitute for nascent democratic processes.

Downward accountability of leaders to citizens is the substantive essence of democracy [*Moore, 1998*]. It is the mechanism by which decentralisations are supposed to secure participation, even when representative, elected local governments tend to have a poor record in terms of serving women, the poor and other marginalised populations – unless required to do so by central government [*Crook and Sverrison, 2001*]. Nevertheless, elected local authorities appear to be the most systematic means of broad-based inclusion. However, the essays in this volume indicate concerted resistance even to establishing this basic level of local democracy. Central governments are choosing upwardly accountable institutions to receive decentralised powers or responsibilities as part of their strategy to maintain central control over natural resources [*Ribot, 2003*]. In the names of 'pluralism' and 'civil society', development institutions and non-governmental organisations (NGOs) appear to be choosing to transfer powers to less-than-democratic 'traditional' authorities, committees and local NGOs, either due to a naive populism, an uncritical acceptance of everything 'indigenous', or an anti-government stance inherited from the Thatcher revolution [*Ribot and Oyono, forthcoming*].[5] The convergence of these anti-democratic tendencies is causing a potentially destructive proliferation of local institutions [*see Ntsebeza, Manor, both this volume; Namara and Nsabagasani, 2003*], which – in turn – is creating competition with fledgling local democratic institutions and undermining their powers and legitimacy. This dynamic also appears to be fragmenting local identities – away from residency-based citizenship and identification with local government as a positive force and toward more divisive ethnic- and lineage-based forms of belonging [*Geschiere, 2003, forthcoming; Ribot, forthcoming*].

Yet, downward accountability of local authority is not the only accountability relation that matters. Central government must be downwardly accountable to local elected authorities for effective decentralisations. Local governments need services from central government – such as expertise, heavy machinery, financial support and market access. Central government also has responsibility for clarifying laws, mediating major disputes, and providing guidelines and means to assure the inclusion of marginal groups. There must be mechanisms for local representatives to hold higher-level bureaucrats accountable to them [*Ntsebeza, this volume; Xu and Ribot, this volume*]. Xu and Ribot [*this volume*] imply that in China local authorities cannot achieve downward accountability of higher-level government since the only level of democratic government is the most local; these elected authorities have little leverage over higher-level authorities. Holding the state accountable means having a real counter power in the local arena – indeed, accountability itself can be defined as counter power [*see Agrawal and Ribot, 1999*]. It may mean having democratic institutions at higher levels (whether this is at intermediate levels of decentralised authority or in state and national legislatures [*see Veit, forthcoming*]) – and there does appear to be a need for multiple channels of influence over the state. It also means local governments must be sufficiently strong, politically organised and federated, and backed by real popular demand for their political and technical functions. Local popular demand for decentralisation must also be enabled and fostered [*see, in this volume, Larson; Oyono; Pacheco; Resosudarmo; Meynen and Doornbos*].

Furthermore, for the state to play a supportive role, central government also needs to be strong [*see, in this volume, Cousins and Kepe; Meynen and Doornbos; Resosudarmo; see also Ribot, 2002b*]. Although the downsizing of government – through structural-adjustment policies – has often led to decentralisation policies, there is no contradiction between a strong state and decentralisation. Decentralisation should strengthen both central and local government. It is not about dismantling the state in order to replace it with local democratic sovereigns. It is about creating local democracy that can build legitimate states and governments – writ large – by playing the inclusive and democratic role that many of us hope governments can play and which are the foundation of democratic systems. Decentralisation is about bringing the state back in, but this time as a positive and legitimate democratic institution.

Decentralisations are not working as some theories suggest. The essays in this volume illustrate that this 'failure' is partly because of the fact that decentralisations are not being implemented, but is also due to the factors that democratic decentralisation theories cannot or do not account for. Most decentralisation theory stems from a mix of new institutionalist 'if-then' propositions: if the institutions (that is, actors, powers and accountability) are right, then the outcomes will be positive. We cannot yet say whether these 'if-then' propositions are right, because, for many reasons, decentralisations are not getting to 'if' [*see Ribot, forthcoming*]. The failure to establish decentralisations – the failure to get to 'if' – is partly due to the practical complexities of implementation, to factors external to the models, to the multiple and alternative motives behind power transfers to the periphery when they do happen,[6] and to the larger political economy in which attempts at these institutional changes are embedded [*see Larson, 2003b*]. When factors outside of the models dominate outcomes, it is time to rethink those models or to systematically locate them in a broader political economy [*see Cousins in Latif, 2002*].[7]

The degree of decentralisation and its outcomes are shaped by many factors: local capacities; incentive structures; ideologies; political and social histories; forms of local social organisation; degrees of local stratification; unresolved land and forest tenure relations; failure to account for time and insecurities (and often retrenching) produced by change; the strength and manipulations of elite actors; state and government resistance; and government, NGO and development agency commitment to 'traditional' or private and third-sector institutions over democratic authorities. Moreover, decentralisations are often implemented with the primarily instrumental goals of intervening agencies, such as improving environmental management, pacifying local opposition or meeting donor demands, rather than as a complex, integral political project. Unfortunately, the commitment to democratisation and popular participation may be minimal or secondary. Whether it is due to practical difficulties of reform, government resistance strategies or the naive populism of development agents and NGOs, non-implementation takes several forms and can still be, at least partly, measured against the models that are used to justify these reforms. Models help us to recognise decentralisation when we see it: we know they are not being implemented because governments transfer inadequate *powers* to *actors* who are not *accountable* to local populations.

II. THE ESSAYS IN THIS VOLUME

Each essay in this volume is discussed below with an eye to highlighting the newest insights.

Amita Baviskar's essay throws into relief the often-seen chasm between decentralisation discourse and practice. In Baviskar's case study of Madyha Pradesh, India, the chasm is produced by the contradiction between procedural participatory objectives of decentralisation and the instrumental objectives of donor programs [*see also Shivaramakrishnan, 2000*]. Donors pre-specify the objectives that local people are supposed to adopt as their own – or 'participate in' – while creating incentives for project managers to achieve these objectives through specific success indicators. In Baviskar's case, this development formula made a watershed management project into a theatre where successful participation and ecological improvement were performed for the donor audience. The performance was enabled by separating participation from power – that is, by using or creating representative structures but locating real decision making elsewhere. In this case, structures of representation and participation are well crafted, but project decisions are made by project personnel who must perform successfully and are accountable to their bosses to demonstrate success through overly specified indicators of preconceived outcomes.

Baviskar shows the process by which donor-required success is manufactured, how the local elite and project managers participate and benefit, and how the ecology and well being of the population remains unchanged. To avoid delays and the 'politics' of the *panchayat* (elected local government), the administrators, in collaboration with local elite farmers, circumvent the committees and the inconvenience of local democracy [*see also Ferguson, 1994*], avoiding the 'politics' that are the heart of democratic decentralisation [*see also Manor, this volume*]. In short, Baviskar points out that project and funding imperatives and the incentives they create for administrators can lead projects to undermine the very processes they purport to be supporting [*see also Mosse, 2001; Hirschmann, 2003; Vivian and Maseko, 1994; Kassibo, 2002*]. The need to identify such 'successes' subverts any real attempt at building longer-term, locally rooted and locally accountable institutional processes.

Ben Cousins' and Thembele Kepe's contribution describes a 'decentralised' natural resource management initiative in South Africa's Wild Coast that also purports, but fails, to promote local participation and empowerment. In spite of its accompanying rhetoric, the Spatial Development Initiative (SDI) in Mkambati fails to establish the kind of decentralisation that would make local participation possible. Instead of working through democratic local authorities, decision-making powers remain centralised or are given to elite actors unaccountable to local people. Democratic participation is minimal, hence the local realities of resource use never enter the decision-making processes, and local institutions that frame resource access, rights and conflicts are marginalised. The case reflects how the disenfranchising of people through the disabling of democratic processes disenfranchises their local experience, knowledge and institutions. As the authors argue, prospects for development interventions to integrate successfully with the lived realities of local peoples would be significantly enhanced if they were based on locally accountable institutions that effectively represent local understanding, needs and aspirations [*see also Oyono, this volume*].

The Mkambati case also illustrates the destructive confusion that arises when privatisation is done in the name of decentralisation [*see also Johnson and Forsyth, 2002*]. Privatisation is not decentralisation – its accolades are attributed to its exclusive logic rather than the inclusive logic that is behind the efficiency and equity benefits of decentralisation [*Ribot, 2002b*]. The two are often conflated since decentralisation and privatisation are both possible routes to state downsizing. Yet decentralisation is about strengthening local government – something that these and other authors point out is also enhanced by the presence of a strong and dedicated central state [*see also Meynen and Doornbos, this volume; Xu and Ribot, this volume; Ribot, 2002b*]. While privatisation is an option for powers pried from central governments under dominant and widespread neo-liberal economic policy – including structural adjustments – it is not the only option.

In the Makambati case, privatisation through 'outsourcing' facilitated elite capture by providing 'opportunities for opportunists'. Prospects for local democratic institutions to contribute to development were further undermined as local political and business elites harnessed development committees (set up for popular 'empowerment') for personal accumulation [*see also, in this volume, Manor; Baviskar; Oyono*]. Furthermore, this privatisation was undertaken in a context of deep social conflict, and both privatisation and elite capture were met with disputes and resistance – undermining the project itself. Without local input into decisions and the fair resolution of deep-seated land-tenure disputes, for example, projects like the SDI in Mkambati are doomed. Strong central intervention may be needed to apply new decentralisation laws and help clarify conflictual land-tenure arrangements.

Anne Larson's essay encourages us to explore the ways in which decentralisation is leveraged from below. Definitions of decentralisation usually refer explicitly only to the formal, legal process of power and resource redistribution as designed and implemented by central governments. As we see in many of the cases in this volume, central governments resist institutionalising the formal structures necessary for local participation and democracy to flourish. Larson argues from the Nicaraguan experience that formal decentralisation needs grass-roots demand to overcome central resistance [*see also, in this volume, Baviskar; Meynen and Doornbos*]. In Nicaragua, as the formal structures have been put in place, local capacity to make demands has increased, the political power and legitimacy of local governments has grown, and central leaders have begun to see political advantages in making local government allies – which makes them more amenable to furthering the formal process, and so on. Larson refers to the local dynamic – whereby local leaders make decisions, with or without formal decentralised authority, in a context of increasing local legitimacy – as decentralisation 'from below'.

Moreover, Larson argues that natural resources are particularly amenable to decentralisation from below, at least in part because they are already physically located in the local arena, and within a particular history and tradition of everyday resource use and management [*see also Kaimowitz and Ribot, 2002*]. Local leaders, however, may be more likely to ignore natural resources and concentrate on the service and infrastructure investments that many consider to be their top development priority, or they may only be interested in resource exploitation as an economic opportunity. Like central governments, though, local governments respond to grass-roots pressure from constituents [*see also Brannstrom, this volume; Gibson and Lehoucq, 2003; Larson and Ferroukhi, 2003*], who increasingly turn to their local elected officials to address resource-related problems and conflicts. Effective and responsible decentralised natural resource management will arise, therefore, from a dynamic process involving decentralisation not only from above but also from below. Decentralisation reforms from above create the infrastructure of participation by broadening opportunities for people to influence government. Decentralisation from below is when people use that infrastructure along with other channels of political leverage to seize and realise the new opportunities.

However, demand cannot come from below when people are subject to arbitrary authority. Lungisile Ntsebeza's essay is about tension between 'traditional' chiefs and local democracy where contradictory laws recognise both. Due to their historical relevance to local populations, traditional leadership is often celebrated as being a more legitimate or appropriate recipient of decentralised land decisions than are elected local authorities [*see also, for example, Oyono, this volume*]. But conflicts over a new system of land administration in post-apartheid South Africa illustrate that some chiefs are not downwardly accountable. Drawing on Mamdani [*1996*], Ntsebeza argues that rural residents who are dependent on hereditary traditional leadership are not citizens, but subjects. Though some traditional leaders promote local participation, leaders who cannot be selected – or removed – by constituents have only limited downward accountability. Ntsebeza argues that democracy should be both participatory and representative, and that rural citizenship requires that the South African government return to its commitment to create and support democratically elected local governments.

Ntsebeza's South African case also highlights the importance of central government accountability to local authorities and the complexities of transition. Ntsebeza shows that higher-level governments must also be accountable to lower level elected authorities [*see also Xu and Ribot, this volume*]. Local government needs the support of central government to carry out its functions and to gain local people's confidence. In Transkei, rural South Africa, central government administrators failed to even acknowledge local government in their constitutionally sanctioned role in land allocation and integrated rural planning. The failure of elected local government to perform this role undermined the authority of local representatives and forced local residents to turn back to tribal authorities for access to basic resources – although many residents would have preferred to work with their elected authorities. Because central authorities do not support new local governments, apartheid-era laws remain in force. Furthermore, the failure to resolve conflicting authority over land has led to a breakdown of old resource management systems – also largely under the authority of traditional leaders – without the clear establishment of new ones. The resulting state of confusion and insecurity leads to an absence of rules and an 'open access' problem for natural resources. Similar concerns affect Mongolia and Indonesia [*see Mearns, this volume; Resosudarmo, this volume*].

Pablo Pacheco's contribution provides a detailed study of Bolivia, where significant forest management responsibilities have been decentralised to local governments. It shows that local governments have been given powers to allocate forest resources to local populations, and central authorities have provided these local authorities with technical support. In contrast, most of the outcomes observed in the essays presented in this volume are often not the outcomes of democratic decentralisation but rather of hybrids, deconcentration, privatisation, or partial, poorly designed or highly circumscribed decentralisation. Nevertheless, there is enough evidence to indicate that, under the right circumstances, the theory can hold true: democratic decentralisation can improve efficiency, equity, democracy and resource management [*see also Ferroukhi, 2003; Larson, 2003a; Ribot, 2002a, forthcoming*].

Bolivia's decentralisation, although more advanced than others in Latin America, is, however, only partial. Though some powers are being transferred in Bolivia, like other cases in this volume, local-government decision making, and access to and control of benefits from the forestry sector, is still limited and circumscribed by government controls. Furthermore, despite authorities being elected locally, downward accountability remains highly problematic [*see also Resosudarmo, this volume*]. Pacheco points out that the structure of elections – particularly party involvement – does not foster downward accountability [*see also Ribot, 1996, 1999, 2002b; Larson and Ferroukhi, 2003*]. Outcomes associated with Bolivia's decentralisation are highly diverse – both positive and negative for local populations and for the forest. Pacheco finds that whether outcomes improve the lot of marginal people or reinforce asymmetries of local power relations in favour of the elite depends on the degree to which authorities are accountable to local constituents. The involvement of elected authorities in forest management is a function of the degree of local livelihood dependence on the resource.

Ida Adu Pradnja Resosudarmo and Robin Mearns describe decentralisations in Indonesia and Mongolia that cannot be understood in isolation from other sweeping national reforms occurring simultaneously. The rapid transition from strong, authoritarian central government to more decentralised, democratic structures has led to what is – hopefully – a temporary breakdown of each nation's natural resource management systems. In the midst of the crisis of change, the rules of natural resource governance are highly vulnerable to insecurity, particularly where resources are valuable – as in Indonesia – or under common property management – as in Mongolia. In Indonesia, where central authority included violent repression, decentralisation has mirrored central behaviour, fostering violence [*see also Peluso, 2002*].

Resosudarmo's contribution highlights the importance of the historical context for understanding the response of local governments and citizens to new opportunities such as those offered by decentralisation. In Indonesia, 30 years of authoritarian central government ended in political and economic crisis in the late 1990s. Citizens in the Outer Islands in particular deeply resented years of marginalisation and, above all, ongoing exclusion from the lucrative timber trade. When political reforms finally began, local governments scrambled to find new sources of income to assert their political autonomy from central government. Logging contracts became one of those sources, leading to the proliferation of small-scale contracts. In the reforms, central government transferred to lower-level governments the rights to a significant portion of the income and the power to allocate harvesting and use in areas of up to 100 hectares of highly lucrative forest resources. The result has been a substantial increase in logging with little regard for environmental consequences, as local people and governments take advantage of a new income-generating opportunity. Resosudarmo attributes over-exploitation to insecurity and a lack of confidence that these new local rights will last – especially since central authorities have already tried to re-concentrate some of these powers.

Resosudarmo, moreover, also shows that local authorities have only limited downward accountability to the population, since the popular vote is restricted to the election of a political party list rather than individual candidates chosen locally – as is true in most developing countries; this is a major problem for decentralisations [*see also Pacheco, this volume*].[8] While local people have benefited to some degree from new access to forest resources, the primary benefits have not gone to those who need them most. The Indonesia case highlights the importance of downward accountability as well as the need for a balance of powers between central and local authorities in periods of decentralisation. It highlights the danger of decentralisation that happens too fast and with almost no central-government supervision and the dangers of reactionary re-centralisation threats that increase insecurity.

Mearns' contribution illustrates similar problems in Mongolia. At present, decentralisation in Mongolia's pasture management is structured as deconcentration, as the local authorities being given management powers are not elected but rather appointed by the central government; elected local authorities have little power and almost no fiscal resources. In the case of Mongolia, ambiguous authority and power transfers make it unclear which rules take precedence in determining who grazes where and when. As a result, it is increasingly common for the herders themselves to make unilateral decisions. While the passage of time – which should lead to the gradual consolidation of new institutions – may be an important part of the solution to these problems, Mongolia's pastures could benefit from greater transparency and downward accountability of those with resource-management powers – including public participation in land management decisions and greater clarity in terms of the definition and use of those powers.

Furthermore, Mearns argues that for pastoralists in Mongolia, incomplete or 'empty' decentralisation has increased social differentiation and vulnerability, and led to an 'open-access' crisis of the commons. Transfer of responsibilities to local levels of government constituted a withdrawal of the state, rather than decentralisation. Without the devolution of fiscal resources or means for holding local authorities accountable, Mongolia's post-socialist transition produced increased need – in the form of unemployed urban labourers who returned to the countryside to herd – and a provision vacuum – in the form of unfinanced and unaccountable local government. This effective disengagement of the central state resulted in: increased vulnerability for pastoralists; increased social vulnerability as the newer, less-experienced and least socially connected herders failed and dropped out of herding; and the reconfiguration of grazing patterns with profound consequences for the pastoral environment. Poorer herders remained close to settlements, which led to overstocking, while vast more-distant areas remained underused due to the lack of investment in water supply, transport infrastructure and service provision – all resulting from the fiscal constraints on local government.

Jianchu Xu and Jesse Ribot's essay shows how the provincial government of Yunnan, China undermines its tentative moves toward decentralised forest management by continuing to allow powerful central policy makers to implement far-reaching decisions that affect peoples' livelihoods without any local participation or accountability. The provincial government's fairly weak decentralisation efforts are completely overshadowed by drastic top-down measures that have severely undermined local livelihoods by limiting economic alternatives in the interest of protecting forests and watersheds. These higher-level authorities have failed to account for livelihood needs in their conservation-oriented decisions. The essay implies that because the democratic part of decentralisation involves only the lowest level of political administration – the 'administrative village', there are no democratic mechanisms in place to hold higher-level government offices downwardly accountable to the local elected administrative village heads or to the local population. Because of this, decentralisation remains limited. The essay also suggests that this downward accountability of higher-level authorities will be essential to establishing effective democratic decentralisation and bringing indigenous people's livelihood concerns into decisions [*see also Ntsebeza, this volume; Cousins and Kepe, this volume*].

Phil René Oyono's contribution emphasises the sociological context of decentralisation initiatives, arguing that decentralisation does not lead to automatic benefits but must be implemented in such a way that reinforces democratic practices and social responsibility. Even where systems are established for elected committees with local leaders to receive important decision-making powers, as in Cameroon, the results may not benefit either local peoples or the forest. Rather, in spite of committee elections, some local leaders do not represent local peoples' interests but rather are establishing themselves as a new local elite, as we have seen in several cases. Not all communities are able to demand or enforce the downward accountability of their leaders. In contrast with Nstebeza's contribution discussed above, Oyono argues that the failure of this new local leadership is partly related to the marginalisation of traditional leaders, who have greater legitimacy but have been left out of this process. In addition, many local villagers – as well as these new forestry committees – believe it is time to get their 'fair share' from the forest, and support rapid and extensive logging to increase local revenues. This is in part because of the history of forest centralisation and elite exploitation in Cameroon and because decentralisation has been implemented as an administrative procedure with purely instrumental managerial interests rather than as a value-laden package for good governance and resource management in the common interest.

James Manor's contribution outlines a major shift in the local institutional basis of the current decentralisation movement. The first wave of the current movement, in the 1980s, transferred powers to multi-purpose (hence integrative) local governments. In recent years, however, international donors and central governments are increasingly turning toward single-purpose user committees. Manor argues that donors see user committees as a mechanism to give local peoples greater say over the development decisions that affect them. Central government officials, however, establish user committees at the insistence of donors but then manipulate them to their own ends by limiting their downward accountability – through the selection of committee members – and by reigning in their powers and jurisdiction [*see also Baviskar, this volume*].

While Manor argues that these committees are less democratically accountable and less representative than local government, they are often justified in the name of keeping politics out of what are purported to be 'scientific' or 'technical' decisions [*see also Baviskar, this volume; Ferguson, 1994*]. Yet, as Manor (and Baviskar [*this volume*]) makes evident, keeping politics out of decision making is far from the central government's intention – which is simply to maintain its own hegemony. Besides, politics is not to be avoided – as if it could be – as an inconvenience; rather, it should be embraced as the mechanism by which local preferences and needs are registered, integrated and responded to.

Manor's contribution emphasises how these proliferating single-purpose committees are undermining the democratic processes that were presumably institutionalised with the creation and strengthening of elected local governments in Third World countries.[9] Grass-roots participation is fragmented, reducing its coherence and effectiveness, and the poor may even be worse off than before. Fundamentally, these user committees, which tend to be 'over-funded' when compared to under-funded, elected, multi-purpose local government bodies, generate confusion over the division of responsibilities, usurp local-government functions and deprive local governments of revenues [*see also Ribot, 2002b*]. These myriad problems result in destructive conflicts and the undermining of local-government authority. Ironically, governments, donors and NGOs – in the name of participation and democracy – are undermining democracy through the naivety of their actions, their failure to recognise the eminently political nature of decentralisation, and, in some cases, their effort to destroy local democratic processes. Manor suggests that the solution is to place local committees under the authority of elected local governments [*see also Ribot and Oyono, forthcoming; Blair, 2000*].

Christian Brannstrom's essay focuses on larger-scale, single-purpose watershed management committees that encompass multiple local jurisdictions (what Ostrom, Schroeder and Wynn [*1993*] call 'special districts'). Territories of elected political institutions are rarely contiguous with larger ecologically defined watershed or forest zones. Their jurisdiction is often too small for the scale on which these resources require management. As such, integrated management of these resources poses a challenge for decentralisation. Usually, these larger-scale resource zones are managed by technical ministries of the central state. Some countries, such as Bolivia, Honduras and Nicaragua, are approaching decentralised management of such resources by creating federations or consortiums of local governments [*Larson, 2003c; Pacheco, 2003; Vallejo, 2003*]. In other places, new jurisdictions are created with elected authorities in order to govern such specially defined ecological districts [*Ostrom, Schroeder and Wynn, 1993*].

In Brazil, other alternatives have been tried. Brannstrom compares three different committee-based approaches to watershed resource management in the three Brazilian states. In spite of the presence of local governments (as a minority of members) on two of the regional (catchment-scale) committees, the author argues that all three cases represent decentralisation largely to upwardly accountable actors. Unlike Manor, who argues that elected local governments are critical for user-committee accountability and democracy, Brannstrom argues that only in the state that mandated the inclusion of *civil society* representatives on the water resources committee was there a degree of downward accountability. He presents evidence that civil society groups exerted significant pressure on other members to be downwardly accountable and played an important role in opening debate on controversial water issues and in organising water user groups. Obviously, the civil society and local government approaches are not mutually exclusive. Brannstrom also points out that local governments tend to demand short-term political returns on their decisions, whereas other groups may have longer-term horizons. Brannstrom emphasises that decentralisation is most productive when the state creates new ways to pry open government to multiple influences and to find ways for local government and civil society to work together.

Brannstrom's essay also indicates some important limits to civil society approaches. In the case where civil society organisations were committee members, there were no organisations representing shantytown dwellers or water consumers. The government did, however, organise small farmers into associations to include them in decision making – indicating that central government can play a role in assuring broad-based inclusion, especially of marginal segments of the population [*see also Crook and Sverrison, 2003*]. Brannstrom makes the further point that although NGOs may be able to hold government accountable, it remains unclear what or whom these NGOs represent [*see also Manor, this volume; Ribot, 2002a*]. In addition, Brannstrom points out that the committee in São Paulo became the focus for grass-roots activists, 'who previously would have lobbied individual municipal governments or bureaucratic headquarters'. This is another illustration of Manor's [*this volume*] point that these committees take powers and relevance away from elected local governments [*see also Ribot, 2002a, b, forthcoming*]. Inclusion of 'civil society' institutions in public decision making can certainly be a positive force – but it probably does not hurt to keep it in check via dependence on representative authorities [*Manor, this volume; Blair, 2000*].

Wicky Meynen and Martin Doornbos's essay articulates the often unstated conceptual differences and policy objectives regarding decentralisation and natural resource governance, which often give rise to conflicting institutional arrangements that are not compatible with democratic decentralisation or sustainable resource management. In particular, the authors argue that the same donor agencies often promote, on the one hand, market liberalisation and privatisation of natural resources for commercial exploitation and decentralisation, and on the other hand, popular participation and community-based approaches to enhance subsistence strategies. While it is not clear that donor agencies in fact view local participation through decentralisation as limited to defending subsistence interests, this essay elucidates the problems that can arise when different priorities, power struggles and inaccurate conceptions of 'the local' result in a mixture of contradictory policies at the national level and conflicting institutional arrangements locally.

Drawing on examples from India in particular, Meynen and Doornbos demonstrate the following responses to decentralisation: active state opposition to devolving power and resources; conflicting relations among state agencies, local user groups and local elected officials; intra-village conflicts over new boundaries; and selective privatisation and other forms of exclusion that discriminate against marginal groups. While similar problems are apparent in many of the essays, this essay is particularly useful because of the way in which the authors link these institutional outcomes to unresolved conceptual contradictions. For effective democratic decentralisation, the authors highlight the importance of a strong central state [*see also Cousins and Kepe, this volume*], particularly for redressing inequalities and resolving conflicting or exclusionary natural resource management initiatives, and flexible implementation in order to address diverse local realities. Fundamentally, however, they argue that decentralisation will continue to be fraught with contradictions unless there is organised and effective civil society pressure combined with countervailing global forces that would fundamentally reverse current priorities.

III. WAYS FORWARD/RESEARCH AGENDA

The first step forward from the current impasses would be to implement the decentralisation experiment. This might involve identifying the appropriate powers to transfer (and those to keep central) and building the kinds of representative, locally accountable institutions that make decentralisation effective. It would involve opening *public* dialogues with governments, development institutions, NGOs and local communities on which powers should be public and which private, and which central and which local [*see Larson, 2003b, 2003d*]. It would involve public dialogue on the implications of the mix and hierarchy of local institutions that governments, development agencies and NGOs are choosing to work with and on the constitution of representation in the local arena. Promoting local enfranchisement through decentralisation will also involve thinking through the timing and sequencing of reforms to reduce uncertainties and the shocks of change, and giving the experiment time to take root. Decentralisation should, if established, also create multiple channels of influence that grass-roots movements and individuals can use to discipline the authorities who wield power over them; such influence is a key part of the production of citizenship. Yet citizens also need civic education to know that they have channels of influence, and they also must learn to exercise the powers that are available. Testing democratic decentralisation will most certainly also involve developing effective strategies for avoiding elite capture and for countering government resistance to dialogue and change at every turn.

Baviskar's contribution to this issue indicates three arenas in which the link between the people and the state can be opened. First, strong grass-roots organisation, particularly of subaltern groups, is imperative to overcome central government resistance to democratic decentralisation. Where local people are unable or unwilling to make demands on state administrators or even on their own elected committee members or local governments, they become collaborators in the charade of decentralisation – even more so when they participate in corruption, help manufacture the charade of success and/or benefit economically from it. Second, she suggests the importance of understanding the complex history of relations between the state and local populations in order to understand the furthering of such collaboration. Third, she points out the need for researchers and other third parties to take a closer look at decentralisation processes and publicise their findings as another important accountability mechanism. Research has an important role to play in identifying positive alternatives and in 'raking the muck' to force governments and development agencies to act according to their promises.

Further research will help us to clarify where decentralisations are falling short, where they are moving forward to produce positive outcomes and how we can leverage productive change.[10] Some research needs to focus on seemingly technical matters. For example, better subsidiarity principles are needed to guide the choice of powers – to identify which should remain public, which can serve society best when privatised, and to indicate which belong at each level of the political-administrative hierarchy. Such research could then feed into the public dialogues mentioned above. Institutional choices also require guidelines and public debate. More research is needed on the implications of local institutional proliferation, inter-institutional relations, arrangements of nesting and hierarchy, and mechanisms of inter-institutional accountability. More must be understood also about the scale of institutions and how to match larger ecological scales of management to political-administrative districts without undermining fledgling local democratic institutions. Additional work is also needed on how 'rights-based' approaches [*see Johnson and Forsyth, 2002*] and minimum-standards approaches (also about establishing a domain of local freedoms) [*Ribot, 2002b, forthcoming*] can enhance the domain of discretion, the powers, the effectiveness and ultimately the legitimacy of local democratic authorities.

As Martin Luther King [*1963*] said, 'freedom is never voluntarily given by the oppressor; it must be demanded by the oppressed'. Further research is needed to understand how local people come to demand representation and services. To what degree is local mobilisation a matter of producing empowered and representative local authorities that people feel they have a reason to influence, and to what degree is it about civic education, political organising or even rebel rousing? How do people become engaged as citizens rather than managed as subjects? Of course, while technical criteria can be produced to guide decentralisations, ultimately decentralisations are always political and therefore require public engagement and debate. That debate can be effectively informed by good research on the many factors that appear to shape the establishment of decentralisation and its outcomes. It can also be informed by research on the views of local people, which are often excluded from public debate. Research can shed light on the local legitimacy of different government and non-government regimes, on the preferences and desires of local people and on the structures that exclude these perspectives from public discourse.

Finally, we need to use what we are learning to produce new theories, models and analytic approaches that can help us locate the micro- and macro-structures of decentralisation in a larger political economy of state formation, governmentality, popular movements, resistance and counter resistance. The stomping out of fledgling democratic institutions prescribed by democracy theorists and democratic decentralisation advocates alike is a political problem. It is no wonder that democratic decentralisation as a political solution is threatening many actors and facing widespread resistance.

NOTES

1. It is important to note that the language of rights and enfranchisement was also present in earlier decentralisations. So, this is not a complete change, but rather democratisation and rights issues emerge more frequently in this round [*see Mair, 1936*]. It should be taken as a cautionary note that the earlier decentralisations, which went under such titles as 'indirect rule', were not emancipatory reforms [*Ribot, 1999*].
2. The minutes for this meeting can be found on the World Resources Institute website at http://www.wri.org. See Latif [*2002*].
3. According to the World Bank, decentralisation should improve resource allocation, efficiency, accountability and equity 'by linking the costs and benefits of local public services more closely' [*World Bank, 1988*]. Local governments are in a better position to know the needs and desires of their constituents than national governments, while at the same time it is easier for constituents to hold local leaders accountable [*World Bank, 2000*]. Decentralisations are also expected to promote democracy by 'bringing the state closer to the people', increasing local participation and building social capital [*World Bank, 1997*].
4. Similarly, the use of uncompensated local labour in the name of participation is another common practice; Ribot [*1995*] called this practice 'participatory corvée'.
5. Nevertheless, it is also important to recognise that there are some very real concerns about the accountability as well as capacity of more 'democratic' structures, such as local elected governments. We believe, however, that the short-term gains that may be made by circumventing them only serve to undermine democratic processes in the long term. It is also important to recognise that traditionally marginalised populations, such as indigenous groups, peasants and women, will probably need direct interventions in their favour in order for their livelihoods to improve, whichever type of decentralisation is implemented. See Edmunds and Wollenberg [*2003*].
6. When real power transfers take place to the periphery, it is usually due to economic crisis, political crisis, successionist movements or conditionalities from international donors. In exceptional cases, as in Kerala State in India, it has occurred due to ideological commitment to decentralisation and popular participation [*see Ribot, 2002b*]. Bazaara [*2002*] and Muhereza [*2003*] have argued that decentralisation in Uganda, which is publicly justified on the grounds of efficiency, equity and democracy, is actually about the resolution of fiscal and political crises.
7. As Cooper [*1993: 89*] commented, if the 'model treats the most important problems as exogenous factors to be invoked to explain why things do not work out correctly, perhaps the model and exogenous factors should change places'. Yet, it is important when making such changes not to throw out what the models have to offer. We may be able to keep the 'if-then' propositions while querying the problems of getting to 'if'.

8. For notable exceptions, see the cases of Mali and Uganda [*Kassibo, 2002; Bazaara, 2002, 2003*].
9. In a WRI-organised workshop on 'Decentralization and the Environment' held in Cape Town in March 2001, Agrappinah Namara and Dr. Nyangabyaki Bazaara presented arguments on what they called 'the committee effect' in Uganda. They noted the proliferation of committees and many of its negative effects – including the creation of a professional class of committee members.
10. For an extensive research agenda on democratic decentralisation, see Ribot [*2002b*].

REFERENCES

Agrawal, A., 2001, 'The Regulatory Community: Decentralization and the Environment in the Van Panchayats (Forest Councils) of Kumaon, India', *Mountain Research and Development*, Vol.21, No.3, pp.208–11.

Agrawal, A. and J. Ribot, 1999, 'Accountability in Decentralization: A Framework with South Asian and African Cases', *Journal of Developing Areas*, Vol.33, pp.473–502.

Alden Wily, L., 2000a, *Democratic Woodland Management in Eastern and Southern Africa: What's Happening?* Mimeo (later published as Drylands Issue Paper No.99, London: IIED).

Alden Wily, L., 2000b, *Sharing Products or Power? Intentions, Meanings and Approaches to Community Involvement in Forest Management in East and Southern Africa*, draft paper, mimeo, 7 Nov.

Anderson, J., J. Clément and L. Van Crowder, 1998, 'Accommodating conflicting interests in forestry: Concepts emerging from pluralism', *Unasylva*, Vol.49, No.194, pp.3–10.

Bazaara, N., 2003, *Decentralization, Politics and Environment in Uganda*, Environmental Governance in Africa Working Paper No.7, Washington: Institutions and Governance Program, World Resources Institute, Jan. 2003; available at http://www.governance.wri.org/publications. cfm.

Bazaara, N., 2002, 'Actors, Powers and Environmental Accountability in Uganda's Decentralisation', Paper presented at the Conference on 'Decentralization and the Environment', 18–22 Feb., Bellagio, Italy; available at http://www.governance.wri.org/publications.cfm.

Blair, H., 2000, 'Participation and Accountability at the Periphery: Democratic Local Governance in Six Countries', *World Development*, Vol.28, No.1, pp.21–39.

Buell, R.L., 1928, *The Native Problem in Africa*, Vols.1–2, New York: Macmillan.

Carney, D., 1995, 'Management and Supply in Agriculture and Natural Resources: Is Decentralization the Answer?' *ODI Natural Resource Perspectives*, Vol.4, June, pp.1–4.

Conyers, D., 2000, 'Decentralisation: A Conceptual Analysis (Parts 1 and 2)', *Local Government Perspectives: News and Views on Local Government in Sub-Saharan Africa*, Vol.7, Nos.3/4, pp.7–9, 13, 18–24.

Cooper, F., 1993, 'Africa and the World Economy', in Fredrick Cooper, Florence E. Mallon, Steve J. Stern, A.F. Isaacman and W. Roseberry (eds.), *Confronting Historical Paradigms: Peasants, Labor, and the Capitalist World System in Africa and Latin America*, Madison, WI: University of Wisconsin Press, pp.84–204.

Crook, R.C. and J. Manor, 1998, *Democracy and Decentralization in South-East Asia and West Africa: Participation, Accountability and Performance*, Cambridge: Cambridge University Press.

Crook, R.C. and A.S. Sverrisson, 2001, *Decentralization and Poverty-Alleviation in Developing Countries: A Comparative Analysis or, is West Bengal Unique?* IDS Working Paper 130, Brighton: Institute of Development Studies, University of Sussex.

De Valk, P., 1990, 'State, Decentralization and Participation', in P. de Valk and K. Wekwete (eds.), *Decentralizing for Participatory Planning: Comparing the Experiences of Zimbabwe and Other Anglophone Countries in Eastern and Southern Africa*, Aldershot: Avebury Press, pp.62–84.

Dillinger, W., 1994, *Decentralization and Its Implications for Urban Service Delivery*, Urban Management Program Discussion Paper No.16, Washington, DC: The World Bank.

Edmunds, D. and E. Wollenberg (eds.), 2003, *Local Forest Management: The Impacts of Devolution Policies*, Bogor, Indonesia: CIFOR.

Ferguson, J., 1994, *The Anti-Politics Machine: "Development", Depoliticization, and Bureaucratic Power in Lesotho*, Minneapolis, MN: University of Minnesota Press.

Ferroukhi, L., 2003, *Gestión Forestal Municipal en América Latina*, mimeo.

Fisher, M.H., 1991, *Indirect Rule in India: Residents and the Residency System, 1764–1858*, New Delhi: Oxford University Press.

Geschiere, P., 2003, 'Autochthony and the Struggle over Citizenship: New Modes in the Politics of Belonging in Africa and Elsewhere', Draft discussion paper for SSRC, July 2003, mimeo.

Geschiere, P., forthcoming, 'Ecology, Belonging and Xenophobia: The 1994 Forest Law in Cameroon and the Issue of "Community"', in H. Englund and F.B. Nyamnjoh (eds.), *Rights and the Politics of Recognition in Africa*, mimeo.

Gibson, C. and F. Lehoucq, 2003, 'The Local Politics of Decentralized Environmental Policy', *Journal of Environment and Development,* Vol.12, No.1, pp.28–49.

Helmsing, A.H.J., 2001, *Local Economic Development: New Generations of Actors, Policies and Instruments*, Summary report for the UNCDF Symposium on 'Decentralization and Local Governance in Africa', Cape Town, South Africa, 26–30 March, New York: UNCDF.

Hirschmann, D., 2003, 'Aid Dependence, Sustainability and Technical Assistance: Designing a Monitoring and Evaluation System in Tanzania', *Public Management Review*, Vol.5, No.2, pp.225–44.

Johnson, C. and T. Forsyth, 2002, 'In the Eyes of the State: Negotiating a "Rights-Based Approach" to Forest Conservation in Thailand', *World Development*, Vol.30, No.9, pp.1591–605.

Kaimowitz, D. and J.C. Ribot, 2002, 'Services and Infrastructure versus Natural Resource Management: Building a Base for Democratic Decentralization', Paper presented at the Conference on 'Decentralization and the Environment', 18–22 Feb., Bellagio, Italy; available at http://www.governance.wri.org/publications.cfm.

Kaimowitz, D., C. Vallejos, P. Pacheco and R. Lopez, 1998, 'Municipal Governments and Forest Management in Lowland Bolivia', *Journal of Environment and Development*, Vol.7, No.1, pp.45–59.

Kassibo, B., 2002, 'Gestion participative et décentralisation démocratique – Étude de cas: La gestion de la forêt du Samori dans la commune de Baye Région de Mopti (Mali)', Paper presented at the Conference on 'Decentralization and the Environment', 18–22 Feb., Bellagio, Italy; available at http://www.governance.wri.org/publications.cfm._

King, M.L., 1963, 'Letter from Birmingham Jail', 16 April; http://www.almaz.com/nobel/peace/MLK-jail.html.

Larson, A., 2003a, 'Decentralization and Forest Management in Latin America: Toward a Working Model', *Public Administration and Development*, Vol.23, No.2, pp.211–26.

Larson, A., 2003b, 'Local Governments and Forest Management in Central America: Conceptions of Decentralization in National Context', Paper presented at the 'Open Meeting of the Human Dimensions of Global Environmental Change Research Community', International Science Planning Committee, Montreal, Canada, 16–18 Oct.

Larson, A., 2003c, 'Gestión forestal municipal en Nicaragua: Descentralización de cargas, centralización de beneficios?' in L. Ferroukhi (ed.), *Gestión Forestal Municipal en América Latina*, Bogor, Indonesia: CIFOR/IDRC.

Larson, A., 2003d, 'Mejores prácticas para la gestión descentralizada de los recursos forestales en Centroamérica', Report to the SIDA-IDB Partnership, 20 June.

Larson, A., 2002, 'Natural Resources and Decentralization in Nicaragua: Are Local Governments Up to the Job?' *World Development*, Vol.30, No.1, pp.17–31.

Larson, A. and L. Ferrouhki, 2003, 'Conclusiones', in L. Ferroukhi (ed.), *Gestión Forestal Municipal en América Latina*, Bogor, Indonesia: CIFOR/IDRC, pp.213–33.

Latif, M., 2002, 'Minutes of the World Resources Institute Conference on Decentralization and the Environment', Bellagio, Italy, 18–22 Feb.; available at http://www.governance.wri.org/publications.cfm.

Mair, L.P., 1936, *Native Policies in Africa*, New York: Negro University Press.

Mamdani, M., 1996, *Citizen and Subject: Contemporary Africa and the Legacy of Late Colonialism*, Princeton, NJ: Princeton University Press.

Manor, James, 1999, *The Political Economy of Democratic Decentralization*, Washington, DC: The World Bank.

Mansuri, G. and V. Rao, 2003, 'Evaluating Community Driven Development: A Review of the Evidence', First draft report to Development Research Group, The World Bank, Feb., mimeo.

Margulis, S., 1999, 'Decentralized Environmental Management, Decentralization and Accountability of the Public Sector', in S.J. Burki and G.E. Perry (eds.), *Annual World Bank Conference on Development in Latin America and the Caribbean*, Washington, DC: The World Bank.

Mawhood, P., 1983, *Local Government in the Third World*, Chichester: John Wiley.

Mbassi, J.P. Elong (ed.), 1995, *La décentralisation en Afrique de l'Ouest*, Report of the Conference on 'Decentralization in West Africa', Ouagadougou, 5–8 April, Cotonou, Benin: PDM and CEDA.

Meinzen-Dick, R. and A. Knox, 1999, 'Collective Action, Property Rights, and Devolution of Natural Resource Management: A Conceptual Framework', Draft paper for workshop, 15 July, mimeo.

Meinzen-Dick, R. and R. Pradhan, 2000, *Implications of Legal Pluralism for Natural Resource Management*, Paper presented at the workshop on 'Institutions and Uncertainty', IDS, Brighton, 6–8 Nov., mimeo.

Moore, M., 1998. 'Death Without Taxes: Democracy, State Capacity, and Aid Dependency in the Fourth World', in G. White and M. Robinson (eds.), *Towards a Democratic Developmental State*, Oxford: Oxford University Press.

Mosse, D., 2001, '"People's Knowledge", Participation and Patronage: Operations and Representations in Rural Development', in Bill Cooke and Uma Kothari (eds.), *Participation: The New Tyranny?* London: Zed Books, pp.16–36.

Muhereza, F.E., 2003, *Environmental Decentralization and the Management of Forest Resources in Masindi District, Uganda*, Environmental Governance in Africa Working Paper No.8, Washington: Institutions and Governance Program, World Resources Institute, Feb.; available at http://www.governance.wri.org/publications.cfm.

Namara, A. and X. Nsabagasani, 2003, *Decentralization and Wildlife Management: Devolving Rights or Shedding Responsibility? Bwindi Impenetrable National Park, Uganda*, Environmental Governance in Africa Working Paper No.9, Washington: Institutions and Governance Program, World Resources Institute, Feb.; available at http://www.governance.wri.org/publications.cfm.

Olowu, D., 2001, *Local Political and Institutional Structures and Processes*, Summary report prepared for the UNCDF Symposium on 'Decentralization and Local Governance in Africa', Cape Town, South Africa, 26–30 March, New York: UNCDF.

Ostrom, E, 1990, *Governing the Commons: The Evolution of Institutions for Collective Action*, Cambridge: Cambridge University Press.

Ostrom, E., L. Schroeder and S. Wynne, 1993, *Institutional Incentives and Sustainable Development: Infrastructure Policies in Perspective*, Boulder, CO: Westview.

Oyugi, W.O., 2000, 'Decentralization for Good Governance and Development', *Regional Development Dialogue*, Vol.21, No.1, pp.3–22.

Pacheco, P., 2003, 'Municipalidades y participación local en la gestión forestal en Bolivia', in L. Ferroukhi (ed.), *Gestión Forestal Municipal en América Latina*, Bogor, Indonesia: CIFOR/IDRC, pp.19–56.

Peluso, N., 2002, 'Some Questions about Violence and Decentralization: A Preliminary Exploration of the Case of Indonesia', Paper presented at the Conference on 'Decentralization and the Environment', 18–22 Feb., Bellagio, Italy; available at http://www.governance.wri.org/publications.cfm._

Prud'homme, R., 2001, *Fiscal Decentralization and Intergovernmental Fiscal Relations*, Summary report for the UNCDF Symposium on 'Decentralization and Local Governance in Africa', Cape Town, South Africa, 26–30 March, New York: UNCDF.

Resosudarmo, I.A.P., 2002, 'Closer to People and Trees: Will Decentralization Work for the People and the Forests of Indonesia?' Paper presented at the Conference on 'Decentralization and the Environment', 18–22 Feb., Bellagio, Italy; available at http://www.governance.wri.org/publications.cfm.

Ribot, J.C., forthcoming, *Democratic Decentralization of Natural Resources: Encountering and Countering Resistance*, Washington, DC: World Resources Institute.

Ribot, J.C., 2003, 'Democratic Decentralization of Natural Resources: Institutional Choice and Discretionary Power Transfers in Sub-Saharan Africa', *Public Administration and Development*, Vol.23, No.1, pp.53–65.

Ribot, J.C., 2002a, *Democratic Decentralization of Natural Resources: Institutionalizing Popular Participation*, Washington, DC: World Resources Institute.

Ribot, J.C., 2002b, *African Decentralization: Local Actors, Powers and Accountability*, Democracy, Governance and Human Rights Working Paper No.8, Geneva: UNRISD and IDRC.

Ribot, J.C., 2002c, 'Workshop on Decentralization and the Environment: Assessing Participation for Rio+10', Workshop Concept Paper, Feb. 2002, Bellagio, Italy, World Resources Institute; available at http://www.governance.wri.org/publications.cfm; also in Latif [*2002*].

Ribot, J., 2001, 'Some Concepts and a Proposed Framework for Contributions', Concept paper for the Workshop on Decentralization and the Environment: Assessing Participation for Rio+10, The Rockefeller Foundation Bellagio Study and Conference Center, 18–23 February 2002. Paper prepared 28 August 2001.

Ribot, J.C., 1999, 'Decentralization, Participation and Accountability in Sahelian Forestry: Legal Instruments of Political-Administrative Control', *Africa*, Vol.69, No.1, pp.23–65.

Ribot, J.C., 1996, 'Participation without Representation: Chiefs, Councils and Forestry Law in the West African Sahel', *Cultural Survival Quarterly*, Vol.20, No.1, pp.40–44.

Ribot, J.C., 1995, 'From Exclusion to Participation: Turning Senegal's Forestry Policy Around', *World Development*, Vol.23, No.9, pp.1587–99.

Ribot, J.C. and René Oyono, forthcoming, 'Resisting Democratic Decentralization in Africa: Some State and Elite Strategies for Holding onto Power', in B. Wisner and C. Toulmin (eds.), *Toward a New Map of Africa*, London: Earthscan Press.

Roe, E.M., 1995, 'More than the Politics of Decentralization: Local Government Reform, District Development and Public Administration in Zimbabwe', *World Development*, Vol.23, No.5, pp.833–43.

Rothchild, D., 1994, *Strengthening African Local Initiative: Local Self-Governance, Decentralisation and Accountability*, Hamburg: Institut für Afrika-Kunde.

Shivaramakrishnan, K., 2000, 'Crafting the Public Sphere in the Forests of West Bengal: Democracy, Development and Political Action', *American Ethnologist*, Vol.27, No.2, pp.431–61.

Smith, B.C., 1985, *Decentralization: The Territorial Dimension of the State*, London: George Allen.

Smoke, P., 2000, 'Fiscal Decentralization in Developing Countries: A Review of Current Concepts and Practice', in Y. Bangura (ed.), *Public Sector Reform, Governance and Institutional Change*, Geneva: UNRISD.

Therkildsen, O., 1993, 'Legitimacy, Local Governments and Natural Resource Management in Sub-Saharan Africa', in H.S. Marcussen (ed.), *Institutional Issues in Natural Resources Management*, Occasional Paper No.9, Roskilde Denmark: The Graduate School of International Studies.

Totemeyer, G., 2000, 'Decentralization for Empowerment of Local Units of Governance and Society: A Critical Analysis of the Nambian Case', *Regional Development Dialogue*, Vol.21, No.1, pp.95–118.

UNCDF, 2000, 'Africa: Decentralisation and Local Governance Conference Concept Paper', Prepared for the UNCDF Symposium on 'Decentralization and Local Governance in Africa', Cape Town, South Africa, 26–30 March, New York: UNCDF, mimeo.

UNDP, 1999, *Taking Risks: United Nations Capital Development Fund*, New York: UNDP.

Uphoff, N.T. and M.J. Esman, 1974, *Local Organization for Rural Development: Analysis of Asian Experience*, Special Series on Rural Local Government Paper No.19, Rural Development Committee, Ithaca, NY: Cornell University.

Utting, P. (ed.), 1999, *Forest Policy and Politics in the Philippines: The Dynamics of Participatory Conservation*, mimeo (later published by UNRISD and Ateneo de Manila University Press, Quezon City, Philippines, 2000).

Vallejo, M., 2003, 'Gestión forestal municipal: una nueva alternativa para Honduras', in L. Ferroukhi (ed.), *Gestión Forestal Municipal en América Latina*, Bogor, Indonesia: CIFOR/IDRC, pp.57–88.

Veit, P.G., forthcoming, *Serving Constituents, Servicing Nature: Legislative Representation and Natural Resource Politics in Africa*, Washington: Institutions and Governance Program, World Resources Institute, mimeo.

Vivian, J. and G. Maseko, 1994, *NGOs, Participation and Rural Development: Testing the Assumptions with Evidence from Zimbabwe*, UNRISD Discussion Paper No.49, Geneva: UNRISD.

Wollenberg, E., D. Edmunds and J. Anderson, 2001, 'Pluralism and the Less Powerful: Accommodating Multiple Interests in Local Forest Management', *International Journal of Agricultural Resources, Governance and Ecology*, Vol.1, Nos.3/4, pp.199–222.

World Bank, 2000, *Entering the 21st Century: World Development Report 1999/2000*, Oxford: Oxford University Press.

World Bank, 1997, *World Development Report*, New York: Oxford University Press.

World Bank, 1988, *World Development Report*, New York: Oxford University Press.

Between Micro-Politics and Administrative Imperatives: Decentralisation and the Watershed Mission in Madhya Pradesh, India

AMITA BAVISKAR

I. INTRODUCTION

The principle of decentralised management of natural resources has gained considerable legitimacy among policy makers and practitioners in India [*Kolavalli and Kerr, 2002*]. Since the 1990s, legal and administrative provisions have facilitated the creation of new participatory institutions for managing degraded forests, branch canals and micro-watersheds. In some cases, however, the consensus in development circles about the virtues of decentralisation has created a curious paradox, leading to a situation where centralised strategies are employed to demonstrate the 'success' of decentralisation. In this essay, I examine the Watershed Development Mission in the state of Madhya Pradesh in central India in order to argue that the pressure to show tangible results, combined with the bureaucratic imperative to retain control, has subverted the decentralised structure of resource management. Project and funding imperatives have helped to undermine the very processes that they purport to support, such that neither the goal of ecological restoration nor social justice is achieved. At the same time, decentralised management is not simply empty rhetoric that can be dismissed as a top-down, donor-driven discourse. Instead, it is based on existing political networks and transactions between the state government and villagers, and its success or subversion depends on their active collaboration. What does decentralisation actually accomplish and for whom? I attempt to answer this question by drawing attention to the differentiated nature of village communities as well as state bureaucracies operating under historical conditions of structured inequality. This essay argues that villagers and lower-level bureaucrats bring diverse agendas and perspectives to bear on development projects, co-opting newly created institutions of decentralised

Amita Baviskar is a Ciriacy-Wantrup Fellow at the Institute of International Studies, University of California at Berkeley. The author would like to thank Anne Larson and Jesse Ribot for their detailed comments on this essay, as well as the two anonymous reviewers.

European Journal of Development Research, Vol.16, No.1, Spring 2004, pp.26–40
ISSN 0957-8811 print
DOI:10.1080/09578810410001688716

management and assimilating them into ongoing individual and collective projects of social survival and gain. In conclusion, I suggest some directions for analysis and action that may help to make the new structures and processes of resource management more accountable to their members.

II. MADHYA PRADESH AND THE WATERSHED MISSION

The Area and People

This essay is based on a larger study conducted in Jhabua district, Madhya Pradesh (MP),[1] an area notorious as being drought-prone and poverty-stricken. Jhabua has a history of a sharply fractured polity, where the tribal population of Bhil and Bhilala *adivasis* (Scheduled Tribes) has been dominated by a bureaucracy of caste-Hindus and a trading class of caste-Hindus and Muslims. According to the 1991 census, 86 per cent of Jhabua's population belongs to the Scheduled Tribes. The MP Human Development Report 1998 notes that 75 per cent of Jhabua's population lives below the poverty line. The literacy rate for rural Jhabua is 14 per cent, with rural female literacy at seven per cent. The infant mortality rate in rural Jhabua is 130 per thousand live births. The average life expectancy is 51 years. Only about nine per cent of the district's agricultural land is irrigated [*GoMP, 1998a*].

Jhabua's landscape, once described by the distinguished environmentalist Anil Agarwal as a moonscape, is semi-arid, undulating terrain, where *adivasis* customarily supplement the small plots of farmland that they legally own with *nevad* (literally, new field) clearings in the forest. Since *nevad* is carved out of land held by the Forest Department, the state treats it as an encroachment. The illegality of *nevad* enables field-level forest officers to bully and extort money from farmers, enmeshing *adivasis* in an insecure, impoverished existence. Unable to invest in making agriculture more productive, denied access to forest-based resources and deprived of state developmental inputs, *adivasis* increasingly migrate out of the district in search of work.[2] Besides *nevad*, conflicts over dam-induced displacement and the failure of social welfare programs in the district have also been central in shaping *adivasi* consciousness about the state. *Adivasi* political mobilisation in the district has taken a variety of forms [*Baviskar, 1997*], ranging from participation in a militant peasants and workers' union (KMCS) in south Jhabua to participation in the ruling Congress party to membership in religious sects.

The Watershed Mission

In the last five years, the government of Madhya Pradesh has been receiving rave reviews because of the success of its Watershed Development programme in Jhabua district in bringing about an ecological and social transformation through successful decentralisation [*Agarwal et al., 1999: 33–56;*

Hanumantha Rao, 2000: 3945; Shah, 2001: 3407].[3] Jhabua's transformation is attributed to 'political and administrative will for decentralizing administration' in the sphere of environment and development [*Hanumantha Rao, 2000: 3945*]. Led by the Congress government of chief minister Digvijay Singh, decentralisation has been effected under two broad heads: one, the Rajiv Gandhi Technology Missions, and, two, the *panchayati raj* (local government) system.

Formal political decentralisation in Madhya Pradesh has been effected under the provisions of the *Panchayats* (Extension to Scheduled Areas) Act of 1996. This Act applies to those parts of the state that are designated as Scheduled Areas under the Indian Constitution by virtue of having been numerically dominated by Scheduled Tribes (*adivasis*). In these areas, the work of the village *panchayat* (elected local government) will now be monitored by the *gram sabha* (body consisting of all adults in the village). The power to approve the *panchayat's* plans regarding local resources, including forests and minor water bodies, is now vested with the *gram sabha*. While this appears to be a radical transformation towards participatory development – a movement from representative to direct democracy, a closer examination of the provisions of the Act shows critical lacunae and ambiguities: no financial powers are allocated to the *gram sabhas*; control over forests is still vested with the Forest Department; and the *gram sabha* is powerless to stop land acquisition by the government. Thus what appears to be a far-reaching move towards making *panchayats* more accountable to the people they represent may be greatly limited by its failure to specify powers and procedures for the *gram sabha*. Notably, the decentralised management of watersheds was not entrusted to the *panchayats* but to separate bodies formed under the rubric of the Rajiv Gandhi Technology Missions.

Under the Technology Mission for Watershed Management, the MP government has used funds from the central government Ministry of Rural Development to design a programme combining integrated natural resource planning and decentralised management. Integrated natural resource use planning adopts the watershed (and its division into smaller micro-watersheds) as its unit of operation. Action is oriented towards regulating the movement of water through the ecosystem, encouraging water percolation and storage through stabilising catchment area soils and improving vegetative cover. In addition, the watershed mission also encourages the establishment of women's micro-credit groups, grain banks and other developmental activities that combine savings and income-generation for improved livelihood security.

It is claimed that the transformation of the physical landscape – the increased availability of subsoil moisture, greater vegetation and increased agricultural productivity – has been achieved through decentralised management. At the grass roots, a Watershed Development Committee (henceforth Committee), elected by the *gram sabha* and representing one to five villages, is free to decide and implement various activities. The Committee consists of elected members of whom at least three must be women and another three *panchayat* (local government) representatives, an appointed secretary (a local unemployed youth who is paid a salary to maintain records and oversee the work) and a 'project in charge', who is a representative from the Project Implementing Agency;[4] a villager is elected president of the Committee. The Committee's work is facilitated by a Community Organiser, generally a social science graduate or a retired development official, appointed and paid by the District Rural Development Agency. In addition, there is a 'project implementing team' that includes members from the agriculture, animal husbandry, health, public works, public health engineering, and forest departments, which provides technical assistance to the Committee. The tasks of planning and execution, and the finances that underwrite these, are vested with the Committee, subject to review and sanction from a state-appointed Technical Committee. The Watershed Development Committee is thus empowered, on paper, to determine how village common resources should be managed in the collective interest of villagers and to devise context-specific plans. In addition, funds placed at its disposal enable the Committee to translate plans into reality. Using Agrawal and Ribot's analysis of powers of decision-making [*1999: 276*], the watershed mission seems to empower village Committees to create and implement rules, make decisions about resource use, ensure compliance and adjudicate disputes.

The combination of integrated natural resource planning and decentralised management is being attempted through an unlikely vehicle – a centralised, singe-focus Technology Mission. The Madhya Pradesh government adopted the Rajiv Gandhi Technology Missions in 1994 for the tasks of watershed management as well as universal primary education, control of diarrhoeic diseases, elimination of iodine disorders, and rural industries and fisheries development. According to the government, 'the challenges of underdevelopment in these areas required unconventional and radical responses that hinged on concentrated action to make the state take rapid strides' [*GoMP, 1998b: 1*]. A mission-mode entails 'clarity of strategies and objectives, action within a definite time-frame, fast-track procedures, committed team, inter-sectoral effort, collective action, close monitoring and transparent evaluation' [*GoMP, 1998b: 2*]. The mission approach is singularly suited to achieving 'targets', preferably single-point objectives that can be secured through rapid co-ordinated action that is centrally directed (for instance, immunisation campaigns). Goals that are not supposed to be target-driven but where process dynamics are important in themselves, and where simultaneous monitoring and evaluation is critical for self-correction, fit awkwardly into the mission approach.

The mission approach tries to energise and enthuse the MP bureaucracy, which is widely perceived as being corrupt and incompetent, by generating the collective effervescence and momentum of an intensive campaign. The negative image of the state administration is not only resented by the MP-cadre officers of the Indian Administrative Service (IAS),[5] but is also a liability in terms of receiving development assistance. The goal of breaking out of this rut and fashioning a more dynamic image and persona for the administration received encouragement from the chief minister Digvijay Singh.

Achieving Targets, Avoiding 'Politics'

To become a mission, the objectives of watershed development had to be recast into 'targets' – as measurable inputs to be achieved within a set time frame. The meeting of targets and deadlines has inexorably shaped the programme: how many committees formed? How much money in the village account? How many compost pits dug? How many contour trenches? How many check dams built? How many trees planted? How much area treated? Achieving these physical, measurable targets requires that the slow and arduous work of social organisation, for which the Project Implementing Agency is anyway ill-equipped, be rushed through or dispensed with. The obsession with physical targets reflects not only the desire for demonstrating tangible 'success' and generating enthusiasm for the mission among villagers, politicians and fund-providers, but also stems from the need to be financially accountable – to physically prove to state auditors that money has indeed been spent on approved works.[6]

The mission approach, making the administrator in charge of the project accountable to his bosses for the production of visible results, also means that the structures and procedures according primacy to the village committee have to be short circuited to avoid delays and ensure measurable outcomes. The elaborate technical rules and specifications about the tasks to be conducted under the watershed mission and the intricate recording and accounting procedures are, in any case, well beyond the grasp of most villagers, including literate ones. The guidelines issued by the government dictate everything from the exact dimensions of a contour trench to the amount of labour that villagers must contribute 'voluntarily'. No village Committee has yet managed to master these norms and employ them to get administrative sanction for its own plans. Most Committee plans therefore conform to a blueprint devised by officials for ensuring a smooth passage through the process of getting administrative approval.

The watershed mission is supposed to work through a divestment of state power and its transfer to institutions at the village level. Curiously, the mission creates an entirely new structure in the form of the watershed Committee instead of using the already existing elected body of the village, the *panchayat*.

An administrator explained: 'The *panchayat* is not participatory; it is too political'. This reflects official perceptions that *panchayats* were part of the wheeler-dealing of larger provincial electoral politics. Factionalism and political party affiliations were understood by state officials to be undermining the consideration of the welfare of the village as a whole. In contrast, the watershed Committee as a body constituted to manage a specific set of natural resources, strongly guided by the state's developmental bureaucracy, was seen as more 'participatory'. This response shows the official's perceived tensions between the idea of democratic decentralisation as a process that could become 'too political' and the watershed mission as a project that needed to be kept away from politics. This perception reflects the idea of watershed management as a development programme, where politics is seen as antithetical to development. State officials' anxieties about keeping the mission 'free from politics' are used to justify the political move of separating the watershed Committee from the *panchayat*. Once formed, the watershed Committee's working is not monitored by the *gram sabha*, limiting downward accountability to four-year intervals of re-election and, in extraordinary cases, recall through the filing of no-confidence motions against its members.

In addition, the move towards decentralisation is tightly leashed by ensuring that every proposed plan has to be scrutinised and sanctioned by a Technical Committee of government officials. Villagers' work must be inspected and found satisfactory by the Technical Committee before they are fully paid for their labour. Continued state control is justified on the ground of safeguarding public welfare; the state is represented as the bulwark against private appropriation and subversion. Yet, the rules and procedures designed to keep politics out insinuate into the watershed mission state officials' agendas of gatekeeping and rent seeking. Not only must watershed Committees follow stringent state specifications about the work that they undertake, but even if they follow the guidelines to the letter, they cannot get plans and bills passed without paying off engineers, clerks, etc. The notion that watershed work is apolitical introduces into the mission the politics of the state in various ways: it legitimises bureaucratic control, it allows corruption and it enables collaborations between state officials and particular individuals and social groups [*cf. Ferguson, 1990*].

Participatory Rural Appraisals and the Paper Trail

The principle of decentralised management in the watershed mission is not only compromised by the bureaucratic mode of ensuring success but also, paradoxically, by the practice of the very procedures established to ensure villagers' participation. The initial process of planning calls for Participatory Rural Appraisal, a collective activity. Government officials see no reason for going through this exercise; it does not influence any watershed outcomes since the plans are already indicated by the government guidelines. However, if the project bosses require information, the *sarpanch* (elected village head) can simply be summoned and asked to provide the data. The rules of the mission also mandate that decisions be taken in meetings of the watershed Committees, the proceedings of which must be recorded in writing. A decision can only be taken when there is a quorum of one third of the members for the Committee meetings and one third of the members for the *gram sabha* meetings. In practice, meetings are not conducted thus nor are minutes recorded of the actual proceedings. Most Committee members are illiterate and unfamiliar with the elaborate procedures required by the state. Meetings may be held informally between officials and a few village men, or not held at all (or sometimes villagers sit through a meeting but there is a wide gulf between their recollection of what transpired and what is officially recorded). Since the president and the secretary do not know how to hold meetings as specified by the government, and since the 'decisions' are generally what officials have in mind anyway, the minutes of the meetings are composed by the Community Organiser, a government official. The secretary of the Committee goes to the Organiser's office and copies them out. The minutes of meetings in different villages will often be exactly the same, with only the names changed. In the village, the Committee secretary goes from house to house and collects members' thumb impressions and signatures in a blank register book, where future minutes will be recorded. Thus an instant record of 'participation', of decentralised village institutions at work, is created and authenticated for posterity. This fiction of one kind of villagers' participation, the kind specified by rules, is perpetuated through the bureaucratic record only through most villagers' participation of another kind – in the circumventions invented by state officials. This participation indicates villagers' willingness to go along with the project in the hope that it will benefit them in one way or another.

Short-Circuited Democratic Participation: 'Success' as a Self-Fulfilling Prophecy

The pressure to make evident the success of the watershed mission leads to the creation of spectacular showplaces that visitors can tour.[7] The choice of villages to be adopted for watershed development is guided not by ecological parameters but administrative expedience. Sites are chosen based on accessibility – how close they are to the road, to facilitate official visits. An equally important parameter for selecting the villages where the programme will be initiated is the political orientation of the villagers. Rather than choosing areas where ecological degradation is most severe, and where lands need the most soil and water conservation, the programme is extended to villages where people are likely to be willing partners of the state. Li makes a similar observation in the case of a resettlement scheme in Indonesia: 'The key from the point of view of the … staff is that the people selected should be keen and willing to participate, interested in receiving what the program has to offer, and ready to play their part in making the program a success' [*Li, 1999: 305*]. This may in fact mean *avoiding* the people and places for whom the program is designed, but whose actual involvement may in some way endanger the chances of securing programme 'success' for the administrators. Thus the watershed mission carefully selects villages to ensure that troublemakers are left out. This means that villages organised by political organisations such as the KMCS, which have a history of being critical of the state and vociferously demanding their rights, are excluded. Ironically, the villages with the greatest levels of political awareness and popular mobilisation have the smallest chance of being selected for the watershed project. These villages are probably the most favourably endowed in terms of public participation, transparency and accountability to create viable democratic institutions for watershed management. Yet their very political strength is a liability from the point of view of the state administration.

Avoiding Conflict, Without Ecological Improvement

Even in the villages that are selected, the process of matching management practices to ecological characteristics is compromised by the grounded history of conflicts over access to land. Watershed development demands a ridge-to-valley approach, with soil and water conservation working its way downhill. In practice, however, wherever hill lands are contested terrain, the hills are left untouched. In most villages in Jhabua, the poorer farmers cultivate hill slopes; only some of this land is legally owned – most of it consists of 'encroachments'. These villagers perceive state initiatives to undertake conservation measures on this land as an insidious attempt to reclaim land – the thin edge of the wedge that would result in the farmers' eviction. According to watershed management principles, the hills should not be farmed at all but planted with trees and grasses. However, any state attempts to change land use would be an uphill task, inviting instant opposition by farmers who stand to lose their access to food. The poorest farmers who cultivate the most friable soils are thus unwilling to participate in the watershed programme. Rather than risk getting tangled in the thickets of tenure disputes, the officials in charge of the watershed mission prefer the easier option of working in the valleys.

Government officials' tendency to violate the watershed principle by focusing on the valleys also stems from the imperative that state development projects yield visible, preferably dramatic, outcomes – visible to project bosses, donors, metropolitan visitors and the media. Success is demonstrated by publicising the experience of one or two 'before-and-after cases' where subsistence farmers who grew coarse cereals went on to become prosperous by switching to high-value horticultural crops, thanks to the watershed mission. On closer examination, these success stories turn out to be based on the liberal supply of subsidised inputs such as free seeds, fertilisers and pesticides to a handful of farmers whose valley lands are already well irrigated. Such selective successes cannot be claimed as the outcome of soil and water conservation measures, nor can they be replicated sustainably on a large scale. The partnership between state officials and farmers who are relatively well-endowed with land and irrigation not only violates the principles of watershed management but also the programme's claims of promoting social justice since it exacerbates the disparities between hill and valley farmers.[8] In addition, it makes the mission a self-fulfilling prophecy since many of the people it claims to transform already have the attributes expected as the outcomes of the transformation process.

Participation and Accountability: Villagers' Perceptions of the Watershed Mission

The formal decentralisation effected by the watershed mission is subverted by the administrative imperatives of demonstrating success and the related need to stay in control.[9] Yet, decentralisation is not all smoke and mirrors. By directing public attention and increasing state legitimacy through the media, it has very real effects. It perpetuates a particular notion of neo-Chayanovian rural development that fails to address the political predicament of the vast majority of *adivasis* who are not only land-owning peasant-cultivators but increasingly participate as permanent members of the industrial proletariat in a state where extractive and manufacturing industries are multiplying rapidly. It is important to note, though, that the subversion of the watershed mission's stated principles is made possible by the participation of key villagers, whose actions are informed by their own understanding and expectations of government schemes.

One such 'participant' is Jhetra, the vice-president of the watershed Committee in Kakradara village, the showplace to which all visitors are taken. Jhetra and his wife Badlibai have represented the successes of the watershed mission on several state trips to conferences. The mission had brought considerable work their way: they had started a nursery to sell saplings to the government for distribution, and Jhetra had supervised the digging of three irrigation tanks in the village over three years. Yet, although deeply involved in the mission's activities, his perception of his role differed from the notion of decentralised participatory management envisaged in mission objectives. Jhetra complains that he was given a *theka* (contract) by the government to construct the tanks, for which he was paid Rs 110,000. During a VIP visit, he overheard government officials tell the Minister for Agriculture that the tanks had been built for Rs 200,000. Jhetra believes that government officials embezzled the money and that he has been cheated. When I asked the District Collector about this, he was quick to point out that the discrepancy between what Jhetra was paid and the amount mentioned to the minister was explained by the *shramdaan* (voluntary labour) that villagers were supposed to contribute to the project. The monetary value of the voluntary labour component was Rs 90,000; if the project had been executed by the state it would have cost Rs 200,000.

The confusion around voluntary labour, Jhetra's proprietary attitude towards the tanks and his suspicions about corruption in the disbursement of funds all reveal interesting glimpses of what the mission looks like from his point of view. According to Jhetra, he was awarded a 'contract' by the government to dig the irrigation tanks. An employee of the Public Works Department, he is conversant with the award and implementation process of construction works. He sees himself as a *thekedar* (private contractor), bidding successfully to execute a project for the government upon payment. Yet tank construction and nursery plantation are supposed to be activities undertaken by the watershed Committee, jointly planned and executed by all the members. In Kakradara, the collective effort has been transformed into a private collaboration between government officials and one enterprising household – Jhetra and Badlibai's. As a contractor, Jhetra sees himself as employing wage labourers, not as a part of a committee of equals.

In receiving funds from the state, Jhetra is sure that he has been short-changed, but officials dismiss his suspicions by saying that he does not understand the modalities of accounting for voluntary labour. Yet the decision about how much labour is to be volunteered is not made by the *villagers* who would perform that work, but by the state. There are government rules about 'voluntary' labour in the watershed mission: if the work is on government lands, a portion of the minimum wage is deducted and deposited in a common fund.[10] These rules are not negotiated: they are simply communicated from above. Ironically, villagers don't know that their labour was 'volunteered'; many of them complain that watershed work does not pay as much as other public works. This indicates that they perceive watershed work as yet another form of labouring for the state, and they have no sense of ownership *vis-à-vis* the project. Government officials who explain that wage deductions are due to 'voluntary labour' never ask villagers whether they would be willing to forego their wages in this manner. The rules change and can confuse even project officials; villagers who cannot fathom them simply assume this is one more way that they are being cheated. Jhetra's suspicions about corruption in a project where he is a key actor are telling. Implicit in his complaint is the notion of how a government should work ideally (in an uncorrupt manner), as well as an awareness of the ubiquity of its corruption ('if there is a discrepancy, someone's bound to be cheating') [*cf. Gupta, 1995*]. Yet his critique accompanies his collaboration with the watershed project as designed by the state. Jhetra's participation ensures that the work is done and visible effects are created in the showplace that is Kakradara. For him, the Committee structure is a formality, its processes cosmetic. A perfunctory nod at 'community participation' is all that is necessary before getting down to the *real* business at hand – getting the tanks constructed and the illicit profits shared.

Clearly, the watershed mission creates opportunities for the material and symbolic advancement of entrepreneurs like Jhetra. A project that is supposed to be based on collective planning and implementation can become a vehicle for private profiteering. While elected representatives on the Committee receive no official compensation for their work ('after all, it's a voluntary institution'), there is scope for 'adjustment' by fudging accounts of material and labour. As long as the paperwork is in order, rules can be subverted if officials cooperate. For example, villagers in the next hamlet allege that Jhetra made all the required weekly contributions under the names of different women in his wife's savings group (all the members were his relatives) in order to get a loan for a tractor. Someone who knew how to work the system could thus exploit the availability of soft loans for women's micro-credit groups. The potential for women's empowerment through the savings groups, which has been realised in some other villages, could be negated in Kakradara by the powerful alliance between state actors eager to secure spectacular effects and a male villager willing to supply them with shortcuts for private profit. These collaborations and compromises generally remain unspoken. When I asked the complaining Jhetra why he did watershed work, he replied, '*Gaon ke liye*' (For the village).

The watershed mission has thus brought about a kind of decentralisation in that it has changed the distribution of the proceeds of a government project, creating new transactions where villagers who had so far enjoyed limited scope for corruption can participate in skimming off a percentage of the unofficial earnings. The previous experience of government projects has given entrepreneurs like Jhetra a keen eye for the prospects for economic advancement through these means. At the same time, Jhetra is accountable to kinsmen in his hamlet; he must be able to direct some of the benefits of the watershed mission in their direction to ensure their continued cooperation. As a leader and a broker, he has to skilfully negotiate the demands of his dual constituencies. Delays in the disbursement of wages may erode Jhetra's authority in the village, a factor that state officials can use to their advantage. Left out of this process, however, are other, less favourably situated villagers, who cannot create networks of mutually beneficial transactions with state officials. These include those *adivasis* whose membership in political organisations like KMCS, which demand control over natural resources such as forests and land, threatens to undermine state control.

The above discussion demonstrates that creating the impression of project 'success' depends on collaborations between government officials and villagers. Why do the elected members of a watershed Committee, in theory answerable to fellow villagers, participate in subverting the project's mandated processes? While the opportunity for private profit and increased symbolic capital may explain Jhetra's actions, other Committee members may not be so motivated. Part of the explanation lies in the cultural distance between the formal process of democratic accountability constituted in the watershed project and villagers' political experience. The elaborate procedure for eliciting information through Participatory Rural Appraisal and using it to collectively design a community-monitored watershed-management project runs completely counter to both officials' and villagers' understanding of how decisions are made and implemented. In the absence of political mobilisation, people implicitly interpret the mission within the framework of their lived experience of social inequality and more or less accept its undemocratic working as 'business as usual'. The formal equality mandated by the project flies in the face of people's everyday knowledge and ingrained orientation that decisions are usually made by a handful of village leaders who have cultivated links with government officials that others cannot easily replicate. Challenging leaders' power is a risky enterprise that, even if successful, may simply result in co-optation and accommodation within a patronage network. Resistance to bureaucratic and elite control and the creation of downward accountability is a complex, difficult process at the best of times; in the absence of organised political mobilisation, it seems almost impossible.

III. CONCLUDING DISCUSSION

Such a tale of sordid deals and engineered 'success' is probably depressingly familiar to many development practitioners. What lessons, if any, does it hold for those interested in supporting democratic decentralisation, especially regarding rights to natural resources? Clearly, decentralised resource management, even when supported by government policy and financial assistance, may accomplish outcomes very different from those hoped for by votaries of these efforts. At present, government PIAs are headed by IAS officers who, for the most part, have worked hardest at publicising the successes of the project to metropolitan visitors and political patrons, and at creating a few well-nurtured showplaces where such visitors can be taken. The IAS officers identified with the success of the mission are motivated by the prospect of career advances and other rewards. For the field staff, however, there is little incentive or accountability for achieving anything by way of social organisation or even physical works beyond what is immediately visible to one's superiors. Complex guidelines and norms for undertaking watershed-related activities, and unfamiliar procedures that field staff are reluctant to adopt for reasons of control and comfort, mean that decentralisation is subverted from within. Without radically restructuring the framework within which government officials – both administrative and technical staff – work, decentralisation cannot be achieved. While NGOs are regarded as superior agents for achieving the potential for decentralisation within watershed development [*Kolavalli and Kerr, 2002*] (M. Shah, 2002, 'Rethinking Watershed Strategy', *The Hindu*, 29 Jan., New Delhi edition), their dependence on external funding (and the bureaucratic imperatives of larger NGOs [*Mosse, forthcoming*]) may also create pressures to demonstrate success, especially when project time lines are as short as five years.

How might downward accountability be achieved in this case? Perhaps it is from the tensions within decentralisation, from greater scrutiny and criticism of the experience so far, that more effective structures and practices will evolve. The watershed mission has now spurred *adivasi* political organisations to protest, highlighting how it distorts and deflects attention away from the issue of *adivasi* rights to land and water. Left out, disaffected or even envious villagers look at the mission's operations more critically, voicing demands for a greater share of the fruits of development. Investigative journalists and researchers have begun to probe the consensus around this narrative of success. From this 'crucible of cultural politics' [*Moore, 1999*] may eventually emerge a system of checks and balances [*Agrawal and Ribot, 2000: 478*]. In such a system, every element of the watershed mission would be closely analysed to see whether it promotes downward accountability. At the same time, some external agency would have to play a role to ensure that the decisions regarding land and water management take into account the concerns of subaltern groups within the village. A larger issue, one that determines whether any watershed project will succeed in incorporating the interests of most *adivasis*, is the legal status of *nevad* (Forest Department land illegally cultivated by *adivasis*) farmlands. Without resolving the larger legal and political question of *adivasi* rights to cultivated lands and forests, decentralised watershed development cannot be achieved.

In this essay, I have examined the paradox of state-led projects of decentralisation that ensure their instant 'success' by retaining control in the hands of the bureaucracy. I have also argued that, although such projects are conceived by high state officials, their implementation is only possible through the participation of key villagers. Such collaborations between state officials and villagers help to undermine the project's stated objectives of ecological and social improvement. Attempting to achieve these objectives requires a rethinking of grass-roots political processes. First, strong organisation, particularly of subaltern groups, is essential for overcoming government resistance to democratic decentralisation. Where local people are unable or unwilling to make demands on state administrators or even on their own elected Committee members, they become collaborators in the charade of decentralisation – even more so when they participate in corruption, help manufacture the charade of success and/or benefit economically from it. Second, this essay suggests the importance of the complex history of relations between the state and local populations in understanding such collaboration. Third, this essay reveals the need for researchers and other third parties to take a closer look at such so-called 'successes' and publicise their findings as another important accountability mechanism. Like 'empowerment' and many other aspects of development, decentralisation is a process that must develop over time, not a project that can be implemented and declared a short-term success through the measurement of easily defined target variables. The need to identify such 'successes' subverts any real attempt at building the slower, institutional processes that could bring about sustainable long-term change.

NOTES

1. Baviskar [*forthcoming*].
2. This situation is not unique to Jhabua, but prevails in all the forested parts of MP state [*see Baviskar, 2001; PUDR, 2001*].
3. Curiously, no independent study is cited in support of the claims about the achievements in Jhabua. Agarwal *et al.* [*1999*] quote a GoMP (Government of Madhya Pradesh) study of results from 18 'best case' micro-watersheds. Hanumantha Rao, the chair of the review committee for watershed development programmes under the Ministry of Rural Development's Drought-Prone Area Programme (DPAP), simply asserts that 'the success story of Jhabua is too well known to need repetition … Although only about five per cent of the problem area in Madhya Pradesh is now covered by the watershed development programme under DPAP, anecdotal evidence points to good performance in qualitative terms' [*Hanumantha Rao, 2000: 3945*]. Even a usually meticulous economist like Amita Shah does not cite a source for her statement that 'the watershed project in Jhabua is a testimony of the fact that, if designed and implemented properly, these kind of micro-level initiatives can help check the incidence of outmigration at least during a normal rainfall period' [*Shah, 2001: 3409*]. I would speculate that the desire to identify some sign of hope on the dismal development landscape has overtaken these scholars' critical sensibilities.
4. The Project Implementing Agency (PIA) can be an NGO but, in Madhya Pradesh, the state government has appointed government organisations and line departments such as the Forest Department and the Public Health and Engineering Department to oversee the bulk of watershed work. While NGO PIAs are seen as more effective on a small scale, it is argued that only government PIAs have the institutional capacity to replicate the watershed mission across the entire state.
5. The central administrative service from which officers are assigned to different states. IAS officers occupy the top sub-district, district, divisional and state-level posts in any one state, before being posted in the central government.
6. On this point, see also Mosse [*2003*]. James Scott relates the preoccupation with legibility and simplification to the administrative needs of large, centralised states [*Scott, 1998: 9–83*].
7. See Baviskar [*forthcoming*] for a more detailed account.
8. Other studies also indicate that the benefits of watershed projects are unequally distributed. In their survey of watershed projects in Maharashtra, Kerr *et al.* found that only 35 per cent of respondents reported receiving any benefits; moreover, '*the perception of project benefits rises steadily with landholding size*' [*Kerr et al., 1998, cited in Shah, 2000: 3164*] [emphasis added].

9. I have discussed elsewhere how IAS officers have a stake in demonstrating the success of projects such as the watershed mission, whereas the structure of rewards and penalties for most lower-level staff makes them either apathetic or even hostile to the changes proposed. In addition, advocacy NGOs and donor agencies (such as the Centre for Science and Environment, Ford Foundation) also have a stake in highlighting new environmental success stories [*Baviskar, forthcoming*]. Mosse [*2003*] discusses how NGOs ensure their own reproduction and expansion by promoting participatory development.
10. Ten per cent is deposited in a 'development fund' for the maintenance of physical works and five per cent collected in a 'village fund' to enable further investment in agricultural productivity. If the work is on private land, then only half the minimum wage is paid and there are no deductions for augmenting common funds. I was told this version of the rules by a Community Organiser. The secretary of the Committee in Kakradara told me that 25 per cent of the wage was deducted for the 'village fund' and another five per cent for the 'development fund'. There was also a discussion about how the rules for works on private lands had been changed in the previous year by the Collector.

REFERENCES

Agarwal, A., S. Narain and S. Sen (eds.), 1999, *State of India's Environment: The Fifth Citizens' Report*, New Delhi: Centre for Science and Environment.

Agrawal, A. and J. Ribot, 1999, 'Accountability in Decentralization: A Framework with South Asian and West African Cases', *Journal of Developing Areas*, Vol.33 (Summer), pp.473–502.

Baviskar, A., forthcoming, 'The Dream Machine: Following the Course of the Watershed Mission in Jhabua', in Amita Baviskar (ed.), *Waterscapes: The Cultural Politics of a Natural Resource*, Delhi: Oxford University Press.

Baviskar, A., 2001, 'Written on the Body, Written on the Land: Violence and Environmental Struggles in Central India', in Nancy Peluso and Michael Watts (eds.), *Violent Environments*, Ithaca, NY: Cornell University Press, pp.354–79.

Baviskar, A., 1997, 'Tribal Politics and Discourses of Environmentalism', *Contributions to Indian Sociology*, Vol.31, No.2, pp.195–223.

Ferguson, J., 1990, *The Anti-Politics Machine: "Development", Depoliticization and Bureaucratic Power in Lesotho*, Cambridge: Cambridge University Press.

GoMP (Government of Madhya Pradesh), 1998a, *The Madhya Pradesh Human Development Report 1998*, Bhopal: GoMP.

GoMP, 1998b, *Rajiv Gandhi Missions: Four Years*, Bhopal: GoMP.

Gupta, A., 1995, 'Blurred Boundaries: The Discourse of Corruption, the Culture of Politics, and the Imagined State', *American Ethnologist*, Vol.22, No.2, pp.375–402.

Hanumantha Rao, C.H., 2000, 'Watershed Development in India: Recent Experience and Emerging Issues', *Economic and Political Weekly*, Vol.35, No.45, pp.3943–7.

Kolavalli, S. and J. Kerr, 2002, 'Mainstreaming Participatory Watershed Development', *Economic and Political Weekly*, Vol.37, No.3, pp.225–42.

Li, T.M., 1999, 'Compromising Power: Development, Culture, and Rule in Indonesia', *Cultural Anthropology*, Vol.14, No.3, pp.295–322.

Moore, D.S., 1999, 'The Crucible of Cultural Politics: Reworking "Development" in Zimbabwe's Eastern Highlands', *American Ethnologist*, Vol.26, No.3, pp.654–89.

Mosse, D., 2003, 'The Making and Marketing of Participatory Development', in P.Q. van Ufford and A.K. Giri (eds.), *A Moral Critique of Development: In Search of Global Responsibilities*, London: Routledge, pp.43–75.

PUDR (People's Union for Democratic Rights), 2001, *When People Organise: Forest Struggles and Repression in Dewas*, Delhi: PUDR.

Scott, J.C., 1998, *Seeing like a State: How Certain Schemes to Improve the Human Condition have Failed*, New Haven, CT: Yale University Press.

Shah, A., 2000, 'Watershed Programmes: A Long Way to Go', *Economic and Political Weekly*, Vol.35, Nos.35–6, pp.3155–64.

Shah, A., 2001, 'Water Scarcity Induced Migration: Can Watershed Projects Help?' *Economic and Political Weekly*, Vol.36, No.35, pp.3405–10.

Decentralisation when Land and Resource Rights are Deeply Contested: A Case Study of the Mkambati Eco-Tourism Project on the Wild Coast of South Africa

BEN COUSINS and THEMBELA KEPE

I. INTRODUCTION

This contribution examines a failed community-based eco-tourism development project in one of the poorest rural regions of South Africa – the Wild Coast of the Eastern Cape Province. In the Mkambati project, both local and non-local actors and agencies have been involved in a complex politics of land and natural resource rights, and the question of 'who decides' (and therefore 'who benefits') has been central to the many-sided conflicts that have erupted.

The project is located within the former Transkei 'homeland' of South Africa, one of several targeted for high profile Spatial Development Initiatives (SDIs). The SDI concept involves 'targeted interventions by central government for helping unlock economic potential and facilitate new investment and job creation in a localised area or region' [*Jourdan, 1998: 718*]. These interventions take the form of infrastructure development, mostly in spatially concentrated corridors or nodes and implemented through private-public partnerships, and the promotion of 'anchor projects' such as industrial plants, roads or resorts. A poorly defined version of decentralisation of decision making to the local level is a central feature of the SDI model in two respects: 1) the 'empowerment' of local communities (and local entrepreneurs), and 2) government facilitation of 'partnerships' between private-sector investors and local communities.

In South Africa the distinction between 'decentralisation' and 'privatisation' is currently somewhat blurred, given the dominance of neo-liberal approaches to economic policy making. This case may resonate with experiences elsewhere, as multilateral agencies and donors increase pressure on governments everywhere to promote foreign investment, privatise service

Ben Cousins is Director and Thembela Kepe is a Researcher in the Programme for Land and Agrarian Studies, School of Government, University of the Western Cape. The authors would like to thank Anne Larson, Jesse Ribot and two anonymous reviewers for their incisive comments on a first version of this essay.

European Journal of Development Research, Vol.16, No.1, Spring 2004, pp.41–54
ISSN 0957-8811 print
DOI:10.1080/0957881041000168725

delivery and thus to 'outsource development' in the name of market efficiencies.

The reasons for the failure of the eco-tourism project in Mkambati are many and various [*Kepe et al., 2001; Kepe, 2001*], but include some that speak directly to debates on democratic decentralisation, as well as debates regarding the beneficiaries of eco-tourism projects.[1] Democratic decentralisation grants important decision-making powers to downwardly accountable local actors [*Ribot, 2001*]. Yet for the SDI project, the devolution of effective decision-making powers from central bodies to local actors was not seen as a key issue and was barely addressed, and a rhetoric of 'empowerment' has been employed in its place. Also ignored was the question of the accountability of various local bodies to the community members whose interests they have claimed to represent. Even for local residents, democratisation and accountability were not articulated as key issues. The emphasis on private-sector partnerships and local entrepreneurship within the SDI, as if it were a form of (or substitute for?) decentralisation, fostered the attempted capture of the development project by entrepreneurial elites, which then generated resentment among and fierce resistance by other community members.

One of the key goals of democratic decentralisation is to promote and institutionalise local participation, and hence to operate from a clear understanding of local needs and desires [*Ribot, 2001*]. Nevertheless, SDI project planning and attempts to establish its local institutional framework barely even recognised the subtle realities of the use of natural resources in local livelihood strategies, or the local institutional arrangements through which access to resources is gained. Yet these were central to the actions and motivations of local residents. At the same time, national and provincial government departments that played a key supportive role in the SDI by implementing land-reform policies, securing land and resource rights, and resolving deep-rooted tenure disputes accorded these a low priority. In cases such as these, however, it is clear not only that powers should be devolved to downwardly accountable local actors but also that the devolution of powers must be accompanied by effective tenure reforms. These reforms must clarify each actor's rights as well as strengthen their capacity to exercise them.

Finally, the case evidence supports the argument that effective democratic decentralisation requires a strong central state that is committed to the process, provides adequate resources for the devolution of decision-making powers and facilitates the creation of downwardly accountable local bodies.

II. POLICY FRAMEWORKS

Understanding the local power dynamics in Mkambati is difficult without situating them within the national policies developed and implemented since

1994 by the post-apartheid government. These generally assert that there is an important role for local decision-making (often by 'communities'), and notions of 'participation' and 'consultation' are common in policy documents such as White Papers. However, the locus of decision-making powers and mechanisms to ensure the accountability of decision makers are much less-clearly articulated.

Spatial Development Initiatives (SDIs)

From their inception in the mid 1990s, SDIs were seen as integral to the new government's macroeconomic strategy. Within this, a 'paradigm shift' in economic policy towards international competitiveness, regional co-operation and diversified ownership were emphasised [*Jourdan et al. 1996*], thereby addressing the spatial distortions of apartheid, a 'fast-track and integrated approach' from within government, and the pivotal role of the private sector [*Platzky, 2000*]. The latter in particular clearly aligns the SDI concept with neo-liberal development doctrine [*Rogerson and Crush, 2001*].

The SDIs are premised on the need to attract investment capital to previously neglected areas. Objectives include sustainable job creation, growth and development configured to suit a locality's inherent development potential, the mobilisation of private sector investment and lending, 'economic empowerment' through small, medium and micro-enterprise (SMMEs), and exploitation of under-utilised local resources as the basis for industrial and export-oriented growth [*Kepe et al., 2001; Rogerson and Crush, 2001*].

A number of SDIs are being implemented within the wider Southern Africa region. Thirteen SDIs in different parts of South Africa had been initiated by late 2000. On the Wild Coast of the former Transkei, several development 'nodes' were identified – with the focus on eco-tourism. The existence of five nature reserves, together with the scenic beauty of the coastal zone, is seen to provide a basis for the expansion of both national and international tourism, and a new Pondoland National Park is being planned. Several development nodes have been identified, including Dwesa/Cwebe/Nqabara, Coffee Bay/Hole-in-the-Wall, Port St Johns, Magwa and Mkambati. The aim is to establish eco-tourism ventures in these anchor project sites, with the hope that improvements in infrastructure and other investments will encourage a range of economic initiatives in the surrounding areas. It is hoped that the five nature reserves found along the coast together with scenic areas such as Hole-in-the-Wall, will attract both national and international tourists to the Wild Coast. Agriculture and forestry have also been identified as enterprises with development potential, and government planners estimate that in the Eastern Cape around 120,000 hectares of land could be afforested, mostly in the communal areas of the Wild Coast. Private companies are encouraged to enter into agreements with communities in these areas.

In South Africa the notion of 'empowerment' refers to increasing the level of participation in the mainstream economy by black South Africans. In the SDIs this is supposed to take place through:

- Community control over land;
- Community involvement in the management of productive assets;
- Community-held equity shares in new enterprises; and
- Support for SMME development.

A critical issue for the SDIs is the extent to which these features are compatible with significant levels of private investment, and the need for public agencies to facilitate 'partnerships' between communities and investors. Increasingly, district councils and local municipalities are being seen as the levels of government that should play this role. Here, decentralisation is explicitly allied with neo-liberal conceptions of market-driven development. Not at all clear in the SDI model is the institutional location of decision-making power at local or 'community' level.

Local Government Reform

Following the advent of majority rule in 1994, a transitional local government regime was installed until such a time as the details of a more permanent system could be put into place. Problems experienced in the 1995–2000 period included a lack of experience and skills among elected councillors, inadequate mechanisms for effective consultation with and feedback to constituents, inadequate financial resources, weak decision-making powers and a lack of accountability mechanisms [*Manor, 2000*].

Following new legislation and a second round of elections in 2000, a permanent new system of local government has replaced the transitional arrangements. The number of district councils and primary level bodies has been reduced from 843 to 299, consequently leading to a greatly increased 'distance' between elected representatives and constituents. This, together with a proportional representation system and selection of candidates from party lists, makes accountability to those constituents more difficult. Local government is required to be developmental, and all municipalities must produce Integrated Development Plans. These Plans must provide for extensive public participation in the planning process. Yet municipalities in the poverty-stricken former 'homelands' have a small or non-existent revenue base, meaning that the problem of 'unfunded mandates' [*Manor, 2000*] has been perpetuated if not exacerbated. Also unresolved in both the 'transitional' period and since 2000 is the issue of the roles and powers of traditional leaders in local government [*Ntsebeza, 2001*]. Partly because of serious capacity problems, SDIs have generally not attempted to work through – or even in co-operation with – local government bodies.

Land Reform

The overarching goal of land reform in South Africa is to redress the racially based land dispossessions of the apartheid era and the resulting highly inequitable distribution of land ownership. Other goals include land-tenure security for all and the enabling of land-based economic development. The three main components of land reform are land redistribution, land restitution and tenure reform [*Department of Land Affairs, 1997*]. Restitution policy aims to restore land and provide other remedies (that is, alternative land or financial compensation) to people dispossessed by racially discriminatory legislation and practice. Policies and procedures are based on the Bill of Rights and the Restitution of Land Rights Act of 1994. A programme of land tenure reform has been slow to emerge [*Cousins and Claassens, 2003*].

The land-tenure system in the former 'homelands' is usually described as 'traditional' in character but, as elsewhere in Africa, chiefs and headmen formed an integral part of a colonial system of indirect rule in which customary law and communal land rights were administered by chiefs. The legacy of this history is that communal land is still owned by the state, and the land rights of the occupants are not well defined and protected by law. For most rural people, rights still take the form of permits. Land administration is currently in a state of chaos, and there is widespread confusion over who may make decisions on land in cases where development projects such as housing schemes are planned. Tensions and disputes over land rights are common. In response to increasing political pressure, government is currently drafting a Communal Land Rights Bill.[2] Among other provisions, this will define the powers of local land administration bodies. A central issue is the accountability of such bodies to rights holders.

III. THE CASE STUDY AREA AND LOCAL INSTITUTIONAL FRAMEWORKS

The area known as 'Mkambati' is situated in north-eastern Pondoland (31°13'–31°20'S and 29°55'–30°4'E), in the Eastern Cape Province, South Africa. It is inhabited by the mPondo people, who speak a Xhosa dialect (IsiMpondo). The case study focuses on three sub-areas within the wider Mkambati area that are under different tenure regimes: communal tenure settlements to the west; 11,000 hectares of state land in the centre, formerly used by a now defunct parastatal agricultural project (the Transkei Agricultural Development Corporation, or TRACOR); and the 7,000-hectare state-owned Mkambati Nature Reserve to the east. The communal tenure area comprises seven villages that make up the Thaweni Tribal Authority. Of these, Khanyayo is the village that has been at the centre of conflict over the Mkambati SDI.

The inhabitants of the seven villages generate their livelihoods through a mixture of arable and livestock farming and the collection of a range of natural resources as well as various off-farm sources, including remittances and pensions. Access to natural resources is mediated by a variety of formal and informal institutions. These include national and provincial laws and regulations, official land and resource tenure regimes, embedded (but not officially recognised) systems of property rights, customary norms and practices around resource sharing, and illegal (but socially structured and locally legitimate) means of access.[3]

Of the seven villages within the Thaweni Tribal Authority, Khanyayo has the closest ties, in terms of both history and proximity of settlement, to the Mkambati Nature Reserve and the TRACOR state farm. In 1920 the Khanyayo people were forcibly removed from an area of about 18,000 hectares – which they used for settlement, livestock grazing and other resources – to make way for a leper colony. For over 70 years the Khanyayo have aggressively attempted to regain their land rights, and they have continued to hunt and harvest natural resources within the area that they lost – legitimising this use through the informal institution of *ukujola* (see note 3). Following the closure of the leper colony in 1976 and its conversion into the Mkambati Nature Reserve and TRACOR state farm, tension between the state and the Khanyayo increased, particularly over grazing rights. In 1997, following the official end of apartheid in 1994, the residents of Khanyayo lodged a claim against the state for restitution of their land.

Throughout the early 1990s, the Khanyayo had relied on moral support from the other six villages in their fight for their rights to the nature reserve land and the TRACOR state farm. Initially, this support was a result of common political affiliation, which at the time was unanimously in favour of the African National Congress (ANC). However, it was also during the early 1990s that the political landscape in Mkambati area began to blur due to strained relations between the traditional leadership (chiefs and headmen) and democratic political organisations. The traditional leadership was challenged by the rise of local civic organisations affiliated with the ANC. Former migrant workers who had returned to the villages established civic associations throughout the area, some as branches of the South African National Civic Organisation (SANCO). Control over land allocation was a major bone of contention.

In Khanyayo village, a civic organisation – the Khanyayo-Mkambati Development Forum (KMDF) – was formed by local political activists in 1996, mainly to spearhead the fight to regain their land rights. The formation of the KMDF was not welcomed by leaders in the other six villages, who tended to support the senior chief at the head of the Thaweni Tribal Authority – Chief Mhlanga. In 1992 the chief and his supporters (who were mainly from the wealthier and politically powerful elite) had formed an organisation known as the Joint Management Committee (JMC), supposedly in order to facilitate development in the Mkambati Nature Reserve. The JMC argued that all seven villages under the Thaweni Tribal Authority should be co-claimants to the land in question as they were all under a single chief.

By 1994 two members of the original JMC had taken political office – one in the national parliament and one in the local Transitional Representative Council. The JMC has continued to use these politicians as advisors, and they have assisted the JMC in securing the support of senior officials in the provincial government, including the premier, in their struggle to be seen as the only legitimate local institution within the Mkambati area.

Initially, the conflict over the land claim between the Khanyayo people, on the one hand, and the chief (together with the JMC), on the other, appeared to be a microcosm of countrywide conflicts between traditional authorities and democratic political structures [*Ntsebeza, 1999*]. However, in the Mkambati area the formally elected local government structures have not been major players in struggles over land and development. Between 1995 and 2000 a small number of councillors sat on the Transitional Representative Council of the nearby Lusikisiki municipality, but were not widely known to their constituents and were not very active in promoting local development.

This lack of a strong local presence by elected councillors has continued since the restructuring of local government in 2000. Mkambati now falls within the Ingquza Hill municipality, which is split into separate wards. Neither of the two current councillors reside in any of the villages involved in the disputes over land in Mkambati. The central government's continuing indecision regarding the roles and powers of traditional leaders contributes to ongoing uncertainty within Mkambati as to where real political and administrative authority at the local level resides.

Given this uncertainty, as well as the long-term conflict over land rights in Mkambati and TRACOR, any development targeting the disputed land could be expected to face numerous challenges. As it turned out, these issues did indeed plague the SDI project in Mkambati.

IV. THE SDI AND DEVELOPMENT POLITICS IN MKAMBATI

SDI Planning and Community 'Empowerment'

In line with the SDI's goal of targeting areas that have both needs and economic potential, the Mkambati area was identified as one of the five 'development nodes' along the Wild Coast.[4] The nature reserve was central to SDI plans for encouraging large-scale foreign investment in eco-tourism ventures in this node. Private investment would focus on the extension and upgrading of tourist facilities to cater to local and international tourists and sport hunters; the facilities would include accommodation for a total of 90 visitors. The government's contribution would be to improve infrastructure – including roads, electricity and telephones – in the reserve area as well as in the communal-tenure settlements. Outside the nature reserve, forestry companies were encouraged to consider planting commercial forests in sections of TRACOR state land as well as in the surrounding communal areas. It was envisaged that local people would benefit from the SDI in a number of ways, such as employment, opportunities for local entrepreneurs and rental payments to the community by investors.

When the SDI began, the Department of Trade and Industry, together with the Eastern Cape provincial government, invited the private sector to submit proposals for investment in Mkambati and other development nodes on the Wild Coast. Among other things, private-sector proposals had to address a key principle of social empowerment established by government [*Government of Eastern Cape, 1998*]: the 'community' must benefit directly from the proposed developments in the short, medium and long term. Consultants suggested a number of models for community participation and empowerment in Mkambati, and government and SDI implementers focused on three [*Koch et al., 1998*].

The first empowerment model involved the private sector entering into a lease agreement or management contract to operate facilities developed by communities on communal land. Under this model, the community would remain responsible for the development and maintenance of infrastructure and facilities. The private sector would be responsible for environmental management and for facilitating SMME development and support. In this model, tourism remained under the private sector. Under the second model, the community that requested proposals from the private sector for partnerships would (with assistance from the state) develop, operate and maintain all required tourism facilities, and assume responsibility for environmental management and SMME development and support. The third model involved 'state-owned land'. Here the state would request private-sector proposals for all three functions – to develop, operate and maintain tourism, as well as environmental management and SMME development and support. The private sector would be instructed to build into the proposals options for facilitating community empowerment. This model required that communities adjacent to the state land be given the opportunity to purchase or access equity in the tourism operation. It was this model that was adopted in the Mkambati case, notwithstanding the restitution claim to the land within the nature reserve and the TRACOR estate.

The SDI implementing team for the Mkambati node comprised officials from the Development Bank of Southern Africa (DBSA) and the Department of Trade and Industry, as well as consultants employed by the provincial government. The empowerment model they adopted involved a clear role for a local organisation to represent 'community interests' in the form of a 'community-private sector partnership'. This body would connect the ecotourist project to local development planning processes, and actively facilitate projects to produce the spin-off benefits which they hoped would flow from external investment in upgraded tourist facilities in the nature reserve. To play this role, it should have powers to negotiate on behalf of the beneficiary community, distribute income from leases or other sources of revenue and oversee the allocation of employment in public works programmes such as roads.

In 1997 the SDI implementing team formed the Mkambati SDI Committee, which was to act as this link between the 'local community', the SDI team and investors. This committee was mainly composed of JMC members, who worked closely with the chief. This committee became locked in disputes with the KMDF, which represented Khanyayo villagers in the fight to regain land rights. Consequently, residents of Khanyayo village did not recognise the legitimacy of the SDI Committee. Uncertainty about institutional responsibilities, together with ongoing tensions between traditional authorities and elected local government in the area, hampered attempts to resolve disputes between the KMDF and the SDI Committee (or the JMC).

The Politics of Land and Resource Rights in the Mkambati SDI

The advent of the SDI soon after the lodging of a land restitution claim exacerbated the conflict between Khanyayo residents and leaders of the other six villages in the Mkambati area, but also brought new tensions and disputes of its own. Largely unresolved to date, these have effectively stalled the proposed SDI. Consequently, among other things, no eco-tourism development has taken place in the area, and by June 2003 the nature reserve was still operated by the provincial department responsible for conservation. We argue that in order to have any chance of success, the SDI project cannot proceed without first resolving land claims, and, second, building acceptable institutions for resolving local disputes.

A host of actors and interest groups has pursued a variety of competing objectives, and just who should be 'empowered' has been fiercely contested. The different groupings have engaged in a number of power plays and entered into complex and shifting relationships with each other at different moments in time, ranging from alliances or collaboration at one end of the spectrum, through wary neutrality or relative indifference, to outright hostility and confrontation at the other. Since 1990 the political terrain in Mkambati has become steadily more complex – and less stable. Three key issues are at the heart of the conflicts that have emerged.

1) Which 'community' is to be the beneficiary of the SDI?
When the SDI was introduced, the 'Mkambati community' was an abstract concept, adequate perhaps for purposes of initial planning. The SDI's first definition of the 'local community' was based on geographical location [*Kepe, 1999*] and thus favoured the Khanyayo villagers, who are the immediate neighbours of Mkambati Nature Reserve. Members of the other six villages within the Thaweni Tribal Authority were unhappy with this and campaigned through the JMC for all six to be included within the definition of 'beneficiary community'. When the JMC (now composed mainly of the local business and political elite, including some in government posts) threatened violence, the SDI implementation team quickly yielded to their demands. This decision has contributed in great part to the ongoing tensions between Khanyayo villagers and people living in the other six villages. Lack of clarity on this fundamental issue persists, despite attempts to find a mediated solution to the centrally important and still unresolved problem of the land claim [*Kepe, 2001*].

2) Who owns the land on which the SDI eco-tourism project was to be located?
The SDI, with its empowerment models that offered significant benefits for land-owning communities, seems to have intensified the conflict over land rights in Mkambati. The Khanyayo people appeared confident that, based on history, their land claim would succeed and they would be regarded as the land-owning community for the purposes of the SDI development. However, a year after the Khanyayo lodged their claim, the JMC followed with a counterclaim for the wider 'community'. The Restitution Commission was legally bound to treat both claims as potentially legitimate until proven otherwise, hence the Khanyayo and the JMC were to remain potential land owners of Mkambati Nature Reserve and TRACOR until the claim was resolved.

Concerned that the SDI project was being stalled by land disputes, the government commissioned several mediation processes between the warring factions. In 1999 mediation by facilitators on behalf of the provincial office of the Department of Land Affairs managed to get the JMC to withdraw its claim with the promise that they would be regarded as equal shareholders of any development taking place on the disputed land. While this did not please the Khanyayo, they appeared to agree to this compromise. However, with the land claim still unresolved by the beginning of 2003, tensions in the area have mounted and the SDI has ground to a complete halt.

3) Which institution represents local people's interests?
The question of which local body can claim to legitimately represent the interests of the 'local community' has been a central point of contention in the muddied waters of Mkambati's institutional landscape. Perhaps surprisingly,

the main contenders have been neither local government bodies nor traditional leaders.

Local government bodies have been only peripherally involved in the struggles over land rights and SDI planning in Mkambati, perhaps because of their 'distance' from the local level and the fact that most ward councillors were not themselves residents of any of the affected villages. Traditional leaders have aligned themselves with either the JMC and the SDI Committee (Chief Mhlanga) or with the KMDF (the headman of Khanyayo village), but have generally not asserted an active leadership role for themselves. They have attempted to maintain their status as accepted local leaders, with a central role in land allocation, dispute resolution, etc., but have not been willing to risk losing support by attempting to take the lead in high-profile land struggles or arguments over the distribution of benefits from the SDI eco-tourism project. Ironically, SDI policy documents state that the SDI seeks to work with local leaders, who include traditional authorities as well as elected local government bodies [*Mahlati, 2000*]. These local leaders are supposed to act as 'community' representatives in SDI negotiations, as well as mediate in disputes.

But the SDI team, backed by both a powerful national government department and the provincial government, were willing to recognise another, more locally based 'representative' body in this role. The JMC (and later the Mkambati SDI Committee) received such recognition, despite having no statutory status and the absence of any formal guidelines as to what their decision-making powers were; nor were any mechanisms established to ensure transparency and accountability. Instead, the JMC instituted a strategy that was clearly designed to capture the SDI and its benefits. These included using mobile phones to contact government and SDI personnel to convey what they claimed were messages from 'local people', occupying empty buildings inside the Mkambati Nature Reserve, failing to announce community meetings when important visitors were coming and monopolising committee appointments.

The KMDF (sometimes acting in concert with the Khanyayo headman) has refused to acknowledge the authority of the JMC/SDI Committee. For them, powers such as the control of income flows from natural resources (for example, trees and river sand) clearly derive from ownership of the land and the resources on it.

V. CONCLUSIONS

The Mkambati case is one of contestation over land, natural resources and the spoils of development. Different actors have engaged in a diverse set of strategies and tactics aimed at increasing their power to further their own objectives, but none have articulated democratic decentralisation as a goal.

The absence of a politics of democracy has been the key to stalling development in Mkambati. Central issues in democratic decentralisation are the establishment of downwardly accountable bodies that have appropriate powers and are composed of appropriate actors. As the Mkambati story shows, failure to explicitly address these issues can create opportunities for opportunists, resistance and intractable conflict, rather than concerted collective action in community-based development planning and natural resource management.

Another lesson from Mkambati relates to land and natural resources. Where these are central to people's livelihood strategies, and in particular where they are not held in private property regimes, the formal and informal institutional arrangements that mediate their use will deeply influence local decisions and actions in development initiatives such as the Wild Coast SDI. External agencies must understand these realities and make them central in development planning. Prospects for such 'realism' would be enhanced by building downwardly accountable institutions that take seriously the task of facilitating local participation in decision making.

On the evidence of this case, private-sector oriented forms of decentralised development planning can be highly problematic. An emphasis on external investment and 'community-private sector partnerships', without a clear role for representative decision-making bodies that are accountable to their constituencies, can easily lead to elite capture. Alternatively, as in Mkambati, local resistance to such capture can lead to disputes that stall investment and development. Functional and legitimate local institutional frameworks, together with the resolution of competing claims to land and resources, are preconditions for the success of partnerships such as those envisaged within the SDI.

The Mkambati case also suggests that the central state has an important role in facilitating democratic institutional development at the local level and in clarifying and supporting land and resource rights. Poorly planned and implemented programmes such as the Wild Coast SDI, with ineffective support from provincial and national government agencies, have hindered rather than assisted local processes and helped entrench intractable conflict. National programmes of tenure reform and land restitution have failed miserably in clarifying and securing local rights. Government actions have weakened rather than strengthened prospects for democratic governance as the local political and business elite have used their connections to provincial politicians to secure recognition of their committees, which are used as vehicles for personal accumulation. This suggests that effective government oversight of local processes is critical, and that 'even civil society depends on strong government' [*Ribot, 2001: 20*].

NOTES

1. In acknowledging that many eco-tourism projects in poor countries often do not benefit poor people, Ashley and Roe [2002] suggest that a conscious effort should be made to implement 'pro-poor tourism' strategies.
2. Controversy has erupted in relation to several features of the draft law. Critics have highlighted the following problems: the transfer of ownership of communal land from the state to communities and/or individuals will trigger massive boundary disputes and hinder service provision by municipalities; proposed levels of state support to local land administration bodies are inadequate; and giving chiefs a prescribed level of representation on land administration bodies will exacerbate tensions with local government [*Cousins and Claassens, 2003*].
3. A key informal institution is that of *ukujola*. This refers to illegal but locally legitimate forms of natural-resource use, such as hunting wildlife or gathering medicinal plants and other floral resources in the Mkambati Nature Reserve [*Kepe, 1997*].
4. The others were Dwesa/Cwebe/Nqabara, Coffee Bay/Hole-in-the-Wall, Port St Johns and Magwa.

REFERENCES

Ashley, C. and D. Roe, 2002, 'Making Tourism Work for the Poor: Strategies and Challenges in southern Africa', *Development Southern Africa*, Vol.19, No.1, pp.61–82.

Cousins, B. and A. Claassens, 2003, 'Communal Land Tenure in South Africa: Livelihoods, Rights and Institutions', *Development Update*, Vol.4, No.2, pp.55–77.

Department of Land Affairs, 1997, *White Paper on Land Policy*, Pretoria: Department of Land Affairs.

Government of Eastern Cape, 1998, 'Formal Invitation to Submit Pre-Qualification Proposals', Bisho: Ministry of Economic Affairs, Environment and Tourism.

Jourdan, P., 1998, 'Spatial Development Initiatives (SDIs) – The Official View', *Development Southern Africa*, Vol.15, No.5, pp.717–25.

Jourdan, P., K. Gordhan, D. Arkwright and G. de Beer, 1996, 'Spatial Development Initiatives (Development Corridors): Their Potential Contribution to Investment and Employment Creation', Unpublished paper.

Kepe, T., 2001, *Waking up from the Dream: The Wild Coast SDI and the Pitfalls of 'Fast Track' Development*, Research report No.8, Cape Town: Programme for Land and Agrarian Studies, School of Government, University of the Western Cape.

Kepe, T., 1999, 'The Problem of Defining "Community": Challenges for the Land Reform Programme in Rural South Africa', *Development Southern Africa*, Vol.16, No.3, pp.415–33.

Kepe, T., 1997, *Environmental Entitlements in Mkambati: Livelihoods, Social Institutions and Environmental Change on the Wild Coast of the Eastern Cape*, Cape Town: Programme for Land and Agrarian Studies, University of the Western Cape.

Kepe, T., L. Ntsebeza and L. Pithers, 2001, 'Agro-Tourism Spatial Development Initiatives in South Africa. Are they Enhancing Rural Livelihoods?' *Natural Resource Perspectives*, No.65, Jan., London: Overseas Development Institute, pp.1–4.

Koch, E. with G. de Beer, S. Elliffe and others, 1998, 'SDIs, Tourism-led Growth and the Empowerment of Local Communities in South Africa', *Development Southern Africa*, Vol.15, No.5, pp.809–26.

Mahlati, V., 2000, 'Integrated Planning and Implementation in Rural Areas: Experiences from Agri-tourism Spatial Development Initiatives (SDIs)', in B. Cousins (ed.), *At the Crossroads. Land and Agrarian Reform in South Africa into the 21st Century*, Cape Town: Programme for Land and Agrarian Studies, School of Government, University of the Western Cape/Braamfontein, National Land Committee, pp.111–28.

Manor, J., 2000, 'Local Government in South Africa: Potential Disaster Despite Genuine Promise', Unpublished paper prepared for the United Kingdom's Department for International Development, Brighton: Institute for Development Studies, Sussex University.

Ntsebeza, L., 2001, 'Traditional Authorities and Rural Development in Post-Apartheid South Africa: The Case of the Transkei Region of the Eastern Cape', in J. Coetzee, J. Graaf, F. Hendricks and

G. Woods (eds.), *Development: Theory, Policy, and Practice*, Cape Town: Oxford University Press.

Ntsebeza, L., 1999, *Land Tenure Reform, Traditional Authorities and Rural Local Government in Post-Apartheid South Africa*, Research Report No.3, Cape Town: Programme for Land and Agrarian Studies, School of Government, University of the Western Cape.

Platzky, L., 2000, 'Reconstructing and Developing South Africa: The Role of the Spatial Development Initiatives', Paper presented at the International Conference on Sustainable Regional Development, University of Massachusetts, Lowell, 28 Oct.

Ribot, J., 2001, 'Integral Local Development: "Accommodating Multiple Interests" through Entrustment and Accountable Representation', *International Journal of Agricultural Resources, Governance and Ecology*, Vol.1, No.3, pp.327–50.

Rogerson, C. and J. Crush, 2001, 'New Industrial Spaces: Evaluating South Africa's Spatial Development Initiatives (SDI) Programme', *South African Geographical Journal*, Vol.83, No.2, pp.85–92.

Formal Decentralisation and the Imperative of Decentralisation 'from Below': A Case Study of Natural Resource Management in Nicaragua

ANNE M. LARSON

I. INTRODUCTION[1]

Decentralisation in Nicaragua began in the late 1980s and has generated important changes, both structurally and within civil society. Elected municipal officials, governmental posts introduced in 1990, have been granted important responsibilities for the management of their territories in general as well as for their region's natural resources. As a result, a new local sphere of governance has been created [*Ortega, 1997*], defended by a broad alliance of municipal government representatives, decentralisation advocates and non-governmental organisations (NGOs). Local governments, then, have become strategic allies in national politics.

There is also strong grass-roots support for decentralisation in Nicaragua. A study conducted in 14 northern municipalities in 1996 found that 68 per cent of the people surveyed believed that municipal governments could do things better than the central government. The overwhelming majority, 97 per cent, believed that the best way to solve problems was with citizen participation [*Ortega and Castillo, 1996*].[2]

This apparent generalised enthusiasm for decentralisation, however, contrasts rather sharply with the reality of the official process, which largely stagnated up until 2003 after important reforms were made to the Municipalities Law in 1997. First, decentralisation has been primarily a process of deconcentration and privatisation, and many analysts believe that the central government has no real desire to give up any further power. Second, after a decade of decentralisation rhetoric, the government has still not adopted

Anne M. Larson is a Research Associate at the Center for International Forestry Research and Nitlapán Institute for Research and Development, Managua, Nicaragua. The author would like to acknowledge that this essay would not have been possible without the support of Jesse Ribot and the World Resources Institute and the Center for International Forestry Research (CIFOR). Different phases of the research were funded or sponsored by CIFOR, DFID, Protierra, Profor, the Nitlapán Institute of the UCA, and the SIDA-IDB Partnership. She would also like to thank the anonymous reviewer for their helpful comments.

European Journal of Development Research, Vol.16, No.1, Spring 2004, pp.55–70
ISSN 0957-8811 print
DOI:10.1080/0957881041000l688734

its official decentralisation policy, though a draft finally underwent a national consultation in 2003. Third, Nicaragua is the only Central American country that had no law guaranteeing central government transfers (until that same year), and maintained the lowest annual transfers in the region – at approximately 1.0–1.2 per cent of the national budget.

Natural resource decentralisation has taken place within this broader context, with its own stops and starts and myriad contradictions. Fundamentally, though, laws and regulations are vague and contradictory, and municipal governments have little autonomous decision-making authority with regard to their natural resources. Even where high-level authorities support some form of decentralisation, lower-level bureaucrats often do not. Experience so far suggests that loosening central control requires, among other things, organised demands and mobilisation from local actors and their allies.

In the next section, this essay briefly examines the traditional conception of decentralisation as a top-down process and argues for the importance of recognising decentralisation 'from below'. This is followed by a section on decentralisation in Nicaragua and central government resistance. The subsequent section examines municipal natural resource management and the importance of grass-roots motivating forces, and is followed by the conclusions.

II. DECENTRALISATION FROM ABOVE AND BELOW

Decentralisation is often conceptualised as a top-down process instigated by national governments in order to increase efficiency and equity and/or to promote local participation and democracy. Ribot, for example, writes that 'Decentralization takes place when a central government formally transfers powers to actors and institutions at lower levels in a political-administrative and territorial hierarchy' [*Ribot, 2002*].

While this definition is convenient and precise, it refers only to the formal, legal process of decentralisation. It does not include the way in which local actors make decisions without specific central authority to do so, or the way in which the legitimacy of local elected authorities grows outside of any controlled, formal process. Neither does it conceptualise the political reality of decentralisation as an iterative process that appears to require grass-roots and local government pressure in order to advance. This dynamic reality represents decentralisation 'from below' and is precisely the foundation upon which greater participation and democracy are forged. It is, then, the foundation of democratic decentralisation.

Natural resources appear particularly amenable to decentralisation 'from below'. This is at least in part because they are already physically present in the local sphere and because that physical presence is integrated into a local history and culture of resource use and management [*see Larson, 2003; Kaimowitz and Ribot, 2002*]. It is now fairly widely recognised, however, that local governments often have little motivation to address natural resource problems [*see Ferroukhi, 2003; Gibson and Lehoucq, 2003; Larson, 2002*]; they are more interested in the economic benefits of management than the burdens of environmental problems or conservation.

Yet, local governments are playing an ever-greater role in local resource decisions. This is in part due to the authority they are legally granted and the opportunities that become available by appearing environmentally active [*Larson, 2003*]. It is also in part because where elected local governments have been granted a certain level of autonomy and their authority, capacity and legitimacy have been increasing over time, as in Nicaragua, other local actors turn to them more and more to address local environmental problems as a 'natural' local authority. The evidence from Nicaragua shows that local governments will take action in response to certain incentives, environmental crises and, related to these, pressure from constituents and NGOs [*Larson, 2002*].

III. NATURAL RESOURCE DECENTRALISATION AND CENTRAL GOVERNMENT RESISTANCE

In Nicaragua, municipal governments argue that the powers they have over natural resources are not the ones they want. Rather, in practice they have been given the burdens of certain management responsibilities without either the resources to take on those burdens or other benefits that would arise from having real decision-making authority.

Nevertheless, the Municipalities Law grants municipal governments the rather sweeping responsibility 'to develop, conserve and control the rational use of the environment and natural resources as the basis for the sustainable development of the municipality and the country, promoting local initiatives in these areas and contributing to their monitoring, vigilance and control in coordination with the corresponding national entities' (Leyes No.40 and 261 de los Municipios). This and other laws give municipal governments numerous specific attributions regarding the environment and natural resources.[3] The most important of these is the right to give their opinion, known as an *aval*, prior to central government approval of resource exploitation requests, which include both concessions on national lands and extraction permits on private lands. Municipal governments also have a right to 25 per cent of the income the Tax Office receives from these contracts. Municipal governments must co-ordinate with the Environment Ministry (MARENA), Forestry Institute (INAFOR) and other national entities to undertake various other tasks. These include the establishment of municipal parks for the conservation of important local resources and the development of land-use plans, as well as participating in environmental impact evaluations, managing protected areas, declaring soil conservation areas, controlling forest fires and establishing norms for ecosystem quality.[4]

Despite all of these attributions, the central government reserves for itself, based on Article 102 of the Constitution, the right to make key decisions over natural resource exploitation. Specifically, although legally required to consider municipal government opinion, it is the central government that enters into contracts for forestry, mining and fishing. In reality, local government opinion is sometimes not even requested, and dissenting opinions can simply be ignored.[5] Similarly, the central government failed to turn over the municipal portion of timber and other revenues for several years. There are numerous other problems that can be summarised as a general state of 'legal confusion' (J. Ortega, J., Environmental Lawyer, AMUNIC, Interviews, 7 Sept. 2000, and 17 Nov. 2001).

The bottom line is that the central government has retained control over those aspects of natural resource management that generate income, and retains control over almost all other resource-related tasks by requiring the local government to 'co-ordinate' with central entities – usually without establishing mechanisms to do so. It has also failed to transfer sufficient funds to local governments for these to be able to meet their obligations to constituents. Up until recently, Nicaragua transferred the lowest percentage of the central budget to municipal governments in Central America, though, by law, this should now rise to four per cent in 2004. During the previous government of President Alemán, many people, primarily those who were not members of the governing Liberal Party, complained that the central government managed municipal funds in a way that allowed it to maintain control over, as well as favour, its party members.

The main argument for failing to provide municipal governments with greater financial resources was that they did not have the capacity to manage them. Central government representatives also argued that there were still local funds available that municipal governments were not tapping. While this may be true, it does not fundamentally affect the need or the right of local governments to receive government transfers. Other arguments against prescribed transfers were that legislators 'need freedom at the time of planning the budget' [*see Fitoria, 2001*], as well as, simply, a lack of funds.

Nevertheless, local government administrative capacity increased substantially in recent years, while government transfers did not. A World Bank study in one province, for example, found that ten out of 13 municipalities had 'adequate' or 'very adequate' internal financial controls [*Donkin and Arguello, 2001*]. While it is true that local governments should also increase their capture of local tax revenues, the principal tax they are permitted to charge is the property tax, which requires an updated cadastre.

Moreover, the legislature actually phased out the municipalities' primary source of local funds – the municipal sales tax. With regard to the supposed shortage of funds, there are several existing sources of funding that are directed to municipal projects through central government institutions and through National Assembly legislators that could easily be transferred to local government.[6]

The situation, though, has finally begun to change. The Social Investment Fund (FISE) – the main entity of the government of Nicaragua for promoting municipal 'development' projects, such as the construction of roads, schools and health centres – was entirely centrally managed and controlled, though analysts argued that municipal governments could undertake the same projects for roughly 75 per cent of the cost [*Fitoria, 2001*]. Thanks to municipal and donor pressure, FISE began transferring administration of these projects to municipalities in 2002; over one-third of Nicaragua's 152 municipalities were managing these funds as of May 2003. Most importantly, the Municipal Budget Transfer Law was finally passed in mid-2003, guaranteeing a four per cent transfer to municipal governments in 2004, increasing gradually to ten per cent by 2010.

Less, however, has changed with regard to natural resources. The primary *stated* reason for limiting local government control over natural resources is – as it was with government transfers – low local capacity, in particular that municipal governments do not have the capacity to make technical decisions. An INAFOR official stated that if, for example, a municipal government gave an unfavourable opinion of a logging contract, he would not take that opinion into account unless it was backed up by a rigorous technical argument. Only a few municipal governments have technical personnel, though this is increasing.

Yet it is readily apparent that there are other important reasons for limiting the role of municipal governments. It does not take great technical expertise, for example, to determine whether felled logs have been taken legally or illegally. Nor is a technical degree in forestry required to make what are primarily political decisions about who should benefit from logging or how that income should be distributed [*Bazaara, 2002*]. More importantly, the state forestry institute does not want to give up income. This includes income from logging contracts as well as fines, since INAFOR controls both contracting and illegal logging. Up until mid-2003, with the imminent approval of a new forestry law, INAFOR depended directly on this income for its own operating budget. There is also, moreover, widespread suspicion that some INAFOR employees obtain important income through corrupt activities; in fact, the director was removed in July 2003 after reinstating three staff members who had been fired after the Attorney General's Office identified them as accomplices in illegal timber trafficking. At the same time, the comptroller's office authorised a special audit of INAFOR in response to the number of anomalies reported nationally.

Even honest employees of INAFOR, however, fear not only losing income but their own power, authority and possibly even their jobs. Lower-level technicians have been heard making disparaging remarks about local government officials for their lack of expertise and lower level of education. The control of information is often a source of power and even income – hence, some central officials fail to share even required information with local governments.

Local governments have, though, gained ground through several key mechanisms. First, since 1993, Nicaragua's municipal governments have all been members of the Nicaraguan Municipal Association, AMUNIC. AMUNIC is funded by the municipal governments themselves but also receives international and NGO funding for numerous specific projects. Its paramount goal is to increase local government capacity and political, administrative and financial autonomy. It has played a key advocacy role for municipal autonomy as well as promoting transparency, local participation and effective natural resource management, and has important ties to donors, the central government's Municipal Development Institute (INIFOM) and national NGOs. AMUNIC was behind important amendments to the Municipalities Law that significantly increased municipal autonomy and authority in 1997. Several other laws have been drafted and a few passed, thanks at least in part to AMUNIC's lobbying and networking. AMUNIC has also been active in negotiating the transfer to municipalities of the 25 per cent of tax income on resource extraction contracts. Central government allies, as well as donor pressure, are also essential. The delivery of timber revenues began under an INAFOR director who explicitly and actively supported the decentralisation of key forest management activities to local governments.

Second, the political power of local government has increased in more subtle and strategic ways. Two vice presidential candidates for the 2001 elections had previously been directors of INIFOM, including the current vice president. As local government authority and legitimacy has increased in the eyes of local citizens so has the perception of national political leaders that mayors are important for mobilising popular support. In turn, then, national leaders have become more likely to support formal decentralisation initiatives. For example, a political battle between the Legislature and the Executive over the 2003 national budget resulted in a majority alliance in the Legislature in support of an unprecedented 3.2 per cent fiscal transfer to municipal governments. In the final negotiation, the Legislature backed down on this demand, but several months later the Executive offered municipal governments an even higher percentage for 2004 and the Municipal Budget Transfer Law was negotiated and passed unanimously by the National Assembly.

Third, through political pressure and organisation individual municipalities have also had some success at getting INAFOR and other central agencies to hear their demands. In general, the municipality of Managua, probably due to its size, appears to have little problem engaging central resource ministries in negotiation. Smaller municipalities, however, have had to resort to other means. For example, four municipalities in the north of León province joined together in a threat to pass ordinances banning logging. INAFOR responded by agreeing to approve all logging contracts only with municipal government consent, rather than just their official 'opinion'.

Finally, it is important to mention that numerous foreign aid agencies, particularly the World Bank, have played an important role by lending legitimacy and funding to the decentralisation process – both in general and with regard to natural resources. Many of these agencies have also directly promoted capacity-building for local officials.

IV. MUNICIPAL RESOURCE MANAGEMENT

As mentioned earlier, municipal governments have in general shown greater interest in natural resources and resource issues where the generation of income is concerned. They also may be motivated by the more intangible benefits of actually having decision-making authority, though this is more difficult to study given the current limits on this authority. This section first reviews a few of the different kinds of management activities or other specific resource-related initiatives in which local governments have been involved, then looks at the question of motivation more closely.

Resource-Related Initiatives

Logging Permits. According to law, the municipal government must give its opinion on all resource extraction permits prior to their approval by the central government. At least with respect to timber, almost all of the nation's municipalities participate in this process, though in the end there may be more illegal loggers than legal ones. The municipal government usually charges a fee for this *aval*.

As of 2002, INAFOR sometimes transferred responsibility for the approval of domestic permits – small amounts, determined by region, for household use – to local governments. All permits for larger quantities, however, required management plans and INAFOR approval.[7]

Personnel. Municipal governments increasingly have their own personnel specifically assigned to the task of reviewing permit applications in order to give a more informed opinion. These personnel should visit the site in question, confirm that the applicants are in fact the landowners and guarantee that the trees to be logged are of sufficient width and in an appropriate location. In some municipalities, a community representative undertakes this on-site review rather than the government, and the application is passed on to the local government with that representative's approval.

Personnel are also sometimes hired, particularly in wealthier municipalities, to monitor protected areas, manage nurseries and reforestation projects, direct agroforestry projects and support INAFOR in the control of logging. Nevertheless, it is often the poorest and most rural forest-rich municipalities that most need personnel to independently review logging requests but have the least resources with which to contract qualified people. When there are technicians in these municipalities, they are almost always financed, at least in part, with donor funds.

Fees for Resource Extraction and Related Activities. Many municipal governments have charged fees of all kinds for resource use and extraction. These include the *aval* fee mentioned above, fees for the use of transit routes and fines for unauthorised extraction. In other cases, local governments have sought to charge a registration fee for all kinds of machinery and equipment used for resource extraction, such as chainsaws. In some cases, municipal governments charged their own logging fees in order to compensate for INAFOR's failure to transfer their legally allocated portion to them. The problem with this is that the majority of these charges are illegal, though it is not entirely clear which are and which are not.

Ordinances and Resolutions. Many municipal governments have begun to try to protect local resources by issuing municipal ordinances and resolutions. Many of these ordinances address problems of contamination, deforestation or over-exploitation by stating local government policy and often, again, establishing fees for resource use and/or fines for non-compliance. Many of these have been passed at the pressure or urging of NGOs working in those municipalities and could, if enforced, improve environmental conditions or prevent deterioration.

Municipal Environmental Commissions (CAMs). The CAMs are the most common way in which local governments have promoted intra-governmental co-ordination and civil society participation in addressing natural resource or environmental concerns. They are advisory bodies made up of representatives of local government, central government, civil society and sometimes private enterprise. As of 2002, over half of Nicaragua's municipalities had established CAMs, though few actually met on a regular basis with a clear and dynamic agenda. Some particularly active CAMs, however, have drafted important municipal ordinances controlling resource extraction, manage environmental education campaigns, co-ordinate activities among INAFOR, MARENA and the local government, and investigate complaints by citizens of 'irrational' or illegal extraction.[8]

Fire Controls. MAGFOR and MARENA have actively promoted fire prevention since a drought in early 1998 led to massive forest fires throughout Nicaragua and the rest of Central America. Officially, this has often been co-ordinated by the mayor's office with the participation of the local representatives of several central government entities and local civil society (NGOs, projects and farmers). Unofficially, the primary role of the Municipal Council has been to issue an appropriate fire ordinance establishing requirements for burning permits and fines for burning without a permit, and declaring local government support for the campaign – which is then usually managed by NGOs.

Nevertheless, a few municipal governments have actually fined or jailed farmers who lost control of their fires and damaged other people's property. Also, since a pine blight struck a large portion of Nicaragua's northern pine forests, leading to the felling of thousands of trees in 2001–2, municipal governments were seen, perhaps for the first time, taking active leadership in fire prevention during the 2002 dry season.

Preventing Extraction. Local groups protested against central government-approved mining concessions in the municipalities of El Castillo and in Bonanza, and in both cases convinced their local governments to take their side. The central government did not actually cancel the concession in either case, but neither of the two companies involved has ever chosen to act on its concession. In other cases, local protest is directly aimed at local government. Community members from one district of El Sauce objected to logging being carried out by a company from a neighbouring municipality. They demanded that the government take action, and threatened to blockade the logging road if it did not. When the municipal government failed to respond, the population fulfilled its threat, blockaded the roads and forced the government to negotiate a municipal ordinance that suspended existing logging permits for six months and required district council approval of new permits.

Corruption. Some local governments have taken advantage of their new power to reap economic benefits at the expense of their constituents and their local resources. The mayor and two councillors from Waspán, for example, were – together with the INAFOR delegate and others – accused of illegal wood trafficking, and were placed under investigation (*La Prensa*, 18 January 2001). In other cases, municipal governments have accused INAFOR of corruption.

The mayor of Bilwi (Puerto Cabezas) told *La Prensa*, 'It is time for the Environmental Attorney General and the Comptroller's Office to investigate the logging, marketing and illegal trafficking of wood and the complicity of INAFOR' (*La Prensa*, 15 November 2002).

Marginal Groups. In a few cases, marginal groups are clearly better off under decentralised management. In Bonanza, the indigenous Mayangna population has increased its power and authority in the region by participating in the traditional political system and getting several members elected to local office, including, as of 2001, the mayor. This has made it possible to put indigenous concerns, such as the legal demarcation of indigenous territories, on the political agenda.

Other Initiatives. In addition to these initiatives, some local governments have declared municipal protected areas, sought actively to support existing national parks, developed land-use plans and undertaken environmental planning exercises. Many have promoted reforestation projects and a few have undertaken broader-scale watershed or agroforestry projects.

Motivation

In spite of all of these initiatives, there is little investment in the forestry sector; the initiatives, moreover, have been fairly haphazard, uncoordinated and unplanned. In general, municipal priorities tend to be urban and geared toward the provision of services and infrastructure, even in rural areas where natural resources are essential for local livelihoods and development. Neither local governments nor local citizens tend to associate natural resource or environmental concerns with 'development', but rather with conservation – which they associate not with local government but with MARENA. In a study of 21 municipalities in 2001, only two appeared close to considering these issues integral to the overall management, organisation and development of the municipality [*Larson, 2001*]. In part, this is an issue of tradition that requires a change in the conception of development.

As local governments tend to become increasingly involved in natural resource initiatives and as, at the same time, this changing conception of development evolves, the question of motivation becomes key to understanding the future of decentralised forest management. Why do local governments get involved in natural resource management at all, and what motivation do they have to make responsible resource decisions?

As political leaders, elected officials are usually interested in maintaining public support and being remembered for the initiatives taken during their administration.[9] This is often one of the reasons officials give for investing in visible, often urban, infrastructure projects such as roads, sidewalks, schools or community buildings; but reforestation, fire prevention or watershed projects also provide a simple and reasonably inexpensive way to take recognisable initiatives in rural areas.

Perhaps more importantly, environmental management initiatives, as well as local government transparency and accountability, are high on the agenda of many donor organisations. Several national NGOs and other agencies even give out awards to municipal governments for exceptional performance in these two arenas. Hence, promoting environmental initiatives increases visibility and can provide a platform for attracting funding to the municipality – and to the local government in particular. Recognition, such as through national awards, can provide incentives for interested politicians to increase their own legitimacy and respectability as political leaders.

These strategic political interests provide the context for understanding the responses of local leaders to the immediate pressures or opportunities found to have played a key role in government action highlighted in the Nicaragua research. Four factors were found to be important: an economic interest in generating municipal revenue; specific legal responsibility; a conflict or crisis; and NGO or project pressure or influence [*Larson, 2002*].

The nature and quantity of the initiatives taken make it clear that many municipal governments' main interest in natural resources is in generating revenue. It is often this possibility that, at least initially, attracts their attention to the issues when pressured or lobbied by civil society organisations or other parties interested in promoting local resource management by municipal governments. This has occurred in a context where the central government controls the vast majority of resource revenues and has often failed to hand over the legally required share to local governments.[10]

At the same time, having legal responsibility for a particular issue also appears to encourage local governments to perform the indicated task. For example, whether they take it seriously or not, all the municipalities studied provide *avals* when they are requested. Having legal responsibility or the right to make certain decisions also clearly affects the nature of the initiatives taken, the way in which central government and donor support is directed, and the expectations of the local population [*see also Larson, 2003*].

In other cases, conflict or crisis leads to action: the mayor's office in Posoltega promoted watershed protection after over two thousand people died in a devastating landslide provoked by Hurricane Mitch in 1998. In Bonanza, El Castillo and El Sauce, local citizens chose to fight outside logging or mining interests and turned to their local governments for support and action, and in some cases actually forced the local government's hand in the matter. Local governments appear less likely to intervene, however, when conflicts involve two or more *local* groups.

Municipal governments have also sometimes avoided intervening, even when a serious problem arises. In Jalapa, neither local government nor INAFOR personnel took action to address the pine beetle problem until it had seriously escalated. Municipal authorities said they did not have the technical expertise to manage forestry problems or the funds to hire technical personnel. It is also not entirely clear, given the legal framework, that it was their responsibility rather than INAFOR's. Nevertheless, logging is one of the most important economic activities in the region. Once the problem became critical enough, both INAFOR and the local governments began to take action.

In many cases, NGOs and other donors have provided important incentives and pressure on local governments through their initiative, influence and persistence. This includes threats to withdraw funding, persistent lobbying and negotiation, hiring 'municipal' personnel, and drafting ordinances themselves and presenting them to the Municipal Council for approval. For example, in El Castillo, the Danish aid agency DANIDA threatened to withdraw funding in three different cases between 1996 and 2001 if the local government did not do as it requested.[11] In another example, an NGO in Cua-Bocay organised an alliance of community groups to oppose a mining concession in the municipality and convinced the local municipal council to vote against the concession.[12] Some NGOs, as well as AMUNIC and MARENA, have pressured or encouraged local governments to form CAMs and institutionalise their participation, as well as, at times, the participation of other groups. Not all of these activities promote government assimilation or understanding of the problem, however. They do, though, represent the leverage of certain sectors of civil society. The best projects have worked closely with local peoples and sympathetic municipal government representatives to build a clear understanding of the issues and an institutional framework for the future.

All of these factors suggest the paramount role of economics and political pressure in such situations [*see also Gibson and Lehoucq, 2003*], as well as the importance of understanding the possible strategic interests of local leaders. The interest in generating income from natural resources is a political concern where existing budgets are limited by political decisions at the central government level and where central authorities fail to provide legally mandated funds. The legal responsibility for certain tasks is delegated by central politicians or won through the lobbying efforts of local governments and their allies. Local politicians respond to the opportunities, as well as the realities, presented by local crises and conflicts – and may avoid responding if there is no grass-roots or other political pressure, no clear benefit or no mandate that makes it their responsibility to do so. NGOs and other pressure groups exert their democratic right to influence local government through whatever means they believe appropriate.

Municipal government leaders have their own interests in pleasing their constituents and responding to their concerns, highlighting their own abilities to act responsibly, being seen as committed to natural resource and environmental concerns, and winning broader recognition. Yet in many cases, local people and organisations have to apply pressure on local governments in order for them to take action. Also, without grass-roots democracy, local politicians may have a stronger incentive to pursue their personal interests rather than their constituents' interests. Whether their local elected officials have a specific legal responsibility or not, local people are increasingly turning to these leaders as the appropriate authority to address local problems.

V. CONCLUSIONS

By definition, decentralisation is a political process because it involves the redistribution of power and resources. Those who have to give up power and resources – in this case central governments – will often, naturally, resist doing so. The decentralisation of natural resource management is even more likely to provoke resistance, because natural resources are often economically valuable. They generate income for central government agencies, maintain jobs for central government employees and even provide 'perks' – through corrupt activities – to individuals in certain positions of responsibility.

It is not surprising, therefore, that central governments resist decentralisation. What is surprising is how rare it appears for donors who promote decentralisation to recognise and take into account this political resistance.[13] It is precisely the dynamic grass-roots political process – which, in itself, should be reinforced by democratic decentralisation – that makes it possible to overcome central resistance. Decentralisation from below, combined with donor pressure, is what makes the formal decentralisation process from above possible, as well as being a key factor in making it effective.

Similarly, the political process is clearly critical in decentralised natural resource management by local governments. Many local governments appear to have little interest in taking resource-related initiatives unless these generate short-term economic and/or political benefits. Development priorities are elsewhere. Yet, as local elected governments gain authority and legitimacy, they are increasingly pressured by constituents to address all kinds of issues relevant to local livelihoods – including concerns about natural resources. Donors and NGOs can increase the incentives for responsible environmental initiatives by raising the profile of, and hence the political benefits for, the elected leaders who take them. How these pressures and incentives are directed will play an important role in affecting the kinds of decisions local governments make as well as the outcomes for local people and natural resources.

A specific and clear legal mandate for local governments creates political opportunities both for pressure groups and for local government officials themselves. This legal mandate reflects the conception of formal democratic decentralisation, where downwardly accountable local actors are given significant powers in an autonomous decision-making sphere [*Ribot, 2002*]. But the Nicaraguan case, as well as many others documented in this volume, suggests that effective democratic decentralisation – and particularly the democratic decentralisation of natural resource management – will not, and perhaps cannot, be implemented only from above.

NOTES

1. This essay is based on several years of research and analysis of decentralisation and municipal natural resource management in Nicaragua, with a primary focus on forest management [*see Barahona and Mendoza, 1999; Fauné and Kaimowitz, 1999; Fauné and Martínez, 1999; Fauné and Mendoza, 1998; Larson, 2001, 2002; Larson and Barahona, 1999a, b; Martínez and Mendoza, 1999; Martínez and Rocha, 1999; Mendoza and Artola, 1999; Mendoza and Martínez, 1999; Parrilli, 2000; Rocha and Barahona, 1999*]. Additional interviews were conducted for an earlier version of this essay. My conception of decentralisation 'from below' has benefited in particular from conversations with David Kaimowitz.
2. Still, 66 per cent said that a person could only get something from a municipal government if s/he was well connected. This contrasts with a more recent poll (in a different region) that found that only ten per cent of the people surveyed believed friends of the mayor were the primary beneficiaries of INIFOM-funded projects (G. Boyer, World Bank Municipalities Project, email communication, 7 Dec. 2001).
3. These are granted by the Municipalities Law (Nos.40 and 261), the General Law of the Environment and Natural Resources (Law 217) and related enabling legislation (Decrees 9-96, 45-94 and 14-99). Fire control was established by Decree 207 in 1972.
4. The only specific arena that is the exclusive responsibility of local governments is waste management.
5. In the case of the Regional Governments of the Atlantic Coast, the central government is required by law to get their approval for concessions, though it has sometimes failed to do so.
6. These include the Social Investment Fund (FISE), Rural Development Institute (IDR) and the Presidency [*Baltodano, 2002*].
7. Administrative procedures established in 2002 by INAFOR changed the standards from a consideration of the amount to be logged to the size of the area to be logged. Thus, 'domestic permits' disappeared in favour of 'areas under ten hectares' – only these, too, now require a management plan. A new Forestry Law was approved by the National Assembly as this essay was going to press, which would allow INAFOR to sign accords with local governments – permitting them for the first time, in special cases, to authorise commercial logging permits.
8. Some, however, have overstepped their authority and tried to impose their decisions on municipal governments (J. Ortega, J., Environmental Lawyer, AMUNIC, Interviews, 7 Sept. 2000 and 17 Nov. 2001).
9. In Nicaragua, mayors are not permitted to run for immediate re-election, but may serve for a total of two terms during their lifetime.
10. It is also important to remember that some of these charges are illegal.
11. These requests involved rejecting a central government mining concession, reinstating technical assistants who had been trained by the project (fired in a change of administration) and taking action to evict colonists from inside a forest reserve.
12. The mining company, however, lobbied councillors as well as the community that would be directly affected; the council voted in favour of the concession in its next session.

13. One form of resistance includes the manipulation of decentralisation discourse while actually *increasing* central government control over remote regions and undermining traditional local resource management [*see Wittman, 2002, on Guatemala*].

REFERENCES

Baltodano, M., 2002, 'Cambiar esquemas en manejo de recursos', *Municipalidades*, Vol.2, No.9, pp.18–21.

Barahona, T. and R. Mendoza, 1999, 'Chinandega: El manejo de una reserva natural en un mundo de agricultores', Managua: CIFOR/Nitlapán/Protierra.

Bazaara, N., 2002, 'Actors, Powers and Environmental Accountability in Uganda's Decentralization', Paper prepared for the 'Workshop on Decentralization and the Environment', Bellagio, Italy, 18–22 Feb.

Donkin and Arguello, 2001, 'Evaluación del Control Interno, Departamento de Chinandega', Nicaragua. Consultants' report, unpublished.

Fauné, A. and D. Kaimowitz, 1999, 'Posoltega: La necesidad de articular esfuerzos y recursos en torno a la reforestación', Managua: CIFOR/Nitlapán/Protierra.

Fauné, A. and T. Martínez, 1999, 'Achuapa: Capacidades locales para la gestión de recursos naturales', Managua: CIFOR/Nitlapán/Protierra.

Fauné, A. and R. Mendoza, 1998, 'Bosawas: La gestión de los recursos naturales en el territorio: Estado, gobierno y poderes locales', Unpublished report, Managua: CIFOR/Nitlapán.

Ferroukhi, L. (ed.), 2003, *Gestión Forestal Municipal en América Latina*, San José: CIFOR/IDRC.

Fitoria, D., 2001, 'Descentralización: Tarea Pendiente', *Confidencial*, Vol.6, No.257.

Gibson, C. and F. Lehoucq, forthcoming, 'The Local Politics of Decentralized Environmental Policy', *Journal of Environment and Development*, Vol.12, No.1, pp.28–49.

Kaimowitz, D. and J. Ribot, 2002, 'Services and Infrastructure versus Natural Resource Management: Building a Base for Democratic Decentralization', Paper prepared for the 'Workshop on Decentralization and the Environment', Bellagio, Italy, 18–22 Feb.

Larson, A., 2003, 'Decentralization and Forest Management in Latin America: Toward a Working Model', *Public Administration and Development*, Vol.23, No.2, pp.211–26.

Larson, A., 2002, 'Natural Resources and Decentralization in Nicaragua: Are Local Governments Up to the Job?' *World Development*, Vol.30, No.1, pp.17–31.

Larson, A., 2001, *Recursos Forestales y Gobiernos Municipales en Nicaragua: Hacia una Gestión Efectiva*, Managua: CIFOR/Nitlapán.

Larson, A. and T. Barahona, 1999a, 'San Carlos: Una oportunidad despreciada?' Managua: CIFOR/Nitlapán/Protierra.

Larson, A. and T. Barahona, 1999b, 'El Castillo: La colonización y las empresas madereras en una zona de amortiguamiento', Managua: CIFOR/Nitlapán/Protierra.

Martínez, T. and R. Mendoza, 1999, 'Somotillo: La gestión de cuencas una necesidad impostergable', Managua: CIFOR/Nitlapán/Protierra.

Martínez, T. and J.L. Rocha, 1999, 'El Sauce: La organización comunitaria como base para el desarrollo', Managua: CIFOR/Nitlapán/Protierra.

Mendoza, R. and N. Artola, 1999, 'León: Dilemas en la gestión del bosque seco y del área manglar', Managua: CIFOR/Nitlapán/Protierra.

Mendoza, R. and T. Martínez, 1999, 'Villanueva: Los recursos naturales en un municipio empobrecido', Managua: CIFOR/Nitlapán/Protierra.

Ortega, M., 1997, *Nicaragua: Políticas de descentralización y capacidades de gestión administrativa y financiera de las municipalidades*, San Salvador: FLACSO.

Ortega, M. and M Castillo, 1996, 'Informe de Resultados: Cultura Política Local y Percepción Cuidadana sobre su Participación en el Proceso Electoral', IPADE/CASC-UCA/DANIDA, Managua.

Parrilli, M.D., 2000, 'Reactivando la Cadena de los Pinares en las Segovias: Análisis de conclusiones a partir del study-tour realizado en Dipilto, Santa Clara, Jalapa, Ocotal y Estelí en mayo del 2000', Managua: CIFOR-Nitlapán.

Ribot, J., 2002, 'Democratic Decentralization of Natural Resources: Institutionalizing Popular Participation', Washington, DC: World Resources Institute.

Rocha, J.L. and T. Barahona, 1999, 'Puerto Morazán: La camaronicultura: Un espejismo en tierra salada?' Managua: CIFOR/Nitlapán/Protierra.

Wittman, H., 2002, 'Negotiating Locality: Decentralization and Communal Forest Management in the Guatemalan Highlands,' Masters thesis, Cornell University.

Democratic Decentralisation and Traditional Authority: Dilemmas of Land Administration in Rural South Africa

LUNGISILE NTSEBEZA

I. INTRODUCTION

Since the advent of democracy in 1994, South Africa has embarked on its own version of democratic decentralisation in a range of areas. In this contribution, the issue of decentralisation will be interrogated primarily through a focus on local government reform and land administration. This focus illuminates problems that are on the horizon for natural resources, such as forests, wildlife and fisheries, especially as these latter resources are to be managed through similar structures that are being constructed and contested in the local government and land-policy arenas. Within this context, the role of traditional authorities and municipal councillors will be assessed.[1]

The Constitution of the Republic of South Africa establishes three distinct, interdependent and interrelated spheres of government: national, provincial and local.[2] The local sphere of government is made up of municipalities. In terms of the Constitution, municipalities must be established throughout the country, including rural areas.[3] The Constitution further states that the national or a provincial government 'may not compromise or impede a municipality's ability or right to exercise its powers or perform its function'.[4] The Constitution and White Paper on Local Government define post-1994 local government as 'developmental', involving integrated development planning. This requires municipalities to coordinate all development activities within their areas of jurisdiction [*Pycroft, 1998: 151*].

Developmental local government thus seeks not only to democratise local government, by introducing the notion of elected representatives even in rural areas, but also to transform local governance, with a new focus on improving the standard of living and quality of life of previously disadvantaged sectors of the community [*Pycroft, 1998: 155*]. In addition, developmental local

Lungisile Ntsebeza is Associate Professor in the Department of Sociology, University of Cape Town, South Africa.

European Journal of Development Research, Vol.16, No.1, Spring 2004, pp.71–89
ISSN 0957-8811 print
DOI:10.1080/0957881041000168874

government requires that citizens should actively participate in development initiatives in their areas [see *ANC, 1994: 2–3; Ntsebeza, 1999; 2001*].[5]

As a legacy of the colonial and apartheid periods, most land in the rural areas of the former Bantustans is owned by the state and the Development Trust, and administered and managed (during the apartheid period) by government-created Tribal Authorities. Although rural inhabitants are the effective owners of land in the sense that they have lived in these areas for long periods of time, landholding based on the permit-to-occupy (PTO) system does not provide them with a legally secure title comparable to a freehold title. It is, above all, this insecurity of tenure that has created conditions for the exclusion of rural inhabitants from the administration and management of what is essentially their land. Land-tenure reform aims to correct these imbalances.

Tenure security is addressed in South Africa's Constitution as follows: 'A person or community whose tenure of land is legally insecure as a result of past racially discriminatory laws or practices is entitled, to the extent provided by an Act of Parliament, either to legally secure tenure or to comparable redress.'[6] These constitutional provisions, coupled with the democratic principles enshrined in the Constitution and in various pieces of post-1994 legislation, establish conditions for new democratic and accountable institutions – with significant community participation – for land administration and management. The new structures that will perform the land administration and management functions will not necessarily be the new developmental local governments. However, whether land administration and management functions are performed by local government or not, local government will still be obliged to play its former regulatory and control roles, and, since 1994, fulfil its developmental mandate.

Despite the fact that a large number of traditional authorities became collaborators and stooges in the colonial and apartheid systems, the institution of traditional leadership gained recognition in South Africa's 1993 Interim Constitution and 1996 Final Constitution. However, in these documents there was no clarity as to the precise roles, functions and powers of traditional authorities in rural local government or land administration. The recognition of the institution of traditional authorities raises a host of questions about the nature of democratic decentralisation in the rural areas under traditional authorities. In particular, it raises the conceptual question of whether an inherently undemocratic, hereditary institution can exist in a South African democracy purportedly modelled on the liberal tradition of representative government. Indeed, upholding a constitution that enshrines democratic principles in a Bill of Rights, whilst acknowledging a political role, or roles, for unelected and unaccountable traditional authorities, is inconsistent and contradictory. This contradiction also raises questions about the possible resolution of the identity of rural inhabitants in the former Bantustans in post-1994 South Africa. The issue here is whether rural residents will continue to be subjects under the political rule of unelected traditional authorities or will enjoy the citizenship rights, including the right to choose leaders and representatives, that the South African Constitution confers on all South Africans.

This contribution examines the institutional arrangements put in place in the name of decentralisation and the impacts of these arrangements on, in particular, land administration in the rural areas of the former Bantustans of South Africa.[7] Of critical importance will be a discussion of the role of traditional authorities in post-1994 South Africa, particularly how they have responded to current policies and laws. At the heart of the discussion will be an assessment of the relationship between theory and practice.

II. DECENTRALISATION: KEY CONCEPTS

An outline of two key concepts, 'decentralised despotism' and 'political/democratic decentralisation', is a useful starting point for understanding South Africa's dilemma of democratising rural areas while recognising hereditary traditional authorities.

Mamdani's [*1996*] thesis is that the colonial state in Africa was 'bifurcated', with different modes of rule for urban 'citizens' and rural 'subjects'. The colonial strategy of 'divide and rule' took two related forms: an enforced division of Africans along ethnic lines, and an enforced division between town and countryside. The African was 'containerised', not as a native or indigenous African but as a 'tribesperson'. Colonialists justified 'indirect rule' on the basis that 'tradition' and 'custom' were indigenous forms of social organisation. Moreover, they reinforced and used these identities to divide and manage rural Africans. In order to enforce their dual policy of 'ethnic pluralism' and urban–rural division, colonialists exercised 'force to an unusual degree'. In this way, colonial despotism was highly decentralised [*Mamdani, 1996: 22–4*].

The chief, according to Mamdani, was a pivotal actor in the local state: the Native Authority. His authority was rooted in the fusion of various powers – judicial, legislative and executive – in his office, rather than the classic liberal democratic notion of a separation thereof. Mamdani uses the analogy of a 'clenched fist' to delineate this concentration of power. Native Authorities, according to him, were protected from threats by anyone but their colonial rulers. Their officials were appointed from above and never elected. They had no term of office, and remained therein for as long as they enjoyed the confidence of their superiors.

Mamdani argues that the colonial legacy was reproduced after independence. However, no nationalist government was content to reproduce the colonial legacy uncritically. Each attempted to reform the colonial state, but in doing so reproduced a part of that legacy, thereby creating its own variety of despotism. Post-colonial African states, whether conservative or radical, de-racialised the colonial state, but did not democratise it. On democratic transformation, Mamdani proposes 'nothing less than dismantling' the 'bifurcated state'. This will entail 'an endeavor to link the urban and the rural – and thereby a series of related binary opposites such as rights and custom, representation and participation, centralization and decentralization, civil society and community – in ways that have yet to be done' [*Mamdani, 1996: 34*].

These features of Native Authorities aptly capture the central features of Tribal Authorities that were set up during the apartheid period in South Africa. It is arguably in response to these that the post-apartheid state is making efforts to 'dismantle' Tribal Authorities. It is not clear, however, how far these new local political–administrative arrangements move away from the system of 'decentralised despotism' and towards a more democratic form of rural governance. The constitutional recognition of the hereditary 'institution of traditional leadership' without any clarity as to its roles, functions and powers makes these questions about democratising rural governance even more urgent.

'Political/democratic decentralisation' is said to occur when powers and resources are transferred to authorities that are 'downwardly accountable to local populations' [*Agrawal and Ribot, 1999: 478*]. The aim is to increase public participation in local decision making. Advocates of this kind of arrangement believe that locally accountable representatives with real public powers and greater community participation in decision making will increase efficiency and equity in the use of public resources. This notion of decentralisation can be contrasted with other kinds of decentralisation reforms taking place in the name of democratisation and development. For example, deconcentration – or 'administrative decentralisation' – and privatisation, which are not democratic in nature, often accompany or take place in the name of democratic decentralisation reforms. Deconcentration occurs when the central state transfers some responsibilities to its local branches. In this regard, local branches are primarily upwardly accountable to the central state, and not necessarily downwardly accountable to the communities they are serving. Proponents of democratic decentralisation consider deconcentration as 'weak' decentralisation precisely because it is not downwardly accountable and therefore not democratic.

Whether privatisation can be regarded as a form of decentralisation is a hotly debated issue. Those in dispute argue that decentralisation concerns public resources, while privatisation entails transferring public resources to private groups and individuals that may or may not serve public interests. As with deconcentration, these groups and individuals are not necessarily obliged to be 'downwardly accountable' to the communities they serve. Also, the logic of privatisation is quite different from that of decentralisation [*Agrawal and Ribot, 1999*].

Manor has recently argued that studies of democratic decentralisation indicate three essential conditions for democratic local government: substantial resources (especially financial resources) from higher levels of government; substantial powers to be devolved to local authorities; and mechanisms to ensure that bureaucrats are accountable to elected representatives, on the one hand, and mechanisms to ensure that elected representatives are accountable to voters, on the other [*Manor, 2001: 2*].

Through the lens of land tenure and control, this contribution investigates the degree to which rural political administration is shifting away from the closed-fist policies of colonial and apartheid decentralised despotism towards more democratic and enfranchising forms of rural authority.

III. CURRENT DYNAMICS IN SOUTH AFRICA'S COUNTRYSIDE

Almost ten years since the advent of democracy in South Africa, there is still confusion as to the form local government and land administration will take within its borders, including the precise role of traditional authorities. In the run-up to the 1994 elections, the majority of rural areas in the former Bantustans were characterised by deep tensions and clashes between traditional authorities and groups in civil society led by residents' associations. The most popular civil organisation that emerged from around 1993 was the South African National Civic Organisation (SANCO). At the centre of these struggles was control over land – and land allocation in particular. In many rural areas, residents' associations – led by SANCO – took over the land allocation functions from traditional authorities. By 1994, there was a breakdown in land administration, including the issue of PTOs, in many rural areas.

After the 1995/96 local government elections, these tensions manifested themselves between elected rural councillors and SANCO on one side, and traditional authorities on the other. The majority of rural councillors were drawn from SANCO activists. The confusion as to whose function it was to allocate land continued unabated. This was particularly true in the case where civic structures and traditional authorities had equal popular support. There are two levels at which this dilemma could be understood and explained: the law and practice. The laws governing the allocation of land in the rural areas of the former Bantustans have not been repealed. In this regard, the South African Constitution is clear that existing laws will remain in force until such time as they have been replaced by appropriate legislation. As will be seen below, the processes of establishing legislation to clarify land allocation procedures in post-1994 rural South Africa have borne no fruit. Hence, apartheid laws regarding allocation of land in rural areas remain in force.

Most rural residents, including rural councillors, and indeed many South Africans thought that land allocation was to be one of the responsibilities of the newly elected councillors. After all, control over land was the cardinal issue in rural struggles in the early-to-mid 1990s. The perception of most rural residents was that all the functions that were performed by Tribal Authorities, including land allocation, would be taken over by elected councillors. These residents, and rural councillors in particular, got a rude shock when it turned out that the old apartheid laws were still in place. Above all, government officials still use, with minor adjustments, the apartheid procedure and do not recognise elected councillors as having the powers required to allocate land. The extent of the above confusion, the dilemma of rural residents, and the role of government officials over land allocation in areas falling under the jurisdiction of traditional authorities are well captured in the testimony of one rural resident who was sympathetic to SANCO:

> This is the reason why we still use chiefs. Rural councillors run in circles. This makes us a laughing stock and divides us. People will tell you: 'Go to your rural councillor, you won't succeed'. You end up going to the chief, even if you did not want to. At the magistrate's offices they ask you about the stamp [of the Tribal Authority]. If you do not have the stamp, they will say: 'Don't waste our time'. The land issue is complex. There is a struggle between TrepCs [Transitional Representative elected rural Councillors] and the headman. The former brought electricity and telephones, but land is in the hands of chiefs. You are forced to be flexible (*kufuneka ubemvoco*), otherwise you won't get your benefits. When we wanted land for pre-schools we were told to go to the headman, something that made the headman boastful. Sometimes you may have spoken badly about the headman, and you end up bowing down to it, as it is often necessary that you get what you want. With chiefs and headmen it takes a few days to get what you want, whereas with rural councillors it takes months, and even then you end up not succeeding.[8]

The above statement reflects experiences in one administrative area in the Transkei where inhabitants were divided between supporters of the headman, and civic structures and rural councillors. In this area, civic structures under the auspices of SANCO demarcated land and allocated plots to its supporters, an indication that control of local governance by elected officials rather than traditional authorities is possible. However, those who were allocated plots were not granted PTOs as the government officials did not recognise their process. It is partly to this dilemma that the above informant was referring.[9]

The above statement also says something about the performance of rural councillors. It is quite clear from interviews with many rural inhabitants across gender and generation that there was a lot of expectation that a developmental local government would transform their lives. By the end of the transition period in 2000, though, rural councillors had lost the confidence of ordinary rural residents who initially supported them. The main cause of the disgruntlement seems to have been lack of delivery of even basic services such as water and road maintenance. There are a number of reasons why performance has been poor, but especially lack of adequate support from government in the form of allowances that could attract capable and skilled people, and a budget that could provide capacity building for councillors and finance essential services.[10] The lack of skill among councillors became evident when Integrated Development Plans (IDPs), so critical to developmental local government, had to be prepared. In many parts of the countryside, the IDP process was either not started or never finalised. Where it was ‘completed’, consultants were the driving force behind the process and there was barely any participation of communities as required by the Constitution and legislation. In short, serious deficiencies among rural councillors, partly as a result of lack of government support, have the potential of weakening democracy as rural residents lose confidence in their elected representatives and end up preferring unaccountable Tribal Authorities and their incumbents.

Before embarking on a further analysis of the current dilemma in the democratisation of rural areas, it is worth situating the issue of traditional authorities in a brief historical context.

IV. TRADITIONAL AUTHORITIES IN HISTORICAL PERSPECTIVE

Prior to the introduction of democracy in South Africa in 1994, and especially during the apartheid period, local government and land administration were concentrated or fused in Tribal Authorities. These structures, which were made up of chiefs, headmen and councillors and a tribal secretary, were imposed on resisting rural inhabitants and were an extended arm of the central state. They were, not surprisingly, undemocratic, unaccountable, autocratic, and, in many instances, feared [*Ntsebeza, 2001, 1999; Manona, 1998; Mbeki, 1984; Lodge, 1983*]. The allocation of land provides an excellent example.

The process of allocating land started at a local, sub-headman area and was finalised with the issuing of a PTO by the magistrate/district commissioner.[11] In theory, a person, usually a man, who wanted land first identified the land and approached people in the neighbourhood to establish if there were other claimants and solicit their support. In the event that the land was available, the applicant approached the sub-headman of the ward in which the property was situated. The sub-headman then called a ward general assembly (*imbizo*), at which the purpose was to offer people an opportunity to comment on the application. If there were no objections, the sub-headman submitted the application to the headman of the administrative area. The headman verbally verified that the general assembly was called, and that no objections had been lodged. In addition, the headman established whether the applicant was a married, registered taxpayer. In this regard, the sub-headman had to produce a receipt issued by the magistrate as proof. If the applicant could not produce a receipt, the headman would have to accompany the applicant to the magistrate's office, where he would be duly registered. The applicant could not go to the magistrate's office on his own: he had to be accompanied by a headman or the chief.

Upon production of the receipt, the headman then normally granted the application; this was seen as a formality. As one headman stated: 'As a headman, I accept and respect the decision of the sub-headman.' The headman then submitted the application to the Tribal Authority; this was also seen as a formality. The Tribal Authority completed the application form that was submitted to the district commissioner. The application form had to be signed by the chief, the councillors and the Tribal Authority Secretary. At this point the applicant was expected to pay an application fee to the Tribal Authority; this was the only fee that the applicant was supposed to pay.

In practice, though, the system of land allocation was complex and often did not adhere to the letter of the law. The main problem was how to monitor the system and make local authorities accountable. In the majority of cases, traditional authorities were upwardly accountable to the government, not to the rural residents. The apartheid and Bantustan regimes gave traditional authorities such powers that they were feared rather than respected by their communities [*Delius, 1996; Ntsebeza, 1999*]. This made it extremely difficult for ordinary rural residents to hold traditional authorities accountable.

Some traditional authorities, moreover, exploited the lack of 'checks and balances'. There were basically two forms of violations: allocating land without going through the procedure, and illegal taxation. Traditional authorities abused their power by charging unauthorised fees to applicants in the name of the 'rights of the great place' (*iimfanelo zakomkhulu*). These included alcohol, poultry, sheep, and even an ox. This practice reached its zenith in the early 1990s when, for instance, some cottage sites were illegally allocated to some 'whites' along the Wild Coast in the old Transkei. These sites were dubbed 'brandy sites', as it was imperative that applications be accompanied by a bottle of brandy. It was standard practice in some parts that ordinary rural residents present the sub-headman with a bottle of brandy (or some suitable gift) [*De Wet and McAllister, 1983: 50*]. Furthermore, in a number of cases traditional authorities allocated land to rural residents, bypassing the district commissioner. These rural residents were consequently not issued a PTO.

It is against the background of collapse in land administration, tensions between traditional authorities and democratically elected civic structures, and the imperative of democracy following the first non-racial elections in 1994 that policy on rural governance and its implementation in South Africa should be understood.

V. POLICY ON RURAL LOCAL GOVERNMENT AND LAND ADMINISTRATION IN POST-1994 SOUTH AFRICA

The post-1994 ANC-led South African government has attempted to separate, among others, local government, land ownership and administration functions and powers and decentralise them to democratically accountable local institutions, with an emphasis on the active participation of communities in decision-making processes. The tension though, as will be seen below, is that the same government also recognises the hereditary 'institution of traditional authorities' without, it appears, questioning its role during the colonial and apartheid periods, and without clarifying its roles, functions, and powers in post-1994 developmental local government and land administration and management.

Rural Local Government

The local sphere of government, according to the Constitution, consists of municipalities, which are established throughout the country – including rural areas. A 'transitional' policy on rural local government in the former Bantustans was initially established in 1995. This comprised a two-level structure, consisting of a district council at a subregional level and a range of possible structures at the local (primary) level.[12] In rural areas, the primary structures, established at the magisterial district level, would either be transitional rural councils (TRCs) or transitional representative councils (TrepCs). The main difference between TRCs and TrepCs was that the former were accorded the powers of a fully fledged local authority while the latter were accorded far fewer powers and were seen as fulfilling representative and brokering functions. The District Council performed local authority functions on behalf of TrepCs. In theory, TrepCs could eventually evolve into effective and democratic local authorities. In practice, however, these structures did not evolve into local authorities at the end of the transitional period in 2000. This is an important point to keep in mind given that almost all the rural areas in the former Bantustans had TrepCs.

An integral aspect of developmental local government is integrated development planning, which requires that municipalities – in addition to providing services – co-ordinate all development activities within their jurisdiction in order to improve the standard of living and quality of life of previously disadvantaged sectors of the community. In this regard, all municipalities are required to produce IDPs and Land Development Objectives (LDOs). According to the White Paper on Local Government [*DPACD, 1998*], the LDOs should be seen as part of the IDPs and not as a separate planning process. Both the Constitution and legislation emphasise the need for community participation in the formulation of IDPs to ensure that these plans are expressive of the needs and priorities of local people, rather than central government.

The role of traditional authorities (chiefs of various ranks) in a post-1994 democracy, including local government, was never explicitly stated from the beginning of the political negotiation process that led to the first democratic election in 1994. In the past, as already shown, these authorities enjoyed unrivalled powers over a range of activities in the rural areas of the former Bantustans. Both the interim and final constitutions merely incorporated a clause recognising 'the institution of traditional leadership' without any clarity or guidelines as to its roles, functions and powers. The Local Government Transitional Act of 1993, as amended in 1995, provided an extremely limited, if not vague, role for traditional authorities in local government. Defining them as an 'interest group' along with women and farm workers, the Act gave traditional authorities not more than ten per cent representation in an *ex officio* capacity.

Land Administration

Attempts to empower rural residents by involving them in decision-making processes on land issues were given a boost with the launch of the White Paper on Land Policy in April 1997 [*DLA, 1997*]. The White Paper drew a crucial distinction between 'ownership' and 'governance' in land issues in rural areas. This distinction was blurred in the colonial and apartheid eras, as the state was both legal owner and administrator of land. By drawing the distinction, the White Paper introduced a separation of the functions of ownership and governance, 'so that ownership can be transferred from the state to the communities and individuals on land' [*DLA, 1997: 93*].

By the beginning of 1998, the Department of Land Affairs (DLA) had developed principles that would guide its legislative and implementation framework. These included the following:

- These rights should be vested in the people who are holders of the land and not in institutions such as tribal or local authorities. In some cases, the underlying rights belong to groups and in other cases to individuals or families. Where the rights to be confirmed exist on a group basis, the rights holders must have a choice about the system of land administration, which will manage their land rights on a day-to-day basis.

- In situations of group-held land rights, the basic human rights of all members must be protected, including the right to democratic decision-making processes and equality. Government must have access to members of group-held systems in order to ascertain their views and wishes in respect of proposed development projects and other matters pertaining to their land rights.
- Systems of land administration that are popular and functional should continue to operate. They provide an important asset given the breakdown of land administration in many rural areas. The aim is not to destroy or harm viable and representative institutions. Popular and democratic tribal systems are not threatened by the proposed measures [*Thomas et al., 1998: 528*].

Three issues need to be highlighted in this regard. First, we should consider the distinction between land ownership and governance. Following the DLA principles, members of particular communities become co-owners of land. This is an ownership issue. As co-owners, the principles imply, it will be up to them to decide how they want their land to be administered. The latter is an issue of governance.

A further implication of this distinction is that the concentration or fusion of functions in Tribal Authorities would be undermined. There would, instead, be a clear separation of the functions. The four main actors are: landowners (the broad community), land administrators or managers (the officials/ bureaucrats), traditional authorities and local government. The latter two will not be the owners of land, and will not necessarily have the right to allocate land, unless specifically asked by the landowners to do so. However, as a body representing public interests, local government will continue to perform its control, regulatory and (in terms of the Constitution) development functions.

Lastly, it is quite clear from the above that the Department of Land Affairs intended to subject traditional authorities to a system that would make them more representative and accountable to their communities. However, as already noted, establishing democratic and accountable structures while recognising an undemocratic and unaccountable institution of traditional leadership, especially in the form that has been inherited from the apartheid past, is a fundamental contradiction. I develop this point further below.

Furthermore, law that would give effect to the above policies laid down in the White Paper on Land Policy has yet to see the light of the day. The unresolved question of the role of traditional authorities in local government and land reform seems central to this delay.[13]

VI. TRADITIONAL AUTHORITIES AND GOVERNMENT SHIFT

Traditional authorities are vehemently opposed to the moves of the ANC-led government to introduce decentralisation and democratisation in rural areas under their jurisdiction. What is striking about the post-1994 period is that traditional authorities, despite earlier divisions, seem to be drawing closer and closer to one another [*Ntsebeza, 2001, 1999*]. While the initial collaboration was around local government, it is quite clear that the main issue that brings traditional authorities together is their opposition to the notion of introducing new democratic structures. They would be happy to be the only primary structure in rural areas and insist on preserving the concentration of functions they enjoyed under apartheid. With regard to land-tenure reform, traditional authorities agree with government that land in the rural areas of the former Bantustans should not be the property of the state. But they want land to be transferred to them or their structures – the Tribal Authorities – rather than transferred to individuals or democratically constituted and accountable legal entities such as Communal Property Associations.

Government seems to have succumbed to the above pressure exerted by traditional authorities. As we have seen, policy and legislation in the immediate post-1994 period seemed, on the whole, to have been driven by a commitment to extend participatory and representative notions of democracy to rural areas. An expression of this radicalism was the promulgation of the Regulation of Development in Rural Areas Act, 1997, by the Eastern Cape Legislature. This Act sought to divest traditional authorities of all their development functions and transfer these to elected councillors. This, of course, was in line with new functions of local government. However, since the end of 1997, the pendulum seems to have swung in favour of traditional authorities [*Ntsebeza, 2001*].

The White Paper on Local Government published in March 1998 makes broad and sweeping statements about the possible role that traditional authorities can play. Traditional 'leadership' is assigned 'a role closest to the people'. On the issue of development, a task that has been added to local government by the Constitution, the White Paper boldly asserts: 'There is no doubt that the important role that traditional leaders have played in the development of their communities should be continued' [*DPACD, 1998: 77*]. The recommendation in the White Paper that 'the institution of traditional leadership' should 'play a role closest to the people' flies in the face of the recommendation of the 1994 ANC election manifesto, formulated in the Reconstruction and Development Programme (RDP). The RDP was emphatic that democratically elected local government structures should play this role. The White Paper thus marks a major shift in government policy, and has grave consequences for the possibility of democracy in rural areas. Similarly, the Constitution has explicitly added development functions to democratically elected local government structures. Yet, the White Paper recommends that traditional authorities should continue performing these tasks. Moreover, the statement that traditional authorities played an important role in development among their communities must be viewed with suspicion. No evidence is adduced to support this statement. Existing evidence shows that traditional authorities were never directly involved in development projects. These projects were implemented by government line departments. Where traditional authorities acted as a link between government departments and their communities, research has shown that they have often been corrupt. An example is the illegal taxes that traditional authorities imposed in the land allocation process [*Ntsebeza, 1999*].[14]

The issue of the role of traditional authorities was the subject of much discussion and negotiation in the run-up to the second democratic local government election in December 2000. It was, moreover, instrumental in causing the postponement of announcing the date for the election. The position of the government was, in the run up to the election, still ambivalent. After a series of meetings between the government and traditional authorities, the government made some concessions. The first significant one was an amendment of the 1998 Municipal Structures Act that was successfully rushed through parliament just before the local government elections. The amendment increases the representation of traditional authorities from ten per cent to 20 per cent of the total number of councillors. Furthermore, traditional authorities would not only be represented at a local government level but also at a district and, in the case of KwaZulu-Natal, metropolitan level. Traditional authorities, though, would not have the right to vote.

This concession seemed to have encouraged traditional authorities to ask for more. They rejected the 20 per cent increase. They wanted nothing short of amending the Constitution and legislation emanating from it regarding municipalities in rural areas in the former Bantustans. They wanted municipalities to be scrapped in these areas in favour of apartheid-era Tribal Authorities as the primary local government structures. Traditional authorities have claimed that the president had promised them, in word and in writing, that their powers would not be tampered with. If anything, they would be increased.[15] For his part, the president has neither denied nor endorsed these claims. This makes it difficult to know the implications of these claims in terms of policy, law and practice.

The manner in which this vexed issue of the role of traditional authorities in a post-1994 democratic South Africa is handled and negotiated is intriguing. In so far as local governments are concerned, traditional authorities fall under the Department of Provincial and Local Government. In practice, though, traditional authorities do not seem to be recognising this Department.

They prefer that the president and the deputy president handle their matters. For example, traditional authorities have submitted almost all their requests to the office of the president. They seem to think that the Minister of Provincial and Local Government is not as favourably disposed towards them as the president. Alternatively, this might be a deliberate strategy to pit the president against the minister.

The response of the government to the requests by traditional authorities was, for the second time in as many months, to present a bill to parliament to amend the Municipal Structures Act. The bill did not address the central demand of traditional authorities – the scrapping of municipalities in rural areas in favour of Tribal Authorities, but merely sought to give local government powers to delegate certain powers and functions to traditional authorities. In addition, a range of peripheral duties would be assigned to traditional authorities. Predictably, traditional authorities rejected the bill and threatened to boycott the 2000 local government election. They also threatened that there would be violence in their areas if their demands were not met. The bill was subsequently withdrawn on a technicality. It would seem that the president made some undertakings, given that traditional authorities eventually participated in the election.

A much shorter draft amendment of the Municipal Structures Act was published on 20 November 2000 for public comment. It seems clear from this draft amendment that a trade-off is proposed. The government has resisted amending the Constitution regarding municipalities in rural areas. However, the draft amendment to the Municipal Structures Act gives traditional authorities control over the allocation of land in so-called 'communal areas', as stated in Section 81(1) (a) of the Municipal Structures Second Amendment Bill, 2000:

> Despite anything contained in any other law, a traditional authority observing a system of customary law continues to exist and to exercise powers and perform functions conferred upon it in terms of indigenous law, customs and statutory law, which powers and functions include – (a) the right to administer communal land … .

The South African Legal Resources Centre, a public-interest law clinic with offices in key South African cities, has, with due cause, objected to this clause. In its submission to the Portfolio Committee on Provincial and Local Government, the Legal Resources Centre has pointed out that the phrase 'Despite anything contained in any other law' has the effect of overriding 'a vast but indeterminable number of laws in a vast but indeterminable number of areas of our national life'. The Legal Resources Centre interpreted the phrase to mean that, 'as far as development and the management and use of natural resources are concerned, this Act overrides the requirements of other critical national laws'.[16] These national laws would include laws on environmental affairs and local government, and insist that citizens should be accorded the right to democratic participation in decisions that affect them. At the time of writing, however, the draft amendment had not been discussed in the Portfolio Committee. In this committee, the public is given an opportunity to make an input before the bill is presented to parliament.

VII. DECENTRALISATION IN RURAL SOUTH AFRICA: WHAT TYPE?

It is difficult to neatly classify decentralisation in rural South Africa into the two categories described above: decentralised despotism and democratic/political decentralisation. There is a sense in which it could be argued that by insisting on decentralised representative and participatory structures, post-1994 policies on local government and land reform, for example, meet the requirements of political decentralisation. Problems, though, arise when the thorny issue of the role, functions and powers of traditional authorities has to be considered, especially given the constitutional recognition of the 'institution of traditional leadership'. The key question that needs to be addressed is whether the institution of traditional leadership is compatible with democratic decentralisation or not.

At this juncture, two cardinal principles of democratic decentralisation are worth recalling: downward accountability of public officials and of elected representatives. The institution of traditional leadership can potentially be democratic in one important respect: the involvement of rural residents in decision-making processes. This was indeed the hallmark of governance in most southern African societies at the advent of colonialism.[17] However, during colonialism and apartheid, decisions taken at these gatherings – including land allocation decisions – were merely advisory, and needed the final endorsement of the magistrate. In addition, as has been shown, the system was open to abuse. There is, however, a critical sense in which the institution of traditional leadership in South Africa cannot be democratic. In so far as so-called 'traditional leadership' is based on ascribed, hereditary rule, the possibility of rural residents having the freedom to choose which institution and/or individuals should rule them is automatically excluded. Yet, it is precisely this right upon which democratic decentralisation and indeed the South African Constitution are based.

The Department of Land Affairs has attempted to marry the two systems by suggesting that there may be examples of a 'popular and democratic tribal system'. However, it is not clear what this statement means. More precisely, what is the mechanism for determining the popularity of traditional authorities and their institutions? The argument that traditional authorities and their structures are popular because rural residents utilise them is specious because using alternative authorities is not practical and the options of rural residents to oppose the present structures are very limited. The interview with the rural resident of Transkei, quoted above, clearly illustrates this point.

How do we explain the South African government's ambivalence on the issue of traditional authorities? The reason could be that the government is mindful of the bloody conflict in rural KwaZulu-Natal in the 1980s and 1990s and the need to avoid a repetition. Lodge has argued that government accommodation of traditional authorities was

> a compromise to avert a threatened boycott of the first general elections by the Inkatha Freedom Party [IFP] if the institution was not recognised and protected in the constitution. If it was not for the pressure from the IFP, the institution would have been destroyed by now ... Rather than abolishing it, the ANC is creating legislation conditions through local government that will allow for the gradual phasing out of the institution which is done to avoid resistance from traditionalists ... the ANC has become more tactful and has recognised that abolishing the institution will cause serious political conflict in the country' [quoted in *Dladla, 2000: 15*].

Another reason could be that government does not have the capacity to set up and monitor new structures.

However, even if this were the case, the issue of the meaning of 'democracy' in post-1994 rural South Africa would stand. More specifically, whether rural residents should continue to be 'subjects' after 1994, when their counterparts in urban areas enjoy citizenship rights, would still haunt us. My position is that democracy should, at least, be both participatory and representative, rather than one or the other. Ensuring that rural residents enjoy the right to choose their representatives remains one of the key challenges of the ANC-led, post-1994 government.

It is important to note that the system of electing representatives in rural South Africa is not without its problems. During the transition period, the system adopted for rural areas was proportional representation. This contrasted with the situation in the urban areas, where the electoral system was based on a combination of constituency and proportional representation. Following the demarcation of municipal boundaries in 2000, new municipalities were established. A model amalgamating several urban and rural municipalities was adopted. The electoral system combining constituency and proportional representation that applied to urban areas was extended to all post-2000 municipalities with wards. The proportional representation system, it must be noted, is the dominant one. According to this system, citizens vote for political parties. In terms of the constituency system, on the other hand, voters vote for a candidate. The main problem with the proportional representation system is that councillors are prone to be primarily accountable to their political parties – or the leadership thereof – rather than downwardly accountable to voters.

The main difference between elected rural councillors and traditional authorities in South Africa, though, is that there is always the possibility of replacing councillors or their political party in an election – an option that is not available with traditional authorities.

Stated succinctly, the ambivalence of government regarding the role of traditional authorities in a democratic system and the lack of support for elected rural councillors throws the prospects of democratic decentralisation in rural areas into serious doubt. Clearly, the unresolved question of the role of traditional authorities creates a state of confusion on the ground, especially as to who has rights over land administration in rural areas between traditional authorities and rural councillors.

VIII. CONCLUSION

Post-1994 South Africa is moving from an authoritarian apartheid regime to a democracy strongly influenced by liberal democratic values that include representative government. But how far has this transition gone? This contribution employed two key concepts to analysc the implications of decentralisation reforms in rural South Africa: decentralised despotism [*Mandani, 1996*] and democratic decentralisation [*Manor, 2001; Agrawal and Ribot, 1999*]. It examined the institutional arrangements put in place to give effect to decentralisation, and their impact on land administration in the rural areas of South Africa's former Bantustans.

It is not possible to assess the impact of democratic decentralisation in rural South Africa for the simple reason that decentralisation in this sector is at best incomplete. In the area of land administration, the law that would establish a post-1994 system of land ownership and administration has – after almost ten years – not been promulgated. Although laws exist to establish developmental local government, full implementation has yet to happen.

The major stumbling block to implementing democratic decentralisation is the unresolved question of the roles, powers and functions of traditional authorities in land and local government reform. Democratic decentralisation, with its insistence on elected representatives, is incompatible with the recognition of a hereditary institution of traditional leadership. The lack of adequate government support for the newly established democratic structures also poses a serious obstacle. Both these problems have led to a state of confusion with potentially disastrous consequences for land administration. The absence of rules, formal and informal, in many rural areas in the Eastern Cape with regard to grazing and to harvesting of natural resources raises serious questions about the future of these resources and the impact on the environment.

The post-1994 ANC-led government must reformulate the roles, functions and powers of traditional authorities in a democracy, taking into account the incompatibility of democratic decentralisation with the hereditary rule that underlines traditional authority. The central issue that the government must resolve is whether rural residents should continue to be subjects when their counterparts in urban areas enjoy full rights as citizens. Ensuring that rural residents enjoy the right to choose their own representatives and leaders is the key challenge.

NOTES

1. The term 'traditional authorities' is used in this contribution as an all-encompassing term to refer to 'chiefs' of various rank. It is thus used to refer to *people*, not structures. The term used to refer to structures is 'Tribal Authorities', which were set up by the Bantu Authorities Act of 1951 and are composed of chiefs, headmen, appointed councillors and a tribal secretary. The term that is used in government documentation is 'traditional leaders', which is used without any clarity as to whom precisely this term refers. For example, are headmen 'traditional leaders'? The extent to which traditional authorities/leaders are legitimate leaders is highly disputed. This partly explains the range in terminology.
2. See [*DPACD, 1996: Section 40(1)*].
3. See Section 151 (1).
4. Section 151 (4).
5. See Section 152 (1) (e).
6. Section 25 (6).
7. Bantustans/reserves/homelands are areas that colonialists put aside for African occupation as early as the nineteenth century. The size of this land comprised about 13 per cent of the South African land. After the 1994 democratic elections, these areas were reincorporated into South Africa.
8. Interview with Mr Jama, Cala, South Africa, 9 September 2000.
9. There are many similar cases.
10. For details, see Ntsebeza [*2001; 1999*].
11. This account is based on interviews with various rural residents, sub-headmen, headmen, chiefs and government officials.
12. The subregional level consisted of three to five magisterial districts. A magisterial district consisted of a district town and a number of administrative areas.
13. It is worth noting that a draft Communal Land Rights Bill was gazetted on 14 August 2002. This bill proposes the transfer of registrable land rights to individuals, families and communities. On land administration, it divests traditional authorities of their land administration functions, including land allocation, in favour of democratically elected administrative structures. Where applicable, 'legitimate' traditional authorities are accorded *ex officio* representation not exceeding 25 per cent. It is difficult to predict how events will unfold, and whether a clear-cut piece of legislation defining a clear role for traditional authorities in land and local government will finally emerge.
14. This shift in ANC thinking regarding traditional authorities should be seen against the backdrop of a wider conservative shift in the ANC soon after the 1994 election. The announcement of the Growth, Employment and Redistribution (GEAR) economic policy was the first major expression of this shift [*Fine and Padayachee, 2001; Bond, 2000; Marais, 1998*].
15. It has not been possible to get a copy of or verify this commitment on the part of the president.
16. Submission by the Legal Resources Centre to the Portfolio Committee on Provincial and Local Government, 18 January 2001.

17. It should be pointed out, though, that only men participated in these gatherings (*iimbizo/pitso/kgotla*). Furthermore, these systems differed, with some being more autocratic than others [*Ntsebeza, 1999*].

REFERENCES

Agrawal, A. and J. Ribot, 1999, 'Accountability in Decentralization: A Framework with South Asian and West African Cases', *Journal of Developing Areas*, Vol.33, pp.473–502.

ANC (African National Congress), 1994, *The Reconstruction and Development Programme: A Policy Framework*, Johannesburg: Umanyano Publications.

Bond, P., 2000, *Elite Transition: from Apartheid to Neoliberalism in South Africa*, Pietermaritzburg: University of Natal Press.

Delius, P., 1996, *A Lion Amongst the Cattle: Reconstruction and Resistance in the Northern Transvaal*, Johannesburg: Ravan Press.

De Wet, C.J. and P.A. McAllister, 1983, 'Rural Communities in Transition: A Study of the Socio-Economic and Agricultural Implications of Agricultural Betterment and Development', Working Paper No.16, Grahamstown: Department of Anthropology in collaboration with the Institute of Social and Economic Research, Rhodes University.

Dladla, S., 2000, 'Slow Fall of the House of Chiefs', *Land & Rural Digest*, March/April, pp.14–17.

DLA (Department of Land Affairs), 1997, 'White Paper on South African Land Policy', Pretoria: DLA.

DPACD (Department of Provincial Affairs and Constitutional Development), 1998, *The White Paper on Local Government*, Pretoria: DPACD.

DPACD (Department of Provincial Affairs and Constitutional Development), 1996, *The Constitution of the Republic of South Africa*, Pretoria: DPACD.

Fine, B. and V. Padayachee, 2001, 'A Sustainable Macroeconomic Growth Path for South Africa?' in J.K. Coetzee, J. Graaff, F. Hendricks and G. Wood (eds.), *Development: Theory, Policy and Practice*, Oxford: Oxford University Press, pp.268–81.

Lodge, T., 1983, *Black Politics in South Africa since 1945*, Johannesburg: Ravan Press.

Mamdani, M., 1996, *Citizen and Subject: Contemporary Africa and the Legacy of Late Colonialism*, Cape Town: David Phillip.

Manona, C., 1998, 'The Collapse of the "Tribal Authority" System and the Rise of Civic Associations', in C. De Wet and M. Whisson (eds.), *From Reserves to Region: Apartheid and Social Change in the Kieskamahoek District of (Former) Ciskei, 1950–1960*, Grahamstown: Institute of Social and Economic Research, Rhodes University.

Manor, J., 2001, *Local Government in South Africa: Potential Disaster despite Genuine Promise*, Sussex: Institute of Development Studies, University of Sussex.

Marais, H., 1998, *South Africa, Limits to Change: The Political Economy of Transformation*, London: Zed Books.

Mbeki, G., 1984, *South Africa: The Peasants' Revolt*, London: International Defence and Aid Fund.

Ntsebeza, L., 2001, 'Traditional Authorities and Rural Development', in J. Coetzee, J. Graaff, F. Hendricks and G. Wood (eds.), *Development Theory, Policy and Practice*, Oxford University Press, pp.316–29.

Ntsebeza, L., 1999, 'Land Tenure Reform, Traditional Authorities and Rural Local Government in Post-Apartheid South Africa: Case Studies from the Eastern Cape', Research Report No.3, Bellville: Programme for Land and Agrarian Studies.

Pycroft, C., 1998, 'Integrated Development Planning or Strategic Paralysis? Municipal Development during the Local Government Transition and Beyond', *Development Southern Africa*, Vol.15, No.2, pp.151–63.

Thomas, G., S. Sibanda and A. Claassens, 1998, 'Current Developments in South Africa's Land Tenure Policy', Proceedings of the International Conference on Land Tenure in the Developing World with a Focus on Southern Africa, University of Cape Town, 27–29 Jan.

What Lies behind Decentralisation? Forest, Powers and Actors in Lowland Bolivia

PABLO PACHECO

I. INTRODUCTION

In recent years, developing countries around the world have begun to give local governments greater rights and responsibilities. This trend has resulted either from country initiatives to democratise national political systems or the influence of international organisations. Decentralisation has emphasised the provision of social services (that is, health and education), although several countries are transferring rights over natural resources – specifically forests – to regional and local governments.

There are several arguments that support the transfer of responsibilities to the local level. These include the following: decentralisation reduces government bureaucracy, democratises decision-making and improves efficiency of public service delivery [*Omar et al., 2001*]. In the forestry sector, transferring powers to the local level might contribute to distributing benefits from forest resources more equitably and to regulating forest utilisation more effectively [*Ribot, 2001*], and it may in some cases contribute to supporting the collective action of institutions governing forest resources [*Andersson, 2002*]. If the latter conditions are achieved, decentralisation could then have positive implications for improving the livelihoods of the multiple users of forest resources, as well as for forest conservation [*Kaimowitz and Ribot, 2002*].

Nevertheless, the implications of decentralisation in practice are not so simple. Transferring responsibilities to local governments may lead to contradictory results, and not necessarily the kinds of outcomes decision-makers

---

Pablo Pacheco is consultant to the Center for International Forestry Research (CIFOR), Indonesia, and Research Associate at the Institute of Environmental Research for Amazônia (IPAM), Brazil.
The author would like to thank CIFOR, the United States Agency for International Development (USAID) and the Project for Sustainable Forest Management (BOLFOR) for their institutional support, which made this research possible. He would also like to thank the staff of the Forestry Superintendence of Bolivia for their permanent collaboration with his research on the decentralisation of forest management, and express his gratitude to Jesse Ribot, Anne Larson and two anonymous reviewers for their comments on a previous version of this essay.

European Journal of Development Research, Vol.16, No.1, Spring 2004, pp.90–109
ISSN 0957-8811 print
DOI:10.1080/09578810410001688752

predict [*Ribot, 1999*]. While some evidence suggests that decentralisation can improve people's welfare by more effectively providing public services to the population and reinforcing a 'good governance' of forest resources, it also can achieve the opposite outcome by reinforcing asymmetric local power relationships – which tend to benefit some local elites to the detriment of more marginalised social groups [*Larson, 2003; Ferroukhi, 2003*]. In this light, the conditions shaping a successful decentralisation process are quite complex and depend on a wide array of factors at different levels of government (central to local), as well as on the interactions among these levels.

The conditions shaping decentralisation may vary depending on the type of decentralisation being discussed; that is, on the type of powers and resources that are transferred to lower levels of government. A democratic decentralisation occurs when powers and resources are transferred to local authorities representative of and downwardly accountable to local populations [*Crook and Manor, 1998*], while an administrative decentralisation concerns transfers of powers to local branches of the central state [*Manor, 1999*]. It is believed that democratic decentralisation, in contrast to administrative decentralisation, might promote better outcomes with regard to social equity and forest conservation [*Ferroukhi, 2003; Kaimowitz and Ribot, 2002*]. However, even as part of a democratic decentralisation, governments may transfer only limited powers and resources to local levels of government, and local technical units may be seen simply as implementation units for policies devised at the central level. The latter case is labelled here an 'incomplete democratic decentralisation'.

Agrawal and Ribot [*1999*] argue that the relation between decentralisation and its outcomes can be better understood by analysing it in terms of actors, powers and accountability. Two relations thus become relevant for analysing the change in power distribution and accountability that constitutes decentralisation: between the central state and local governments, and between the latter and local populations [*Ribot, 1999, 2001*]. The latter relation basically implies analysing the actors who receive the powers being allocated and how they interact to address issues regarding the design of regulations governing the use of natural resources, the enforcement of such regulations and the potential conflicts emerging from either the enforcement of those regulations or the distribution of economic benefits.

The actors, powers and accountability approach, though relevant to understanding the outcomes of decentralisation, does not, however, capture the structural conditions shaping decentralisation outcomes for forests and people. In this line of reasoning, Larson [*2003*] proposes a framework for understanding the environmental and social outcomes of decentralisation. Yet, this framework fails to distinguish properly the attributes of local governments from the exogenous factors shaping their institutional action, and does not acknowledge the influence of other social actors in local governance – except as they influence local government itself.

It is obvious that different types of decentralisation will have different outcomes on forest resources and people. In the same way, the conditions shaping decentralised forest management (that is, government policies, economic incentives, attributes of the forest resources, social and environmental ideologies, local power relationships and local political economy) are going to have differentiated implications depending on the type of decentralisation in effect [*Ferroukhi, 2003; Gibson et al., 2000; Kaimowitz et al., 1999; Larson, 2003; Ribot, 2001*]. Under the assumption that democratic decentralisations may allow for more discretionary decisions by local government authorities, the influence of local politics and the local political economy can be even greater. To date, there is no definitive evidence as to what set of factors has greater relevance for explaining specific outcomes.

Nevertheless, rather than a few specific factors, what defines the final outcome of decentralisation is the interaction between the type of decentralisation and the conditions under which it takes place. Specifically, then, it is most important to understand the combination of powers transferred to the local level, the way these are used to make decisions about natural resources, and the social, political and economic mediations operating at the local level that influence such decisions. In this regard, for instance, the way local authorities negotiate decisions over forest resources with local populations is as relevant as the extent to which local actors depend on forest-related activities for survival or economic accumulation.

This essay discusses the implications of decentralisation on forest resources in the Bolivian lowlands. Bolivia has decentralised forest management responsibilities to municipalities to the greatest extent of any Latin American country [*Ferroukhi, 2003*]. It has also institutionalised a process of popular participation. Nevertheless, though Bolivia has made important progress in promoting a political environment that enables social participation and in delegating responsibilities to local governments (municipalities) on forest-related issues, the powers that municipalities have received are limited, and most decisions over forest resource allocation and resource use norms and regulations are still made by the central government. This case exemplifies well what we label here an incomplete democratic decentralisation.

While in some cases local governments have become key players with regard to forestry issues within their respective territorial jurisdictions, in others they have played a marginal role. The involvement of municipalities in forestry has mainly resulted in the creation of technical forestry units (*Unidades Forestales Municipales* – UFMs) to implement the responsibilities transferred to them, such as: monitoring forest extraction, controlling forest crime, creating municipal forest reserves and granting them as forest concessions to local forest users, and helping local groups develop their logging operations according to official forest management regulations. Nevertheless, not all UFMs have been able to undertake the diverse functions that central government delegated to them, and most have emphasised some functions over others.

Various factors explain these diverse results. To simplify, they can be grouped into two areas: 1) the attributes of the municipalities (that is, the extent to which local authorities are willing to support the process, and the availability of financial and technical resources), and 2) structural variables such as the type and magnitude of forest resources, local power relationships, and the local political economy.

The Bolivian case points out limits to decentralisation in practice. It also shows that decentralisation can be beneficial to marginal groups and the environment, but that outcomes are highly varied and have a complex array of causal factors – both related and unrelated to decentralisation itself. Moving the process forward demands a better understanding of the attributes of local governments and of the range of factors that shape the outcomes of decentralisation. This essay seeks to contribute to that objective using the Bolivian case. By so doing it aims to identify the main shortcomings and prospects of the forest management decentralisation process in lowland Bolivia and to propose policy recommendations that would adjust the Bolivian model towards a more democratic decentralisation that recognises the role of local actors in natural resource governance.

This essay consists of seven parts, including this introduction. The second part describes the characteristics of forests in lowland Bolivia; the third analyses the decentralisation model in Bolivia as part of a broader state policy reform undertaken in the mid-1990s; the following section describes the characteristics of local governments and actors, as well as their inter-relationships; the fifth part analyses the main forestry-related initiatives undertaken by the municipalities; the sixth analyses the implications of such actions for people and forests; finally, the last section summarises the main conclusions.

II. FORESTS IN LOWLAND BOLIVIA

Bolivia is a country covering an area of 1,098,581 square kilometres, of which about 70 per cent is located in areas below 500 metres above sea level [*Montes de Oca, 1989*]. About 80 per cent of the country's forest (53 million hectares) is located in these lowlands. The lowland economy consists of commercial farming and ranching, small-scale food production, coca cultivation, mining, and petroleum and natural gas production. The forestry sector's contribution to the national economy, including logging and the collection of non-timber forest products, is very low – less than two per cent of the GDP on average during the 1990s [*Cámara Forestal, 2000*].

A large portion of the lowland forest has already been selectively logged, an activity that has become increasingly important since the 1970s. Four species, mahogany (*Swietenia macrophylla*), cedar (*cedrela sp.*), oak (*Amburana cearensis*), and *ochoó* (*Hura crepitans*) accounted for 60 per cent of the timber produced between 1985 and 1994 [*Quiroga and Salinas, 1996*]. These species are now the least abundant because unsustainable rates of extraction have threatened their natural regeneration. Both timber companies and local users have thus begun to exploit less valuable species, though their market conditions are far less attractive [*Dauber et al., 1999*].

Deforestation in Bolivia has been relatively low compared to other forested countries of the region, though forest clearing has increased rapidly, particularly during the last two decades. Deforestation was estimated at about 80,000 ha/year nationally in the early 1980s, increasing to 250,000 ha/year (0.4 per cent per year) from the mid-1980s to 1992–94 [*Steininger et al., 2000*]. Most of this increase resulted from the expansion of large-scale mechanised agriculture for the production of soybeans, currently one of Bolivia's main exports, and to a lesser degree from cattle ranching and small farmers' shifting cultivation [*Pacheco, 1998*].

Increasing forest depletion, as well as a general rise in environmental consciousness, has led the Bolivian government to promote land use planning and expand its protected areas. In the late 1990s, the three departments covering most of the Bolivian lowlands formulated a land use plan, and several land use planning exercises are underway at the municipal level. The central government's original goal in promoting such plans was to identify areas for conservation, forests for timber production and, in particular, areas for potential agricultural expansion. Nevertheless, the plans are not often taken into account in development initiatives.

The portion of the country incorporated into the national system of protected areas has become quite significant since the mid-1980s. By the late 1990s, 17 per cent of the country's total area was assigned some form of protected status, although the legal designation of 1.9 million hectares of this land had not yet been specified and only a small fraction of the total had, in practice, been effectively protected [*World Bank, 2000a*]. Resources from international donors are crucial to maintaining the areas prioritised for conservation under management plans.

In the mid-1990s, lowland Bolivia had approximately 2 million inhabitants, of whom 800,000 lived in rural areas – implying an average rural population density of only slightly more than one person per square kilometre. Of these, between 180,000 and 200,000 were indigenous people, and approximately

500,000 to 600,000 people were concentrated in the agricultural colonisation areas of the plains near the city of Santa Cruz or in the *Yungas* region of Cochabamba and La Paz [*Muñoz, 1996*].

Lowland Bolivia is a very heterogeneous region in terms of existing land tenure systems, ranging from indigenous communal systems to private property regimes, and in terms of its population. Rural actors include indigenous people, small-farmer colonists with both communal and individual land tenure systems, and a diverse group of small-scale timber extractors, as well as collectors of non-timber forest products – particularly Brazil nuts (*Bertholletia excelsa*) and palm heart (*Euterpe precatoria*). There are also large and medium landholders and cattle ranchers, as well as forest concessionaries who mainly reside in the region's main towns or cities.

It is unclear how much land is held by each of these groups, though in government redistribution programmes, which gave away some 30 million of the region's 76 million hectares, about 23 million hectares went to medium and large commercial farms and ranchers, and 3 million to small-scale agricultural colonists. By 2001, a total of 5.3 million hectares of state public forest had been granted as forest concessions to logging companies and approximately 2 million hectares had been claimed as municipal forest reserves, but only 430,000 hectares granted as concessions to small-scale loggers within such municipal forest reserves had management plans [*Superintendencia Forestal, 2003*]. Furthermore, indigenous people have claimed a total area of 22.3 million hectares to be recognised as indigenous territories (*Tierras Comunitarias de Origen* – TCO), from which about 5 million hectares are suitable for logging [*Stocks, 1999*]. By the late 1990s, only 3 million hectares had been titled as TCO [*Martinez, 2001*].

III. THE MOVE TOWARDS DECENTRALISATION

Since the mid-1980s, the Bolivian government has been implementing a structural adjustment programme, entailing an aggressive process of both external and internal market liberalisation and the reduction of public spending by cutting, among other things, investment projects and productive sector subsidies [*World Bank, 1994*]. In the early 1990s was launched a 'second generation' of reforms aimed to drastically shrink the state apparatus and promote private investment. The government privatised state-owned companies and decentralised the state administrative system to achieve the first goal. The second required modifying a set of legal instruments regulating the country's strategic economic sectors, including forestry [*Bolivian Government, 2000*].

Decentralisation, therefore, was part of a larger package of reforms.[1] The cornerstone of these reforms was to attack poverty on the assumption that higher social investment at the local level and, in particular, the creation of conditions enabling economic growth might help the population overcome its precarious living conditions. This discourse of development was not made explicit until the late 1990s [*World Bank, 2000b*].

The most important step towards the administrative decentralisation of the state was taken with the approval of the Popular Participation Law (*Ley de Participación Popular* – LPP) in 1994. This law initiated a top-down process to transfer responsibilities to municipal governments – the country's smallest administrative unit – and to enhance institutional mechanisms for grassroots participation in both public investment planning and the monitoring of public expenditures. Key provisions of the LPP expanded the municipal government's jurisdiction beyond the urban centres to their entire territory, and made municipalities responsible for local schools, health facilities, roads and water systems. To finance these new responsibilities, the law requires that the central government allocate 20 per cent of its annual budget to the municipalities in proportion to their population. Furthermore, the administration of rural and urban property taxes was transferred to municipal governments, which now collect them and decide where to invest these revenues.

The LPP was intended to go beyond a simple change in the country's administrative system because it was also designed to address pressing social and economic problems by attempting to reverse a chronic lack of investment in social infrastructure and the marginality of rural populations from decisions about public investment [*Pérez and Baldivia, 1997*]. The way the LPP proposed to achieve such aims was to redistribute national resources in a more egalitarian manner according to the rule of one *boliviano* (national currency) for each Bolivian [*Centellas, 2000*].

The LPP approval entailed a dramatic change with respect to pre-LPP reality. Previously, nearly 92 per cent of national spending went to three cities – La Paz, Santa Cruz and Cochabamba – with most of the remainder flowing to the other six departmental capitals. Hence, social investment in rural areas was very low and was not a priority except for a few specific projects [*Rojas, 1996; Centellas, 2000*].

The Administrative Decentralisation Law was passed one year later. It abolished the previously existing regional development corporations,[2] and transferred their functions and most of their assets to the prefectures (departmental governments), which would then become more involved in technical issues in addition to their traditional role of maintaining public order. This law also created councils to oversee the prefects, elected by the municipal councils from each province [*Urioste, 2001*]. It did not change the fact that governors were – and are – still nominated by the central government.

In 1996, both forest and agrarian laws were reformed.[3] These two laws dramatically changed the way public forest and land are allocated and their use monitored. The Forestry Law created a new monitoring and enforcement system, along with market-oriented regulations and taxes intended to make unsustainable forestry operations unattractive.[4] The main purpose of the agrarian law is to clarify land ownership rights through a process of title regularisation (*saneamiento*), new titling and the consolidation of the rural property cadastre. The agrarian law has merged the rights over the land and forest, and, since its approval, social, economic and ecological considerations constitute legitimate ways to justify land ownership.[5]

The Forestry Law has also dramatically changed the way forest resources are managed by creating a new set of regulations for forest management and clear cutting. It is worth mentioning that it was also aimed at democratising access to forest resources by recognising private landholders' and indigenous peoples' forest rights. Furthermore, it allocated a portion of public forest to municipalities as municipal forest reserves. These areas must be granted as forest concessions to small-scale loggers. Previously, these groups of loggers had no formal access to forest resources and were forced to operate illegally within areas granted as forest concessions [*Kraljevic, 1996; Pacheco and Kaimowitz, 1998*].

The Forestry Law, moreover, transferred a number of powers to prefectures and municipalities. Current prefectures' responsibilities include implementing forestry research and extension programmes and forest conservation at the departmental level, as well as developing programmes for strengthening municipal institutional capacity in the forestry sector. Municipal governments' new responsibilities include monitoring logging activities and inspecting raw material supply and processing programmes. Municipal governments are also in charge of delimiting municipal reserves to be assigned as community concessions for local forest users in up to 20 per cent of the total public forest within their jurisdiction. In order for local forest users to gain access to municipal reserves, they must fulfil several requirements to be recognised as a 'local social association' (*Asociación Social del Lugar* – ASL) by the Ministry of Sustainable Development and Planning (*Ministerio de Desarrollo Sostenible y Planificación* – MDSP).[6]

In order to carry out their new functions, municipal governments are expected to create municipal forestry units (UFMs). The law also allows municipalities to form consortiums with other municipalities to create such units. The UFMs are accountable to the municipalities, but they have to comply with the orientations and guidelines defined by the Forestry Superintendence (*Superintendencia Forestal* – SF) – which is the national entity, under the MDSP, in charge of implementing the new forestry regime. The SF is the primary entity responsible for allocating concessions and forest permits, authorising and monitoring forest management plans, collecting forest taxes, and controlling illegal logging and forestry crime. This institutional system, in theory, should be entirely financed with the revenues coming from both forest extraction and clear cutting fees.[7] It is worth mentioning that municipalities have not received any specific responsibilities related to promoting forest initiatives within indigenous territories.

Under the new regulatory framework, indigenous people have exclusive rights to use the forest resources within their territories; private property owners, moreover, have acquired rights over the forest resources on their lands. The state, though, still reserves the right to allocate public forests through a system of long-term forest concessions to private companies, in addition to approving applications as requested by the ASLs. In practice, the definition and enforcement of these rights, such as the titling of indigenous territories and the creation of municipal forest reserves, depends on a long and bureaucratic process of title regularisation over which municipal governments have little influence [*Contreras and Vargas, 2001; Pacheco, 2000*]. Since 2002, municipalities have begun to participate in land titling issues, mainly by prioritising the areas in which the agrarian reform agency has a title regularisation process underway.

The forest actors mentioned above are all required to formulate and implement forest management plans as a requisite to extracting timber or non-timber forest products. Land use plans at the farm level are also required for farmers to obtain clear cutting permits. The SF is the entity responsible for approving those management plans. The supervision of such plans is also in the hands of the SF, though as was mentioned earlier, forest-monitoring activities should be implemented in coordination with the UFMs.

In summary, the transfer of powers to municipal governments has been a gradual process that has progressively incorporated forest management responsibilities. Key decisions about *who* has the right to access forest resources and regulations for the use of forest resources have been retained at the central level. Forest monitoring and promotion of local forest management initiatives are shared with the municipal governments. The departmental governments have become responsible for forestry research and extension systems, and should develop programmes to strengthen the institutional capacity of the municipal governments.

There is an apparent paradox in the way the Bolivian model was formulated and implemented. On the one hand, since the Popular Participation Law was launched there has been an ongoing process aimed at strengthening the political role of municipal government and promoting broad social participation in the local arena. On the other hand, only limited powers and responsibilities are transferred to the municipal level regarding forest management, and municipal governments have little voice in decisions regarding who has access to forest resources and the rules for the use of such resources.

IV. MUNICIPAL GOVERNMENTS AND LOCAL ACTORS

Decentralisation in Bolivia has reshaped the nature of power relations at the local level. Before 1985, mayors were appointed by the central government and municipalities had very few financial resources. In 1985 a new municipalities law was approved. It established the election of municipal governments, though there were no other mechanisms in place to guarantee the downward accountability of these leaders to the population. Thus, mayors were primarily accountable to their political parties.

Municipal governments were restricted to making decisions about a limited range of urban services, since their jurisdiction was only urban. Mayors themselves had little influence on local politics, which were dominated by non-resident landholders as well as merchants, professionals, ranchers and sawmill operators. Traditional organisations for both small farmers and indigenous peoples, which were important at the community level, had little influence in the municipal arena because their main interlocutors were rooted at the departmental and national levels respectively.

In 1994, the LPP strengthened municipal governments, made them more democratic and expanded their jurisdictions. Rural populations gained the right to participate in municipal elections and to run for election to the municipal council for a five-year period. Nevertheless, national political parties still mediate all individual candidates, a mechanism which allows political parties to maintain their control over local political agendas and reproduce a system of political patronage. Municipal councils are responsible for appointing mayors among their elected members, which is done, in practice, through political alliances negotiated by political parties at the national level. They may also remove mayors through the so-called 'constructive censure' that every year makes it possible for municipal councils to vote out mayors for poor performance. This system is still in place despite an intense debate in Bolivia about the perverse effects it may be producing.

The LPP has also sought to introduce community control over municipal governments by recognising local social organisations (that is, farmer organisations, neighbourhood committees and indigenous groups) as territorially based grassroots organisations (*Organización Territorial de Base* – OTB). These are permitted to influence municipal investment decisions through a participatory planning process conducted by the municipalities, which should result in the formulation of a medium-term Municipal Development Plan. Each year, as part of this Plan, the municipalities have to develop a participatory operational plan. Furthermore, local organisations are allowed to constitute a community-based vigilance committee in each municipality which oversees municipal financial management and can request Congress to 'freeze' a municipal account if there are suspicions of fraud or severe mismanagement.

Although the mechanisms described above constitute innovative ways to allow citizens and communities to hold municipal governments accountable [*World Bank, 2000c*], in practice they are not what they seem for at least two reasons. First, the 'constructive vote' does not necessarily reflect whether it was a 'bad' or 'good' administration but rather the political intentions of the councillors. The latter have led to an indiscriminate replacement of mayors [*Rojas, 1998*]. Second, even though the given mechanisms are intended to democratise public investment decision-making, the planning process has not been particularly participatory. Moreover, the formulation of these plans depends on external expertise and they are rarely implemented fully. Furthermore, the vigilance committees do not always work in practice; when they do, their composition is usually biased in favour of urban residents or they have been co-opted by the locally hegemonic political parties [*Urioste, 2001*].

On the other hand, small farmers and indigenous people have been elected to office for the first time in many lowland municipalities. In those cases, municipal governments have politically supported local actors' claims for resource access.[8] These local actors and their claims fall generally into three groups: indigenous groups reinforcing their land claims, small-scale loggers negotiating temporary logging authorisations, and small farmers modifying land use and forest regulations. This has also occurred in areas where these groups have strong organisations with the capacity to influence municipal decisions or where they represent the majority of voters. In these cases, municipal governments may amplify the social actors' demands.

In other cases, transferring responsibilities and resources to municipalities has led to the reinforcement of pre-existing local elites, particularly in northern Bolivia – where cattle ranchers are highly influential in local politics. These local elites have, in some cases, influenced municipal governments to build local alliances against indigenous land claims [*Kaimowitz et al., 1999*].

Moreover, the political mediations that political parties introduce at the municipal level have often led to distortions in local political representation. This factor can impede indigenous and peasant leaders in attempts to run in municipal elections, or force them to negotiate with national political parties at the risk of losing their ties with the social groups from which they emerged. The politicisation of oversight committees and their co-optation by political parties constitutes an associated phenomenon.

V. MUNICIPAL GOVERNMENTS AND FOREST MANAGEMENT

Although it is hard to generalise, the findings suggest that decentralisation has changed national public investment patterns, particularly in the sectors of education, water management and sanitation, health and transport. Faguet [*2001*] argues that municipal investment might now be reflecting real local needs. Yet evidence also suggests that this investment may be disproportionately oriented towards the urban centres, thus largely discriminating against rural populations [*Vargas, 1998*]. In that context, municipal governments have neglected natural resource-related projects – except for a few dispersed initiatives to maintain tree nurseries and support occasional agroforestry activities in rural communities [*Pacheco and Kaimowitz, 1998*]. Municipalities have little interest in spending resources on land use planning or conservation.

Nevertheless, resources spent on the forestry sector have sharply increased in relation to the past, mainly because of the portion of forest taxes that 109 municipalities with forest resources began to receive since 1997. In 1998, municipalities received over US$2 million, but that amount decreased to half during the next year, and in 2001 the SF transferred only US$460,000 to the municipalities. This drastic reduction in four years is because most forest concessionaries have not been paying their taxes. In March 2003, a government decree was issued stating that the companies with forest concessions no longer have to pay for the total concession area but rather for the area annually logged. This measure will, therefore, consolidate the reduction of municipal income from concessions.

In addition, the distribution of these resources is quite uneven, with half of them going to only 13 municipalities. By 2002, most municipalities in the lowlands had created their UFMs, even though a large proportion had to fully allocate the financial resources from concessions to support these units due to the limited funding they received for this purpose. The limited budgets of these units make it difficult for them to operate with little more than basic personnel and equipment [*de Urioste, 2000; Pacheco, 2000*]. Furthermore, municipal governments are unwilling to budget their own resources to support the operational costs of the UFMs, and the municipalities that receive the larger proportion of resources from forest taxes tend to spend those resources on other sectors besides forestry [*Flores and Ridder, 2000; de Urioste, 2000*].

In practice, few municipalities are able to implement all the responsibilities that they have received. This is because their investment priorities lie in other sectors, and because of the lack of financial resources. The municipalities most interested in building some technical capacities in forestry were those receiving the largest proportion of resources from forest fees, reflecting the importance of forestry in their local economies. Other factors influencing the establishment of UFMs were the political will of mayors, the existence of forestry projects funded by foreign donors and social pressures to set up these units [*Pacheco and Kaimowitz, 1998*].

The UFMs have spent most of their efforts and resources on delimiting the municipal forest reserves and establishing agreements with groups of small-scale loggers on how forest concessions should be allocated.

Furthermore, they have had to carry out inspections in those areas in order to avoid encroachment from illegal loggers. Nevertheless, the process of creating municipal forest reserves has been slow and bureaucratic. By March 2000, 16 municipalities had requested a total of 2.4 million hectares to be declared as municipal reserves by the MDSP. Two years later, the MDSP had only declared 681,315 hectares as municipal forest reserves [*Pacheco, 2003*]. In the same year, the SF had approved forest management plans for a total area of 430,000 hectares, favouring 16 local forest user groups [*SF, 2003*]. The ASLs produced about 16,000 cubic metres of timber in 1999, representing five per cent of the country's legal production of timber [*Contreras and Vargas, 2000*].

The challenge for the municipalities that have been able to allocate concessions for local forest users within their municipal forest reserves has been to find some way to support the ASLs (in terms of forestry inventories, forest management plans and organisational support) in developing their logging operations. The UFMs, in general, have been unable to meet such demands without the support of one of several forestry projects that have begun to collaborate with municipalities. Nevertheless, a few municipalities have oriented resources to the support of ASL operations through road improvements to facilitate access to their forest areas.

In terms of controlling illegal logging, the response of the UFMs has been ambivalent. On the one hand, the units intervene to monitor logging when there is pressure from the SF to do so, rather than on their own initiative. The UFMs have, though, been more active in patrolling the municipal forest reserves as a way to avoid illegal extraction of forest resources. On the other hand, UFMs tend to collaborate with the SF in inspections aimed at controlling the forestry operations of absentee forest concessionaires more than those of producers residing in the area.

The UFMs are, however, much more active in monitoring and penalising illegal clear cutting, because the municipalities receive a portion of the fines imposed on producers who clear cut without authorisation. The municipalities, however, have not established systems for monitoring forest clearing, and their attention is most often drawn to illegal clearing as a result of specific denouncements from citizens [*Kaimowitz et al., 1999*].

VI. IMPLICATIONS FOR PEOPLE AND FORESTS

It is difficult to separate the implications of the decentralisation process itself from the effects of the other policy reforms that were undertaken along with it. Furthermore, the overall process of popular participation and decentralisation has some effects that are indirect but have decisive importance in shaping outcomes. For example, even though both popular participation and decentralisation have opened opportunities for groups previously marginalised to access and benefit from forest resources, forestry regulations have discriminated against small-scale farmers and loggers and limited their ability to take full advantage of such opportunities.

The direct effects of decentralisation in the Bolivian lowlands are as follows: the municipalities have begun to receive resources from forestry fees; they have gained rights to manage a portion of public forests as municipal forest reserves; and some small-scale loggers can make legitimate use of such resources through a system of forest concessions as well as obtain some technical assistance from the technical units created within the municipalities with forest resources. Furthermore, municipalities have become active players in issues related to forest management and the control of forest crime, and there are an increasing number of initiatives to develop agroforestry projects, fire control and environmental education programmes, among others. The next paragraphs will discuss the indirect and direct implications introduced here.

To some extent, decentralisation has created new opportunities for indigenous people, small farmers and small-scale timber producers by increasing their bargaining power with other social actors. Yet most pre-existing local elites have not lost their power, and a large number of forested municipalities are still dominated by local merchants, professionals, ranchers and sawmill operators; strengthening municipal governments has reinforced these groups as well. However, they are under increasing pressure to acknowledge the presence of and negotiate with groups that have been previously marginalised. In any case, the complexity of the power dynamics in these relationships makes it difficult to generalise [*Pacheco and Kaimowitz, 1998*].

Indigenous groups have obtained lands through a land tenure system of common property and, as was mentioned earlier, have exclusive rights to use and manage the forest resources within their territories. Land regularisation, however, has become a long and bureaucratic process, and only a currently incalculable portion of the claimed land will likely be titled as indigenous territory. Municipal governments have had an ambiguous position regarding indigenous territories. In some cases, they have been supportive of indigenous demands, mainly when indigenous groups are important actors in the municipality and have gained some political representation within the local government. However, in the cases where local elites are hegemonic, they have resisted the creation of indigenous territories within their jurisdictions [*Pacheco and Kaimowitz, 1998*].

A large group of small-scale loggers have had difficulties in exploiting timber, and along with indigenous people have been compelled to adjust their management practices to standards determined as part of the new forestry regulations (that is, rotation cycles and cut diameters, among others). These groups also lack the managerial skills necessary to undertake post-harvest operations, and some forest-use regulations like the prohibition of chainsaw use has limited their options for using forest resources. Where these loggers have been able to influence the municipal governments, the latter's intervention has been key in creating a political platform to support demands to accelerate the process of municipal reserve creation and service provision.

Small-scale farmers have been affected by the regulations governing clear cutting and logging on their plots because an unknown proportion have been unable to meet the conditions for formulating farm-level land use plans. The main obstacle has been the lack of land titles and the costs of title regularisation. There have also been cases where small farmers have used clear-cutting authorisations to justify logging because the cost of formulating land use plans was lower than the cost of formulating forest management plans. In general, the actions intended to control illegal logging have made life difficult for small farmers and small-scale loggers [*Pacheco, 2000*]; the UFMs have rarely intervened in such situations.

The allocation of up to 20 per cent of public forests for local community groups recognised as ASLs potentially represents an important opportunity for groups of small-scale loggers to exploit forest resources legally. Yet the process of delimitation and allocation has been extremely centralised in the MDSP. To date, there is no quick and easy mechanism allowing municipalities to delimit those reserves as the process largely depends on land-rights regularisation by the National Agrarian Reform Institute (*Instituto Nacional de Reforma Agraria* – INRA). In some municipalities, the areas chosen as municipal reserves have overlapping conflicts with indigenous territories and other private property land claims [*Pacheco, 2000, 2003*].

Moreover, a large portion of ASLs lack the managerial and financial capacities necessary to develop their forestry operations efficiently. Even though the municipal forest units have gained direct control over a portion of timber royalties, these resources are not sufficient to support the social forestry initiatives within the municipalities' jurisdictions. This scheme, therefore, becomes highly dependent on technical and financial assistance from international co-operation, public projects and non-governmental organisations [*Kaimowitz et al., 1999*]. Thus, it is not clear to what extent the livelihoods of the groups recognised as ASLs have improved.

Although it is not a priority, some municipal governments are willing to spend resources on agroforestry projects to support demands from small farmers and indigenous communities. A few are also interested in developing environmental education programmes, particularly those that have a portion of their territory in protected areas. In recent years, a few forest projects (such as the forest management project BOLFOR) have developed a system of fire control initiatives involving municipalities.

The effects of decentralisation on forest conservation are not yet known. It could be assumed, however, that if decentralisation supports groups that manage forests better, then it should have positive effects on maintaining forest conditions. Thus, actions such as giving greater control over forest resources to indigenous people and facilitating access to forest resources for small-scale loggers could have some positive effects on forest conservation and improve these people's livelihoods. Nevertheless, those actions might not achieve their expected outcomes if such groups do not have the technical and financial capacities and incentives needed to build a competitive forest management system with clear rules for the distribution of economic benefits. Municipalities alone can do little to guarantee that this system will work.

Similarly, enforcing a system of regulations aimed at managing forest resources in a sustainable manner may have positive implications for forest conditions. Yet the standards these regulations impose are difficult for some of the local populations who depend on forest resources to implement. Also, the fact that forest regulations are hard to enforce makes it difficult to control forest crime in lowland Bolivia. Furthermore, the decentralised forest management model has largely emphasised the monitoring role of the UFMs within an institutional context of little collaboration among the different public entities. Within this context, there is low motivation for local authorities to sanction forest crimes, particularly if this means penalising influential local actors.

VII. CONCLUSIONS

The main lessons that emerge from the Bolivian case are that municipal governments are becoming more involved in forest-related activities, but that outcomes are diverse. Nevertheless, the Bolivian case shows that strengthening the role of municipal governments in forest management can lead to greater social equity and perhaps to more sustainable resource use. It also shows that these outcomes are by no means assured. Decentralisation has created new opportunities for indigenous people, small farmers and small-scale loggers, but these groups lack access to the financial resources and markets that would allow them to take full advantage of these opportunities – and municipal government assistance in forest management has so far been quite limited.

The extent to which municipal governments have undertaken their responsibilities (facilitating local groups' access to and helping them benefit from forest resources, or implementing actions to control forest crime and penalise illegal logging or forest clearing) has mainly depended on local power relations, the degree to which local governments are accountable to their constituents and the extent to which the local economy depends on forest resources. In other words, the type of activities the municipalities implement in practice depends on which social actors benefit from forest resource use, and how influential they are in local decision-making. Yet decisions also depend in important ways on how accountable the municipal authorities are to their constituents and how willing they are to resolve disparate demands coming from diverse local groups, or to support them at higher levels of decision-making. Furthermore, authorities from municipalities where the local economy and, hence, people's livelihoods depend more extensively on forest resources will tend to privilege the forest sector in their agenda of priorities. In contrast, local governments are less willing to become involved in forest management and monitor illegal clearing in cases in which local economies depend on activities that demand forest clearing.

It has been mentioned that although municipalities receive a portfolio of responsibilities they often prioritise the most locally relevant ones. The efficiency with which they implement such tasks depends on the attributes of the technical units (availability of financial and human resources with good technical skills and equipment to operate) and the political support local authorities give these technical units. Many of the decisions the UFMs should make are political rather than technical, but, in practice, they do not have the legal authority to make political decisions. Therefore, the little discretionary power that municipal governments hold over political decisions regarding forest resources has limited the impact of the UFMs, mostly on issues regarding access to and use of forest resources.

Some of the municipalities have been able to negotiate financial resources from external sources to support their forest programmes, but in most cases the forestry projects and NGOs working closely with municipalities have tended to replace – rather than complement or reinforce – the UFM's role, particularly regarding the provision of technical assistance to local forest users. Though this may have increased short-term results, the way in which technical assistance is being developed tends to create a strong dependence on projects and international donors in the long term. This could be overcome through actions that strengthen the creation and consolidation of municipal consortiums. Such initiatives are still in their infancy.

The main lesson from the Bolivian case is that the model implemented had the embedded notion that all municipalities were somewhat homogeneous, hence the reality of forests and actors was reasonably uniform. Thus, the instruments that have been proposed for promoting forest conservation and improving local livelihoods at the same time do not work properly when faced with local realities that are more complex. In this light, it is important to advance towards a real democratic decentralisation whilst acknowledging the lack of homogeneity as well as understanding that local systems of forest resource governance are not completely embedded within municipal governance systems.

This, then, means that not all responsibilities should be transferred equally to every municipality, and that a better system of checks and balances – involving the whole public system (both vertically and horizontally) – must be implemented to ensure greater transparency and accountability in decision-making. At the same time, local actors require greater scope for establishing forest resource use contracts and agreements, as do municipalities for intervening in decisions about forest resource allocation. There should also be greater flexibility in the design of mechanisms of service provision to local populations that account for different economies of scale and differentiated social group preferences.

NOTES

1. This reform package included the *Ley de Reforma Educativa* (Law of Educational Reform), *Ley de Capitalización* (Law of Capitalization), *Ley de Pensiones* (Law of Pensions) and the *Ley de Reforma Administrativa* (Law of Administrative Reform), all of which were passed in the first half of the 1990s.
2. The development corporations were set up in the 1970s. Their main functions were to plan and implement development projects for both urban and rural areas. The corporations' income came mostly from petroleum, gas, mineral and timber royalties, with a portion from the national treasury.
3. This was done through the approval by Congress of the new Forestry Law (Forestry Law, No.1700) in July 1996, followed by the implementation of its regulations some months later, and the National Service of Agrarian Reform Law (*Ley del Servicio Nacional de Reforma Agraria*, known as INRA law, No.1715) in October 1996.
4. Forest logging fees are equivalent to US$1 per hectare/year. Forest concessions were originally mandated to pay for the concessions' total area; indigenous people and private landholders were to pay only for the total area to be annually logged. Clear cutting fees are equivalent to US$15, plus 15 per cent of the estimated value of the timber from the cleared area (see Forestry Law, No.1700, Art.37).
5. This has implied a drastic shift in agrarian ideology from the old concept 'land for those who work it' to a new one in which conservation is also legitimate for ownership. The reality, however, is a bit different.
6. The requisites for small-scale loggers to create an ASL are as follow: 1) their members have to reside in the same municipality where they are claiming forest concessions; 2) the organisation should be in existence for at least five years; and 3) a minimum of 20 people must be affiliated (see DS 24453, Titulo I).
7. Prefectures receive 35 per cent of concession fees and 25 per cent of the fees charged for clear cutting operations. Municipal governments receive 25 per cent of both types of fees. FONABOSQUE – the entity in charge of funding sustainable forest management projects – receives ten per cent of the concession fees and 50 per cent of the clear cutting fees; the SF gets 30 per cent of the concession fees (see Forestry Law, No.1700, Art.38).
8. Three main exceptional regimes have been approved by the SF: one allowed logging in private properties of 200 hectares or less, and lasted longer than expected – being extended until August 1998; another allowed small farmers to log timber in areas under three hectares without the presentation of a farm-level land use plan; and another permitted local forest user groups (ASLs) to initiate their forestry operations without having had their Forest Management Plans formulated and approved or their forest concessions formally allocated within the municipal forest reserves [*Pacheco, 2000; Contreras and Vargas, 2001*].

REFERENCES

Andersson, K., 2002, 'Explaining the Mixed Success of Municipal Governance of Forest Resources in Bolivia: Overcoming Local Information Barriers', Center for the Study of Institutions, Populations and Environmental Change, Indiana University.

Agrawal, A. and J.C. Ribot, 1999, 'Accountability in Decentralization: A Framework with South Asian and West African Cases', *Journal of Developing Areas*, Vol.33, pp.473–502.

Bolivian Government, 2000, 'Informe anual para el XIII Grupo Consultivo', La Paz.

Cámara Forestal de Bolivia (CFB), 2000, 'Plan estratégico para el desarrollo forestal de Bolivia', Santa Cruz, Bolivia.

Centellas, M., 2000, 'Decentralization and Democratization in Bolivia', Paper prepared for the 22nd Congress of the Latin American Studies Association, Miami, March.

Contreras, A. and M.T. Vargas, 2001, 'Social, Environmental and Economic Impacts of Forest Policy Reforms in Bolivia', Washington, DC: Forest Trends and CIFOR.

Crook, R.C. and J. Manor, 1998, *Democracy and Decentralization in South-East Asia and West Africa: Participation, Accountability and Performance*, Cambridge: Cambridge University Press.

Dauber, E.R., A. Guzmán and J.R. Terán, 1999, *Potencial de los bosques naturales de Bolivia para producción forestal permanente*, Santa Cruz, Bolivia: Superintendencia Forestal.

de Urioste, J.L., 2000, 'Informe final: proyecto de apoyo a la gestión forestal municipal', Santa Cruz, Bolivia: Superintendencia Forestal (unpublished draft).

Faguet, J.F., 2001, 'Does Decentralization Increase Responsiveness to Local Needs? Evidence from Bolivia', Washington, DC: World Bank.

Ferroukhi, L. (ed.), 2003, *La gestión forestal municipal en América Latina*, Bogor, Indonesia: Center for International Forestry Research, International Development Research Center.

Flores, G. and M. Ridder, 2000, 'Experiencias con el proceso de fortalecimiento forestal municipal en Santa Cruz', Santa Cruz, Bolivia: Programa de Apoyo Forestal.

Gibson, C., M.A. McKean and E. Ostrom (eds.), 2000, *People and Forests: Communities, Institutions and Governance*, Cambridge, MA: The MIT Press.

Kaimowitz, D. and J. Ribot, 2002, 'Services and Infrastructure versus Natural Resources Management: Building a Base for Democratic Decentralization', Submitted for the 'Conference on Decentralization and the Environment', Bellagio, Italy: World Resources Institute, February.

Kaimowitz, D., P. Pacheco, J. Johnson, I. Pavez, C. Vallejos and R. Vélez, 1999, 'Local Governments and Forests in the Bolivian Lowlands', *Rural Development Forestry Papers (RDFN)*, No.24b, London: Overseas Development Institute.

Kraljevic, I., 1996, Estudio exploratorio del sector maderero local de la provincia Velasco en el departamento de Santa Cruz, Documento Técnico 48/1996, Santa Cruz: Proyecto BOLFOR.

Larson, A., 2003, 'Decentralization and Forest Management in Latin America: Toward a Working Model', *Public Administration and Development*, Vol.23, No.3, pp.211–26.

Manor, J., 1999, *The Political Economy of Democratic Decentralization*, Washington, DC: The World Bank Group.

Martinez, J., 2001, 'Proceso de titulación de las tierras comunitarias de origen (TCOs)', in M. Urioste and D. Pacheco (eds.), *Las tierras bajas de Bolivia a fines del siglo XX*, La Paz: Programa de Investigación Estratégica en Bolivia, pp.385–418.

Montes De Oca, I., 1989, *Geografía y recursos naturales de Bolivia*, La Paz: Ministerio de Educación y Cultura.

Muñoz, J.A., 1996, 'Access to Land and Rural Poverty in Bolivia', in *Bolivia: Poverty, Equity and Income*, Washington, DC: The World Bank Group, pp.159–193.

Omar, A., S. Kahkonen and P. Meagher, 2001, 'Conditions for Effective Decentralized Governance: A Synthesis of Research Findings', Center for Institutional Reform and the Informal Sector, University of Maryland.

Pacheco, P., 2003, 'Municipalidades y participación local en la gestión forestal en Bolivia' in L. Ferroukhi (ed.), *La gestión forestal municipal en América Latina*, Bogor, Indonesia: Center for International Forestry Research, International Development Research Center, pp.19–56.

Pacheco, P., 2000, 'Avances y desafíos en la descentralización de la gestión de los recursos forestales en Bolivia', Bogor, Indonesia: Center for International Forestry Research and Project of Sustainable Forest Management BOLFOR.

Pacheco, P., 1998, *Estilos de desarrollo, deforestación y degradación de los bosques en las tierras bajas de Bolivia*, La Paz: Center for International Forestry Research, Centro de Estudios para el Desarrollo Laboral y Agrario, and Fundación TIERRA.

Pacheco, P. and D. Kaimowitz (eds.), 1998, *Municipios y gestión forestal en el trópico boliviano*, La Paz: Center for International Forestry Research, Centro de Estudios para el Desarrollo Laboral y Agrario, Fundación TIERRA, and Project for Sustainable Forest Management BOLFOR.

Pérez de Castaños, M. I. and J. Baldivia, 1997, *Participación popular: Primeras visiones sobre logros y limitaciones*, La Paz: Grupo Esquivel.

Quiroga, M.S. and E. Salinas, 1996, *Minerales y madera, temas para el debate ambiental*, La Paz: Grupo de Acción y Reflexión sobre el Medio Ambiente.

Ribot, J., 2001, 'Local Actors, Powers and Accountability in African Decentralizations: A Review of Issues', Paper prepared for IDRC, Assessment of Social Policy Reforms Initiative, Washington, DC: World Resources Institute.

Ribot, J., 1999, 'Accountable Representation and Power in Participatory and Decentralized Environmental Management', *Unasylva*, Vol.50, No.4, pp.18–22.

Rojas, G., 1996, *La participación popular: avances y obstáculos*, La Paz: Secretaría de Participación Popular.

Rojas, G., 1998, *Censura constructiva: inestabilidad y democracia municipal*, Descentralización y Participación No.1, La Paz: ILDIS/Friedrich Ebert Stiftung.

Steininger, M.K., C.J. Tucker, J.R. Townshend, T.R. Killeen, A. Desch, V. Bell and P. Ersts, 2000, 'Tropical Deforestation in the Bolivian Amazon', *Environmental Conservation*, Vol.28, No.2, pp.127–34.

Stocks, A., 1999, 'Iniciativas forestales indígenas en el trópico boliviano: realidades y opciones'. Documento Técnico 78/1999, Santa Cruz, Bolivia: Project for Sustainable Forest Management BOLFOR.

Superintendencia Forestal (SF), 2003, *Informe Anual 2002*, Santa Cruz, Bolivia: Sistema de Regulación de Recursos Naturales.

Urioste, M., 2001, 'Bolivia: descentralización municipal y participación popular', La Paz: Fundación TIERRA.

Vargas, H., 1998, 'Los municipios en Bolivia: son evidentes los avances con participación popular', Cochabamba, Bolivia: Centro de Estudios para la Realidad Economica y Social.

World Bank, 1994, 'Bolivia: Structural Reforms, Fiscal Impacts and Economic Growth', Washington, DC: Latin America and the Caribbean Region Office.

World Bank, 2000a, 'Project Appraisal Document. Support of the First Phase of the Sustainability of the National System of Protected Areas Program in Bolivia', Report No.21447-BO, Washington, DC: Latin America and the Caribbean Office.

World Bank, 2000b, 'Bolivia: Country Assistance Evaluation', Report No.21412, Washington, DC: Operations Evaluation Department.

World Bank, 2000c, 'Bolivia: Decentralization Reform Project', Report No.PID9249, Washington, DC: Latin America and the Caribbean Office.

Closer to People and Trees: Will Decentralisation Work for the People and the Forests of Indonesia?

IDA AJU PRADNJA RESOSUDARMO

I. INTRODUCTION

Indonesia is an archipelago with 17,000 islands spread over an area of 1.9 million square kilometres. It is a country characterised by large geographical, economic and social disparities, particularly between the island of Java and the Outer islands.[1] About 60 per cent of the 210 million population live on Java, though it comprises only seven per cent of the country's land area. In 2000, Java accounted for more than half of the national Gross Domestic Product (GDP), and the capital city of Jakarta 15 per cent [*Economist Intelligence Unit, 2002*]. Located on Java, the central government has played a dominant political and administrative role throughout most of the country's history [*MacAndrews, 1986: 9*].

Following Indonesia's 1997–98 economic and political crisis, there were widespread demands, both in Jakarta and in the regions,[2] for political, administrative and economic reforms – which Indonesians frequently refer to as *reformasi.* In Jakarta people focused on bringing the fallen New Order government's leadership and cronies to trial for corruption and on the formulation of new laws allowing for democratic and other reforms. For the regions, the fall of the previous regime and *reformasi* has meant that citizens were now able to express their long-felt objections to policies biased in favour of Java, which had created a large gap in their respective levels of development [*Ferrazzi, 2000: 108*]. All over the country, people demanded a greater role in managing their local affairs [*Ahmad and Hofman, 2000: 1*]. In particular, resource-rich regions demanded a greater share of the revenue from the natural resources produced there [*Kantaprawira, 2002: 12*] ('Kalimantan Menuntut Peran Putera Daerah', *Kompas*, 21 Dec., 1998; 'Pembagian Keuangan Pusat

Ida Aju Pradnja Resosudarmo is a PhD scholar in the School of Resources, Environment, and Society at The Australian National University. This essay was first prepared for the World Resources Institute 'Workshop on Decentralisation and the Environment' in Bellagio, Italy, 18–22 Feb. 2002. The author is grateful to Anne Larson and Jesse Ribot for their extensive and detailed comments at various stages of the revision of this essay. Comments from an anonymous reviewer were also very helpful.

European Journal of Development Research, Vol.16, No.1, Spring 2004, pp.110–132
ISSN 0957-8811 print
DOI:10.1080/0957881041000168876l

Daerah tidak Mengarah ke Federalisme', *Kompas*, 19 Oct., 1998; 'Kalsel Minta 70 Persen', *Kompas*, 1 Oct., 1998; 'Perimbangan Keuangan Pusat dan Daerah. Irja Minta 70 Persen, Kaltim 75, Riau 10', *Kompas*, 10 Sept., 1998). The resource-rich provinces of Papua, Aceh and Riau threatened to secede from the Republic ('Otonomi Daerah Irja', *Kompas*, 3 Sept., 1998).

The inability of the centralised governance system to respond to the economic and political crisis raised serious questions regarding its effectiveness [*Rasyid, 2002: 1*]. Increased autonomy in decision-making and a more just distribution of resources came to be perceived as crucial to prevent national disintegration, hence decentralisation became the alternative [*Van Zorge Report, 1999: 4*]. In November 1998, the People's Consultative Assembly, the highest authority of the state, held a special session resulting in a statement of principles for the 'Organization of Regional Autonomy, Equitable Arrangements, Division and Utilization of National Resources, and Balanced Finance of the Central and Regional Government in the Context of the Unitary State of the Republic of Indonesia'.[3] With great haste and little public debate, the House of Representatives passed two decentralisation laws in April 1999: Law No.22/1999 on Regional Governance and Law 25/1999 on the Balance of Funds – both of which were signed in May by then President Habibie. These two laws were to come into effect on 1 January 2001.

The passage of these decentralisation laws marked the beginning of a fundamental political and administrative transformation of Indonesia, as they legislate the devolution of a wide range of public service functions, the strengthening of elected local legislative assemblies, and the financial and economic empowerment of the regions.[4] They also stipulate the transfer of natural resource management authority to regions, albeit with ambiguities and contradictions, and increase the regions' share of natural resource revenues. Later that same year, however, a new forestry law was introduced that tended to maintain forest decision-making authority at the centre.

Proponents of decentralisation argue that it is good for natural resource management, since it can incorporate local knowledge about the diverse resource base. By bringing decision-makers physically closer to citizens, public access is improved – thereby promoting a greater sense of ownership of rules about resource use that should result in an increased willingness to abide by them [*Carney, 1995: 2*]. In contrast, distant state authorities face significant constraints in allocating resource use rights effectively, leading to overexploitation and disadvantages for the poorest sectors [*Carney and Farrington, 1998: 14*].

Decentralisation, however, also has several shortcomings. Non-local groups may have better appreciation for long-term or large-scale concerns, such as conservation [*Lutz and Caldecott, 1996: 2*], and equitable distribution of benefits of high-value natural resources such as forests may be hindered, since decentralisation can increase the likelihood of elite domination [*Carney, 1995: 5*].

Many countries around the world have adopted some form of decentralised governance [*Agrawal and Ribot, 1999: 473*]. The outcomes vary among countries and regions, and, particularly in the context of natural resource management, there is limited evidence that decentralisation has benefited forests and the people who depend on them [*Kaimowitz et al., 1998: 45*]. This essay examines this question in the context of Indonesia's recent efforts to decentralise forestry authority.

A number of variables are likely to determine the outcomes of decentralisation. Crook and Sverrisson suggest factors such as the variations in administrative and financial resource allocation systems and in relations between central and local governments, configurations of local economic, political and social structures, and the length of time decentralisation has been implemented [*Crook and Sverrisson, 2001: 2–5*]. Local governments need four elements for successful democratic decentralisation: adequate power, financial resources, administrative capacity and reliable accountability mechanisms. The last of these – ensuring both the accountability of elected politicians to citizens, and of bureaucrats to elected politicians – is identified as the most important [*Manor, 1999: 55; Piriou-Sall, 1998: 12*]. Governments' different political motivations for decentralising also affect outcomes [*Crook and Sverrisson, 2001: 2*]. In addition, historical legacies shape present-day politics and social dynamics, and can either facilitate or impede decentralisation [*Manor, 1999: 58–9*]. All these factors have played a role in shaping the process of forest sector decentralisation in Indonesia.

Indonesia's decentralisation laws promised a significant shift in decision-making authority over natural resources to local governments, but their implementation has been challenging. Legislation was formulated with insufficient preparation and planning [*Alm et al., 2001: 87*], resulting in inconsistencies and ambiguities within and among different laws and regulations. Inconsistencies between decentralisation laws and sectoral laws, such as the forestry law, as well as the regions' accumulated historical frustrations and distrust of the centre's real intentions in the devolution of authority, have given rise to conflicts among different tiers of government.

At the same time, a substantially increased percentage of income from lucrative forest resources has been transferred to lower-level governments, as well as the right to allocate forest-harvesting rights. These changes have occurred as a result of the broad political and economic reforms that increased the authority of local governments in general and decreased the power of provincial governments, while the central government scrambles to maintain its own authority and legitimacy. Although it may be too early to draw firm conclusions from these still-recent changes, the results so far indicate a substantial increase in logging with little regard for environmental consequences as local people and governments take advantage of new income-generating opportunities. This increase is likely to lead to forest deterioration and conversion, as well as, in some ways, increased benefits to local peoples.

At the same time, local authorities have only limited downward accountability to the population – the popular vote is restricted to the election of a political party rather than individual candidates. And while local people have benefited to some degree from new access to forest resources, the primary benefits have not gone to those who need them most.

The Indonesian case highlights the importance of downward accountability as well as the appropriate balance of powers between central and local authorities in decentralisation [*World Bank, 2000: 112*]. It underlines the dangers of a substantial and abrupt loss of central authority [*Prud'homme, 1995: 213–19*] and raises important issues regarding historical and national context and the insecurity of change in the generation of outcomes.

This essay describes the broad dynamics of decentralisation's early stages in Indonesia, focusing on some of the major trends that began to emerge at the district level, and explores the initial impacts of decentralisation on forests and local communities. The following section summarises the recent decentralisation reforms. The next section briefly reviews forest management prior to the reforms. The essay then examines how forestry decentralisation has unfolded, focusing particularly on key district-level dynamics and the relationship between the Ministry of Forestry and local governments. Finally, it identifies some of the preliminary outcomes of the process to date, then draws some conclusions.

A substantial part of this analysis is based on the findings of CIFOR (Center for International Forestry Research) research on decentralisation and the administration of policies affecting forests in Indonesia, conducted in collaboration with Institut Pertanian Bogor, University of Adelaide, Murdoch University and the Australian National University (ANU), and on preliminary findings of research on the same topic in collaboration with Universitas Tanjungpura, Universitas Hasanuddin and Brandeis University. Fieldwork was conducted in nine districts in 2000 and three districts in 2001. Updates and revisions of this essay were done since the author became affiliated with the School of Resources, Environment and Society at ANU.[5]

II. CURRENT DECENTRALISATION REFORMS

Given Indonesia's diversity, a unitary state with centralised power and decision-making authority was for a long time considered the appropriate form of government for maintaining national unity and integration [*Malo, 1995*].

Indonesia has several times attempted to decentralise but, until very recently, implementation was limited to a shift of administrative responsibilities rather than the transfer of political or decision-making power and authority to locally elected representatives [*Devas, 1997: 361*]. The 1999 decentralisation laws restructured the political and organisational arrangements of the regional governments, their relationship with the centre, and established a new framework for the intergovernmental fiscal system.

Law 22/1999 on Regional Governance

Two sections of the law on Regional Governance are pertinent to our discussion of natural resource decentralisation. Article 7 transfers the authority over all sectors of governance except those considered strategic – such as foreign affairs, the judiciary, security and defence, monetary and fiscal matters, and 'authority in other sectors' – to regions. 'Authority in other sectors' is explained further as including natural resource use and conservation. However, Article 10 of the same law appears to contradict this, stating that 'regions have the authority to manage national resources within their jurisdictions and are responsible for maintaining the environment according to law'. Consequently, these two articles easily invite a variety of interpretations.

One important change provided by the decentralisation framework has been the 'downgrading' of the provinces and the 'upgrading' of districts/municipalities. First, power and resource transfers from the centre are aimed at districts and municipalities as opposed to the provinces. Although many argue that district-level capacity is lower [*Van Zorge Report, 2000a: 5*] ('Tim Unhas: Otonomi Sebaiknya di Dati I', *Kompas*, 30 June, 1998), the common justification for this decision is that, being closer to the people, district and municipal governments are best placed to make decisions and provide public services in line with the people's needs and aspirations [*McLeod, 2000: 30; Usman, 2001: 4*]. At the time, increasing power to the provinces was perceived as encouraging separatist tendencies and, hence, a threat to national unity [*Usman, 2001: 4*] – an unlikely scenario with regards to the smaller and weaker districts [*Van Zorge Report, 2000a: 5*].[6] Moreover, increasing provincial power is perceived as too similar to federalism *[Van Zorge Report, 2000a: 5, 1999*], a concept that was promoted by the Dutch shortly after independence in an attempt to maintain control over parts of Indonesia and is therefore unpopular to many Indonesians.

Second, there is no longer a hierarchical relationship between the provinces and districts/municipalities. Whereas previously district or municipality heads reported to their respective governors, they are now directly accountable to local legislative assemblies. This is a marked difference from the past centralised era and has changed the relationship between provincial and district officials.

Another important aspect of the law is that it separates local legislative and executive powers, thus effectively boosting the power of local legislatures. Local legislative assemblies now elect the district head or *bupati* who is, accordingly, responsible to the legislative assembly (district Dewan Perwakilan Rakyat – DPRD).[7] Previously DPRDs were part of the executive body of regional governments and were subordinate to the executive [*CSIS, 2001: 8*]. Their major functions are no longer merely to 'endorse' regional legislation but to produce it together with regional governments and provide the checks and balances to control and monitor regional governments. The *bupati* is also required to work with the DPRD in the planning of district budgets.

In theory, real power should ultimately rest with citizens through their representatives. But Indonesia has a proportional representation system to elect members of the legislative assemblies at national, provincial, district and municipal levels. As stated earlier, under this system constituents vote only for political parties, thus members of the assembly represent political parties that have secured a sufficient number of electoral votes and may not necessarily secure their own position due to their skills or knowledge of local affairs.

Law 25/1999 on the Fiscal Balance between the Central Government and the Regions

The fiscal balance law provides the legal framework for building regional financial capacity to carry out tasks associated with regional autonomy. It establishes the major components of regional revenue sources, reorganises the system of central government fiscal transfers and structures revenue-sharing from natural resource exploitation.

Decentralisation has thus not only expanded districts' regulatory functions and political authority but also the responsibility and opportunity to meet their budgetary and development needs that are not sufficiently covered by central transfers. In response to this new opportunity, immediately after the decentralisation laws were passed the regions began to calculate expected government transfers – particularly concerning revenue-sharing arrangements – and to look for innovative ways to raise revenues locally. As we will see below, local government financial concerns are key to the way in which decentralisation has proceeded.

Central State Relations with Provincial and Local Institutions

The implementation of decentralisation depends to a great extent on the relationship between the central government and local institutions. This is shaped by two factors. First, the new legal power structures have changed the relationship between state and local institutions, as well as between provincial and district institutions. Second, the historic failure of the central government to devolve power has left the regions with lingering distrust of such promises [*Suharyo, 2000*].

The regions' distrust of the process was documented in the early stages of decentralisation. In 2000, many district and provincial officials expressed scepticism with references to regional autonomy as 'half-hearted autonomy', criticism of the laws as false promises, or statements like 'the central government continues to hold the head of the snake and will only give us the tail' [*Potter and Badcock, 2001: 16; Casson, 2001b: 26*].

The provinces have also demonstrated resistance to the present configuration of regional autonomy for handing over power to district governments, which in effect bypassed provincial governments. Resistance from the provinces is not without reason. Several districts and municipalities have shown a tendency to disobey or ignore provincial government instructions ('Mendagri Hari Sabarno: Bupati/Walikota Memandang Sebelah Mata pada Gubernur', *Kompas*, 11 April 2002; 'UU Otonomi Diminta Diamandemen', *Kompas*, 13 Feb. 2001). In addition, many government positions at the provincial level were abolished as a result of decentralisation. As a result, the provincial government association reportedly requested that the House of Representatives and the central government amend the two regional autonomy laws, particularly regarding the elimination of the hierarchical relationship between provincial and district and municipal governments ('UU Otonomi Diminta Diamandemen', *Kompas*, 13 Feb. 2001). Discussions among central government authorities regarding plans to amend the laws are ongoing.

III. FOREST MANAGEMENT IN INDONESIA

Approximately 120 of the 190 million hectares of Indonesia's land area are officially classified as forest estate, that is, under the legal control of the Ministry of Forestry. The forest estate is further classified into production forests, for timber production (57 million hectares); conservation and protection forests (55 million hectares); and conversion forests, for conversion to non-forestry uses such as plantations and agriculture (eight million hectares) [*FWI/GFW, 2001*]. Not all of these areas are actually forested: estimates range from 89 to 98 million hectares [*FWI/GFW, 2001: 17*]. From 1985 to 1997, the annual deforestation rate was estimated at 1.7 million hectares [*Holmes, 2002: v*].

For many years these forests have made substantial contributions to national and local economies, and to the livelihoods of forest communities. In 2002, though significantly lower than preceding years, the export value of forestry products was US$5 billion, or 12 per cent of the value of total non-oil and gas exports [*Bank Indonesia, 2003*]. The industry provides direct employment for approximately 2.5 million workers and indirect employment for 1.5 million others [*Sarjono, 2002*]. An estimated 30 million people depend on forests for their livelihood [*FWI/GFW, 2001: 3*].

Prior to 1967, most of Indonesia's natural forests were in effect controlled and managed by forest dwellers, and logging was limited to small-scale activities supplying local timber markets [*Ross, 2001: 165*].[8] Decentralisation of government forestry institutions in 1957 had granted forest management authority to provinces. Provincial bureaucrats were then accountable to the governor, rather than to the forestry department in Jakarta. The Basic Agrarian Law of 1960, recognising customary property in so far as it did not conflict with national interests, further weakened the forestry department's power [*Ross, 2001: 165*].

When the New Order government came to power in 1966, the country urgently needed new sources of revenue to resolve its economic crisis. Its vast forests were seen as an untapped resource that could be utilised for this purpose. In 1967, the government adopted the Basic Forestry Law, which placed all of Indonesia's forests under central government authority. For several years, however, provincial governors retained the power to grant concessions of up to 10,000 hectares, district heads up to 5,000 hectares and sub-district heads up to 100 hectares, while the forestry department awarded concessions for areas over 10,000 hectares [*Ross, 2001: 173; Magenda, 1991: 78*]. In 1970, the forestry department set a new minimum concession size of 50,000 hectares, effectively revoking regional and local government authority to grant licences [*Ross, 2001: 174*]. From that time, the forest department granted large-scale forest exploitation rights – or *Hak Pengusahaan Hutan* (HPH) – covering tens of thousands and even hundreds of thousands of hectares to domestic, private and state-owned logging companies. These HPH activities, through the imposition of fees such as concession rights levies, royalties, and reforestation funds, have been an important source of government income.

Over the years, New Order government policies resulted in the concentration of forest industries into a few large conglomerates, and logging concessions became a form of patronage bestowed to secure the financial and political interests of state elites. Meanwhile, forest dwellers, who had depended on forests for generations, were systematically marginalised [*Fay and Sirait, 2002: 126; Potter, 1991: 180*].

IV. FOREST MANAGEMENT UNDER DECENTRALISATION

The current decentralisation process again brought about significant changes in forest management, including the way in which logging activities are carried out and the emergence of local government timber-licensing schemes. It needs to be noted, however, that some of these trends predate decentralisation legislation, and were associated with the broader atmosphere of *reformasi*.

Legal Framework for Forestry Decentralisation

As explained above, Law 22 provided the basis for transferring power over forest resources to regions, but with contradictions and ambiguities that easily allowed for multiple interpretations. Like other Indonesian laws, the law itself is broad, further requiring an implementing regulation,[9] which, unfortunately, was not ready until a year later – in part due to conflicting interests.

Complicating matters further, a new forestry law (Law 41/1999) was passed in September 1999 to replace the Basic Forestry Law (1967). This new law does not mention the transfer of forest authority to regions, implying that it remains with the Ministry of Forestry. As a result, local governments have based their actions on their interpretation of Law 22. The Ministry of Forestry, on the other hand, clings to its power by relying on the new forestry law.

Power struggles in several sectors led to intense negotiations between the Minister of Regional Autonomy and sectoral representatives in the preparation of the implementing regulation of Law 22 [*Van Zorge Report, 2000b: 12*]. The Ministry of Forestry strongly resisted surrendering authority, arguing that districts lack the capacity to manage Indonesia's forests [*Van Zorge Report, 2000a: 6*].

In May 2000, the government finally passed the much-awaited regulation.[10] Interestingly, though expected to clarify Law 22's ambiguities, it failed to explicitly clarify district responsibilities. Instead, it specified only the powers and responsibilities of the central and provincial governments. Implicitly, therefore, it assumes that all other authorities beyond those mentioned in the regulation lie with district governments.

The regulation gave the Ministry of Forestry a number of important powers that reaffirm its policy-making role in forest management, particularly in setting criteria and standards. This includes: classifying forest areas and changing their status and functions; setting criteria and standards for tariffs on forest use licence fees, royalties and reforestation funds; setting criteria and standards for licensing forest area use; and setting standards for the management of forest products, including planning the management, use, maintenance, rehabilitation and control of forest areas, and for natural resource conservation in forests and plantations. Provinces are given authority over forestry issues affecting more than one district within the province. It is presumed, therefore, that the responsibilities of districts/municipalities are limited to day-to-day forest management functions.

Previously, however, the Ministry of Forestry had promoted other policies as part of the '*reformasi* package', ostensibly to respond to demands for a more just and equitable distribution of forest benefits. In January 1999, a few months prior to the introduction of the decentralisation laws, the government issued a regulation concerning forest exploitation (Government Regulation No.6/1999), and the Ministry of Forestry issued its implementing regulation

(Ministerial Decision 310/1999). This legislation granted district governments the authority to issue small-scale timber concession licences to co-operatives, individuals, or corporations owned by Indonesian citizens for areas of up to 100 hectares within conversion forests and production forests slated for reclassification to other uses. It did not allow for their issuance in areas where large-scale concession permits (HPH) had already been granted. This legislation has been a key source of contention between the ministry and local governments, as we will see below.

Other important legislation includes the Ministerial Decree on the Criteria and Standards of the Licensing of Forest Products and the Harvesting of Forest Products in Natural Production Forests. The Ministry of Forestry issued this decree towards the end of November 2000, about one month before the formal implementation of regional autonomy was effectively to begin. It granted district leaders the authority to issue concession licences, within their jurisdiction, for areas up to 50 thousand hectares, governors to issue licences that crosscut two or more districts and the central government to issue licences over areas crossing provincial boundaries.

Forest Revenue-Sharing

Many local governments believe that the successful implementation of decentralisation will depend on their ability to raise local revenues to support themselves as autonomous areas [*McCarthy, 2001a: 7; Usman, 2001: 6–7*]. The discussion of forestry issues, therefore, has evolved in this context.

Briefly, district incomes are composed principally of locally generated revenues, balance of funds or central government transfers, regional loans and other sources. The central government transfers most relevant to our discussion include the local share of natural resource revenues and the specific allocation funds, which, with regard to forestry, are composed of reforestation funds.

Of the new transfer provisions above, the implementation of natural resource revenue-sharing has been one of the most contentious issues, particularly for resource-rich regions. This is hardly surprising, since these arrangements allowed natural resource-rich regions to enjoy a substantial portion of their riches – particularly of oil, gas and forests – for the first time in 30 years.

With regard to forestry fees, 30 per cent of the revenue from the forest concession rights levy was previously retained by the central government, while the remainder was distributed to the provincial governments. Now only 20 per cent is retained by the centre and 16 per cent is distributed to the provincial governments, while 64 per cent goes to the producing district. Similarly, 20 per cent of the forest royalties is now retained by the centre and 80 per cent distributed to the regions – the province receives 16 per cent and the producing district 32 per cent, while the remaining 32 per cent is distributed equally among the other districts within the province. Previously, revenue from forest royalties was divided as follows: 30 per cent to the provincial governments, 15 per cent to districts, 40 per cent for national forestry development and 15 per cent for regional forestry development.[11] The new arrangement for reforestation fees is 40 per cent for producing regions – the distribution among producing district, province and the remainder of the districts in the province is not specified – and 60 per cent for the central government.

Several forest-rich districts were unhappy with the new formulae for revenue distribution and sought to secure a larger portion [*Alqadrie et al., 2002: (3) 29–30; Casson, 2001b: 15; Barr et al., 2001: 11*]. Alqadrie *et al.* reported that Kapuas Hulu district of West Kalimantan delayed the transfer of timber-related payments collected within its jurisdiction in an attempt to demand a greater share [*Alqadrie et al., 2002: (3) 30–31*]. This occurred despite the fact that the Ministry of Forestry and the governor of West Kalimantan issued specific procedural directives to submit these payments on time, directly to the central government. Moreover, the most lucrative forestry revenues – the reforestation funds – have also been a source of dispute between districts and the central government, and between districts and provinces. To access these funds, each district must submit proposals for approval by the province [*Potter and Badcock, 2001: 42*].

The transparency of calculations and transfer procedures are as important to the districts as the predetermined formulae of their share. Districts must keep track of all payments associated with timber produced within their jurisdictions to ensure that they receive their proper share. The timing of transfers – such as the delayed distribution of reforestation funds in 2001 ('Dana Reboisasi Akan Digunakan Untuk Memagar Hutan Lindung', *Kompas*, 27 Oct., 2001) – has also raised concerns, because it affects districts' cash flows ('Kaltim Minta DR Cair Tahun Ini', *Kompas*, 26 July, 2001).

New District Timber Regimes: Emphasis on Economic Considerations[12]

With decentralisation, local governments perceive that the generation of substantial local revenue is necessary not only to finance their development priorities but also to maintain their independence from central government [*Saad, 2001: 10*]. Immediately after parliament approved the decentralisation laws – months before they legally took effect – many districts passed regulations aimed at increasing local revenue.

Local governments, particularly in forest-rich districts, have sought to generate cash by applying new timber-related fees, such as taxes and levies on forest products transported through their jurisdictions. To support this effort, local governments lobbied the central government to revise the 1997 taxation law that prohibited regions from levying taxes (including taxes on timber and forest products);[13] the new law was passed in December 2000.[14] Some districts, however, applied these new levies on forest products even before the new law was introduced [McCarthy, 2001b: 8–9].

One of the most appealing income-generating opportunities was that presented by the small-scale (up to 100 hectare) logging licences mentioned earlier. When this legislation was passed, district leaders immediately seized the opportunity to allocate large numbers of these licences. In practice, however, many of the areas licensed have fallen within the boundaries of centrally issued HPHs, thereby threatening their operations [*Universitas Cenderawasih, 2002; Barr et al., 2001: 19; Casson, 2001a: 16; KK-PKD Kutai Barat, 2001: 48; Suparna, 2001: 167*]. The Indonesian Forest Concessionaire Association – the body representing the large logging companies – lobbied at both the national and provincial levels to halt the extensive allocation of these small-scale permits [*Barr et al., 2001: 23*].

In response, in September 1999 the Ministry of Forestry requested the governors' assistance to suspend the further issuance of these permits, but district officials did not comply. By that time, the decentralisation laws had been approved, and although they were not yet in force, they allowed for the interpretation that the position of the district leader *vis-à-vis* the governor had changed: district leaders were not required to comply with the governor's instructions because they were no longer the governor's subordinates. In April 2000, as districts still refused to stop issuing small-scale logging licences, the Ministry of Forestry issued a decree suspending the ministerial decision that had given the district governments this authority.[15] Several district governments, however, ignored the decision, arguing that they retained the right to issue these permits because only the ministerial decision was repealed, while Government Regulation 6/1999 – which has higher authority than a ministerial decision – was still in force [*McCarthy, 2001b: 10–11*]. Other districts argued that small-scale logging ensured that local people directly benefit from forest resources [*Casson, 2001a: 17*]. Typically, local legislative assemblies fully supported the issuance of district licences [*McCarthy, 2001b: 11*].

The environmental implications of these small-scale logging licences are not insignificant, particularly in terms of the area logged and the volume of timber removed. To give three examples: by July 2000, the district of Kapuas had granted 60 small-scale logging permits [*McCarthy, 2001b: 11*]; in December 2000 the district of Kutai Barat in East Kalimantan had issued 622 similar licences [*KK-PKD Kutai Barat, 2001: 43*]; and the timber harvest from the 409 licences issued by Sintang district of West Kalimantan was estimated at 1.2 million cubic meters [*Witular, 2003c*]. Moreover, the case of Malinau district illustrates that, in practice, one 'small-scale' permit could extend far beyond the 100-hectare limit specified by the decree. In addition, the short, one-year duration of these permits means a high rate of forest removal, as new permits need to be granted when they expire.

Many of the new small-scale permits were issued prior to the establishment of a regulatory agency at the district level [*Barr et al., 2001: 17*]. Districts also generally lacked the capacity to monitor the implementation of licences [*Alqadrie et al., 2002; Barr et al., 2001: 17; Casson, 2001a: 16*], which were not infrequently granted without the necessary field inspection [*Barr et al., 2001: 36*] – resulting in inappropriate assignments. Moreover, there are indications that the approval of permits has been based on informal incentives rather than environmental and social considerations [*Alqadrie et al., 2002: (4) 10; Barr et al., 2001: 19; McCarthy, 2001b: 13*] ('1, 2 Juta Kubik Kayu Hasil Tebangan Liar di Kalbar', *Kompas*, 16 Oct., 2001).

While there are variations in the types of fees and royalties imposed on these small-scale logging activities, they generate substantial revenues for district governments. District governments have introduced new fees on small-scale licences, including 'third party contributions' – a one time fee, usually based on the size of the concession – and a 'retribution' fee based on volume of timber harvested. For example, Kapuas district raised US$37,500 in just one month after it applied retribution fees on timber [*McCarthy, 2001b: 9*].[16] By August 2000, small-scale logging activities in Kutai Barat district had generated more than US$30,000 for the district [*Casson, 2001a: 16*]. In the same year, third-party contributions from similar activities in Berau district, East Kalimantan, had generated US$400,000 – or half of the district's GDP for that year [*Casson and Obidzinski, 2002: 2141*].

Some aspects of the new district timber regime have directly or indirectly encouraged illegal logging [*Casson and Obidzinski, 2002: 2138*]. For example, some districts issued regulations validating timber harvested outside the formal forestry regime. Instead of auctioning confiscated timber, as was done previously, district governments simply imposed fees. Hence timber can be transported out of a district and traded legally provided that those involved pay the corresponding central government and district fees [*McCarthy, 2001a: 26*]. Such regulations in effect 'legalise' illegal timber. In this case, local governments appear to be particularly interested in the revenues generated from timber, rather than where or how it was harvested.

Moreover, the districts' poor monitoring capacity has encouraged logging in areas outside those delineated by the permits. It has been reported that some small-scale permit holders start by logging areas outside the boundaries of their permits, with the intention of saving their designated areas 'for later' [*Alqadrie et al., 2002, (3) 39*]. It has also been common for small-scale licensees to provide documentation for the transport and trade of logs cut illegally by others, claiming that the logs originated in their own concession areas [*Alqadrie et al., 2002: (3) 40*].

The Challenge of Maintaining Conservation and Protected Areas

One of the most urgent challenges of forest management today concerns the maintenance of conservation and protected areas, particularly given the widespread increase of illegal logging – defined here as the harvesting of timber in violation of the law. Other threats include increased pressures to reclassify protected areas for other uses and conversion to small-scale agriculture. Many of Indonesia's national parks and protected forests are experiencing serious levels of encroachment in one form or another [*Alqadrie et al., 2002: (5) 1; Soetarto et al., 2001: 64–5*] ('Lindu Lore National Park Looted', *The Jakarta Post*, Feb. 9, 2003; M. Kurniawan, '18% of Protected Forests Already Destroyed: Government', *The Jakarta Post*, 13 Feb., 2003; M. Kurniawan, 'Money, Guns Destroy Protected Forest in Central Kalimantan', *The Jakarta Post*, 10 Feb., 2003; 'Kayu Taman Nasional Ditebang, Pemda Kapuas Hulu Diam Saja', *Kompas*, 23 Aug., 2001; 'Penebangan Kayu Liar Masih Marak di Way Kambas', *Media Indonesia*, 6 Aug., 2002).

The decentralisation laws place the responsibility for both the management and financing of conservation areas with the central government (that is, the Ministry of Forestry). Since the beginning of *reformasi*, however, the government has been unable to enforce controls as it did during the New Order period [*Casson and Obidzinski, 2002: 2136; Potter and Badcock, 2001: 39*]. The military, for their part, are now reluctant to exert control for fear of being accused of authoritarianism and becoming the target of community violence [*Soehartono, 2001: 42*]. In addition, the economic crisis resulted in a huge decline in government budget allocations for the management of protected and conservation areas [*Merrill et al., 2001: 39*]. At the same time, the crisis has forced many people to find alternative sources of livelihood and, hence, turn to forests. Together, these circumstances stimulated an increase in illegal logging and protected area encroachment. Although these problems may not be associated exclusively with decentralisation, their escalation and the penetration of the last remaining good forests demonstrate the urgency of addressing this issue under decentralisation.

The central government's capacity to manage and secure protected and conservation forests has been regarded as far from adequate, yet it is being increasingly stretched. The lack of personnel and supporting infrastructure limit the government's ability to carry out efficient monitoring and enforcement [*Wardojo, 2001: 5*]. For example, in Betung Kerihun National Park, West Kalimantan, one park personnel attends to 27,580 hectares [*Merrill et al., 2001: 44*]. These difficulties are aggravated by the way illegal logging activities are carried out: through violent opposition to whoever stands in the way [*Potter and Badcock, 2001: 38*].

Under decentralisation, the issue of conservation and protected areas must also ultimately be placed in the context of opportunities for local revenue-generation. Some districts have issued small-scale logging permits in protected areas [*Barr et al., 2001: 36*] ('1, 2 Juta Kubik Kayu Hasil Tebangan Liar di Kalbar', *Kompas*, 16 Oct. 2001), and district-licensed logging operations have reportedly 'spilled over' into protected forests ('Hutan Sumatara Utara Dikorbankan untuk PAD', *Kompas*, 9 Sept. 2002). Districts perceive conservation areas as a lost revenue opportunity [*Wardojo, 2001: 7; Sembiring, 2001: 28*], and there are indications that some are tempted to convert them to other uses. At least two districts with vast conservation forests have suggested that they be compensated by the central government if they are to maintain them ('Daerah Konservasi Harus Mendapat Kompensasi', *Kompas*, 3 Sept. 2003; 'Samarinda dan Pulau Kumala Terendam', *Kaltim Post*, 2 Sept. 2003; 'Tuntut Kompensasi Hutan Lindung Rp 1 T', *Equator*, 18 Nov. 2000, see http://www.equator-news.com).

Nevertheless, there are also a few encouraging examples. The provincial DPRD of West Sumatra, for example, has suggested that they reject a coal mining permit application in the Kerinci Seblat National Park for environmental reasons ('Coal Mining Ban Proposed in Kerinci National Park', *The Jakarta Post*, 25 Aug. 2001), and Jambi province in Sumatra has taken a firm stand towards supporting the maintenance and expansion of Bukit Tiga Puluh National Park ('DPRD Jambi Dukung Rasionalisasi TNBT', *Kompas*, 23 June 2001). Provincial and local governments have also shown some desire for greater authority over these areas [*Sembiring, 2001: 28; Soetarto et al., 2001: 65*], though this is limited to management aspects with prospects for financial gain – such as tourism [*Barr et al., 2001: 12, 39; Billa, 2001; Soetarto et al., 2001: 67–8*].

Power Struggles between the Ministry of Forestry and Local Governments

The Ministry of Forestry has not been particularly content with local developments. It has persevered, unsuccessfully, in its attempt to halt the issuance of district logging licences through repeated warning and threats and the revocation of, ironically, its own earlier policies. Rather than reaching a successful resolution, the tug-of-war between the Ministry of Forestry and local governments that began from the outset of decentralisation remains intense.

As suggested by the provisions of the Ministry of Forestry's November 2000 decree (see above), local governments were actually authorised to grant not only small-scale licences, but also medium- and large-scale ones. Realising the consequences, the Ministry of Forestry revoked this decree in February 2002 in a desperate effort to halt the proliferation of local timber licences. As with the small-scale licences, however, the regions ignored the new decree. In October 2002, the Ministry of Forestry issued a circular to governors, district leaders and heads of municipalities requesting them to stop issuing such licences and report all those already issued to the ministry.

In June 2002, three years after the passage of the new forestry law, the government produced its implementing regulation, which swings authority for forests back to the centre.[17] For example, it states that the Minister of Forestry has sole authority to issue large-scale HPHs, on the recommendation of lower levels of government.[18] The head of the association of district governments responded that the regions are strongly opposed to the regulation [*APHI, 2002: 12*] (Syaukani, 'Sentralisasi vs Otonomi dalam Pengelolaan Hutan', *Media Indonesia*, 31 July 2002).

Confusion over the hierarchy of laws and regulations has accentuated the conflict between the ministry and local governments. For example, one decree issued by the People's Consultative Assembly in 2000 explaining the hierarchy of Indonesian laws and regulations made no mention of ministerial decrees, providing a loophole for district leaders to ignore them.[19]

As of January 2003, the Ministry of Forestry estimated that the total area of logging concessions granted through local government licence schemes had reached two million hectares (R.A. Witular, 'Deforestation Accelerated as Regions Issue Concessions', *The Jakarta Post*, 27 Jan., 2003), including both small-scale and medium-scale licences ('Regions Race to Issue Licenses', *The Jakarta Post*, 27 Jan. 2003). The province of Papua is reported to have granted medium- and large-scale logging concessions to 44 private firms covering an area of 11.8 million hectares (R.A. Witular, 'Papua refuses to revoke logging licenses', *The Jakarta Post*, 25 March 2003).

The Ministry of Forestry acknowledges that it is losing authority over forests: local governments now reject its orders and regulations (Witular, 'Deforestation Accelerated as Regions Issue Concessions'), and the ministry has no power over them. Administratively, districts are not subordinate to the Ministry of Forestry, but rather to the Ministry of Home Affairs. Meanwhile, the Ministry of Forestry's efforts to gain the Ministry of Home Affairs' approval to impose sanctions on 'defiant' local governments have not been successful (R.A. Witular, 'Ministry Deplores Lack of Support in Saving Forests', *The Jakarta Post*, 27 March 2003).[20]

V. WILL DECENTRALISATION WORK FOR FORESTS AND FOR LOCAL COMMUNITIES?

The general tendency of district governments under decentralisation, at least in the first few years, has been to secure short-term economic gains with inadequate attention to long-term environmental, social and economic considerations. Few district officials demonstrate concern over the ecological consequences of forest over-exploitation [*McCarthy, 2001a: 16*]. Moreover, it appears that the regional governments' enthusiasm to earn as much income as possible from forest resources has not been accompanied by an eagerness to invest a share of the benefits in forests. Little attention, for example, has been given to reforestation or forest rehabilitation [*Casson, 2001a: 16*].

While the effects of decentralised forest management on forests tend to be undesirable, the preliminary implications for local communities are mixed. One of the district officials' main arguments in favour of allocating large numbers of small-scale logging permits is that they give local communities greater opportunity to benefit from forests – benefits that previously went mainly to outsiders [*McCarthy, 2001b: 12; Casson, 2001a: 16*]. So far, however, current dynamics indicate that communities have not been the primary beneficiaries. Typically, licences are granted to local individuals, community groups and village co-operatives, but as they usually lack the required capital and expertise they have had to collaborate with 'partners' or investors – either local or even foreign (such as Malaysian) firms or entrepreneurs [*Alqadrie et al., 2002: (3) 34–5; Barr et al., 2001: 18*], and in some cases large-scale HPH holders [*McCarthy, 2001b: 13*]. In many Kalimantan districts, for example, though the formal licensing fees are relatively low, informal costs are very high, adding up to US$3,000–7,500 to obtain a permit [*Alqadrie et al., 2002: (4) 28; McCarthy, 2001b: 13; Barr et al., 2001: 19*]. In Berau, unofficial contributions to the district office for a 100-hectare area add up to US$1,500 [*Casson and Obidzinski, 2002: 2141*]. McCarthy estimates that the total cost of logging a 100-hectare area amounts to at least US$12,000 [*McCarthy, 2001b: 13*], well beyond the reach of most local people. Despite the stated purpose of the new small-scale licence regime, these high costs limit the actual involvement of local people in logging. Rather, local communities living in and around forest areas participate in these concessions by providing forest areas for logging and receiving fees, which are usually based on the volume of timber harvested [*Casson and Obidzinski, 2002: 2142*].

Though local communities receive some income from these arrangements, most of the profits accrue to the capital provider and other actors [*McCarthy, 2001b: 13*]. At the level of local government, the main beneficiaries are the district office and the district forestry office [*Casson and Obidzinski, 2002: 2142*]. Also, communities are vulnerable to companies' abuse of their contractual agreements with regard to small-scale licences: they often fail to employ locals in logging operations as promised or to assist communities in replanting cleared land with cash crops [*Casson and Obidzinski, 2002: 2141; Barr et al., 2001: 30–31*].

The prospect of economic gains from small-scale logging has intensified conflicts among local individuals and communities, such as disputes over village borders [*Universitas Cenderawasih, 2002; Barr et al., 2001: 33; KK-PKD Kutai Barat, 2001; Rhee, 2000: 37*]. Moreover, because these gains have been primarily captured by local elites with strong political or economic connections [*Barr et al., 2001a: 39; McCarthy, 2001a: 27, 2001b: 16*], a gap has emerged between those who can and cannot take advantage of the opportunities offered by decentralisation and the new small-scale licensing regime.

The decentralisation process in the forest sector has, however, had some positive effects for local people. Compared with the New Order period, they now enjoy greater access to forest resources. Not only is there increased formal recognition of communities [*Rhee, 2000: 36*], but also – at least in the short term – communities can expect to gain some direct income from logging activities in local forests. While the income generated may be meagre, it is probably more than before [*Casson and Obidzinski, 2002: 2142*].

VI. CONCLUSION

The decentralisation process in Indonesia, particularly in the forestry sector, is facing tremendous challenges. The pace of change has been incredibly rapid, with *de facto* decentralisation occurring more quickly than *de jure* decentralisation. Impelled by *reformasi*, the weakening of the existing legal order and future promises of autonomy, decentralisation on the ground began before the January 2001 date set for the implementation of autonomy laws – and long before the necessary supporting regulations were in place.

In practice, then, decentralisation, fostered by local policies and initiatives more than by central government dictates, has been disorderly. A number of interconnected factors have contributed to this. First, part of the problem is the confusion and uncertainty stemming from inconsistencies and legal contradictions within the decentralisation framework, between decentralisation laws and sectoral laws (in this case the forestry law), and regarding the relative authority of certain regulations in the legal hierarchy. Laws and regulations were formulated too hastily and with little public involvement. Consequently, the legal framework leaves room for multiple interpretations, and local governments have justified their actions based on their own analysis. Second, the central government's motivations, by decentralising at a time of political instability while struggling with its declining legitimacy, have played a role in spawning local actions that infringe on national legislation and policies and foster what traditionally have been considered illegal activities. Third, decades of historical neglect of the Outer islands' development, through forest-extraction policies in which benefits primarily accrued to non-local actors, have resulted in deep resentment of central government policies. Furthermore, the rhetoric and failures of earlier decentralisation attempts have sowed the seeds of local distrust in the devolution of power and resources. This distrust has increased due to the centre's ongoing demonstrated reluctance to hand over power in the current process. This has motivated 'opportunity-grabbing' behaviour on the part of local governments and communities, who fear losing these opportunities in the future.

What we have seen, therefore, at least in the first few years of implementation, is a decentralisation process that has led district governments to emphasise economic interests, particularly in forest-rich areas. Meanwhile, the Ministry of Forestry has been losing control over forest resources in terms of its ability both to assign forest use or exploitation and to protect it. Clearly, a more appropriate and, most importantly, legitimate balance of power between the centre and the local levels of government is needed to ensure resource protection.

Effectively, local governments now have more power and authority, but a critical element providing the checks and balances for exercising this power is missing. While district leaders are now accountable to district assemblies, assembly members are accountable to their political parties but not directly to constituents. There is no institutionalised mechanism in place to ensure that district governments use their power and authority in ways that benefit citizens.

The choice to decentralise to districts rather than provinces was based, in part, on the argument that decisions made closer to the people would respond better to citizens' needs and aspirations. Even so, however, Indonesian districts, particularly those of the Outer islands, may cover vast geographical areas with dispersed and remote populations. In addition, transportation and communication infrastructures are often rudimentary or non-existent, hindering meaningful information sharing and interaction between decision-makers located in the district centres and citizens – another obstacle to downward accountability and real citizen participation in decision-making.

Concerns about district-level capacity are also relevant and have clearly had an effect in the forestry sector. Logging concessions have been allocated with minimal control or monitoring mechanisms in place, leading to unsustainable practices. Scale issues are also important: the need to make some decisions based on environmental considerations that cross administrative boundaries suggests that provincial authority over a wider territory may be necessary and appropriate.

Decentralisation has provided greater opportunities for local communities to engage in timber-related activities, enabling them to gain some benefits from this resource. Nevertheless, most of the benefits appear to accrue to other actors, including local elites. A segment of the local population – those who are in less of a position to take advantage of these opportunities – risks being left behind.

Under decentralisation, Indonesian forests have been put to a difficult test. Though it is too early to establish definitive outcomes – as the dynamics are continually changing, there are early signs both that the process has thus far followed a desirable route on the one hand, and a path that needs to be much improved on the other. A greater portion of forest riches is now retained and enjoyed at the source, and local leaders are now making their own decisions regarding forests. Nevertheless, this new power and authority has been exercised primarily in ways that encourage short-term exploitation over long-term sustainability. Future efforts must seek mechanisms to strengthen the gains while discouraging and minimising the losses.

NOTES

1. Large disparities in many aspects have almost exclusively differentiated the island of Java from the other islands, which are commonly referred to as Outer islands – the largest being Sumatra, Kalimantan, Sulawesi and Papua.
2. 'Regions' in general refers to areas outside the capital city of Jakarta, where the central government operates. Regions as specified in the 1999 decentralisation laws pertinent to the focus of this essay refer explicitly to provinces (the first tier of local government, which is directly below the central government), districts and municipalities (rural and urban areas respectively, which are the second tier of local governments).
3. Decree of the People's Consultative Assembly of the Republic of Indonesia No.XV/1998.
4. In the Indonesian context, decentralisation is commonly referred to as 'regional autonomy'; these terms are often used interchangeably.
5. The opinions and interpretations expressed in this essay are those of the author and do not necessarily represent the official policy or position of CIFOR or ANU.
6. Note, however, that the size of district and municipal governments in terms of their populations and areas vary widely. Their populations range from 24,000 to 4.1 million people [*Esden, 2002*]. Some districts cover vast areas. For example, of the districts pertinent to our discussion, Kapuas district in Central Kalimantan has an area of 34,800 square kilometres, while the district of Malinau in East Kalimantan comprises 42,000 square kilometres. As of February 2003, there are 32 provinces and 410 local governments, consisting of 324 districts and 86 municipalities [*GTZ, 2003*].
7. Since November 2002, plans for direct elections of regional heads (that is, governors, *bupatis* and mayors) have emerged [*GTZ, 2002*].
8. Discussion of Indonesia's forests in this essay refers mostly to the forests of the Outer Islands, that is, those outside Java. Java has only small remnants of natural forest; most of Java's forests are teak plantations.
9. Indonesian Laws are usually written in a general form, such that their implementation depends on subsequent government regulations. These implementing regulations are further developed by ministerial decisions to determine exactly how they are to be implemented.
10. Government Regulation No.25/2000.
11. Presidential Decree 67/1998.
12. Elements of the following sections were drawn from Resosudarmo [*2003*].
13. Law No.18/1997.
14. Law No.34/2000.
15. It is unclear why the Ministry of Forestry, at the same time it was trying to repeal the small-scale measure, issued the 50,000-hectare regulation mentioned earlier. At least until recently, though, the small-scale concessions had generated more serious problems, and were the focus of the research presented here.
16. One US dollar is equivalent to about 8,000 rupiah.

17. Government Regulation No.34/2002.
18. Many of the provisions of Government Regulation No.34/2002 will be specified in ministerial decisions to be issued by the Minister of Forestry, suggesting further opportunities for the ministry to consolidate its interests.
19. Decree of the People's Consultative Assembly of the Republic of Indonesia (MPR) No.III/2000 stated that MPR decrees stand immediately below the Constitution in Indonesia's legal hierarchy, followed by laws (*undang-undang*), government regulations replacing laws (*peraturan pemerintah pengganti undang-undang*), government regulations (*peraturan pemerintah*) and regional regulations (*peraturan daerah*).
20. The relationship between the Ministry of Forestry and the Ministry of Home Affairs is beyond the scope of this analysis and requires further examination.

REFERENCES

Agrawal, A. and J. Ribot, 1999, 'Accountability in Decentralization: A Framework for South Asian and African Cases', *Journal of Developing Areas*, Vol.33 (Summer), pp.473–502.

Ahmad, E. and B. Hofman, 2000, 'Indonesia: Decentralization – Opportunities and Risks', Jakarta: IMF and World Bank Resident Mission.

Alm, J., R.H. Aten and R. Bahl, 2001, 'Can Indonesia Decentralize Successfully? Plans, Problems, and Prospects', *Bulletin of Indonesian Economic Studies*, Vol.37, No.1, pp.83–102.

Alqadrie, S.I., Ngusmanto, T. Manurung, T. Budiarto, Erdi and Herlan, 2002, 'Desentralisasi Pembuatan Kebijakan dan Administrasi Kebijakan dalam Mempengaruhi Sektor Kehutanan pada Wilayah di Luar Pulau Jawa: Hubungan antara Otonomi dengan Kelestarian Hutan di Kabupaten Kapuas Hulu, Provinsi Kalimantan Barat', Draft paper, Pontianak: Universitas Tanjung Pura.

APHI, 2002, 'Mengembalikan Pengelolaan Emas Hijau ke Pusat', *Hutan Indonesia*, Vol.4, No.20, pp.11–13.

Bank Indonesia, 2003; see http://www.bi.go.id/bankindonesia/utama/datastatistik/.

Barr, C., E. Wollenberg, G. Limberg, N. Anau, R. Iwan, I.M. Sudana, M. Moeliono and T. Djogo, 2001, 'The Impacts of Decentralization on Forests and Forest-Dependent Communities in Malinau District, East Kalimantan', Case Study No.3, Bogor, Indonesia: CIFOR.

Billa, M. (bupati of Malinau district), 2001, Personal communication, May and Aug.

Carney, D., 1995, 'Management and Supply in Agriculture and Natural Resources: Is Decentralization the Answer?' *ODI Natural Resource Perspectives*, London: ODI, Vol.4, June; see http://www.odi.org.uk/nrp/nrp4.html.

Carney, D. and J. Farrington, 1998, *Natural Resource Management and Institutional Change*, London: Routledge.

Casson, A., 2001a, 'Decentralization of Policies Affecting Forests and Estate Crops in Kutai Barat District, East Kalimantan', Case Study No.4, Bogor, Indonesia: CIFOR.

Casson, A., 2001b, 'Decentralization of Policies Affecting Forests and Estate Crops in Kotawaringin Timur District, Central Kalimantan', Case Study No.5, Bogor, Indonesia: CIFOR.

Casson, A. and K. Obidzinski, 2002, 'From New Order to Regional Autonomy: Shifting Dynamics of "Illegal" Logging in Kalimantan, Indonesia', *World Development*, Vol.30, No.12, pp.2133–51.

Crook, R.C., and A.S. Sverrisson, 2001, 'Decentralization and Poverty-Alleviation in Developing Countries: A Comparative Analysis or, is West Bengal Unique?' IDS Working Paper No.130, Brighton: Institute of Development Studies, University of Sussex.

CSIS (Center for Strategic and International Studies), 2001, *Kemampuan Politik Lokal Untuk Pelaksanaan Otonomi Daerah, Laporan Penelitian*, Jakarta: CSIS.

Devas, N., 1997, 'Indonesia: What Do We Mean by Decentralization?' *Public Administration and Development*, Vol.17, pp.351–67.

Economist Intelligence Unit, 2002, *Country Profile Indonesia*, London: The Economist Intelligence Unit Limited.

Esden, B., 2002, 'Indonesia Rising Above Challenges'; see http://www/decentralization.ws/srcbook/indonesia.

Fay, C. and M. Sirait, 2002, 'Reforming the Reformists in Post-Soeharto Indonesia', in C.P. Colfer and I.A.P. Resosudarmo (eds.), *Which Way Forward: People, Forests, and Policymaking in Indonesia*, Washington, DC: Resources for the Future, pp.126–43.

Ferrazzi, G., 2000, 'Avoiding Disintegration: Decentralization Options for Indonesia' in A.F. Bakti (ed.), *Good Governance and Conflict Resolution in Indonesia*, Jakarta: IAIN Jakarta Press and Logos., pp.107–18.

FWI/GWF, 2001, *'Potret Keadaan Hutan Indonesia'*, Bogor, Indonesia: Forest Watch Indonesia and Washington, DC: Global Forest Watch.

GTZ, 2003, 'Parliament Approves 25 New Districts and Cities', *Decentralization News*, No.40, 7 Feb.

GTZ, 2002, 'Revision of Law 22/1999 to Allow for Direct Election?' *Decentralization News*, No.37, 29 Nov, p.5.

Holmes, D.A., 2002, *Where Have All the Forests Gone?*, Environment and Social Development East Asia and Pacific Region Discussion Paper, Washington, DC: World Bank.

Kaimowitz, D., C. Vallejos, P. Pacheco and R. Lopez, 1998, 'Municipal Governments and Forest Management in Lowland Bolivia', *Journal of Environment and Development*, Vol.7, No.1, pp.45–59.

Kantaprawira, R, 2002, 'Disintegrasi dan Upaya Mencegah Keutuhan Bangsa', in Y.M.A. Aziz and A. Priangani (eds.), *Titik Balik Demokrasi dan Otonomi*, Yogyakarta: Pustaka Raja, pp.3–38.

KK-PKD Kutai Barat, 2001, *Potret Kehutanan Kabupaten Kutai Barat*, Kelompok Kerja Program Kehutanan Daerah (KK-PKD), Kabupaten Kutai Barat, Pemerintah Kabupaten Kutai.

Lutz, E. and J. Caldecott, 1996, 'Introduction', in *Decentralization and Biodiversity Conservation: A World Bank Symposium*. Washington, DC: The World Bank, pp.1–5.

MacAndrews, C., 1986, 'Central Government and Local Development in Indonesia: An Overview', in C. MacAndrews (ed.), *Central Government and Local Development in Indonesia*, Oxford: Oxford University Press, pp.6–19.

Magenda, B., 1991, *East Kalimantan: The Decline of a Commercial Aristocracy*, Cornell Modern Indonesia Project Monograph Series No.70, Ithaca, NY: Southeast Asia Program, Cornell University.

Malo, M., 1995, 'Social Sector Decentralization: The Case of Indonesia', IDRC: Social Development Documents; see http://www.idrc.ca/soc.dev/pub/indones/Indones.html.

Manor, J., 1999, The Political Economy of Democratic Decentralization, Washington DC: The World Bank.

McCarthy, J., 2001a, 'Decentralization, Local Communities, and Forest Management in Barito Selatan District, Central Kalimantan', Case Study No.1, Bogor, Indonesia: CIFOR.

McCarthy, J., 2001b, Decentralization and Forest Management in Kapuas District, Central Kalimantan, Case Study No.2, Bogor, Indonesia: CIFOR.

McLeod, R., 2000, 'Survey of Recent Developments', *Bulletin of Indonesian Economic Studies*, Vol.36, No.32, pp.5–40.

Merrill, R., D. Rothberg and E. Effendi, 2001, 'Meningkatkan Pendanaan Taman Nasional: Memperkuat Sistem Pengelolaan Taman Nasional dalam Era Transisi dan Otonomi Daerah', in R. Merrill and E. Effendi (eds.), *Memperkuat Pendekatan Partisipatif dalam Pengelolaan Kawasan Konservasi di Era Transisi dan Otonomi Daerah*, Jakarta: Natural Resources Management Programme.

Piriou-Sall, S., 1998, 'Decentralization and Rural Development: A Review of Evidence', Washington, DC: The World Bank.

Potter, L., 1991, 'Environmental and Social Aspects of Timber Exploitation in Kalimantan, 1967–1989', in J. Hardjono (ed.), *Indonesia: Resources, Ecology, and Environment*, New York: Oxford University Press, pp.177–211.

Potter, L. and S. Badcock, 2001, 'The Effects of Indonesia's Decentralization on Forests and Estate Crops in Riau Province: Case Studies of the Original Districts of Kampar and Indragiri Hulu', Case Study Nos.6 and 7, Bogor, Indonesia: CIFOR.

Prud'homme, R., 1995, 'The Dangers of Decentralization', *World Bank Research Observer*, Vol.10, No.2, pp.201–20.

Rasyid, R.M., 2002, 'The Policy of Decentralization in Indonesia', Paper prepared for the GSU Conference 'Can Decentralization Help Rebuild Indonesia?' Atlanta, GA, 1–3 May.

Resosudarmo, I.A.P., 2003, 'Shifting Power to the Periphery: The Impact of Decentralization on Forest and Forest People', in E. Aspinall and G. Fealy (eds.), *Local Power and Politics in Indonesia: Decentralisation and Democratisation*, Singapore: ISEAS, pp.230–44.

Rhee, S., 2000, 'De Facto Decentralization and the Management of Natural Resources in East Kalimantan during a Period of Transition', *Asia Pacific Community Forestry Newsletter*, Vol.13, No.2, pp.34–9.

Ross, M., 2001, *Timber Booms and Institutional Breakdown in Southeast Asia*, Cambridge: Cambridge University Press.

Saad, I., 2001, 'Indonesia's Decentralization Policy: The Budget Allocation and Its Implications for the Business Environment', SMERU Working Paper, Jakarta: SMERU Research Institute.

Sarjono, A.P., 2002, 'Forecasting Pengusahaan Hutan Tahun 2002', *Hutan Indonesia*, Vol.3, No.18, pp.15–17.

Sembiring, S., 2001, 'Memperkuat Partisipasi, Transparansi, dan Akuntabilitas Publik melalui Mekanisme Konsultasi Publik dalam Pengelolaan Kawasan Konservasi', in R. Merrill and E. Effendi (eds.), *Memperkuat Pendekatan Partisipatif dalam Pengelolaan Kawasan Konservasi di Era Transisi dan Otonomi Daerah*, Jakarta: Natural Resources Management Program.

Soehartono, T., 2001, 'Mencari Langkah Tepat Pengelolaan Taman Nasional di Indonesia', in E. Marbyanto, I.F.I. Francisca, P. Sidi and S. Iman Pribadi (eds.), *Menguak Tabir Kelola Alam*, Samarinda: Aliansi Pemantau Kebijakan Sumber Daya Alam Kalimantan Timur, pp.37–46.

Soetarto, E., M.T. Felix Sitorus and Y. Napiri, 2001, 'Decentralisasi Administrasi, Pengambilan Kebijakan dan Manajemen Hutan di Propinsi Kalimantan Barat', Draft paper, Bogor, Indonesia: CIFOR.

Suharyo, W.I., 2000, 'Voices from the Regions: A Participatory Assessment of the New Decentralization Laws in Indonesia', Jakarta: United Nations Support Facility for Indonesian Recovery (UNSFIR).

Suparna, N., 2001, 'Forestry Management in the Era of Regional Autonomy', Indonesian Quarterly, Vol.29, No.2, pp.159–67.

Universitas Cenderawasih, 2002, 'Desentralisasi Pembuatan Kebijakan dan Administrasi Kebijakan-kebijakan yang Mempengaruhi Hutan di Luar Jawa: Studi Kasus tentang Peran Lembaga Adat dalam Pengelolaan Hutan di Kabupaten Sorong Propinsi Papua', Draft paper, Feb.

Usman, S., 2001, 'Indonesia's Decentralization Policy: Initial Experiences and Emerging Problems', Paper prepared for the Third EUROSEAS Conference Panel on 'Decentralization and Democratization in Southeast Asia', London, Sept.

Van Zorge Report, 2000a, 'Interview with Ryaas Rasyid, State Minister for Regional Autonomy', Jakarta, 8 May, pp.12–15.

Van Zorge Report, 2000b, 'On the Road towards Autonomy: Can it Work?' Jakarta, 8 May, pp.4–8.

Van Zorge Report, 1999, 'Decentralizing Amid Regional Dissent', Jakarta, 26 Nov., pp.4–13.

Wardojo, W., 2001, 'National Protected Areas Policy under Decentralisation Scheme', Paper presented in the 'Structural Adjustment Workshop' organised by Conservation International Indonesia, Bogor, 4–6 Sep., unpublished.

World Bank, 2000, *World Development Report 2000: Entering the 21st Century*, New York: Oxford University Press.

Decentralisation, Rural Livelihoods and Pasture-Land Management in Post-Socialist Mongolia

ROBIN MEARNS

I. INTRODUCTION AND OBJECTIVES

In 1990 Mongolia embarked on a far-reaching series of political and economic reforms following the demise of the former Soviet bloc, of which it had been a part for some 70 years. In common with post-communist transitions elsewhere, these reforms aimed to bring about a separation of the political, executive and judicial pillars of the state, and to increase the role of markets rather than the state in allocating resources within society. This reform agenda remains far from complete, however, and is far less tidy in practice than the notion of 'transition' implies [see also *Nelson et al., 1997*]. Contemporary Mongolia is characterised by a mosaic of formal and informal institutions, including the results of new experiments in policy-making seen alongside the remnants of old arrangements and patterns of behaviour.

Any attempt to understand the forms that decentralisation has taken in Mongolia to date, and its consequences for natural resource management, must be seen in and distinguished from this broader context of post-socialist transition. A problem of attribution arises. Post-socialist transition and decentralisation both involve the transfer of powers from state to non-state bodies and efforts to increase the accountability of public institutions. 'Decentralisation' is here understood to refer to formal transfers of power 'to actors and institutions at lower levels within a political-administrative and territorial hierarchy' [*Agrawal and Ribot, 1999: 475*]. 'Democratic decentralisation', more specifically, is said to occur when 'power and resources are transferred to authorities representative of and downwardly

---

Robin Mearns is Senior Natural Resource Management Specialist at the World Bank, based in Hanoi, Vietnam. This is a revised version of a paper first presented at the World Resources Institute Conference on 'Decentralisation and the Environment', Bellagio, Italy, 18–22 Feb. 2002. This contribution has benefited from the comments and suggestions of Jesse Ribot, Anne Larson, Nancy Peluso and two anonymous referees, and from discussions with other conferees. The interpretations and conclusions expressed in this contribution are entirely those of the author and do not necessarily represent the views of the World Bank, its Executive Directors, or the countries they represent.

European Journal of Development Research, Vol.16, No.1, Spring 2004, pp.133–152
ISSN 0957-8811 print
DOI:10.1080/0957881041000l688770

accountable to local populations' [*Ribot, 2002: 4*]. Although they have so far been modest in scope, and stronger in rhetoric than in reality, government efforts to advance a democratic decentralisation agenda in Mongolia may be regarded as a subset of the broader domain of transition reforms – which also include some of the institutional prerequisites for decentralisation of natural resource management to work in practice (that is, a closer specification of property and resource-access rights and credible rule-enforcement mechanisms). The problem of attribution arises because of the difficulty of distinguishing the outcomes of these overlapping sets of policy reforms in terms of their consequences for local livelihoods and natural resource management practices.[1]

This contribution makes no claims to resolve this problem of attribution. It begins by describing what is intended by 'decentralisation' in statements of current government policy, contrasting this with the forms decentralisation takes in practice, and offering a brief synopsis of the current status of decentralisation in Mongolia – benchmarked against a number of other developing countries. We then apply the 'actors, powers and accountability' framework [*Agrawal and Ribot, 1999; Ribot, 2002*] to show how certain far-reaching policy reforms over the past decade, including important elements of democratic decentralisation [*Manor, 1999*], have contributed to significant changes in local livelihoods and pasture-land management practices. While the stated intentions of many of the reforms in question are to promote social inclusion and environmental justice[2], their practical outcomes currently have precisely the opposite effects. Finding that these adverse outcomes are in part a reflection of incomplete decentralisation, the contribution concludes with reflections on some of the critical missing elements of a democratic decentralisation agenda that could help to restore social and environmental justice in pasture-land use and management.

This case study is based on field research by the author on pastoral livelihoods in areas representing diverse ecological and market-access conditions throughout rural Mongolia in several periods over the course of the 1990s [*Mearns, 1993a, b, 1996, 1997; NSO and World Bank, 2001*[3]], insights gained from the author's ongoing management of the World Bank's support for 'pro-poor' rural development in Mongolia, and published secondary sources.

II. DECENTRALISATION AS POLICY

To what extent is decentralisation currently claimed as a tenet of policy by the government of Mongolia, both in general and in relation to natural resource governance and environmental justice in particular? Textual analysis of relevant official documents reveals that 'decentralisation' is intended in several different and potentially far-reaching ways. General statements of intent are offered in the government's overall Action Programme, which mirrors the manifesto on which the present government was elected with a landslide victory in June 2000 [*GoM, 2000a*]. This document sets out an ambitious agenda, including: the promotion of regional and rural development, in part to address the over-concentration of economic opportunity in the capital city and central, more market-accessible regions of the country;[4] increasing accountability in the public sector; increasing the capacity of local governments to generate revenues over which they have discretionary control; and offering citizens 'greater opportunity to directly monitor the performance of their elected Citizen's [*sic*] Representative *Hural* [assemblies] and the executive agencies nominated by the *Hural*' [*GoM, 2000a: 53*].

Other relevant declarations of government policy include the recently enacted Public Sector Management and Finance Law (PSMFL), which seeks to increase the accountability and effectiveness of public sector institutions at all levels while also respecting the need for fiscal restraint and sustainability [*GoM, 2002a*]. The PSMFL calls for a shift from input-based budgeting to output- or performance-based budgeting, aims to put more authority in the hands of local assemblies and clarify the responsibilities of local governments, overhauls the existing system of inter-governmental transfers, and devolves service-delivery functions to local providers – under the oversight of local assemblies [*World Bank, 2002*].

The government's Good Governance for Human Security Programme refers to 'decentralizing and empowering local self-governance and local administration' [*GoM, 2001: 12*], and aims to support 'stakeholder consultation, voice, and participation' in the broader policy process, including 'monitoring … citizen satisfaction and recommendations with regard to services, rights, and government responsiveness to citizen demands' [*GoM, 2001: 14*]. The government's Economic Growth Support and Poverty Reduction Strategy (EGSPRS) echoes the broad theme of raising public accountability, notably through greater public voice in and scrutiny of the budget process [*GoM, 2003b*].

Concerning claims for decentralisation as policy with more specific respect to the environment, most official sources [*NCSDM, 1999; GoM, 2000b*] refer principally to the need to enhance citizen voice and participation in decision-making, monitoring and evaluation, usually mediated through civil society institutions. These are not binding policy documents, however, and few concrete, budgeted proposals are made to advance them. In the case of the National Environmental Action Plan, cursory mention is made of the principle of subsidiarity: 'decisions on environmental issues are to be taken at the lowest appropriate level' [*GoM, 2000b: 16*]. The EGSPRS, however, goes further than most other government documents in outlining a strategy with respect to natural resource governance that involves support for herder groups to undertake collective action in grassland and pastoral risk management, and support for effective implementation of the land law. A recently formulated rural development strategy, prepared in part as an input to the EGSPRS, fleshes this out in further detail [*CPR, 2002*].

III. DECENTRALISATION IN PRACTICE

To what extent is this democratic decentralisation agenda being translated into practice? In this section, we consider some of the binding physical, demographic and fiscal constraints before turning to the specific case of pasture-land management.

With a total population of 2.4 million people in an area virtually the size of Western Europe, Mongolia is probably the most sparsely populated country in the world. Excluding the population of the capital city, Ulaanbaatar – in which one-third of the total population lives [*NSO, 2001*],[5] there is an average of roughly one square kilometre of land for every person.

There are three levels of sub-national administration below central government: *aimags* and the capital city have provincial status; next down the hierarchy fall *sums* (rural districts) and *duuregs* (urban districts of the capital city); and lowest of all are *bags* (rural sub-districts) and *khoroos* (urban sub-districts). *Aimags* have an average population of around 75,000; *sums* around 5,000; and *bags* less than 1,000. There is an elected assembly, or *khural*, at each of the three tiers of sub-national government.[6] Each sub-national level also has an executive administration headed by a governor who is nominated by the respective *khural* and formally appointed by the governor at the next-highest level. *Aimag* governors, for example, are appointed by the prime minister.

There is an inherent tension in the PSMFL in seeking to increase public-sector effectiveness in delivering high-quality services to such a dispersed population while also exercising fiscal restraint. One legacy of the former socialist regime, which achieved remarkable (though fiscally unsustainable) health and education outcomes, was a high political expectation that these public services would continue to be delivered at similar levels in the future. This is one half of the twin paradox that the PSMFL struggles to resolve: how to deliver more with less.

Powerful governors at *aimag* and *sum* level are the key actors in local space, but in practice they have little downward accountability to their local constituencies. The primary accountability of governors is upwards to central government. While *aimag*- and *sum*-level assemblies (*khurals*) are elected, their actual role as oversight bodies is very limited. Their functional jurisdiction is vaguely defined and they appear to be more a forum for consultation than for making decisions. This is unlike the state Great

Khural (national parliament), which is empowered to initiate or amend legislation and has a constitutionally defined role in which it must approve and legislate on certain decisions before the executive branch of government can act.

Mongolia has made significant strides since 1990 towards creating a decentralised democracy, including this important separation of citizens' representative assemblies from the executive branches of government which, at least in theory, they oversee. At the sub-national level, however, the system of inter-governmental transfers currently in place has not created fiscally autonomous, self-governing local authorities for three main reasons [*World Bank, 2002*]. First, there are large asymmetries between the expenditure responsibilities of local governments (which have been growing) and their decision-making authority (which is heavily circumscribed by the many mandated functions they are assigned in law, notably in service delivery). Second, local governments have little or no capacity to raise revenues of their own. Third, the system of inter-governmental transfers on which sub-national governments rely for the overwhelming majority of their revenues is unpredictable and inequitable. Overall, levels of fiscal decentralisation are very modest indeed.

The financial autonomy of sub-national governments is currently restricted under the budgetary process and the General Taxation Law (2000), which subjects all major taxes to state legislation – including payment for use of 'state resources' such as mineral deposits, land, timber and water. Sub-national governments have the right to levy user fees for certain natural resources (for example, natural plants other than timber, and mineral springs), but these revenue sources are very small in relation to local budgetary needs – which leads to extreme fiscal dependence on central government. The revenue and expenditure autonomy of *sums* and *bags* is negligible, and accounts for less than one per cent of all budget revenues and expenditures in Mongolia. Local *khurals* can levy taxes on local enterprises, but in practice virtually all enterprises are registered in Ulaanbaatar and a few other urban centres. Inter-governmental transfers are also subject to political bargaining. Horizontal inequities between sub-national jurisdictions are striking, but do not necessarily correspond to the widely varying size of the populations and tax bases.

The other half of the twin paradox facing the PSMFL, then, is how to achieve downward accountability of public sector institutions to their local constituents when the financial resources on which they depend are derived almost entirely from the centre. This creates an inbuilt tendency for upward accountability to predominate. Local people are more likely to demand accountability from public institutions – and local governments are more likely to be responsive – when local resource mobilisation and/or transparency in inter-governmental transfers are more closely matched with public service-delivery obligations. This remains a distant goal in Mongolia.

In summary, a highly imbalanced pattern of decentralisation prevails in Mongolia compared with a sample of 14 other developing countries (see Figure 1). This snapshot captures the intended and unintended consequences of past policies as actually implemented, whether or not those policies were promulgated in the name of decentralisation. Measured against a set of standardised criteria developed by the World Bank for this purpose,[7] contemporary Mongolia has been characterised by substantial though incomplete political decentralisation, but little administrative decentralisation and virtually no fiscal decentralisation [*McLean, 2001*].[8] Administrative decentralisation follows a deconcentrated pattern in which governors and their staffs report upwards to the next-highest level of government, while technical staff report primarily to national line ministries or their respective provincial departments. There is little opportunity for elected assemblies to exert any influence over technical department staff and quality of service delivery at their respective level of government, and therefore little incentive for local populations to use their elected representatives as a channel for articulating concerns and making claims in this respect. Evidence from the Mongolia Participatory Living Standards Assessment 2000 confirms that community members are widely dissatisfied with the extent to which local governors and elected representatives take account of their needs and aspirations [*NSO and World Bank, 2001*].

FIGURE 1

NATIONAL DECENTRALISATION BY DIMENSION IN MONGOLIA AND 14 OTHER COUNTRIES

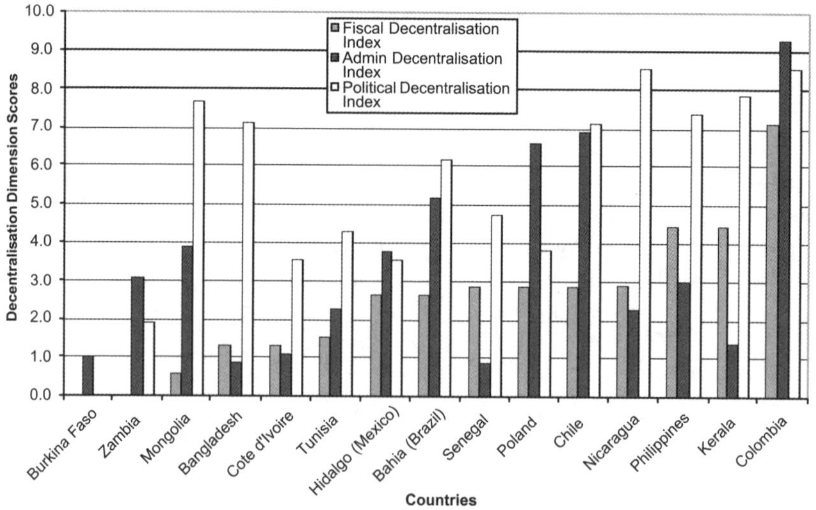

Source: McLean [2001]

IV. DECENTRALISATION AND PASTURE-LAND MANAGEMENT: AN UNFINISHED AGENDA

Against this challenging background within which decentralisation reforms are being pursued, we now examine the forms decentralisation has taken in the specific case of pasture-land management. Under Mongolian conditions, sustainable pasture-land management is primarily achieved by maintaining a spatial separation between the pastures used in different seasons and ensuring that they are grazed only in those seasons ('time-partitioning'). Local patterns of resource use can vary widely from year to year given natural variability in precipitation and forage growth [*Mearns, 1993b*]. Spatial and social (user-group) boundaries therefore tend to be deliberately 'fuzzy', permeable, overlapping and dynamic, which calls for resilient institutional forms to enable groups of resource users to co-ordinate their actions, make internal agreements 'stick' with credible sanctions, and renegotiate access rights on an ongoing basis [*Bruce and Mearns, 2002; Fernández-Giménez, 2002; Goodhue and McCarthy, 2000; Turner, 1999*]. For such local-level collective action to be effective, various forms of support are required from the state, particularly in making essential infrastructure investments and providing inputs and services to help manage risk, in the transparent and fair adjudication of disputes when local mechanisms fail, and in providing for negotiation between higher-level authorities over resource-access rights during times of drought or winter emergency.

Institutional arrangements governing pasture-land management have undergone profound transformation over the past decade in ways that reflect a virtual abdication of public administration rather than decentralisation or purposive intervention. This is in contrast to earlier periods in modern Mongolian history – most notably during collectivisation in the 1950s to 1980s – in which apparently radical changes at the formal level took rather syncretic, adaptive forms in practice [*Mearns, 1993b; Fernández-Giménez, 1999*]. Such adaptive outcomes in the post-transition era may yet emerge. For the time being, however, pasture-land use is characterised more by a breakdown in established co-ordination norms. This is owing to a dramatic rise in the number and heterogeneity of herders combined with the near absence of public support in areas critical to the security and sustainability of their livelihoods.

Significant changes in pasture-land management practice were introduced under collectivisation, including investments in water supply, winter shelters, hay and fodder production, and transportation for making nomadic moves, and species-specialisation in livestock production at the herder camp level [*Humphrey, 1978*]. While some of these changes partially displaced customary forms of collective action in herding, and tended to restrict seasonal nomadic moves within *bag* (then known as 'brigade') territories, they did not alter the basic seasonal rhythm of pasture-land use. In many respects, pasture-land management under collectivisation was marked by the dual control of formal regulatory institutions and informal co-ordination norms [*Mearns, 1993a, b; Fernández-Giménez, 1999*]. Nominal control of decisions concerning who would graze where and when was transferred from individual households to managers of pastoral collectives and state farms, but in practice the outcomes varied little from customary tenure patterns.

During the 1990s, with the onset of economic transition, several important shifts in pasture-land management practice were brought about. One of the most striking features of change in rural Mongolia in the early 1990s was the re-emergence of the *khot ail* as the primary unit of social organisation among herders in all but the most arid regions of Mongolia [*Mearns 1993b, 1996*].[9] The *khot ail* is a fluid group of herding households that co-operates in livestock and pasture management, notably to take advantage of labour economies of scale. It appeared in the early 1990s that *khot ails* might have the potential to 'federate' upwards spontaneously into informal grazing associations and to perform an important function in regulating access to seasonal pastures, mimicking the formal process of 'time-partitioning' of pasture use that prevailed under the collectives. This potential was generally not realised, however, as a result of other driving forces that limited the extent to which herding communities could operate as self-governing grazing associations.[10]

For example, limited livelihood opportunities outside the livestock sector during the harsh economic conditions of the early-to-mid-1990s led to a doubling in the number of herding households, which increased as a share of total population from 17 per cent in 1990 to around 35 per cent by the mid-1990s.[11] As rural communities swelled in size, they also became more heterogeneous. The gains from the privatisation of state and collective assets were unequally distributed, and inequality in livestock holdings began to increase dramatically. Older, more established and new herding households had divergent interests and levels of skill and experience in livestock production, which both contributed to rising inequality and reduced the likelihood of successful collective action in pasture-land management [*Mearns, 1996*].

Newer herding households tended to be formerly non-herding state employees made redundant by economic liberalisation, and were more likely to remain sedentary for much of the year in locations close to settlements where access to markets and social services was more assured. In many places they were often marginalised in the distribution of winter shelters, which rendered them more vulnerable to livestock mortality during harsh winter conditions, and more dependent on social connections with established herders with more secure claims over winter camp sites and associated pastures as a means of gaining access to pasture. The net effect of changes of this sort was a marked decline in pastoral mobility and an over-concentration of grazing pressure around settlements and close to roads. As argued below, this decline in mobility has emerged as one of the principal threats to the sustainability of pastoral livestock production [*WRI, 2000; World Bank, 2003;* see also *Niamir-Fuller, 1999*].[12]

While these changes may not give the appearance of decentralisation, a decentralisation of sorts has taken place as the state has retreated from a direct role in regulating pasture-land allocation and use. In the institutional vacuum that has prevailed, the rules or claims that take precedence in determining who grazes where and when are often unclear. The land law enacted in 1994 appeared to provide a permissive or enabling framework for sustainable pasture-land management, but it contained significant areas of ambiguity – and key actors received little guidance as to how to interpret and apply the law in practice. As a result, divergent approaches to adjudicating claims and resolving the now widespread pasture-land disputes have been adopted in different jurisdictions [*Erdenebaatar and Batjargal, 2001; Fernández-Giménez and Batbuyan, 2000; Hanstad and Duncan, 2001; Mearns, 1997*].

One such source of ambiguity concerned the definition of the term 'common land'. While pasture land is constitutionally protected from privatisation, the ability of herding communities to use the 1994 land law to underwrite controlled-access commons was compromised by a deeply rooted ethic of open access among Mongolian herders. This prevented herder communities from legally denying 'outsiders' or non-members of their communities from gaining access to local pasture, or from insisting that such access be granted only following explicit negotiation. By the late 1990s, many observers had come to the conclusion that controlled-access pastoral commons in Mongolia – while judged to be necessary for the sustainability of pastoral livelihoods and land management – would be unworkable in the absence of flexible guidelines to aid in implementing the relevant provisions of the land law. Such guidelines would, for example, allow self-governing herder groups to hold joint possession of pasture land for use during each season, regulate the time-partitioning of pasture use and exclude non-members – subject to negotiated and reciprocal rights of access to other groups during declared times of drought or winter stress.

V. ACTORS IN DECENTRALISATION OF PASTURE-LAND MANAGEMENT

At the central level, the key actors in pasture-land management are the Ministry of Nature and Environment (MNE) and the Ministry of Food and Agriculture (MFA), but significant tensions exist between these bodies. Briefly stated, the rôle of MFA has been in decline throughout the 1990s while MNE has been in the ascendancy – at least as far as control over land management is concerned. MFA, with authority over all state farms, and its counterpart for pastoral collectives the Supreme Council of Collectives, enjoyed considerable power throughout the state-socialist era, and were jointly responsible for all policies and planning decisions regarding agricultural land use. Responsibility for land management was transferred to MNE in the early 1990s and, under the growing influence of Western notions of environmental management, a series of environmental laws was enacted, including the 1994 land law (effective in 1995) which was regarded as a tool for conservation-oriented rather than production-oriented land management. MFA's role in land management disappeared in the early 1990s, along with any budget for land affairs – ironically, since this coincided with the period in which herders greatly increased in number and as a share of total population – but this loss of influence remains contested within the MFA and its constituent agencies. Some actors within and associated with MFA, for example, have attempted to draft a law specific to pasture-land tenure, although their efforts have been poorly co-ordinated with other initiatives related to the further development of land legislation.

For present purposes, the principal actor with respect to pasture-land management rests at *sum* (rural district) level, in the person of the *sum* governor. The *aimag* (provincial) administration is much less involved in pasture-land management, except (in principle) in setting aside land for use as inter-*sum* grazing reserves during times of drought or *dzud* hazard.[13] During the collective era, the *sum* governor was also the director of the eponymous collective (*negdel*), and the territorial boundaries of the *sum* and the *negdel*, at least by the end of the 1980s, were coterminous. Known as the *sum darga* (boss), he enjoyed considerable discretionary power within his jurisdiction, while being upwardly accountable only to superiors at higher levels in the highly centralised state structure. Following decollectivisation around 1991–92, and the privatisation of the assets of the collective, many *sum dargas* were retained as the managers of the companies and co-operatives that typically acquired the lumpy assets (equipment, buildings, inventory) of the former collectives, and there was often significant continuity in management style and content. Even the upward accountability was retained, as the now ostensibly private companies and co-operatives maintained their federal structure at the national level through membership in the National Association of Mongolian Agricultural Co-operators (the successor to the Supreme Council of Collectives). Land management practice in many of these *sums* continued for a time much as it did during the collective era, albeit driven to generate profits through trading rather than to meet the production quotas of central planning. Other *sum dargas* were quickly appointed as the new *sum* governors.

In practice, *sum* governors currently have considerable discretion to interpret and enforce the land law as they see fit, an activity not generally constrained by their lack of financial resources. This leads to considerable local variation in resolving claims to winter camp sites, often regarded as the key to obtaining secure access to winter pasture (which, in turn, is an important determinant of success in pursuing a pastoral livelihood strategy). For example, in one *sum*, the governor may declare that in privatising the winter shelters created under the collective (*negdel*), preference would be given to those herders who were most frequently allocated those shelters during the collective era. In another, perhaps even adjoining *sum*, the governor may declare that preference would be given to the claims of those who could claim some birthright to the site, perhaps by virtue of their own or their father's residence there prior to the establishment of the collective. Little or no guidance is offered or available to *sum* governors from the centre in resolving such competing claims, and in areas where winter shelters and camp sites are in high demand and short supply (depending on local ecological and topographic conditions and rates of in-migration following decollectivisation) this can be a serious and continuing source of land dispute [*Mearns, 1997; Erdenebaatar and Batjargal, 2001*].

VI. THE NATURE OF POWERS DEVOLVED

For pasture-land management, the key powers in question that are transferred from central to sub-national levels concern the setting of rules to govern the allocation of camp sites and associated sets of pastures among local herders, compliance with those rules and the adjudication of disputes. The principal mechanism for the transfer of these powers is the land law [*GoM, 2002b*]. At the same time, central government has transferred to local governments primary responsibility for drought- and *dzud*-preparedness, but without the budgetary resources needed to ensure that this responsibility will be met adequately.

Chronic under-provisioning of local efforts to support pastoral risk management (for example, through hay and fodder preparation and distribution) throughout most of the decade of the 1990s led to massive livestock mortality in the three consecutive *dzud* years of 1999/2000 to 2001/2002, amounting to a total loss of around one-fifth of the national herd. In early 2001, the government passed Resolution 47 calling for measures to ensure better drought- and *dzud*-preparedness, and specified the roles of each tier of public administration in establishing an effective and co-ordinated national system for pastoral risk management. At the time of writing it remains unclear whether the resources required to implement such a strategy will be provided for in the medium-term framework for national budgeting.

Under the land law, a deconcentrated arrangement of powers and responsibilities is envisaged whereby land disputes arising at any one level of administration are to be passed up to the next higher level for administrative resolution. No clear role is defined for other actors such as civil courts. Considerable ambiguity also exists in practice in specifying the distinct roles of different levels of administration. *Sum* governors appear to believe they have little scope for discretionary decision-making, while in practice they are seen to exercise considerable residual power in the absence of clear guidelines for the interpretation and implementation of the law [*Fernández-Giménez and Batbuyan, 2000*].

A new land law was enacted in June 2002 [*GoM, 2002b*], and came into effect on 1 May 2003. The primary motivation for revising the 1994 land law was to make possible, for the first time and in a limited way, a land market in Mongolia. That is, long-term possession licences over certain types of land may now be transferred by sale/auction and may be mortgaged, in addition to transfer by inheritance as was provided for in the 1994 law. The types of land in question are urban and peri-urban land, household plots in general (including land under herders' winter camps), vegetable gardens, hayfields and arable land, amounting to a total of around two per cent of Mongolia's land area.

The basic provision of the 1992 Constitution and 1994 land law with respect to pasture land (representing 80 per cent of all land) remains unchanged: namely, that pasture land shall be the property of the state and protected from private ownership. However, the new land law also 'clarifies' some of the ambiguity inherent in the 1994 law in such a way as to bring out the sharp internal contradiction between wishing to maintain free access to pastures for all as 'common tenure' [sic] land and wishing to ensure that time-partitioning in pasture use is closely observed at the *bag* level and below [*GoM, 2002b: Art.54*]. That is, 'pasturelands, water points in pasturelands, wells and salt licks' are among those types of land that, 'regardless of whether they are given into possession or use, shall be used for common purpose under government regulation' [*GoM, 2002b: Art.6.2*]. Furthermore, the law specifically provides for the unhindered right of entry or passage for any person in the case of land that is unfenced or not marked by warning signs, regardless of its tenure status [*GoM, 2002b: Art.48*].[14] It also, however, insists that 'winter and spring pastures shall be prevented from livestock grazing during summer and autumn' [*GoM, 2002b: Art.54*] and provides for sanctions (fines plus compensation) to be imposed in cases of out-of-season trespass [*GoM, 2002b: Art.66*].

In early 2001 the MNE at central government level opened up an important channel for downward accountability by agreeing with a civil society lobbying coalition to host a national-level public forum for discussion on the content of the then draft land law. It is not clear why MNE acted in the way that it did, other than being persuaded by leading champions within the coalition of lobbyists. Whatever the origins of the initiative, however, a discussion draft of the revised law was released, comments were invited from the public via print media, a national-level public workshop was held and a televised debate took place, collectively representing an unprecedented step in Mongolian legal history. Not all of the demands of this lobbying group were reflected in the final version of the law, but there is little doubt that the fact this process took place at all represents a significant step forward in promoting downward accountability in legislative development. Many observers, however, would now argue that the major obstacle to transparent and accountable governance of land management, including pasture-land management, lies in implementation rather than in the promulgation of new legislation [*Hanstad and Duncan, 2001*].

VII. SOCIAL DIFFERENCE, ADMINISTRATIVE ACCOUNTABILITY AND REPRESENTATION

In this section, we consider the nature of accountability relationships between herders and local administrators, and show how social networks among them position elite herders to capture a disproportionate share of the benefits in pasture-land access and control – thereby excluding poorer, more vulnerable herders. Herders themselves, recognising the ambiguity that exists in public administration with respect to pasture-land management, are increasingly likely to take matters into their own hands and to act unilaterally in pasture-land use decisions. The increasing heterogeneity of herding communities also makes individual as opposed to collective action more likely. Different types of herders have developed complex strategies to exploit the opportunities open to them, depending on their distinct social and economic positions.

Wealthier herders, with large herds and, typically, better endowments of adult family labour, are likely to employ strategies of family-splitting to ensure that they can guard their valued winter camp sites and associated pastures against out-of-season trespass by others. At least one family member may remain resident all year round at the winter camp, and a permanent wooden structure may be constructed in some areas to reinforce the visibility of the claim being exercised. In such cases, winter shelters and the land on which they stand (though not the pasture land surrounding them) are now commonly privately owned, with documented evidence of possession rights. Serious conflicts may still emerge if competing claims to the surrounding pastures are made by two herders with equally large herds. Herders with small herds will usually be tolerated even if they camp close to the winter pastures claimed by a wealthy herder, since a certain level of 'free riding' is unlikely to undermine the prospects for sustainable pasture-land use [*Mearns, 1996*].

Poorer herders, who are often those with lower levels of skill and experience in herding, and often with large families including the small children of other dependents, have tended to become increasingly reliant on wealthier kin for survival where they continue to pursue livestock-based livelihoods. A form of labour market has emerged, albeit involving in-kind rather than market-based transactions, in which poorer herders will work as labourers for wealthier herders in arduous tasks, such as clearing out winter shelters, herding, or looking for lost animals, in return for the right to join the *khot ail* of the wealthier herder and thereby gain more secure access to grazing for the few animals they own. Those poorer, 'new' herding households without such resources of 'social capital' to draw on often failed at herding within a short space of time, and having 'eaten away' the assets of animals they received at the time of privatisation in the early 1990s they returned to live in *sum* or *aimag* centres – usually dependent on limited social welfare payments [*NSO and World Bank, 2001*].

In this context of divergent livelihood strategies among herders within the same rural communities, the downward accountability of local governors in matters of pasture-land dispute resolution is far from symmetrical and transparent. Wealthier, elite herders frequently enjoy better relations with local governors, and are both able and willing to invest considerable resources in hospitality when the *darga* visits in order to keep open informal channels of communication to encourage the governor to 'turn a blind eye' or to resolve disputes in their favour. Such opportunities to exercise informal influence are not generally available to poorer, more marginal herders, particularly if they have migrated into the area in question from another *aimag*. Inter-regional migrations of this sort became a recognised livelihood strategy in the later 1990s as those able to do so would move to take advantage of the better household-level terms of trade in more central, market-accessible parts of the country [*NSO and World Bank, 2001*].

In the institutional vacuum created by incomplete decentralisation, a 'tragedy of open access' has therefore emerged – with socially differentiated results. Against such a background, some local civil society groups have sought to explore whether opportunities can be exploited to enhance the downward accountability of more receptive *sum* governments in pasture-land management, and recreate 'meso'-level institutional mechanisms to co-ordinate individual herders' actions in pasture-land use and management so as to facilitate more sustainable and socially inclusive outcomes. Some of these groups are beginning to facilitate pilot projects, with donor support, to field-test approaches to group-based pasture-land tenure and management. In some cases, with the moral backing of local administrations, they have been able to go beyond the limits proscribed in the land law to confer possession contracts on groups of around ten to 20 herding households over all sets of pastures customarily used by those groups. Many questions remain to be resolved concerning the representativeness and legitimacy of such groups among other, non-group members in the same districts; the concurrence or otherwise of social group and territorial/resource-unit boundaries; the degree to which such initiatives remain dependent on donor financing; and the operational rules for negotiating reciprocal rights of access to non-group members during times of drought or *dzud*. However, these pilot projects should be recognised as advancing a positive reform agenda that seeks to achieve more environmentally sustainable and socially inclusive outcomes in pasture-land management through efforts to increase the transparency and downward accountability of local governors' offices, elected representatives and *sum*-level technical staff.

VIII. CONCLUSION: TOWARDS A MORE COMPLETE DEMOCRATIC DECENTRALISATION OF NATURAL RESOURCE GOVERNANCE

This contribution has argued that incomplete or 'empty' decentralisation with respect to pasture-land management in post-socialist Mongolia has had adverse consequences for pastoral livelihoods and for the environment. This concluding section first summarises some of the issues raised by this case study and ends by identifying some of the missing elements of a democratic decentralisation agenda that would help to restore environmental and social justice.

In the absence of alternative livelihood opportunities following post-socialist transition, the 1990s saw a dramatic reassertion of the importance of pastoral livelihoods in Mongolia. The number of herding households more than doubled, and herders once again comprise around a third of the national population. While Mongolia may offer valuable lessons to other countries in which pastoralists form a significant share of the population, this trend should not be regarded as an entirely positive one. Economic 'transition' is something of a misnomer; indeed, in relation to natural resource governance, the notion of an institutional vacuum is more fitting. Both rural and urban livelihoods throughout the 1990s were marked by rising vulnerability – pastoral livelihoods in particular became increasingly vulnerable in the face of natural hazards – in the absence of supporting reforms that would match devolution of responsibilities to sub-national governments with the budgetary resources to carry them out, and accountability reforms that would subject the actions of local governments to public scrutiny from their constituents.

Many other changes took place in rural livelihood strategies and dynamics. Distinct patterns of inter-regional and rural–urban migration emerged in response to changing livelihood and market-access opportunities, according to which very different opportunities arose for better-off herders than for poorer herders and other marginal groups in rural society. These patterns have had profound consequences for the distribution of grazing pressure, resulting in an observably adverse impact on the pastoral environment – notably in shrub vegetation communities in the Gobi-steppe transition zone. At the same time, large areas of good grazing remain under-utilised in more remote areas for want of investments in water supply, social service provision and transportation infrastructure, which in turn are severely constrained by the fiscal crisis facing local governments.

The 1990s has also seen a breakdown of the long-standing forms of dual formal/informal regulation of pasture-land management that had persisted throughout the era of agricultural collectivisation. Some of the principal sources of pressure also relate to changing livelihood dynamics, including: rising levels of asset inequality (notably in livestock holdings) combined with limited options for livelihood diversification; population concentration around settlements, roads/markets and points of social service provision; and emergent labour markets in rural areas, which – among other coping and adaptive strategies – have had important consequences for social capital. The rising vulnerability of more marginal groups has resulted from various combinations of declining asset holdings and adverse household terms of trade, and reduced access to common-pool grazing and benefits from increasingly exclusionary forms of social capital.

To what extent are these outcomes attributable to the 'decentralisation' attributes of economic and political transition itself, and to what extent to the consequences of this transition for livelihood opportunities more broadly? While the causal relationships among these factors are attenuated and difficult to disentangle, it is suggested that democratic decentralisation of natural resource governance has had at least some influence on the outcomes under discussion, although it has not yet gone far enough. To date, its scope has been limited to attempts rigidly to prescribe rules of tenure and administrative authority through the introduction of new legislation, rather than to seek clarity and transparency in rules-setting mechanisms to address necessarily 'fuzzy' pastoral-resource access rights. Moreover, the backdrop of institutional flux and uncertainty that characterises all post-socialist transitions has not so far been conducive to fostering the predictability in expectations among social actors that democratic decentralisation reforms demand.

Limited space prevents a full discussion of possible avenues for future research and policy analysis, but some of the missing elements of this unfinished democratic decentralisation agenda include: 1) promoting public access to information on land legislation and the relevant actions and responsibilities of local governments; 2) continuing support for ongoing institutional innovations to increase the downward accountability of local governments in pasture-land management; 3) developing alternative approaches to pasture-land dispute resolution to complement the administrative options enshrined in the land law; 4) fostering public consultation in the further development of national land legislation; and 5) most importantly, elaborating flexible, context-sensitive implementation guidelines and manuals for use by local governors and their staff in upholding the land law in transparent and accountable ways.

NOTES

1. The problem of attribution of environmental outcomes to changes in public policy is not unique to decentralisation or post-socialist transition. A growing literature on the imputed environmental implications of 'structural adjustment' suffers from similar methodological flaws, as discussed elsewhere [*Mearns, 1991*]. Other analytical frameworks that offer insights into the linkages between public policies and livelihood and environmental outcomes include the environmental entitlements framework [*Leach et al., 1999*], the capitals and capabilities framework [*Bebbington, 1999*] and the sustainable livelihoods framework [e.g., *Ellis, 2000*].
2. This has been defined as 'The right to a safe, healthy, productive and sustainable environment for all', irrespective of individual and group identities – including socio-economic status (Environmental Justice Resource Center at Clark Atlanta University, http://www.ejrc.cau.edu/). In this essay the term is used broadly to refer to equitable access to pasture land and associated key resources, such as water sources and salt licks.
3. The Participatory Living Standards Assessment 2000 [*NSO and World Bank, 2001*], led by the author, drew on the experiences and perceptions of some 2,000 rural and urban community members throughout Mongolia, systematically elicited using participatory learning and action methods, in order to compile a profile of livelihood sources, strategies and dynamics throughout the 1990s. These were differentiated according to well-being status, gender, age and geographical (regional and rural/urban) location.
4. See *Law of Mongolia on Regionalized Development Management and Coordination* [*GoM 2003a*] with supporting documents, including the Regional Development Concept (approved by parliament in 2001) and Medium-Term Regional Development Strategy.
5. Anecdotal evidence suggests that the official data from the National Statistical Office of Mongolia underestimate the population of Ulaanbaatar, owing to high rates of influx of unregistered in-migrants in recent years. Some estimates put the true population of Ulaanbaatar at closer to 1 million.
6. An exception to this is the *bag,* in which the *khural* comprises all residents who have reached the age of majority. The *bag* is not formally a territorial or budget entity.
7. The Decentralisation Assessment Module was developed by Hans Binswanger, Andrew Parker, Johan van Zyl, Suzanne Piriou-Sall, Keith McLean, Graham Kerr and Melissa Williams as a product of the 'Decentralisation, Fiscal Systems and Rural Development' research project. Analytical framing for this research was provided by Manor [*1999*].
8. It is important to note that the definitions of these terms as used by McLean [*2001*] differ significantly from those used by Ribot [*2002*]. To assist in making cross-country comparisons, the Decentralisation Assessment Module used by McLean [*2001*] employs a set of indicators to characterise the three dimensions of decentralisation: administrative, fiscal and political. 'Administrative decentralisation' refers primarily to accountability relationships between civil servants and local governments. 'Political decentralisation' refers to the extent and transparency of an electoral system at various levels of government, and the degree to which election outcomes are representative. 'Fiscal decentralisation' refers to the degree of local government autonomy over revenue-raising capacity and expenditure decisions. For Ribot, 'political or democratic decentralisation occurs when powers and resources are transferred to authorities representative of and downwardly accountable to local populations' [*Ribot, 2002: 4*], while fiscal decentralisation is considered to be a cross-cutting element of both deconcentration

(or administrative decentralisation, again *contra* the definition used by McLean [*2001*]) and political decentralisation.

9. *Khot ails* based on kinship ties were suppressed during the collective era of the 1950s–1980s, being temporarily replaced by ostensibly non-kin-based production units of one or two households – known as *suuri*.
10. For further views on the character and historical dynamics of the *khot ail* as an institution, see Bold [*1996*] and Sneath [*1999*].
11. It is important to note that the National Statistical Office of Mongolia distinguishes between full-time 'herding households' (which rely primarily on livestock as a source of livelihood) and 'livestock-owning households' (for which livestock is not the primary source of livelihood), and reports data for both categories. While the number of full-time herding households increased steadily through the 1990s, the total number of livestock-owning households actually declined slightly over the same period, after an initial increase during 1990–92. This initial increase was largely accounted for by household-splitting to form new households so that extended families could maximise their entitlements to livestock from the privatisation of state and collective assets – which were calculated on a per-household basis.
12. In spite of the recent relative decline in pastoral mobility in Mongolia, levels of mobility remain significantly higher than in the neighbouring Inner Mongolia Autonomous Region (IMAR) of China. A graphic illustration of the environmental consequences of this difference in livestock-production strategies is seen in satellite imagery of Mongolia's southern border with China, from which the generally poorer vegetation condition of IMAR compared with Mongolia can be clearly discerned [*Sneath, 1998*]. This simple illustration is a clear demonstration of the importance of pastoral mobility for sustainable grassland management in dryland Inner Asia.
13. *Dzud* is the Mongolian term for a range of winter weather conditions that make forage from natural pastures inaccessible to domestic grazing animals.
14. This currently includes all pasture land. Herders tend to be bitterly opposed to any moves towards fencing pasture land [*Hanstad and Duncan, 2001; Fernández-Giménez and Batbuyan, 2000*].

REFERENCES

Agrawal, A. and J. Ribot, 1999, 'Accountability in Decentralization: A Framework with South Asian and West African Cases', *Journal of Developing Areas*, Vol.33, pp.473–502.

Bebbington, A., 1999, 'Capitals and Capabilities: A Framework for Analyzing Peasant Viability, Rural Livelihoods and Poverty', *World Development*, Vol.27, No.12, pp.2021–44.

Bold, B-O., 1996, 'Socio-Economic Segmentation: Khot-ail in Nomadic Livestock Keeping of Mongolia', *Nomadic Peoples*, No.39, pp.69–86.

Bruce, J.W., and R. Mearns, 2002, 'Natural Resource Management and Land Policy in Developing Countries: Lessons Learned and New Challenges for the World Bank', *Drylands Programme Issues Paper* No.115, London: International Institute for Environment and Development.

CPR, 2002, *Rural Development Strategy for Mongolia*, Draft report to Government of Mongolia, Ulaanbaatar: Center for Policy Research.

Ellis, F., 2000, *Rural Livelihoods and Diversity in Developing Countries*, Oxford: Oxford University Press.

Erdenebaatar, B. and N. Batjargal, 2001, *Pasture Land Disputes and Conflict Resolution: Cases from Mongolia*, Ulaanbaatar: Asia Foundation.

Fernández-Giménez, M.E., 2002, 'Spatial and Social Boundaries and the Paradox of Pastoral Land Tenure: A Case Study from Post-Socialist Mongolia', *Human Ecology*, Vol.30, No.1, pp.49–78.

Fernández-Giménez, M.E., 1999, 'Sustaining the Steppes: A Geographical History of Pastoral Land Use in Mongolia', *Geographical Review*, Vol.89, No.3, pp.315–42.

Fernández-Giménez, M.E. and B. Batbuyan, 2000, 'Law and Disorder in Mongolia: Local Implementation of Mongolia's Land Law', Paper presented at Eighth Biennial Conference of the International Association for the Study of Common Property, Bloomington, IN 31 May–4 June.

GoM, 2003a, *Law on Regionalized Development Management and Coordination*, Ulaanbaatar: Government of Mongolia.

GoM, 2003b, *Economic Growth Support and Poverty Reduction Strategy*, Ulaanbaatar: Government of Mongolia.

GoM, 2002a, *Public Sector Management and Finance Law*, Ulaanbaatar: Government of Mongolia.

GoM, 2002b, *Land Law of Mongolia*, Ulaanbaatar: Government of Mongolia.

GoM, 2001, *The Government of Mongolia Good Governance for Human Security Programme: Policy Document*, Ulaanbaatar: Government of Mongolia.

GoM, 2000a, *Action Programme of the Government of Mongolia*, Ulaanbaatar: Government of Mongolia.

GoM, 2000b, 'National Environmental Action Plan 2000' (final draft dated 9 June 2000), Ulaanbaatar: Government of Mongolia.

Goodhue, R.E. and N. McCarthy, 2000, 'Fuzzy Access: Modeling Grazing Rights in Sub-Saharan Africa', in N. McCarthy, B. Swallow, M. Kirk and P. Hazell (eds.), *Property Rights, Risk, and Livestock Development in Africa*, Washington, DC and Nairobi: International Food Policy Research Institute and International Livestock Research Institute, pp.191–210.

Hanstad, T. and J. Duncan, 2001, 'Land Reform in Mongolia: Observations and Recommendations', *RDI Reports in Foreign Aid and Development*, No.109, Seattle: Rural Development Institute for the World Bank.

Humphrey, C., 1978, 'Pastoral Nomadism in Mongolia: The Role of Herdsmen's Cooperatives in the National Economy', *Development and Change*, Vol.9, No.1, pp.133–60.

Leach, M., R. Mearns and I. Scoones, 1999, 'Environmental Entitlements: Dynamics and Institutions in Community-based Natural Resource Management', *World Development*, Vol.27, No.2, pp.225–47.

Manor, J., 1999, *The Political Economy of Democratic Decentralization*, Directions in Development Series, Washington, DC: World Bank.

McLean, K., 2001, 'An Assessment of Decentralization in Mongolia', Washington, DC: World Bank, mimeo.

Mearns, R., 1997, 'Pasture-land Use and Social Dynamics' and 'Legislative and Institutional Framework for Pasture-land Management' in 'Study of Mongolian Extensive Livestock Production Systems', Final Report to Asian Development Bank under TA No.2602-MON, Calgary: Agriteam Canada Consulting.

Mearns, R., 1996, 'Community, Collective Action and Common Grazing: The Case of Post-Socialist Mongolia', *Journal of Development Studies*, Vol.32, No.3, pp.297–339.

Mearns, R., 1993a, 'Pastoral Institutions, Land Tenure and Land Policy Reform in Post-Socialist Mongolia', PALD Research Report No.3, Brighton: Institute of Development Studies, University of Sussex.

Mearns, R., 1993b, 'Territoriality and Land Tenure among Mongolian Pastoralists: Variation, Continuity and Change', *Nomadic Peoples*, Vol.33, pp.73–103.

Mearns, R., 1991, 'Environmental Implications of Structural Adjustment: Reflections on Scientific Method', *IDS Discussion Paper* No.284, Brighton: Institute of Development Studies, University of Sussex.

NCSDM, 1999, *Mongolian Action Programme for the 21st Century (MAP21)*, Ulaanbaatar: National Council for Sustainable Development of Mongolia.

Nelson, J., C. Tilly and L. Walker (eds.), 1997, *Transforming Post-Communist Political Economies*, Washington, DC: National Research Council, Task Force on Economies in Transition.

Niamir-Fuller, M. (ed.), 1999, *Managing Mobility in African Rangelands: The Legitimization of Transhumance*, London: Intermediate Technology.

NSO, 2001, *2000 Population and Housing Census: The Main Results*, Ulaanbaatar: Mongolian National Statistical Office.

NSO and World Bank, 2001, *Mongolia Participatory Living Standards Assessment 2000*, Ulaanbaatar: Mongolian National Statistical Office and World Bank.

Ribot, J.C., 2002, *Democratic Decentralization of Natural Resources: Institutionalizing Popular Participation*, Washington, DC: World Resources Institute.

Sneath, D., 1999, 'Kinship, Networks and Residence', in C. Humphrey and D. Sneath, *The End of Nomadism? Society, State, and the Environment in Inner Asia*, Durham, NC: Duke University Press, pp.136–78.

Sneath, D., 1998, 'State Policy and Pasture Degradation in Inner Asia', *Science*, Vol.281, pp.1147–8.

Turner, M.D., 1999, 'The Role of Social Networks, Indefinite Boundaries and Political Bargaining in Maintaining the Ecological and Economic Resilience of the Transhumance Systems of Sudano-Sahelian West Africa', in M. Niamir-Fuller (ed.), *Managing Mobility in African Rangelands: The Legitimization of Transhumance*, London: Intermediate Technology, pp.97–123.

World Bank, 2003, *Mongolia Environment Monitor 2003: Land Resources and Their Management*, Washington, DC and Ulaanbaatar: World Bank.

World Bank, 2002, *Mongolia Public Expenditure and Financial Management Review*, Report No.24439-MOG, Washington, DC: World Bank.

WRI, 2000, 'Grassland Ecosystems: Sustaining the Steppe – The Future of Mongolia's Grasslands', in *World Resources Report 2000–2001*, Washington, DC: World Resources Institute with UNDP, UNEP and World Bank, pp.212–24.

Decentralisation and Accountability in Forest Management: A Case from Yunnan, Southwest China

JIANCHU XU and JESSE C. RIBOT

I. INTRODUCTION

China literally means 'The Central Kingdom'. As it is a vast country, China's state administration struggles continuously to maintain the delicate power balance between the political centre and the periphery and between central and local governments.[1] Extension of state control over peripheral areas and resources has long dominated the administration's political agenda [*Harrell, 1995; Menzies, 1992*]. Like Chinese emperors of the past, the Communist Party today remains preoccupied with the issue of stabilising strategic border or peripheral areas.

Today, China has joined the global move towards liberalisation and decentralisation. Economic reforms in recent decades have produced high and sustained economic growth rates and lifted millions of people out of poverty. Concurrent political reforms have decentralised many decision-making processes and created new democratic institutions, especially in rural areas.[2] This process has ceded new political powers and established new economic incentives; it has also transferred some natural-resource management powers to local entities. This decentralisation and power transfer first occurred in the agriculture sector with the introduction of the 'Household Responsibility System' in 1978, which allowed each household or farmer to decide what crops to cultivate, where to cultivate them and how much to cultivate.

These changes have placed additional stress on natural resources and on the livelihoods of indigenous communities in politically and economically

Jianchu Xu is Professor at the Kunming Institute of Botany, The Chinese Academy of Sciences, Kunming. Jesse C. Ribot is a Senior Associate at the Institutions and Governance Program, World Resources Institute (WRI), Washington, DC. The authors would like to thank the Ford Foundation, World Resources Institute and PARDYP (People and Resource Dynamics in Mountain Watershed of the Hindu-Kush Himalayas Project) for funding the field research and writing for this essay. The authors would also like to thank Zheng Lixia, Laetia Kress and Diana Conyers for editing this essay, and owe special thanks to two anonymous reviewers and Anne Larson, whose comments contributed greatly to the development of the essay. Jesse Ribot would like to acknowledge Jianchu Xu for inviting him onboard as co-author: as the former is an Africa specialist with no experience in China, the credit must go to Jianchu Xu for the insights and knowledge about China presented herein.

European Journal of Development Research, Vol.16, No.1, Spring 2004, pp.153–173
ISSN 0957-8811 print
DOI:10.1080/09578810410001688789

peripheral areas. In 1981, the central government responded to poor forest management and to the economic potential of forest resources by decentralising forest management to local communities and individual households under a forestland allocation policy called 'Forestry Three Fixes'.[3] Increasing public awareness of deforestation and its links to soil erosion, loss of biodiversity, floods and other forms of environmental degradation have made the protection of forest ecosystems a central government priority. Conflicts emerged between decentralisation for enhancing local forest management and livelihoods and protecting environmental services that affect larger-scale populations [*Yin, 1998*].

If there is a careful allocation of powers between different levels of authority, decentralisation policies should be able to address any problems therein. However, this has not been the case. Some powers are being transferred to entities such as townships and counties, which are not democratically elected and are too far from the local populations. Meanwhile, inadequate powers are being transferred to the lowest-level elected authorities. Moreover, communities are poorly represented in the decision-making processes concerning these powers, financial and human resources for exercising power at the community level are limited, and performance-monitoring systems are generally absent. Furthermore, in the name of decentralisation, much privatisation is taking place, and a lack of coherence among policies is slowing the reform process.

These problems raise a number of questions. What is the role of decentralisation in empowering local populations and relieving or intensifying pressures on forest resources? Is decentralisation equally appropriate for production forests and for those whose main role is conservation? To what level should forest management functions be decentralised? This essay explores some of these issues by examining the impact of decentralisation on forests in Yunnan Province. It considers how the reform is unfolding, who is receiving which new powers, whether any effects of the reform can yet be measured, and what opportunities and limitations for decentralisation are emerging in the forest sector. It looks first at the cultural and economic environment of Yunnan and the history of forest management in the region. It then examines in more detail the nature of the decentralisation reforms and their impact on forest management and local livelihoods in ethnic minority areas.

II. YUNNAN: AN AREA OF CULTURAL AND ECONOMIC DIVERSITY

Yunnan, word that means 'South of Clouds', is a mountainous, ethnically diverse and relatively poor province. It is located in the south-west of the country, and has borders with Myanmar, Laos and Vietnam. Cross-border trade and marriages have flourished since ancient times.

Yunnan is home to more than 42 million people. Ethnic minorities comprise 31 per cent of the population. They reside in the mountainous areas, which account for 94 per cent of the total area. There are more than 25 distinctly different ethnic groups, 13 of which are also found in neighbouring countries. They have varied agro-ecosystems, including the terraced rice and vegetables cultivation of the Hani and Yi peoples, the paddy agriculture of the Dai and Bai, and the shifting cultivation of the Miao (Hmong), Lisu and Jingpo.[4] The rest of the population is Han Chinese, and is concentrated in lowland valleys and urban areas.

The Chinese government is concerned both about political security in this mountainous area and about the region's environmental impact on the economies of Yunnan and surrounding provinces within the catchments of the Yangtze and Pearl rivers. In Yunnan Province, forests are essential to the livelihoods of marginal groups, including the poor, women and ethnic minorities. While many indigenous people in Yunnan are benefiting from new economic opportunities created by expanding markets and infrastructure development, it is often at the cost of the depletion of forests, forest products and other natural resources such as soil and water. Yunnan's forestlands also play an important conservation role, including the provision of water and nutrients, erosion control and climate regulation, for the lowland areas downstream.

China's transition from a centrally planned economy to a market-based one has triggered many economic and sociocultural changes among Yunnan's various ethnic groups. The reforms have reintroduced the household as the key unit of production and have placed market demand rather than subsistence concerns at the centre of production decisions. Furthermore, they have introduced more-decentralised decision-making systems that should increase local empowerment. Village-level elections are a key part of this change.

Most of Yunnan's natural resources are found on territorial land governed by a range of customary institutions and rules that are monitored and enforced by the village chiefs and elders, and higher-level governors. These institutions structured villagers' attitudes, social relationships and even technology in such a way as to ensure the sustainability of the natural resources and to secure collaboration in managing those resources. The effectiveness of customary institutions depends on cultural identity and local resilience to external influences. Although some cultural practices (such as religious rituals) have changed, especially since the Cultural Revolution (1966–76), most of the earlier rules and norms for forest resource management are still adhered to in some indigenous communities.

However, the ecological health of Yunnan, which is often described as the 'water tower' of Southeast Asia, is at risk due to the construction of major communication and transportation infrastructure in the area as part of the planned development of the Great Mekong subregion. Already several new dams, roads, railways, waterways and airports have been constructed. The problem is that, in planning these developments, insufficient attention has been given to the relationship between the present use of resources and their future sustainability.

III. ETHNIC MINORITIES AND THE PRINCIPLE OF 'LOCAL AUTONOMY'

Historically, Chinese authorities used a variety of measures to bring ethnic minorities and people living on the geographical periphery of the country under central control. These included settlement programmes, which converted wild forestland into agricultural paddies, reducing taxation levels and, during the Yuan Dynasty (1280–1368), marrying members of the royal family to the political elite of these outlying areas.

Since the founding of the People's Republic of China in 1949, there have been many state policies specifically addressing peripheral areas and ethnic minorities in areas bordering international frontiers, such as Yunnan Province. Policies developed for the integration of ethnic minorities have always been closely linked to national development efforts. After 'ethnic classification' in the early 1950s,[5] the State established 'ethnic autonomous' regions and implemented distinct education and development plans. The principle of 'local autonomy', which is defined legally, applies to these regions, and includes political, economic and cultural autonomy. 'Political autonomy' includes provisions such as self-administration and appointment of members of the minority population to leadership positions and offices; it also permits the official use of the local language and writing system. 'Economic autonomy' is defined as self-determination in local economic development within the framework of national development programmes; it includes the prioritisation of local needs and the formulation of policies oriented towards local material improvements. 'Cultural autonomy' consists of the freedom to decide how or if customs are reformed, and the provision of education and health services to meet the specific needs of local minorities [*Xu and Salas, 2003*].

The Minorities Regional Autonomy Law of 1984 elaborates the rights of autonomous administration. Under this law, autonomous administrations are empowered to formulate autonomous and specific regulations regarding the political, economic and cultural features of their respective areas. Based on the situations in each area, they are authorised to make special policies and take flexible measures, provided they are in line with the national Constitution and laws. Also, upon approval from higher authorities, national resolutions, decisions, decrees and instructions may be adjusted or their implementation ceased if they are deemed out of step with local situations. Autonomous administrations are required to independently plan and implement regional economic development under the guidance of the national plan and to manage their own financial affairs and local resources. Furthermore, upon approval by the central State Council, they may take responsibility for law enforcement, in line with the national military system and the practical demands of the local areas. Finally, the law requires that the administrative head of an autonomous region, prefecture, or county shall be a member of the majority ethnic group [*Tan Leshan, 2000*].

IV. FOREST MANAGEMENT IN YUNNAN

Forest management in Yunnan has a long history of political struggle and shifting power between the state and local communities. Three main phases can be distinguished: the period preceding the 1949 Revolution; the era of 'collectivisation', extending from 1950 to 1978; and the post-1978 period of economic reform and decentralisation.

The Period Preceding the 1949 Revolution

In the nineteenth century, during the latter part of the Qing Dynasty, the central government was less interested in natural resources *per se* than in exerting sovereignty over peripheral territories and benefiting financially from the exploitation of their resources [*Menzies, 1992*]. Therefore, rather than controlling the timber industry by regulating its growth, logging, marketing and production, as it does today, it reaped the benefits through taxation. Thus, in the early twentieth century, at the beginning of the Republican period, only 11 per cent of registered forests were in state hands; 55 per cent were under private ownership and 34 per cent were owned collectively [*Yuan, 1924*]. Moreover, large areas of forest in peripheral areas were not registered at all and were managed through customary institutions.

The first survey and reallocation of forestland in Yunnan was undertaken in 1920, during the Republican period. In this survey, the Yunnan Agrarian Association authorised village heads to survey degraded forestlands, which were then divided into plots – each measuring ten *mu*,[6] which were then allocated to individual farmers. For each *mu* of already owned farmland, the farmer received a plot of degraded forestland for reforestation, which they legally owned after reforestation. This ownership, however, was often in name only. Forest laws enacted in 1932 stipulated that 'there is state forest, common forest and private forest', but 'forest is in principle state-owned'. By the1940s, the state had acquired 60 per cent of forestlands, while 40 per cent were privately owned. In Yunnan, private forests, like other resources, were largely in the hands of landlords or *tusi* (local chiefs) and entrepreneurs.

In practice, however, the government never had effective control over the large state-owned forestlands in the peripheral areas of Yunnan. Rather, indigenous people administered these lands through their own methods [*Gao, 1998*]. The customary institutions that were developed dealt effectively with the diversity of cultural communities and the dynamic nature of the environmental and forest resources. Recent field investigations have revealed the different types of customary institutions that operated in the past and have shown that some are still functioning today. One example is the written Customary Forest Laws and Mountain Protection Monument at Ana Village in Chuxiong Prefecture, Central Yunnan, which was established in 1714 during the Qing Dynasty (1644–1912). In translation, it reads as follows:

> A man with a beard is respected (indicative of his seasoned age and rich experience). The same idea applies to mountains too. A person with a beard and hair is like a mountain covered with forest and grass. In the same vein, a mountain sheltered in forest and grass is like a person well clothed. A barren mountain is no different from a naked person, exposing its flesh and bone. An unsheltered mountain with poor soil painfully bears great resemblance to a penniless and rugged man. Even a pine tree or single bamboo grows thousands of leaves and branches, how can a mountain tolerate a treeless state? Yes, indeed, no one does not enjoy being amongst clean streams and green mountains. Everyone understands that only healthy green forest and fertile soil can nurture ever-flowing springs. None doubts the significance of those fundamental elements of nature, such as soil, water and fire. Yet, do we know it is the root of trees and forest that bring us water? It is for our benefit and fortune. Meanwhile, upon the order of the officials, our village has established a tradition of electing a village forest guard since the time of Ch'ien-lung emperor [Qing Dynasty]. Alas, there have been so many generations of the old who have conscientiously protected our village's forest till today. Let us dare not to discontinue this tradition … With this said, we want to reiterate the following: Our elected forest guard should be fair, straight, honest and moral. We have no tolerance for violation, but will elect another. Our villager-rangers should patrol our mountains every day; no slackness should be tolerated, otherwise their salary should be deducted. Felling of trees for timber use should be paid for … Within the Daqin area east to Shangjie road, west to Doupo, north to the peak is to be enclosed for natural forest regeneration and no logging is allowed. Five years later, five trees can be harvested for building one tile-roofed house, and three for grass-thatched houses. Those who want to take the risk to extract more should be fined for five Bi [Qing currency] in addition to community labour at the following locations …

Not only do the indigenous peoples of Yunnan possess profound ecological knowledge, they also already have an established system for local governance and forest resource management.

The Collectivisation Era, 1950–78

The Land Reform Laws enacted in June 1950 provided the legal basis for forest resource management over the next three decades. Between 1950 and 1952, all farmlands and forestlands were nationalised. The state maintained the large forestlands, but allocated farmlands and traditionally managed forestlands to individuals – particularly the poor. In areas thus allocated, customary institutions were largely respected. However, in Yunnan, forestlands were not properly registered and so ownership and access rights to forestland were not legally recognised or respected.

The 'collectivisation' process was initiated between 1952 and 1956. Most farmlands and forestlands were collectivised, although private ownership was still recognised in principle. This was followed in 1958 by the establishment of the 'People's Commune', which had a profound impact on forest ownership and customary institutions. State and collective ownership replaced private ownership and customary public ownership, particularly in mountainous peripheral areas.

The collectivisation policies, particularly those enacted during the 'Great Leap Forward' launched in 1958, resulted in large-scale deforestation. In order to cope with this, the Yunnan provincial government introduced regulations in 1961 to 'ensure forest tenure, protect and develop forests'. These regulations stated that 'the fragmented forest, which is difficult for the state to manage, can be allocated to a nearby village or commune for management'. They further stipulated that 'forest tenure should pay more attention to customary institutions in ethnic areas and take note of the views of ethnic minorities regarding "holy hills" and "sacred forests"'. In order to win the confidence of local villagers, the government emphasised that the village or commune would have security of tenure after the allocation of forestland.

Since then, China has implemented numerous, and sometimes conflicting, policies related to agricultural and forestland ownership [*Liu, 2001*]. After collectivisation came the Cultural Revolution, when campaigns such as that designed to 'eliminate superstitions' eroded traditional cultural practices related to the conservation of forest resources. In addition, the state demanded that local people increase grain production in order to be self-sufficient in food. In Yunnan, this policy resulted in a significant expansion of shifting cultivation and further rapid deforestation during the late 1960s and early 1970s.

Post-1978 Economic Reforms and Decentralisation

The economic liberalisation reforms began in 1978, with the establishment of the 'Household Responsibility System'. Between 1978 and 1981, agricultural lands, such as paddy fields, were contracted out to individual farmers, but forests remained under state control. Since the boundaries between state forests and private agricultural lands were often unclear, there were conflicts between government agencies and local collectives or individuals. In order to stake their claim to contested forestlands, the latter sometimes resorted to clearing the land for agricultural purposes, thereby causing further loss of forest cover.

The reforms in the forestry sector began in March 1981, when the state issued its 'decision on some issues concerning forest protection and forestry development', otherwise known as the 'Forestry Three Fixes', which affected the administration, marketing, investment and management of the forestry sector as well as the tenure of its collective forests [*Yin and Newman, 1997*]. They authorised the decentralisation of authority from central to local government, thereby enabling countries, townships and administrative villages to make an increasing number of decisions [*Liu and Edmunds, 2003*]. The local forest authority together with local communities determined where forestlands were reallocated, how long the contract was to last, and who would benefit from the sharing scheme. The stated objective of this reform was to shift forest management from the state to local communities and individuals. It provided for both private and collectively held plots to be leased to individual households. This was the first time in Yunnan's history that local communities received certificates of forestland ownership and participated in decision-making.

As a result of the implementation of this policy, 13.97 million hectares of land have been transferred from state to local management. This includes 4.84 million hectares of individually held forest (mostly degraded), 6.33 million hectares of contracted (that is, leased) forestlands, 0.86 million hectares of fallow fields previously used for shifting cultivation and 1.94 million hectares of rangelands [*Yunnan Forest Department, 1984: 270–71*].

However, the simplified system of forestland allocation, which was based on the successful 'Household Responsibility System' of farmland allocation, did not work well due to lack of participation by local villagers. This lack of participation can be attributed mainly to demarcation problems, unclear rules over responsibility and benefit sharing, and uncertainty regarding conditions of tenure. In some cases, this resulted in a new wave of deforestation.

The provincial government realised that in Yunnan the rural economy and livelihoods of mountain people were based on forestry. It therefore decided to lease all degraded forestlands – known as 'wastelands' (*huangdi*) – to private individuals or institutions for reforestation. The lessees could be local people or outsiders, but they were required to have the necessary financial and management capacity. The land was leased for periods of between 30 and 70 years at competitive prices and was implemented through 'wasteland auctions'. A pilot auction was held in Yiliang County in 1993, at which 12,000 hectares of wasteland were leased. Over the next four years, 728,725 hectares of wasteland forest, most of which had been owned collectively, were auctioned to individuals [*Zheng, 2001*], thus further 'decentralising' forest tenure and management.

These attempts to decentralise forest management and improve security of tenure over forestlands did not solve the problem of forest degradation, however. The transfer of forest use rights and management responsibility to local farmers was not enough to regenerate the forests, and environmental degradation, soil erosion and flooding continued. On 1 October 1998, after the most extensive flooding ever in the Yangtze basin, the Yunnan provincial government, in response to a state ban on logging, introduced a natural forest protection policy officially called the 'Natural Forest Protection Programme' policy. The logging ban affected 8,480,000 hectares of forestland – almost one-third of the total forested area in Yunnan, and extended across 13 prefectures, most of them in north-western Yunnan. It has had a major impact on the state timber industry, loggers and local-government revenue, as well as on the livelihoods of indigenous communities. Dramatic declines in income from the logging and forest products industry have forced local farmers to look for alternative sources of livelihood, such as livestock production and grazing, and harvesting non-timber forestry products in the forested areas.

The ban on logging was immediately followed by the Sloping Farmland Conversion Programme. This programme was designed to address the problem of cultivation on hill slopes, which was another factor contributing to soil erosion and flooding. According to this policy, any farmland with a gradient of more than 25 degrees must be converted to forest or grassland. To facilitate the conversions, farmers receive seedlings and government subsidies for grain, education and healthcare fees. Combined with the effects of the logging ban, this policy has put indigenous communities in a dire situation.

The two policies imply that the reforms that took place in the name of decentralisation – many of which were in fact privatisation – have failed to achieve their objective of a stable transition of the forest sector. The logging ban demonstrates that the decision-makers failed to understand the dynamics of forest resource management. Field evidence suggests that most over-harvesting and poor logging practices are being carried out by large-scale, state-owned timber enterprises, not individuals, and that forest resources had been depleted before the logging ban in the most accessible parts of the region [*Xu and Wilkes, forthcoming*]. This is indicated in Figure 1, which shows the timber output from Diqing prefecture in northwest Yunnan – one of the areas where large-scale, state-owned logging operations were particularly prevalent. Thus, the main impact of the state's blanket ban on forest harvesting was to undercut the livelihoods of communities that could benefit from sustainable forest management.

V. DECENTRALISATION AND FORESTRY MANAGEMENT

In order to determine the relationship between decentralisation and forest management, this section begins by looking in more detail at the various actors

FIGURE 1
LOGGING IN DIQING PREFECTURE, NW YUNNAN, 1974–99 (1,000m^3)

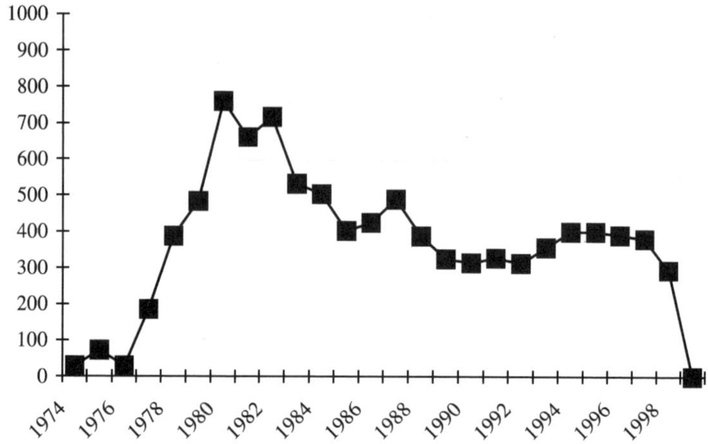

Source: Statistical reports of Diqing Prefecture Forest Bureau 1974–2000, quoted in *Xu and Wilkes, 2004*.

involved in forest management under decentralisation, the nature and scope of the powers that have been decentralised, and accountability in forest management. It then examines the impact of decentralisation on forest management and the livelihoods of those dependent on forestlands.

Actors in Decentralisation

Before the 1950s, most forestlands were governed and controlled by local chiefs (*tusi*). Some of these chiefs inherited their position, while others were either elected by local communities or nominated by higher authorities. Their roles varied from place to place, depending on the complexity of the environment, cultural beliefs and customary institutions [*Xu et al., 1999*]. In the ethnically diverse mountain regions, there were major variations in customary institutions between upland and lowland areas. The centralised planning and decision-making system established during the collectivisation period eroded customary institutions and marginalised traditional actors. However, the state either failed or did not want to address the problem of the delicate social relations among the different customary institutions in the mountain regions. Forest reform in the early 1980s, as outlined above with reference to Yunnan, subsequently transferred ownership and management of some forestlands to local villages and to individuals.

There are six levels of government jurisdiction in China: national, provincial, prefecture, county, township and administrative village. The administrative villages supervise a number of 'natural villages'. The main provincial government departments maintain representative offices at the prefecture level, and often also within the county and township government structures. Townships are the lowest level of government in the official administration. The leaders of administrative and natural villages receive nominal compensation from the government for their services, whereas employees at township and higher levels receive full salaries.

The state forest agencies, along with others such as the environmental protection agencies, have major responsibilities for forest management and conservation of biodiversity. The Ministry of Forestry, which was established in 1951, is responsible for managing the largest territory in China, with mandates for the 'overall protection of forest, forestation of key areas, and rational use and exploitation of forests'. In 1956, a separate Ministry of Forest Industry was set up to meet increasing demands for lumber and wood products and, after two years, the two ministries were merged into what would later become the Ministry of Agriculture and Forestry. In 1979, the Ministries of Forestry and Agriculture were again split, but in 1998 the Ministry of Forestry was integrated into a new Ministry of Land and Resources in order to co-ordinate land administration.

The state forest industry was expanded rapidly in the late 1970s and early 1980s. The state forest agency performed many functions: it served the interests of forest protectors, logging workers and tree planters, as well as providing forestland certification and logging permits. These multiple interests pitted the forest agencies against local communities.

The lowest level of forestry official is the forest guard, who is recruited directly from local villages to keep a look-out for illegal activities and forest fires in state and collective forestlands as well as to report timber permits for township forestry stations. These guards often do very little, either because of the low level of remuneration they receive from the villages or because of conflicts between their accountability downwards to the local communities and upwards to the forest authorities.

The Nature of the Powers Transferred

The 1984 Forest Law, which was revised in 1998, provides for trees and other plants, individually or collectively, to be allocated by contract either to village communities as a whole or to individual villagers. Moreover, Article 9 recognises the special status of indigenous people, giving 'more autonomous rights for forestry development, timber distribution and forestry funds in ethnic autonomy regions' [*Liu and Edmunds, 2003*]. This is in recognition of the fact, acknowledged by lower-level government officials, that local villagers are dependent on forest resources for their livelihoods and for generating cash income.

However, this is not the only objective of the Law. As Article 1 states, it is intended to protect, cultivate and rationally utilise forest resources; speed up the process of 'greening' national territory, thus promoting soil and water conservation, climatic adjustment and other forms of environmental improvement; and meet the needs of socialist construction and people's livelihood. In other words, it emphasises both the ecological and economic functions of forests and recognises the interests of different stakeholders, including both local people and those based elsewhere. The challenge of forest management in contemporary China is to resolve the contradictions between these diverse functions of forest ecosystems and the multiple needs of the various stakeholders.

As the Law has conservation objectives, it exercises rigid control over logging and timber marketing. Thus, Article 29 specifies that a 'limited quota for logging should be made annually (less than the growth volume)', while Article 32 states that 'permission is necessary for logging', and Article 33 specifies that such permission 'should not exceed the annual logging quota'. Logging quotas and timber permits are the main instruments of state control. The forestry bureau usually submits a proposal to the province and a final decision is made by the central government, taking into account national economic demand and the volume of stock in the forestlands.

Under the 1784 forestry law, the main owners of forestland, both local communities and contracted individuals, have little voice in the decision-making process. Many communities are allocated permits without forests or have forests but no permits. Therefore, permits are frequently traded illegally at the county level and below, resulting in several known cases of corruption in Yunnan's county forestry bureaus. In addition, there is no monitoring system under this law to oversee forestland allocation. Forestland certification is another instrument for control of forest resources. However, certification is always linked to short-term campaigns associated with specific policies, such as the 'Three Fixes'.

County forestry bureaus, which provide a direct interface between national government and local communities, have the power to interpret state policies and plans and implement them in a manner relevant to local biophysical and socio-economic environments. For example, township forestry stations may allocate logging permits for less than the prescribed limit in terms of cubic meters, mainly for local subsistence use, and may issue 500 yuan (US$6) fines to those who break regulations. However, lack of transparency in the allocation of timber permits at the county level in the past has reduced the credibility of state forest policies. Moreover, the attitudes and capacity of forestry officials hamper the participation of local people in forest management.

Under these and other new laws, institutions are emerging at the local-community level. These institutions are based on customary institutions but are formed in response to the emerging market economy. Villages are officially encouraged to make their own regulations for community resource management. Such regulations are in line with new trends towards village autonomy, which are reflected in the Village Organic Law.[7] As evidence of the impact of this law, there appear to be increasing struggles between local governments (at both the county and township levels) and emerging community entities over decision-making powers.

The community regulation of non-timber forest products in Lijiashi Village, Xizhang watershed, Baoshan, is a good example of village autonomy and local adaptation of land allocation systems. The Xizhuang watershed, located 20 kilometres northwest of Baoshan City, in western Yunnan Province, covers an area of 3,456 hectares. The watershed supports two administrative villages – Lijiashi and Qingshui. These two village communities have different resources and capacities and have thus developed very different patterns of customary regulation. In Qingshui, village regulation exists in name only, but in Lijiashi it is strong and effective.

Lijiashi Village has a unique land-allocation system. Agricultural land, including land for tea cultivation, is allocated based on need, using the *cheng* system.[8] Each villager under 16 years of age is allocated 0.5 *cheng*, those between 16 and 18 get 0.8 *cheng*, those between 18 and 60 (55 for females) get 1 *cheng*, and those over 60 (55 for females) 0.6 *cheng*. Lijiashi also has a customary forest-tenure policy. Rights to cut timber and gather firewood are allocated to individual households. However, grazing and non-timber forest products (such as pine nuts and mushrooms) are available for the general public – even outsiders. Additionally, the irrigation system in Lijiashi village, which is well managed and maintained by the village community, is a good example of successful community autonomy.

The Lijiashi system is only one of many different types of administrative structures found in Baoshan. Six are listed below, while Figure 2 shows six main models in diagrammatic form [*Zuo and Xu, 2001*]:

1. The traditional centralised model, in which the lower level only has the power to implement central mandates;
2. Administrative powers are transferred to lower levels, such as from county to township, and the lower level not only implements mandates from above but also exercises some discretionary power;
3. The public is involved in the governing process, through research institutions, public hearings and media for monitoring;
4. Administration is entrusted to technical sectors or projects;
5. Administration is shared with other authorities and involves multi-agency co-operation; and

FIGURE 2

POWER RELATIONS BETWEEN UPPER AND LOWER LEVELS OF POLITICAL-ADMINISTRATION

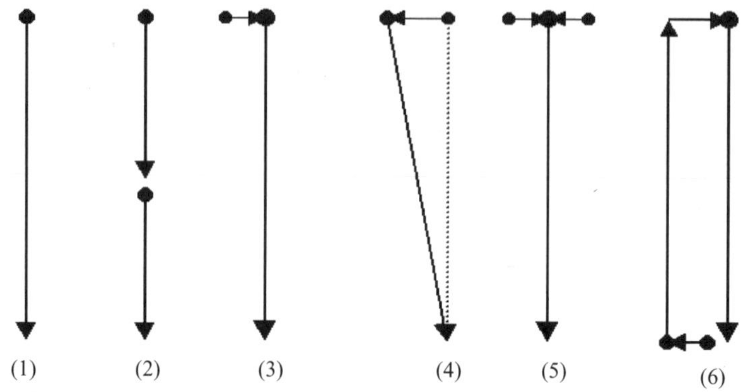

Source: Adapted from Zuo and Xu, 2001.

6. There is ample local participation through community self-organisation and/or representation.

Accountability and Forest Management

High levels of ethnic diversity, cultural identity and socio-economic marginalisation result in two distinct local institutional features that are particularly relevant to forest management. First, there is a comparatively strong sense of community at the village level. Farmers' groups, parent groups, churches, Buddhist monasteries, local language schools and various kinship institutions are active and influential. In addition, long-standing community rules governing resource access are still in effect in many villages; examples include *matsutake* mushroom (*Tricholoma matsutake*) collection, yak grazing and fuel wood collection. Second, local government agencies in these villages tend to be more autonomous, since most officials are from the local area and thus are more closely linked to the members of the local communities than to their provincial government counterparts.

In terms of accountability, there are two dimensions: between villagers and local governments and between resource owners and users and local governments. With respect to the first dimension, recent democratisation and decentralisation reforms are dramatically changing the institutional landscape at the local level. For example, following the introduction and implementation of the Village Organic Law, village heads and village committees are receiving new responsibilities and rights related to local natural-resource management. The local people democratically elect village heads, although the head of the administrative village has to be officially endorsed by township and county government officials. Following the election, a set of officials from various natural villages within an administrative village form an administrative village committee. This committee is the highest level of people's self-governance and the highest level at which the Organic Law has promoted village democracy so far.

However, a number of problems are associated with these processes. Firstly, evidence suggests that there is inadequate external monitoring and evaluation of the village head's performance. Village assembly meetings, which provide internal monitoring, are ineffective for this purpose because the village heads easily manipulate the assembly. Secondly, the election process is often poorly executed due to illiteracy and/or cultural barriers: the processes of candidate selection, voting and vote counting are often riddled with errors. Thirdly, a major task of the administrative village committee is to collect taxes from villagers, but since the villagers receive no services and cannot influence decision-making in higher levels of government, such taxation has created mistrust between the local government and the village and has undermined the creditability of elected village leaders. Furthermore, the elected village leaders have few financial or political incentives to assist villagers. For example, the elected natural-village head receives only US$40 per year. Consequently, nobody wants to be elected since the time required to perform the daily administrative work would limit availability for off-farm work. Most male farmers spend two thirds of their time doing off-farm jobs, which can generate an income of over US$400 per year.

Nobody expects villagers' awareness and capacity for self-government to develop overnight. It takes time to empower the administrative village government and enhance the capacity of natural-village leadership to serve and monitor. However, with the present constraints, electoral accountability becomes essentially a wasted opportunity. Furthermore, it is essential to extend the democratic process to the township level in order to increase accountability and bring material resources and greater decision-making powers to local communities.

The second dimension of accountability concerns the relationship between resource owners and users and the local government authorities. The owners and users of forestland are expected to follow local norms and rules, as determined by the village committee. The state encourages local governing bodies to create new institutions and forms of monitoring. The resulting hybrid of customary institutions and government regulations can be observed in the case of the management of *matsutake* mushrooms among communities in Zhongdian county, in the mountainous Tibetan region of Yunnan [*Yeh, 2000*]. Accountability, in this case, has resulted in flexibility and diversity of social arrangements to adapt to the local sociocultural and biophysical environments.

Zhongdian, recently renamed Shangri-la, is a Tibetan autonomous county in northwestern Yunnan whose economy depended on timber in the past but is now based on *matsutake* mushroom collection. In 1993, approximately 80 per cent of the county's income came from logging. However, the 1998 logging ban has had a tremendous impact on this timber-driven economy. The search for alternative livelihoods has become an urgent priority of the local government. Under these circumstances, *matsutake* mushroom export has begun to provide an alternative income base and thus plays a significant role in local development. At present, the *matsutake* trade generates between 50 and 80 per cent of household cash income, while taxes levied on the trade account for 30 per cent of county revenues.

Recently, however, a lack of clarity regarding *matsutake* property rights, combined with mass commercialisation, was increasingly threatening the sustainability of the mushroom resources. Thus, the production of *matsutake* declined from 530 tons in 1995 to 272 tons in 2000. Such rapid resource degradation called for the attention of both the government and the local community. The government launched a number of regulations and strategies (for example, privatisation) to control the collection and marketing process, but these strategies have proved ineffective due to poor enforcement and excessive transaction costs. Meanwhile, the local community initiated its own collective actions for controlling the *matsutake* collecting groups. These initiatives became the starting point for improved resource management (He Jun, Center for Biodiversity and Indigenous Knowledge (CBIK), Kunming, China, personal communication).

These local arrangements for managing *matsutake* resources exhibit the following characteristics:

- *Well-defined boundaries*. Neighbouring communities negotiate with each other to define the boundaries of the areas where mushroom collection can take place. This also effectively excludes non-community members from access to the resource.
- *Simple rules*. Rules for mushroom collection are generally simple and easy to understand, such as no use of iron tools, three days for collection and one day for closing of the mountain, no gathering of immature or over-mature mushrooms, and so forth. In most cases, there are only five or six terms and conditions.
- *Locally devised rules*. The community devised the rules through collective choice. Moreover, community members gather once a year to hold a village meeting to review the rules implemented over the past year and amend them where necessary.
- *Easy enforcement of rules*. Since the rules are devised through collective choice, enforcement of the rules is easy. These collective actions also build the social capital for institutional durability.

- *Enforceable sanctions*. If a rule is broken the person is subject to a fine; the amount is defined at the village meeting and spelled out in the local rules.
- *Low transaction costs*. Because of the collective action process, the costs of administering the system are low, including the adjudication cost in case of conflicts. This low cost contributes not only to good rule-enforcement but also to institutional development.
- *Accountability of monitors*. Mushroom collection monitors are themselves members of collection groups, usually consisting of two or three people. Moreover, because of the shared norms and rules, the village leader is also accountable to users [*He Jun, 2003*].

In short, rather than privatising resources, these local initiatives have turned an open-access system into one of collective management based on sound institutional arrangements.

The Impact of Decentralisation

There is evidence to suggest that, despite unstable state forestry policies and increasing consumption of forest resources, the overall decentralisation of forest management has contributed to better forest governance and reforestation over the past two decades. According to recent forestry surveys in Yunnan, the forest cover increased from 25.66 per cent to 33.64 per cent during the period 1978–97 (*State Forestry Administration, 2000*). This increase is due partly to the planting of both timber trees (such as pine) and other commercial trees (such as rubber and fruit trees) and partly to natural regeneration. Thus, despite the continued concern about the impact of deforestation that prompted the 1978 ban on logging, the trend of net deforestation has eventually given way to one of net reforestation [*Xu et al., 2003*].

However, while decentralisation in general has been beneficial for forest management, individual policies have had mixed results. For example, in many instances the 'Three Fixes' have increased neither tenure security nor forest cover. The 1998 logging ban, which affected 69 per cent of the natural forests of Yunnan, has also had many adverse effects. Moreover, the monoculture of trees for timber and other commercial forest products has had a negative impact on biodiversity. Increasing forest cover does not necessarily result in a corresponding increase in a region's diversity of plant and wildlife species. Although biodiversity is a property of the natural ecosystem, it is a product of the interaction between the biophysical environment and cultural practices [*Sajise, 1995*]. Therefore, functions and values related to biodiversity and ecosystems should be understood in a much broader context.

China's previous forestry policies and strategies focused only on timber production and the monitoring of forest cover, and thus failed to meet the increasing diversity of demands from local villages. The rural poor depend on common and collectively owned forestlands for their livelihoods, particularly in peripheral areas like Yunnan. Economic reform has had both positive and negative effects on the people in peripheral areas. It has increased productivity and efficiency at the level of household resource management but has not increased the efficiency of the collective. Moreover, it has significantly increased inequalities in household income. Only recently has the Chinese government begun to pay attention to poor groups. For instance, poverty-alleviation policies remain small in significance and are confined to local-level initiatives and, although positive steps are being undertaken, there is still a lack of representation of the poor in decision-making processes.

Various factors, including government policy, market stimuli and development interventions, have already dramatically affected minority societies. Ethnic minorities, particularly those who have lived in the uplands of Yunnan for many generations, are being economically marginalised as a result of China's economic reforms. This is due, in part, to the incompatibility of local vernacular institutions and the difficulties that local communities have in adapting to external institutional change. Some forestry policies have increased the plight of the poor in these areas. For example, the 'wasteland auctions' policy implemented in Yunnan in 1994 deprived the poor of access to forest resources. The term 'wasteland' is actually a misnomer, as such land may be used to meet a critical need for grazing or for gathering fuel and other non-timber forest products. The Yunnan Provincial Government eventually accepted this fact and abandoned the policy.

In general, opportunities for local people to influence forestry policy remain limited. For example, the logging ban was initiated primarily because of concern about the effect of deforestation on other areas, such as watershed areas and those downstream. Planning processes have since been implemented in the downstream areas, but the people living in the forested areas upstream have yet to be involved. Similarly, monitoring and evaluation are still done by forest agencies and remain largely ineffective. There is no channel for farmers to complain. Moreover, individual foresters interpret policies differently. For instance, under the 'sloping land conversion programme' in the county of Lanping, foresters do not allow farmers to plant annual crops even in the first year of conversion, while in some other areas agroforestry practices are permitted.

VI. CONCLUSIONS

Decentralisation in China remains incomplete. Many examples show that there is insufficient transfer of power and decision-making to local institutions, and that the powers they are given can easily be taken away. Although elections are held, the local representatives, supposedly accountable to local communities, remain accountable and subject to higher-level government authorities. This is particularly true among the minority groups in mountainous areas like Yunnan, where communities remain embedded in paternalistic administrative relations. The elected leaders have little political power or voice in the higher governmental decision-making processes. The current decentralisation process in China has only transferred meaningful powers to the township governments, which are still accountable to the central government. Moreover, the local community does not yet enjoy the potential benefits of decentralisation due to limited financial resources and inefficient transfer of powers.

Mechanisms for monitoring the implementation and impact of democratic decentralisation are also lacking. Furthermore, the local community has neither the power nor the access to an independent judiciary system to challenge higher decisions. In many cases, the higher-level government agencies, such as those at the township or county levels, make decisions for local communities due to the lack of local-community representation at higher levels of government.

Unstable policy and frequently shifting property rights in forestlands have destroyed the trust between local communities and the government. Rebuilding this trust would require the establishment of responsible local governments that are accountable and responsive to farmers. There is a need to empower the administrative village governments and enhance their capacity to provide services and monitor the performance of the leaders of natural villages. This will take time, especially in diverse socio-economic and biophysical environments like Yunnan.

Decentralisation, in areas like Yunnan, needs innovative approaches and a flexible political environment. It is essential that decentralisation take place so that decisions can be influenced by existing indigenous knowledge, practices and institutions. The case of Yunnan demonstrates that, in decentralising power from the political centre to the periphery, there is a need to level the playing field by creating a balance of powers in which local authorities can demand higher levels to be downwardly accountable and where indigenous people and local communities have access to and can influence a meaningful decision-making process. Such influence will enfranchise indigenous people and bring their knowledge and practices, as well as aspirations and needs, into the governing process.

NOTES

1. Steven Harrell [*1995*] emphasised that periphery is not only the geographic periphery but is also politically, institutionally and economically far from the power centre. The peripheral people, often named 'minorities', have been subjected over the last few centuries to a series of attempts by the dominant powers to transform them, to make them more like themselves, or to 'civilise'

them. People may be peripheral due to origins, gender, languages, ecological adaptation and livelihood practices, as well as culture.

2. See Ribot [*2002*] and Larson and Ribot [*this issue*] for an elaborated definition of 'decentralisation' as used in this essay – that is, the transfer of powers from central government to lower levels in the political–administrative hierarchy.
3. Under the policy of Forestry Three Fixes (*liangshanyidi*), it determined the ownership of mountains and forests, designated mountain slopes for household use, i.e. shifting cultivation fields (*lunxiedi*), and defined a forest responsibility system, including freehold forestlands (*ziliushan*) and contracted forestlands (*zerenshan*), which were transferred to individual ownership with the objective of stabilising forestlands and fields under shifting cultivation in response to central government policy on decentralisation.
4. Mountain farmers often manage a range of habitats or ecosystems for their livelihoods: hunting, gathering and cultivating in the forest, domesticating species in the upland field and home gardens, selective weeding for favourable species, converting forestland into multiple cropping, etc.
5. In the 1950s, after the foundation of the new Communist-led China, the Chinese government and scholars conducted a systematic scientific classification of the diverse people (*minzu*) within the country. Over 400 potential groups identified, based on local distinctions, were reduced to the officially recognised 56 nationalities *(minzu*) [*Keyes, 2002*].
6. A *mu* is the Chinese measure of land area. There are 15 *mu* in a hectare.
7. The Act of Village Committee Organization of the People's Republic of China was enacted in 1988 and reinforced in 1998 as the Act of Village Democratic Construction, formally called the Village Organic Law. It represents a fundamental policy change in that it allows local villagers to elect their own leaders and village committees. The Law says that the village committee shall support and organise villagers in developing all legal forms of collective economy, coordinate village production, and promote the development of rural socialist production and a socialist market economy; that the village committee should respect the autonomy of collective economic units in conducting economic activities; that it should maintain the dual management system, which is based on the Household Responsibility System and the combination of centralisation and decentralisation; and that it is the village committee's responsibility to protect legal property rights, and other legal rights and benefits of collective economies, individual villagers, contract households, combined households and partners.
8. *Cheng* is a local unit of percentage; one *cheng* = 100%; 0.8 *cheng* = 80%; 0.5 *cheng* = 50%.

REFERENCES

Gao, Lishi, 1998, *On the Dai's Traditional Irrigation System and Environmental Protection in Xishuangbanna*, Kunming: Yunnan Minority Press.

Harrell, S., 1995, 'Civilizing Projects and the Reaction to Them', in S. Harrell (ed.), *Cultural Encounters on China's Ethnic Frontiers*, Seattle, WA: University of Washington Press, pp.3–36.

Keyes, C., 2002, 'The Peoples of Asia: Science and Politics in the Classification of Ethnic Groups in Thailand, China and Vietnam', *Journal of Asian Studies*, Vol.61, No.4, pp.1163–203.

Liu, D.C., 2001, 'Tenure and Management of Non-State Forest in China since 1950: A Historical Review', *Environmental History*, Vol.6, pp.239–63.

Liu, D.C. and D. Edmunds, 2003, 'Devolution as Means of Expanding Local Forest Management in South China: Lessons from the past 20 years', in William F. Hyde, Brian Belcher and Jintao Xu (eds.), *China's Forests: Global Lessons from Market Reforms*, Washington, DC: Resources for the Future and Bogor: Center for International Forestry Research, pp.27–44.

Menzies, N.K., 1992, 'Strategic Space: Exclusion and Inclusion in Wildland Policies in Late Imperial China', *Modern Asian Studies*, Vol.26, No.4, pp.719–933.

Ribot, J.C., 2002, 'African Decentralization: Local Actors, Powers and Accountability', Democracy, Governance and Human Rights Paper No.8, Geneva: United Nationals Research Institute for Social Development.

Sajise, E.P., 1995, 'Biodiversity and Methods: A Synthesis', in S.J. Pei and P. Sajise (eds.), *Regional Study on Biodiversity: Concepts, Frameworks, and Methods*, Kunming: Yunnan University Press.

State Forestry Administration, 1998, *A Documentation of China Forestry Law Amendments*, Beijing: China Forestry Press.

State Forestry Administration (ed.), 2000, *China Forestry Yearbook 1999–2000*, Beijing: China Forestry Press.

Tan Leshan, 2000, 'Autonomy is not what it was', *China Brief*, Vol.2, No.4, pp.1–6.

Xu, J.C., J. Fox, Lu X., N. Podger, S. Leisz and X. H. Ai, 1999, 'Effects of Swidden Cultivation, State Policies and Customary Institutions on Land Cover in a Hani Village', *Mountain Research and Development*, Vol.19, No.2, pp.123–32.

Xu, J.C., Zhang Peifang and Wang Yuhua, 2003, 'Land Use and Land Cover in Lancang Watershed of Yunnan', *Yunnan Botanica*, Vol.25, No.2, pp.45–154 (in Chinese).

Xu, J.C. and M. Salas, 2003, 'Moving the Periphery to the Centre: Indigenous People, Culture and Knowledge in a Changing Yunnan', in M. Kaosa-ard and J. Dore (eds.), *Social Challenges for the Mekong Region*, Bangkok: White Lotus, pp.123–45.

Xu, J.C. and A. Wilkes, 2004, 'People, Plants and Ecosystems in Northwest Yunnan: Biodiversity Impact Analysis in Northwest Yunnan, Southwest China: Biodiversity and Conservation', *Biodiversity and Conservation*, Vol.13, No.5, pp.959–83.

Yeh, E.T., 2000, 'Forest Claims, Conflict and Commodification: The Political Ecology of Tibetan Mushroom-Harvesting Villages in Yunnan Province, China', *China Quarterly*, Vol.161, pp.264–78.

Yin, Runsheng, 1998, 'Forestry and the Environment in China: the Current Situation and Strategic Choice', *World Development*, Vol.26, No.12, pp.2153–67.

Yin, Runsheng and D. H. Newman, 1997, 'Impacts of Rural Reforms: the Case of the Chinese Forest Sector', *Environment and Development Economics*, Vol.2, pp.291–305.

Yuan, Xiang (ed.), 1924, *China Yearbook No.1*, Shanghai: Commercial Press, p.1207.

Yunnan Forestry Department, 1984, *Forestry Information*, Vol.7.

Zheng, B. (ed.), 2001, *Study on Forestland Utilization Rights*, Unpublished report, p.28.

Zuo, T. and J.C. Xu, 2001, *The Impact of Decentralization and Local Participation on Upland Watersheds Management in Yunnan, Southwest China, Progress Report on Resource Policy Support Initiative (REPSI)*, Washington DC: World Resources Institute, mimeo.

The Social and Organisational Roots of Ecological Uncertainties in Cameroon's Forest Management Decentralisation Model

PHIL RENÉ OYONO

I. INTRODUCTION

The end of the 1990s was marked by waves of social and political protest against existing governance systems in Sub-Saharan Africa [*Mamdani, 1990: 53–60; Wunch, 1990: 62–6*]. This was the outcome of the conspicuous socio-economic and political constructions of severe crises [*Synder, 1992: 383–9; Joseph, 1992: 12–16; Robinson, 1994*]. Bratton and van de Walle [*1997: 45–63*], in a study of democratic transitions in Africa, isolated many supra-domestic and domestic explanatory variables behind these crises. In the case of Cameroon, two determinants stand out: first, bad governance, internal imbalances and the collapse of the world market price of cocoa and coffee plunged the country into a deep economic recession in 1986–87; second, at the same time, social and political actors demanded the restructuring and democratisation of domestic political systems. These crises, in many cases, were unexpected by political regimes. Some social and political economy theorists believe that, under such situations, policy-makers or policy managers frequently react to complexity by undertaking system reforms [*Grindle and Thomas, 1992: 3–10*]. Forestry reforms conducted in Cameroon since 1994 are part of official and political responses to the country's systemic crisis.

Ongoing decentralisation of forest management in this country is a central element of these gradual forestry reforms [*Ekoko, 1998: 9–16; Bigombé, 1998: 7–8; Diaw and Oyono, 1998: 25; Vabi et al., 2000: 4–10; Fomété, 2001: 5–8*].

Phil René Oyono is Rural Sociologist and the WRI Research Team Leader at the Center for International Forestry Research (CIFOR), Cameroon. The author would like to thank WRI and CARPE/USAID for funding facilities offered to CIFOR-Cameroon in the study of 'Decentralization, Accountability and the Environment in Cameroon' in 2001 and 2002. He also extends his thanks to CIFOR-Cameroon Research Assistants Charlotte Kouna Eloundou, Samuel Assembe Mvondo and Samuel Efoua for the empirical data they provided during this social and policy research. The author emphasises that this essay is essentially the result of discussions stimulated by Jesse Ribot. Thanks also go to Anne Larson and the anonymous reviewers for the useful comments they made on the first version of this essay, as well as James Murombedzi of IUCN (Southern Africa Regional Office, Harare, Zimbabwe) for comments provided during the oral presentation of this essay in Bellagio, Italy in 2002.

European Journal of Development Research, Vol.16, No.1, Spring 2004, pp.174–191
ISSN 0957-8811 print
DOI:10.1080/0957881041000168798

This contribution examines Cameroon's model of forest-management decentralisation by characterising its organisational infrastructure and by assessing – and anticipating – the ecological effects of those policy changes. The essay is based on environmental governance research conducted in Cameroon during the last three years. Five Community Forests, one Council Forest and nine forestry fee management committees were covered by the study. Methods of data collection included participant observation, analysis of historical trends, semi-structured interviews at the regional level, focus group meetings, historical transects of landscape and future scenarios. Qualitative data analysis aimed to understand forest-management organisations at the local level, modes of representation and accountability mechanisms.

The first section describes the key reforms put in place by the new forest-management regime [*Vabi et al., 2000: 6–7; Ribot, 2002:14; Oyono, 2003: 25–37; Bigombé, 2003: 6–31; Etoungou, 2003: 10–14*], including the institutional and socio-organisational choices legally prescribed for outlying actors in the decentralised management of forests and their revenues. The mechanisms connecting these institutional and socio-organisational choices to implementation – that is, the management of Community Forests, Council Forests and forestry revenues – are examined in the second part of the essay. The third section assesses the social outcomes of these processes. Ecological risks and uncertainties due to the way decentralised management is conducted at both the local and the regional levels are addressed in the fourth section. This is followed by the conclusion.

II. REFORM INITIATIVES AND THE MODEL OF FOREST MANAGEMENT DECENTRALISATION

Policy Change and the Founding Principles of the Model

The colonial logic of resource accumulation, including building financial capital on forest exploitation [*see Schanz, 1914: 4–10; Meniaud, 1948: 112–22*], has been replicated, with some modifications, by the Cameroonian post-colonial state. The legal principle according to which forests belong to the state remains sacred. Focusing on income from timber exports, forest policy managers and political elites produced a highly centralised 'forestry state' during the 70s and 80s [*Brown, 1999: 3–11; Karsenty, 1999a: 10–11; Fomété, 2001: 9–12*]. Under those circumstances, the management of forests as well as related revenue became highly politicised – involving top state authorities and their families – and was transformed into a sensitive issue, a taboo topic, one not submitted to any social or public debate [*Verschave, 2000: 3–12; Mbarga, 2002: 24–5*]. In light of this, politically polarised conflicts of interests and deep *conflits de langage* have continually emerged regarding forest and forestry revenue issues over the last three decades [*Oyono, 2001: 6–8*]. For example, for many years the post-independence state insisted that forest-management issues should remain its 'own affair'. In contrast, local communities in Cameroon's forest zone[1] have continued to claim their rights over forests and substantial portions of income accruing therefrom.

The political rhetoric used by the state regarding forest management up until the launching of the forestry reforms in the mid-1990s had a hegemonic resonance developed in the sense of what Scott [*1990: 7–28*] calls 'public transcript', or a political discourse; that is, a unique version (or translation) of the reality disseminated by the dominant bloc. For local communities and their 'infrapolitical discourse'[2] [*Scott, 1990: 7–28*], forest management and timber revenue are unquestionably social and public issues to be debated in the public sphere [*Hodenthal, 1992: 103–7*]. It is on the basis of these mechanisms of the 'natural' elimination and exclusion of other actors – primarily local communities – from the sphere of forest management and forestry revenue circulation that a *cordon sanitaire* was set up between policy managers, official decision-makers and forestry experts, on the one hand, and the 'others', on the other [*Ribot, 2001a: 3–7*]. In order to implement new modes of action and increase its capacity for socio-political regulation of forest management, as well as to depolarise functional misunderstandings around this issue, the Cameroonian government used decentralisation as a strategic weapon.

'Decentralisation' is defined as a process through which a central government cedes powers and responsibilities to actors and institutions at lower levels [*Mahwood, 1983: 6–14; Smith, 1985: 20–26*]. Democratic decentralisation occurs when powers and resources are transferred to authorities representative of and downwardly accountable to local populations [*Crook and Manor, 1998: 11–14; Agrawal and Ribot, 1999: 475–7; Larson, 2002: 19–22; Ribot, 2003: 2–3*]. Viewed this way, decentralisation in forest management could – in the case of Cameroon – 'decompress', in the short term, the dissident subculture of local communities and dampen their resistance in a number of villages.[3] The first package of policy innovations aimed at decentralising forest management in Cameroon established a new typology of forests (see Table 1) and redefined their social status. Formulated with the close support of the World Bank [*Essamah and Gockowski, 2000: 57–71*], the 1994 forestry legislation generating these legal tools is presented as being the most innovative in the Congo Basin [*Nguinguiri, 1997: 4–7*]. It also inaugurated a pioneering experiment in forest management decentralisation for the whole eco-region.

Council Forests, Community Forests and Forestry Fees

The Cameroonian model of forest-management decentralisation has embraced several specific options. As noted above, the first one is related to the transfer of management responsibilities and powers to councils, known as *communes*, and their elected bodies – the mayor and councillors – for the creation and management of Council Forests (see Table 1). The second is based on the transfer of management responsibilities and powers to village communities for the creation of Community Forests. The third policy option is presented in Table 2. It transfers portions of annual forestry fees or taxes to local communities. It also prescribes the allocation of forestry royalties – a sort of eco-tax – to local communities who have traditional rights over small forest concessions (*ventes de coupe,* see Table 1). These two categories of taxes have led to the decentralised management of forestry revenues – a new taxation system synonymous with fiscal decentralisation [*Karsenty, 1999b: 147–53;*

TABLE 1

CLASSIFICATION OF FOREST TYPES UNDER THE 1994 LEGISLATION

*Permanent forests**

a) *Unités Forestières d'aménagement* (UFA) are concessions of up to 200,000 hectares awarded to logging companies within the permanent forest estate. These replace the former logging licences, which did not require management plans to be formulated before exploitation of the concession areas [*Eba'a, 1998: 4–8*]. These plans must state the subdivision of the UFA that will be exploited annually (these units are called '*assiettes de coupe*').
b) Council Forests (*Forêts Communales*) are managed by elected local councils or municipalities, based on management plans approved by the Ministry of Forests.

*Non-permanent forests***

a) *Ventes de Coupe* are licences awarded for the exploitation of standing volumes on small tracts of land – up to 2,500 hectares in size – in the non-permanent forest. They do not, of themselves, require management plans, though they are subject to limitations as to the levels and type of off-take permitted.
b) *Forêts Communautaires* (Community Forests) are a new and potentially very innovative class of forest exploitation, by which it is intended that, for the first time in Cameroon's history, rural populations can themselves gain direct, legal access to forest products, including timber. The maximum area of any single Community Forest is 5,000 hectares. Exploitation of Community Forests will be by sale of felling rights to licensed companies or other legal entities, though, unlike conventional *ventes de coupe*, the community is required to produce a management plan detailing the terms under which logging will be undertaken.
c) *Personal authorisations* allow individuals to log up to 500 cubic metres of timber for non-commercial use.

Notes: * Permanent forests are lands that are to be used solely for production forestry, preservation and/or wildlife habitats. Their 'permanence' relates to their long-term utilisation: this includes forest concessions, plantations, council forests, national parks, game reserves, forest reserves, botanical gardens, etc.
** Non-permanent forests comprise the rest of the forest estate and include all forestlands that can be converted (temporarily or permanently) to purposes other than forestry, like human settlement and agriculture. This type of forest refers to national domain forests (*Forêts du Domaine Permanent*), community forests and private forests (*Forêts des Particuliers*).

Source: Brown, 1999: 12.

TABLE 2

TRANSFER OF RIGHTS AND POWERS IN THE DECENTRALISING FORESTRY LAW OF 1994

Rights	Aspects concerned	References in the Law
Rights to existing resource management transferred to outlying actors	Exploitation of Council Forests and Community Forests	Articles 7, 16 and 17 of Law 94/01
Customary and use rights	Exploitation of all the products of 'Private Forests' (*Forêts des Particuliers*)	Articles 8, 26 (1), 30 (2), 36 and 86 of Law 94/01
Benefits of part of timber revenue	Revenue from logging	Article 68 (2) (3) of the Law and Article 85 of the Decree of Application
Monitoring and controlling bush fires	Resource conservation	Article 7 of the Decree of Application
Rights of opposition to the classification of protected areas	Exploitation of forest resources	Articles 6, 18 and 20 (1) of the Decree of Application

Carret, 2000: 37–45; Milol and Pierre, 2000: 2–23; Bigombé, 2003: 4–8]. Before the reforms, the crisis of Cameroon's forestry system – a corollary of the whole crisis of the 1980s – was embedded in the issue of inter-generational access to benefits and in bottom-up oriented requirements of equity, security and justice. Decentralisation appeared, at least on paper, to be a response to these needs.

Council Forests. Council Forests are any forests that were classified on behalf of the council/municipality concerned or planted by the council. The act of classification defines the limits and the management objectives of the forest, which can be the same as those of national domain forests, as well as the exercise of users rights for local communities. Council Forests belong to the private domain of the councils concerned. To date, only one non-planted Council Forest has been officially approved; technical studies conducted from 1999 to 2001 established the basis for its management plan.

According to Diaw *et al.* [*2001: 8–14*], social dimensions – that is, the taking into consideration of local communities' collective representations, discourses and practices in an 'interactionist' perspective – were insufficiently captured and, in the final analysis, under-integrated in the operations undertaken by forestry experts at the time. The interactionist perspective refers, among many other things, to the way actors recognise each other in a co-operative process [*Turner, 1982: 390–98*]. In the case of the Dimako Council Forest, experts have simply reproduced the top-down approach in force since the colonial period. This explains how it is possible that farmlands of two villages located in the northern part of the Council Forest were annexed by the delimitation and classification operations [*Assembe and Oyono, 2003: 4–6*]. After the publication of the forest's classification decree on behalf of the rural council, these local communities turned to violence to defend their claims.

Community Forests. A Community Forest is defined as:

> A forest of the non permanent domain, subjected to a 'Convention of Management' between a village community and the Administration in charge of forests. The management of this forest is entrusted to the village community concerned, with the technical support of the Administration … Community Forests are equipped with a 'Simple Management Plan'… a contract by which the Administration entrusts [to a village] a parcel of forest from the national domain, for its management, conservation and exploitation for the interest of the community … and which fixes the activities to carry out [Article 3 of the Decree].

Between April 1998 and November 2001, the Community Forestry Unit, a technical structure created within the Ministry of Forests, received 136 applications from local communities. About 30 Simple Management Plans are already approved and more than 20 Conventions of Management have been signed with village communities to date – that is to say nearly 15 per cent of the requests. About 75 Community Forests are now being managed, among these six in the Lomié region (east Cameroon). Created and implemented with the support of a Dutch Non-Governmental Organisation (NGO) – the *Stichting Nederlandse Vrijvilligers* (SNV) – the Community Forests of the Lomié region are both a policy laboratory and units of scientific observation and monitoring [*Djeumo, 2001: 4–8; Klein et al., 2001: 8; Efoua, 2001: 4–6; Etoungou, 2003: 17–32*].

Although it has been fully demonstrated that NGOs are responsible, in a detrimental way, to the basic operational aspects of the request for and creation of Community Forests [*Etoungou, 2003: 26–30; Oyono, 2003: 34*], these forests are, to some extent, an emanation of powers transferred to local communities as a whole. Community Forest experiments are characterised by a two-level transfer of powers: first, the state transfers management powers to local/village communities requesting Community Forests; second, these communities transfer powers to village committees to represent them in official arenas [*Oyono, 2003: 30–33*].

Forestry Fees. The 1994 Forestry Law articulates the reformist changes offered by an authoritarian state with the continuous demands of local communities for minimum inclusion in the 'forestry game' [*Oyono, 2001: 6–8*]. The law states that, 'for the development of the bordering village communities of national domain forests, part of the income drawn from the sale of forest products must be transferred to local communities, according to mechanisms of the Decree' (Forestry Law, Article 68).

Forestry fees are shared in the following way: 50 per cent to the state; 40 per cent to the council in whose domain the exploited forest is located; and ten per cent to neighbouring village communities. Calculations of the financial sums to allocate to these various actors are made based on exploitation type: CFA francs 2,500 ($4) per hectare exploited in a *vente de coupe*; CFA francs 1,500 ($2.5) per hectare for a forest concession; and CFA francs 1,500 ($2.5) per hectare by holders of a private forest licence. In addition, in *ventes de coupe* bordering villages are given CFA francs 1,000 ($1.7) per cubic metre. Compared with commercial exploitation of Community Forests and Council Forests, forestry fees – as a channel of direct and instantaneous access to cash income – represent more closely local communities' expectations regarding the decentralisation of forest management in Cameroon [*Milol and Pierre, 2000: 10–15*].

Institutional and Socio-Organisational Infrastructure of the Cameroonian Model

In order to promote decentralisation to village communities as defined by the forestry law, policy-makers deemed it appropriate to prescribe the creation of management committees. These organisational constructions were to be village based. Yet such a prescription has the ultimate political intention of justifying reforms with social legitimacies. In 1992, before the forestry reforms, the government of Cameroon – with the support of the International Labour Organization, French Co-operation and the World Bank – carried out an extensive rural reform aimed at establishing efficient social and organisational conditions for agricultural development. As a result, many village organisations were transformed into Common Initiative Groups, which proliferated in an unprecedented manner [*Oyono and Temple, 2003: 67–79*]. On the whole, by prescribing the creation of village community organisations concerned with forestry fees and Community Forest management, the decentralisation model adopted the matrix proposed by the rural reform – which was based on a structural, but not necessarily social, rationality [*Djeumo, 2001: 4–9; Oyono and Temple, 2003: 67–79*].

The law indicates that the village community applying for a Community Forest must be organised as a 'moral entity' (a legally incorporated body) legally recognised by the state.[4] Technical tools developed to facilitate the implementation phase – for example, the Procedural Manual for Community Forest Attribution and other existing legal provisions – have, to that effect, promoted the creation of the management committees mentioned above. Superimposed on village communities, then, Community Forest Management Committees are composed, in general, of less than ten persons. In the case of managing forestry revenue, the law did not propose a specific organisational form but mentioned the need to establish appropriate local institutions. This was further clarified in 1998, when the Ministries of Finance and of Territorial Administration published a joint order prescribing the creation of village committees for the management of forestry fees. As do Community Forest Committees, these committees are structurally uniform – each with a chairperson and a handful of members.

Committees for the management of Council Forests represent the third socio-organisational choice made under the Cameroonian model. As already stated, only one Council Forest – that of Dimako, in the east province – has official recognition in Cameroon so far. It should be managed by a Consultative Committee composed of representatives from the 14 villages under the council's jurisdiction. The creation of that committee is explained, *a priori*, by the need for council authorities to have a space for interaction as a balancing mechanism between the council and constituent villages. The committee is then presented as a tool for local community participation in the management of the forthcoming benefits of logging activities in the Council Forest.

The empirical and theoretical insights of this essay derive from these three socio-organisational choices. The management committees for Community Forests, forestry fees and Council Forests are, in the end, the only officially recognised local actors to be involved in the 'forestry game'. Local communities, by themselves, do not have a significant role to play [*Djeumo, 2001: 7–8; Oyono, 2003: 23–30; Etoungou, 2003: 24–32; Eoné, 2003: 20–24*]. The principal role assigned to these committees 'at the bottom' relates to the defence of local community interests (livelihoods, domestic accumulation and well-being). Thus, committees could be conceived as socio-political resources trying to make 'hidden transcripts' explicit in the sense described by Scott [*1990: 120–25*] – that is, local discourse about justice and claims of rights over forests, and attempts to establish evidence of well-being in the popular imaginary. In short, these committees should be local communities' voices and the translators of the non-dominant discourse.

In the African context, the history of management committees created for rural development programmes and social forestry projects is highly controversial, for most have been external initiatives [*Dia, 1996: 10–19; Ribot, 2000: 33–41; Mapedza and Madondo, 2003: 5–9*]. In the specific case discussed in this essay, the socio-genesis of the new organisations created in Cameroon by the decentralisation process reveals that the role of external actors is central to their emergence and operation, as noted by Assembe [*2001: 15*]:

> On this point, one notes in a recurring way that at the origin of these structures there are external actors. NGOs, project experts, administrative authorities and loggers have encouraged villagers to create these committees, hence the strong implications of these external actors, from their installation phase to the present.

III. THE COMPLEXITY OF THE MODEL AND ITS PARADOXICAL OUTCOMES

Democratic decentralisation theorists argue that public participation and appropriate institutional arrangements at the local level could lead to greater government responsiveness and to positive and sustainable social and ecological outcomes [*Overdevest, 2000: 685–96; Ribot, 2001b: 7–12; Manor, 2002: 2–5*]. Such a postulate appears to be embedded in a causal and positivist axiom in which given determinant causes must always generate precise outcomes. Yet there can be public participation or institutional arrangements without positive effects, or with mitigated effects. Preliminary assessment of the Cameroonian experiment demonstrates that, because this is a process involving powerful actors at national, sub-national (regional) and local levels, its outcomes are paradoxical. In recent studies Oyono [*2003: 30–37*] and Bigombé [*2003: 22–8*] conclude that – though there is participation, through committees, a new regime of forest ownership and a new mode of access to financial benefits – the process of forest management decentralisation is hijacked at the regional level by mayors, administrative authorities, timber companies, politicians and many other interest groups. In some cases, forest concessions and *ventes de coupe* belong to ministers and army generals, who do not want to hand over the local community portion of forestry fees; in other cases, mayors and regional administrative authorities misappropriate the funds in question.

With regard to the issue of power transfers in the framework of environmental decentralisations as a founding principle of rights sharing, the existing configuration of representation arrangements have a questionable capacity to make the co-management of forest resources and benefits socially feasible [*Oyono, 2003: 49–52*]. Many committee members are part of the external, urban elite; they have joined these local initiatives for their personal interests, such as the misappropriation of funds. In addition, important powers are still retained at the national and regional levels.

This said, what is the nature of the outcomes or, short of those 'infra-outcomes' that have emerged from the various village-level committees that have been created for decentralised forest management? In this essay, the concept of 'infra-outcomes' refers to visible signs 'of something' that is still in the maturation process and, in the final analysis, remains in the antechamber of effective outcomes. On the whole, these are mid-term empirical observations in need of confirmation.

Positive Outcomes and Infra-Outcomes

The decentralisation of forest management and its local organisational arrangements are potentially transformational in social and psychological terms. Local communities, by setting up committees, have demonstrated a certain degree of organisational capacity. Moreover, thanks to the decentralisation process, the 'political distance' between communities and forests – and related benefits – seems to be shortened. Kouna [*2001: 6–10*], Oyono *et al.* [*2003: 8–9*] and Bigombé [*2003: 39–42*] provide examples demonstrating that despite bad practices at the regional level, portions of forestry fees are effectively channelled to socio-economic initiatives (classrooms, health centres, etc.) in some villages of the east province. In another effort to demonstrate positive socio-economic effects of forest management reforms, Fomété [*2001: 9–11*] reports that in 2001 42 *communes* of south Cameroon received forestry fees of about $2,666,670 intended, among other things, for development at the village level. In addition, the villages Echiembor and Ngola, in the Lomié region, earned $18,500 and $24,750 respectively in 2002 from the management of their community forests [*Efoua, 2001*: *4*].

In many villages, local actors struggle to promote local democracy in decentralised forestry management. Using available counter-powers such as popular protests, villagers have succeeded in removing corrupt members from their positions on forestry fee and Community Forest management committees – as in the Ebolowa and Mbang regions. This is one example, though isolated, of accountability practices and of a minimal internalisation of the democratic version of local forest management. In addition, the Cameroonian decentralisation model has allowed social groups that have been marginalised for many years to create a new niche. This is the case of the Baka Pygmies of east Cameroon. Considered by historians and ethnographers as the first inhabitants of the Congo Basin [*Bailey, 1992: 43–8; Seltz, 1993: 14–35*], their interests were never taken into account by forestry laws before 1994 [*Oyono, 2003: 12–16*]. To rationalise this marginalisation, official discourse has always asserted that it is a nomadic group without a territorial base. The opportunity to create Community Forests has finally allowed Baka Pygmies the right to manage a forest ecosystem, as in the village Moangué-Le-Bosquet (Lomié region).

The Other Side of the Picture: Negative Outcomes

Nevertheless, financial resources given to local communities are, on the whole, insignificant.[5] In addition, according to reports from Kouna [*2001: 5–7*] and Bigombé [*2003: 32–5*], council authorities and state representatives at the regional level improperly manipulate fees intended for villages. It has also been observed that when these eco-tax or royalty fees are directly transferred to local communities, their destination is socially and economically inappropriate – they are used, rather than for local development, for food and drink [*Bigombé, 2003: 34*]. Village committees created for the management of forestry fees generally engage in rent seeking, in the sense of Eggertson [*1990: 45–67*]; that is, they disconnect themselves from the communities they represent and join the strategic and hegemonic bloc composed of administrative and council authorities and logging companies [*Oyono, 2003: 40–44*]. This misrepresentation, combined with the absence of solid institutional and organisational arrangements for the reliable local management of forestry fees, suggests an 'informalisation' of the fiscal decentralisation option.

The irrelevance – or weakness – of existing institutional and organisational arrangements has also increased insecurity in inter-generational access to resources and benefits. The younger generations, believing they are the losers, seek to negotiate their solid participation in the flow of forestry revenues. The following remark, made by young people of a village in the Lomié region, is revealing: 'The state, those who are dead, the elderly and our fathers have eaten too much from these forests. Now it is our turn.' The prospect 'to eat well and drink well' from forests is leading to a battle of wills at the local level.

Committee members are generally selected from amongst retired civil servants, external elite and urban youth; in short, committees are dominated by 'those who went to modern schools'. Traditional authorities, like elders, heads of lineage, and village chiefs – locally recognised as people who have the power to control nature – have thus been rejected by the new forestry 'game' [*Oyono, 2000: 42–5*]: they have not been taken into account by the social and organisational choices of the official model. As a result, there are prominent indications of ungovernability [*Oyono, 2002: 4–8*] in the villages and areas concerned. The marginalisation of traditional and local authorities in the forestry game has created a 'panarchy', characterised by the coexistence of many centres of power and authority (declining traditional authorities, village chiefs, young people, committee members, external elite, local politicians, etc.). As those who traditionally have held power over nature have been marginalised and replaced by new local actors, the decentralisation model has led to a conflict of authority.

In other cases, outcomes suggest the radicalisation of local communities regarding the management of forestry fees by administrative and council authorities. Bigombé [*2003: 23–5*] notes that in east Cameroon, local communities are protesting against the involvement of these authorities in the 'game' of forestry revenue circulation. He talks of 're-centralisation'. These communities sometimes refuse to participate in village forest management meetings organised by central state representatives [*Efoua, 2001: 5–8*]. For many peasants, the implementation of the decentralisation model around administrative and official logics is indicative of its current limitations.

Analysing the course of these social experiments in the decentralised management of forests, particularly Community Forests, Klein *et al.* [*2001: 16–20*] have argued that the new context has induced a new social stratification. In a development that Institutional Economics refers to as 'egoistic choice' [*North, 1986: 230–37*] – similar to self-interested behaviour – members of committees and other new social agents have come together to constitute a new forestry elite, one that is not at all accountable to those they represent. Djeumo [*2001: 9–11*] has confirmed these social distortions, notably opportunistic behaviours amongst committee members, born from the implementation and management of Community Forests in the Lomié region. Two other factors also help explain these outcomes: first, the lack of administrative order, due to the weakness of the state, which leads many regional representatives and agents to behave as they please – and with impunity; and second, the culture of corruption among state managers, sub-national authorities and state agents, combined with the absence of sanctions.

IV. ECOLOGICAL UNCERTAINTIES

The Congo Basin is home to one of the richest forests in the world, quantitatively and qualitatively. Experts have argued that, because of the abundance of resources, bordering people have never paid attention to the threat represented by the degradation of forest ecosystems. This view is inaccurate: these communities do, in fact, have criteria and indicators for sustainable forest management [*Tiani et al., 2001: 7–13; Oyono and Efoua, 2001: 4–5; Mala and Oyono, 2003: 4–6*]. Ambara [*2003: 7*] notes that due to the 'green delinquency' of members of management committees, many Community forests are being devastated within two months only. In the Lomié region, the 'laboratory of Community Forests management', peasants regularly formulate what, to them, appear to be indicators of good ecological health conditions. As such, they are capable of conducting an ecological assessment of the forest. This does not mean, however, that they are unwilling to trade it in for income, at least to earn something while the state and timber companies take the lion's share.

For the past two years, the commercial exploitation of Community Forests for which Conventions of Management are already signed is at the heart of a triangular conflict among local communities, the Ministry of Forests and the Dutch NGO SNV [*Etoungou, 2003: 32–5; Efoua, 2001: 6*]. The Forestry Administration, with the support of SNV, prescribed small-scale exploitation for Community Forests, which Auzel *et al.* describe as follows:

> This type of logging is based on a number of fundamental rules and techniques: i) the careful selection of trees to be felled, avoiding immature trees; ii) directional felling, to reduce the impact on remaining trees; iii) sawing of logs into planks *in situ* in the forest; iv) the manual transportation of planks to a central area, so as to avoid opening up secondary tracks [*Auzel et al., 2001: 26*].

This formula may be appropriate, somewhere, for meeting sustainability objectives. In contrast, however, its potential for individual or collective accumulation is limited and, thus, underestimated by local communities – particularly in comparison with forestry fees and royalties [*see also Mendouga, 1998: 4–7*]. Villagers argue that it is time to 'live at last with money from forests', and quickly. When exploited according to the formula prescribed by the Ministry of Forests, Community Forests do not fully meet this expectation. Under these circumstances, local communities turn impulsively to the more profitable large-scale logging, which is expected to bring about a collective catharsis by generating important financial benefits and, therefore, eliminating decades of frustration. Community Forest management committees are increasingly ready to negotiate and sign contracts with logging companies. Some of these companies (SFID and PALLISCO, in the east province) are among the giants of commercial timber in Cameroon: they practice both intensive and extensive logging and can devastate a Community Forest in less than two months. It is thus apparent that the eagerness of local communities to generate forestry revenues leads them, 'naturally', to turn to options of accelerated and intensive exploitation. These indications of a shift towards *ventes de coupe* [*Djeumo, 2001: 6–7*] – or towards spaces of anarchistic exploitation – raise concerns about ecological sustainability.

In the pursuit of *ventes de coupe*, the formation of alliances is increasingly apparent between administrative and political elites – who are now deeply involved in the process of creating and acquiring Community Forests in their villages – and logging companies, which finance the technical and administrative operations with the intention of collecting timber in the future. In this regard, there are reports of urban elite attempts to utilise Community Forests to their advantage [*Efoua, 2001: 4–5*]. Local communities – as in the Lomié region, for example – adhere instantaneously to this more profitable strategy because of the cash income it generates.

Djeumo [*2001:10*] has emphasised that the application of certain provisions of the Law of Finances regarding fiscal decentralisation, notably the sum of \$1.7 per cubic metre of timber paid to local communities living beside a *vente de coupe*, has obliged some logging companies to organise – with the support of the regional representatives of the central state – meetings for the official handing over of cheques. Some of these meetings are mentioned in radio programmes and shown on national television. The payment of these forestry fees may have stimulated other communities – conscious of the economic importance of forest products surrounding them and highly interested in exploiting them as fast as possible through Community Forests – to emulate them.

Echoing such empirical statements, Mendouga [*1998: 4–7*] talks of the 'tragedy of 1,000 CFA francs' per cubic metre. In other words, the confluence of many variables – such as access to the eco-tax, the fever of annual forestry fees, and the transformation of Community Forests into disguised *ventes de coupe* – generate within local communities a 'maximalist' and majority faction, primarily of young people, who want 'to eat and drink now with the money from forests'. Fomété [*2001: 12–14*] also presents evidence that local communities largely express the desire to see the forests surrounding them transformed into timber concessions and *ventes de coupe*, to be exploited at once. All of this enriches the thesis that the current model of decentralisation is, at least for the moment, ecologically counterproductive.

V. CONCLUSION

The available evidence demonstrates a significant gap between the experience in Cameroon and arguments that decentralisation should necessarily lead to efficiency, equity and ecological sustainability. This romantic and mechanistic view minimises the fact that the supply/delivery side and the demand side of decentralisation are not centripetal but centrifugal forces. On the one hand, the state does not want to continue to give up powers, and, on the other hand, peripheral actors are increasing their demands for further equity, justice and well-being. To be productive, models of natural-resource-management decentralisation – like the one implemented in Cameroon – need to be substantive and not procedural or instrumental. They must favour basic values and practices, including downward accountability, local democracy, the mystique of responsibility, strong institutional arrangements at the local level and awareness of the common interest.

The Cameroonian decentralisation model, though arising from political calculation, is a courageous initiative. It has, as shown above, already registered some positive infra-outcomes. After all, decentralisation is not mechanical. It is not only explainable by laws and institutional arrangements: its implementation depends on many variables. It therefore requires sufficient time to develop due to the complexity of human and institutional behaviour and because of unpredictability, variability, contingency and change, as well as many other stimuli. In sum, it is a 'story' of adaptation, with successes and failures. Policy innovations and reforms are in themselves experiments and should not be perceived as victories or crises, but, instead, as arenas of ongoing lessons and progressive learning.

Forestry-revenue management and sharing requires a rigorous selection of relevant mechanisms aimed at reducing the involvement of administrative authorities and other interest groups. The institutionalisation of a real representative democracy at the regional and local levels is also a precondition for successful decentralisation of forest management in Cameroon. Collaborative strategies among actors, facilitated by NGOs and action-research programmes, should also reinforce ongoing efforts [*Diaw and Oyono, 2001:4–7*]. The process of decentralisation and the improvement of decentralisation policies also depend on social theory and the strategic information made available by natural resource sociology [*Buttel, 2002: 205–10*].

NOTES

1. The forest zone of Cameroon comprises five provinces and covers 22 million hectares of forest.
2. Scott [*1990: 35–47*] sees in the 'infrapolitics' invisible political strategies carried out by subordinated groups in order to circumvent total control.
3. In many parts of the east and south provinces of Cameroon, local communities are regularly and openly targeting logging companies' interests in their protestations of the 'forestry order'; in such circumstances logging tracks were barricaded and workers and their patrons were kept locked out. Oriented to the requirement of more social equity, the recruitment of young men originating from neighbouring villages was a cyclical social demand. Thus, in 1995, the *Société Foresttère de la Sanaga* was obliged to push out 23 'outsiders' among its workers in order to recruit members of the indigenous population in the Lomié region, east-Cameroon.
4. Forestry reforms have adopted the organisational forms proposed by the Law on the Right of Association of 1990 and by the Rural Reform of 1992 [*Oyono and Temple, 2003: 78–84*]. It is said in these legal frameworks that, to participate in the 'public debate', village communities should be represented in development issues and, for this purpose, in forest management issues by organisations (like committees). In that sense, four types of legal entities are recommended to rural organisations to be officially recognised and institutionalised actors in the game: 1) the common initiative group; 2) the association; 3) the economic interest group; and 4) the co-operative.
5. According to Fomété [*2001: 13–15*], these sums represent approximately US$1.6 per villager for the said operation.

REFERENCES

Agrawal, A. and J.C. Ribot, 1999, 'Accountability in Decentralization: A Framework with South Asian and African Cases', *Journal of Developing Areas*, No.33, pp.473–502.

Ambara, N., 2003, 'Forêts Cameroonaises: La délinquance verte gagne du terrain', *La Nouvelle Tribune,* No.85, p.7.

Auzel, P., G.M. Nguenang, R. Fetéké and W. Delvingt, 2001, 'Small-Scale Logging in Community Forests in Cameroon: Towards Ecologically more Sustainable and Socially more Acceptable Compromises', *Rural Development Network Paper 25f*, London: ODI.

Assembe, S., 2001, 'Analyse d'une structure née de la gestion décentralisée des forêts au Cameroun: Le Comité Consultatif de gestion de la Forêt Communale de Dimako', *Communautés Africaines*, No.79, pp.13–17.

Assembe, S. and P.R. Oyono, 2003, 'An Assessment of Social Negotiation as a Tool of Local Management. A Case Study of the Dimako Council Forest [east Cameroon]', Paper presented at the International IUFRO Workshop on 'The Forest Science/Policy Interface in Europe, Africa and the Middle-East', Copenhagen, Denmark 24–27 June; in review for *The Scandinavian Journal of Forestry Research.*

Bailey, R.C., 1992, 'Forest People', in J.A. Sayer, C.S. Harcourt and N.M. Collins (eds.), *The Conservation Atlas of Tropical Forests: Africa*, Gland, Switzerland: IUCN, pp.43–8.

Bigombé, P., 2003, 'The Decentralized Forestry Taxation System in Cameroon: Local Management and State Logic', Working Paper, Washington, DC: WRI.

Bigombé, P., 1998, 'Vers la décentralisation de l'aménagement forestier au Cameroun: Dynamique de contestation entre l'Etat forestier et de la construction de la gestion participative des ressources forestières', *Bulletin Arbres, Forêts et Communautés Rurales*, No.15/16, pp.6–13.

Bratton, M. and N. van de Walle, 1997, *Democratic Experiments in Africa: Regimes Transitions in Comparative Perspective*, Cambridge: Cambridge University Press.

Brown, D., 1999, 'Principles and Practices of Forest Co-Management: Evidence From West-Central Africa', Draft of report, Washington, DC: CARPE.

Buttel, F.H., 2002, 'Environmental Sociology and the Sociology of Natural Resources: Institutional Histories and Intellectual Legacies', *Society and Natural Resources*, No.15, pp.205–11.

Carret, J-C., 2000, 'La réforme de la Fiscalité Forestière au Cameroun: Débat Politique et Analyse Economique', *Bois et Forêts des Tropiques*, No.264, pp.37–51.

Crook, R.C. and J. Manor, 1998, *Democracy and Decentralization in South-east Asia and West Africa: Participation, Accountability, and Performance*, Cambridge: Cambridge University Press.

Dia, M., 1996, *Africa's Management in the Beyond: Reconciling Indigenous and Transplanted Institutions*, Washington, DC: The World Bank.

Diaw, M.C. and P.R. Oyono, 2001, 'Developing Collaborative Monitoring for Adaptive Co-management of Tropical African Forests. Cameroon extract', European Union Report, Yaoundé: CIFOR.

Diaw, M.C. and P.R. Oyono, 1998, 'Instrumentalité et Déficit des Itinéraires de la Décentralisation de la Gestion des Ressources Naturelles au Cameroun', *Bulletin Arbres, Forêts et Communautés Rurales*, No.15/16, pp.23–7.

Diaw, M.C., P.R. Oyono and V. Robiglio, 2001, 'Les Dimensions Sociales du Classement et de l'Aménagement des Unités Forestières de Gestion. Enseignements Théoriques sur la Démarche et l'Expérience du Projet "Forêts et Terroirs" de Dimako (Sud-Est Cameroun)', Working Paper, Yaoundé, Cameroon: CIFOR/IITA.

Djeumo, A., 2001, 'Développement des Forêts Communautaires au Cameroun: Genèse, Situation Actuelle et Contraintes', *Rural Development Network Paper 25b*, London: ODI.

Eba'a, A.R., 1998, 'Cameroon's Logging Industry: Structure, Economic Importance, Effects of Devaluation', CIFOR Occasional Paper No.14, Bogor: CIFOR.

Efoua, S., 2001, 'Statut des Forêts Communautaires de Ngola, Eschiembor/Melen, Koungoulou et Bosquet. Arrangements et processus de négociation en cours', Unpublished field report, Yaoundé, Cameroon: CIFOR.

Eggertson, T., 1990, *Economic Behavior and Institutions*, Cambridge: Cambridge University Press.

Ekoko, F., 1998, *Environmental Adjustment in Cameroon: Challenges and Opportunities for Policy Reforms in the Forest Sector*, Washington, DC: WRI.

Eoné, M.E., 2003, 'Stratégies de gestion durable des forêts communautaires de Lomié sur la base des expériences acquises par les communautés: aspects socio-économiques', Unpublished M.Sc. dissertation, Dschang, Cameroon: University of Dschang.

Essama N. and J. Gockowski, 2000, *Cameroon Forest Sector Development in a Difficult Political Economy*, Washington, DC: The World Bank.

Etoungou, P., 2003, 'Decentralization Viewed From Inside: The Implementation of Community Forests in east-Cameroon', Working Paper, Washington, DC: WRI.

Fomété, T., 2001, 'La Fiscalité Forestière et l'Implication des Communautés Locales à La Gestion Forestière au Cameroun', *Rural Development Network Paper 25b*, London: ODI.

Grindle, M. and J.W. Thomas, 1992, *Public Choice and Policy Change: The Political Economy of Reform in Developing Countries*, Baltimore, MD and London: The Johns Hopkins University Press.

Hodenthal, U., 1992, 'The Public Sphere: Models and Boundaries', in C. Calhoun (ed.), *Habermas and the Public Sphere*, Cambridge, MA: MIT Press, pp.103–46.

Joseph, R., 1992, 'Africa: The Rebirth of Political Freedom', *Journal of Democracy*, No.2, pp.11–25.

Karsenty, A., 1999a, 'Vers la fin de l'Etat forestier? Appropriation des espaces ou gestion intégrée des massifs forestiers', *Bois et Forêts des Tropiques*, Vol.251, No.1, pp.8–16.

Karsenty, A., 1999b, 'Vers la fin de l'Etat forestier? Appropriation des espaces et partage de la rente forestière au Cameroun', *Politique africaine*, No.75, pp.147–61.

Klein, M., B. Salla and J. Kok, 2001, 'Attempts to Establish Community Forests in Lomié, Cameroon', *Rural Development Forestry Network Paper 25f*, London: ODI.

Kouna, C., 2001, 'Décentralisation de la gestion forestière et développement local: Performance et "*accountabilité*" dans la gestion locale des revenus forestiers à l'Est-Cameroun', Unpublished field report, Yaoundé, Cameroon: CIFOR.

Larson, A.M., 2002, 'Natural Resources and Decentralization in Nicaragua: Are Local Governments Up to the Job?' *World Development*, Vol.30, No.1, pp.17–31.

Mahwood, P., 1983, 'Decentralization: The Concept and the Practice', in P. Mahwood (ed.), *Local Government in the Third World. Experience of Decentralization in Tropical Africa*, Chichester: John Wiley & Sons, pp.1–22.

Mala, W. and P.R. Oyono, 2003, 'Social Ecology, Self-Organizing Systems and Adaptive Practices of Natural Resource Management in the Central African Region', Paper presented at the International IUFRO Workshop on 'The Forest Science/Policy Interface in Europe, Africa and the Middle-East', Copenhagen, Denmark, 24–27 June; in review for *The Scandinavian Journal of Forestry Research.*

Mamdani, M., 1990, 'State and Civil Society in Contemporary Africa: Reconceptualizing the Birth of State Nationalism and the Defeat of Popular Movements', *Africa Development*, Vol.15, Nos.3/4, pp.47–70.

Manor, J., 2002, 'Democratic Decentralizations and the Issue of Inequity', Paper presented at the Conference on 'Decentralization and the Environment', Bellagio, Italy, 18–22 Feb.

Mapedza, E. and A. Madondo, 2002, 'Co-management in the Mafungautsi State Forest Area of Zimbabwé-What Stake for Local Communities?' Working Paper, Washington, DC, WRI.

Mbarga, N.L., 2002, 'L'exploitation des ressources forestières au Cameroun: entre raison d'Etat et raison marchande', *Enjeux*, No.12, pp.24–5.

Mendouga, L., 1998, 'La tragédie des mille francs', *Bulletin du Réseau Arbres, Forêts et Communautés Rurales*, No.15/16, pp.35–9.

Meniaud, J., 1948, 'Le Développement de l'Exploitation Forestière au Cameroun', *France Outremer*, Vol.227, No.160, pp.112–24.

Milol, A. and J.M. Pierre, 2000, 'Volet additionnel de l'audit économique et financier du secteur forestier: Impact de la fiscalité décentralisée sur le développement local et les pratiques d'utilisation des ressources forestières au Cameroun', Study report, Yaoundé, Cameroon: The World Bank.

Nguinguiri, J.C., 1997, 'Les approches contractuelles dans la gestion des écosystèmes forestiers d'Afrique centrale', Working Paper, Pointe-Noire, Congo: CORAF.

North, D.C., 1986, 'The New Institutional Economics', *Journal of Institutional and Theoretical Economics*, No.142, pp.230–37.

Overdevest, C., 2000, 'Participatory Democracy, Representative Democracy, and the Nature of Diffuse and Concentrated Interests: A Case Study of Public Involvement on a National Forest District', *Society & Natural Resources*, No.13, pp.685–96.

Oyono, P.R., 2003, 'Institutional Paralysis, Representation and Decentralized Forest Management in Cameroon: Elements of Natural Resources Sociology for Social Theory and Public Policy', Working Paper No.15, Washington, DC: WRI.

Oyono, P.R., 2002, 'Characterizing Conflicts of Access to Forest Benefits: Legal Gangterism and "Ungovernability" in Rural Cameroon', Paper prepared for the IASCP Meeting, Harare, Zimbabwe, June.

Oyono, P.R., 2001, 'Visiting Change in the Management of Tropical Forests: Systemic Review and a Transcript of Indigenous Discourse', Paper presented at 'ACM Writing Workshop', Bogor, Indonesia, Nov.

Oyono, P.R., 2000, 'L'effectivité du processus d'acquisition et de gestion des forêts communautaires et de la redevance forestière par les populations locales au Cameroun: Bilan critique et perspectives d'évolution', in P. Bigombé (ed.), *La Décentralisation de la Gestion Forestière au Cameroun: Situation Actuelle et Perspectives*, Yaoundé, Cameroon: Editions CERAD/FTPP-Cameroun/Knowledge For All, pp.35–52.

Oyono, P.R. and S. Efoua, 2001, 'Rapport de l'atelier de partage du principe de "critères et indicateurs de gestion des forêts" et d'analyse des systèmes dans le site de Lomié', Workshop report, Yaoundé, Cameroon: CIFOR.

Oyono, P.R. and L. Temple, 2003, 'Métamorphoses des organisations rurales au Cameroun et implications pour la recherche agricole et la gestion des ressources naturelles', *Revue Internationale de L'Economie Sociale*, No.288, pp.67–79.

Oyono, P.R., C. Kouna and W. Mala, 2003, 'Benefits of forests in Cameroon: Global Structure, Issues Involving Access and Decision-Making Hiccoughs', *Forest Policy and Economics* (forthcoming).

Ribot, J.C., 2003, 'Democratic Decentralization of Natural Resource. Institutionalizing Popular Participation', Policy Paper, Washington, DC: WRI.

Ribot, J.C., 2002, 'African Decentralization. Local Actors, Powers and Accountability', Democracy, Governance and Human Rights Paper No.8, Geneva: UNSRID.

Ribot, J.C., 2001a, 'Science, Use Rights and Exclusion: A History of Forestry in Francophone West Africa', Issue Paper No.104, IIED: London.

Ribot, J.C., 2001b, 'Local Actors, Powers and Accountability in African Decentralizations: A Review of Issues', Paper prepared for the International Development Research Center of Canada and the United Nations Research Institute for Social Development, Washington, DC: WRI.

Ribot, J.C., 2000, 'Decentralization, Participation, and Representation: Administrative Apartheid in Sahelian Forestry', in P.E. Peters (ed.), *Development Encounters: Sites of Participation and Knowledge*, Cambridge: Harvard University Press, pp.29–60.

Ribot, J.C., 1999, 'Représentation et pouvoirs responsables dans la gestion participative et décentralisée de l'environnement', *Unasylva*, Vol.50, No.199, pp.18–24.

Robinson, P., 1994, 'The National Conference Phenomenon in Francophone Africa', *Comparative Studies in Society and History*, No.36, pp.575–610.

Seltz, S., 1993, *Pygmées d'Afrique Centrale*, Paris: Editions Peeters/SELAF.

Schanz, M., 1914, 'Le régime forestier dans les colonies Allemandes', Hamburg: Bibliothèque Coloniale Internationale.

Scott, J., 1990, *Domination and the Arts of Resistance: Hidden Transcripts*, New Haven, CT: Yale University Press.

Smith, B.C., 1985, *Decentralization: The Territorial Dimension of the State*, London: George Allen.

Synder, R., 1992, 'Explaining Transitions from Neopatrimonial Dictatorships', *Comparative Politics*, No.24, pp.379–400.

Tiani, A-M., J. Nguiébouri and M.C. Diaw, 2001, 'Criteria and Indicators for Collaborative Monitoring and Adaptive Co-Management of Tropical Forests', *ACM News*, Vol.2, No.3, pp.4–5.

Turner, J.H., 1982, 'A Note on G.H. Mead's Behavioristic Theory of Social Structure', *Journal for The Theory of Social Behavior*, No.12, pp.213–22.

Vabi, M., C. Ngwasiri, P. Galega and P.R. Oyono, 2000, 'The Devolution of Management Responsibilities to Local Communities: Context and Implementation Hurdles in Cameroon', Working Paper, Yaoundé, Cameroon: World Wide Fund for Nature-Cameroon Program.

Verschave, F-X., 2000, *Le Silence de la Forêt: Réseaux, Mafias et Filière Bois au Cameroun*, Paris: L'Harmattan.

Wunch, J.S., 1990, 'Centralization and Development in Post-Independence Africa', in J.S. Wunch and D. Oluwu (eds.), *The Failure of the Centralized State*, Boulder, CO: Westview Press, pp.63–72.

User Committees: A Potentially Damaging Second Wave of Decentralisation?

JAMES MANOR

I. INTRODUCTION

This contribution explores the rapid and widespread proliferation of 'user committees' in less developed countries (LDCs) since the mid-1990s. These committees are said to give ordinary people at the local level some voice and influence over the implementation (and, at times, the design) of the development programmes and/or specific projects of individual government ministries.

This proliferation has reached immense proportions. One recent study stated that the 'development landscape is littered with committees … mandated as "user groups"' [*Cornwall and Gaventa, 2001: 9*]. If we consider just one type of such committees (women's self-help groups) in just one Indian state (Andhra Pradesh), fully 10,000 user committees have recently been established. When we take into account the large number of other types of committees (water user committees, watershed development committees, parent–teacher committees, health committees, forest management committees, and many more) and the large number of other countries across Asia, Africa and Latin America where many such bodies have been established, the massive scale of this trend becomes apparent. It follows a first wave that saw more than 60 governments across the LDCs and eastern/central Europe experiment with the devolution of powers and resources to elected councils at lower levels in their political systems.[1] That initial wave began in the early 1980s or in a tiny number of cases even before,[2] and is still proceeding, albeit slowly and with some reverses in very recent years. The second wave has important implications for peoples' participation and

James Manor is a Professor at the Institute of Development Studies, University of Sussex. The author is grateful to Hans Binswanger and Swaminathan Aiyar for sharing material relevant to this study, to Ruth Alsop for sharing evidence and alerting him to numerous references, and to P. Sundaram, Andrea Cornwall and Mark Robinson for useful insights.

European Journal of Development Research, Vol.16, No.1, Spring 2004, pp.192–213
ISSN 0957-8811 print
DOI:10.1080/0957881041000168806

influence, for the issue of equity, for development and for the institutions created in the first wave.

Readers will have noted the question mark at the end of the title of this contribution. It is there because it is impossible on present evidence to resolve the following three questions:

- Since (as we shall see) user committees are often quite dissimilar to the decentralised councils in the 'first wave', is it justified to describe them as a 'second wave' since those words imply that it is akin to the first?
- Since user committees are sometimes (and perhaps usually) largely controlled from above, to what extent does this new trend qualify as an example of 'decentralisation'?
- Is the proliferation of user committees 'damaging' to the first wave, and perhaps to much else? We have clear evidence that it has sometimes but not always proved damaging, but more empirical studies of specific cases are needed before we can speak with confidence about how often that has happened.

Our capacity to answer all three of these questions is limited by the shortage of solid empirical evidence on user committees.[3] This contribution should therefore be seen as a *preliminary* assessment, and as an invitation to others to undertake research in order to develop more satisfactory answers to these questions.

User committees, which go under various names – including 'user groups' and 'stakeholder committees', differ in several ways from the elected institutions created during the first wave.[4] Many of these differences will emerge in the course of this discussion, but five are worth noting here at the outset:

- *Origins*. Their creation has for the most part been driven by international donor agencies' sectoral programs, in contrast to the first wave – which (especially in the early years) was mostly undertaken by LDC governments on their own initiative; donors' interest and support emerged later [*Manor, 1999: 29–31*]. This has meant that, in numerous cases, LDC governments have been less enthusiastic about user committees' initiatives and more inclined to manipulate them in ways that donors do not intend than was true during the first wave.
- *Remits*. The institutions created in the first wave dealt with a *multiplicity* of subjects (education, health, minor roads, sanitation, women and child welfare, etc.), but most (though not all) user committees are *single-purpose* bodies.[5] A committee might deal with primary schools or forest management – to the exclusion of all else.

- *Funding*. User committees tend to be well-funded by LDC governments, often using donor funds – in contrast to elected multi-purpose councils from the first wave, which are frequently very short of resources.
- *Democratic character*. As we shall see, user committee members are often selected by less-reliably democratic means than are most elected councils at lower levels, or by undemocratic means.
- *Lifespan*. In many, though probably not most cases (we badly need evidence on this), user committees are created for a limited lifespan – for the specific period in which a time-bound project or initiative is intended to exist. This appears to dampen popular engagement with some committees, as people reckon that they will not survive long enough to justify participation. And since poorer groups tend to develop the skills, confidence and organisational capacities to participate effectively only over time, this makes it easier for prosperous groups to dominate some user committees than is true with the multi-purpose institutions created in the first wave. The latter, unlike many user committees, are usually permanent bodies that have firmer constitutional or legal status than user committees possess. For these reasons, the work of many user committees – and many of the development outcomes that result from them – appear to be less sustainable than that of elected, multi-purpose councils.

Donor enthusiasm for user committees arises in part because they enable donors to extract themselves from the often-exasperating business of micro-managing development initiatives. Yet an important part of the explanation lies in a growing (and admirable) donor belief in the importance of giving people at the grass roots greater influence over decisions that affect them. Donors believe that this will help bring people's knowledge of distinctive local conditions to bear on the implementation of projects. This is expected to make projects more sustainable because people will feel more inclined to maintain and possibly contribute funds, time and labour to projects over which they have had some say.[6] These perceptions are shared by senior figures in some LDC governments, but by no means all (or perhaps even most) – and there is far less enthusiasm for these views by government actors at *lower* levels.

The proliferation of user committees is in some respects welcome.[7] Many LDCs lack strong, extensive institutional frameworks that draw citizens into consultations with governments and with the policy process. When user committees are established in connection with government programmes, those that actually give local residents significant influence may provide such frameworks.

It is also important to stress that user committees sometimes play quite constructive roles in political systems that are heavily controlled from the top. In such cases, they may provide people at the grass roots with a very rare opportunity to assert themselves, at least to a limited degree. They may also catalyse the beginnings of autonomous civil society activity at the local level, so that a start can be made in prying open such closed political systems – at least a little. There is evidence of these trends from Vietnam, for example.[8]

However, most political systems in LDCs are not as centralised and closed as Vietnam's. In many other cases, as we shall see, the available (and still limited) evidence indicates that the working of user committees is attended by worrying problems and ambiguities that prevent the good things noted in the two preceding paragraphs from happening.

The discussion that follows begins with an assessment of the methods employed to select members of user committees, followed by a more detailed examination of those methods that at least appear to be democratic. It then considers the powers given to non-officials who become members of user committees. These are sometimes quite limited, and when that is taken together with questions about selection procedures it raises suspicions that user committees are often manipulated by LDC governments to catalyse but also to co-opt, contain and even control civil society at the local level – a topic discussed below. A dangerous myth – that user committees can somehow insulate development processes from 'politics' – is then examined. The analysis concludes with an assessment of the often-troubled relations between single-purpose user committees and the multi-purpose elected bodies created in the first wave of decentralisation, and the significant damage clearly being done in some (perhaps many) cases.

II. METHODS OF SELECTING USER COMMITTEE MEMBERS

There are three main methods by which members of user committees are selected: a) they may be composed (largely or entirely) of all persons within a particular category – those who use water for irrigation, parents of school children, etc.; b) they may be largely or wholly appointed from above, usually by officials from government line ministries.; or c) they may be selected by some sort of 'democratic' process. At times, as we shall see, two of these methods – especially the first and third – are combined. Let us briefly consider the first two of these methods, before moving on to a more detailed assessment of the use of 'democratic' means.

It is worth re-emphasising that at present we have only a preliminary and imperfect understanding of how often the three methods (or combinations thereof) are used. Two issues receive special attention in this discussion: 1) the implications of various methods for issues of equity, and, more importantly here, 2) their implications for bottom-up participation in decisions about development.

a) User Committees whose Members are Drawn from a Particular Category

Certain types of user committees are composed of people from a particular category (or persons chosen by the totality of those in such a category). All parents of school children may, as noted, be drawn onto 'education committees' or 'parent–teacher associations'. All of those who collect forest produce or who live in a forested area may be drawn onto a 'Joint Forest Management committee'. And so it goes on.

Despite the apparently neutral nature of this method of selection, some committees composed in this way tend to serve the interests of prosperous groups. This may occur because of the way eligible members of a category are defined. Water users' committees present a clear example. They are often composed not of all people who drink water but of those who use it for irrigation. Such committees usually consist of the owners of plots of irrigated land, a category that often (depending on local conditions) substantially or entirely excludes poor people.

Other types of committees selected in this way contain both prosperous and poor people – for example, those consisting of all parents of school children within a local arena. The usual practice here is to invite everyone within a category to participate, although poorer members of the category may feel too intimidated or incapable to accept or make much use of invitations – hence, prosperous groups acquire disproportionate influence within committees. The voices of poorer members of such committees may carry weight if they greatly outnumber prosperous people on them, but even where this is true the higher status and wealth and the greater self-confidence, political skills and connections of prosperous people may give them a dominant voice. In such circumstances, the poor gain little from the work of these committees, and may actually be placed at a greater disadvantage than before.[9]

Concerns about user committees' impact on equity are reinforced by one further tendency – which is apparent *no matter which* method is used to select members. Special representation for women and members of other disadvantaged groups appears to be provided far less often on user committees than on the multi-purpose decentralised bodies created in the first wave.[10]

It appears that the only situations in which the influence of poor people reliably predominates are those in which committees selected in this way consist largely or entirely of poor people. This can arise in two different ways. First, the category from which committee members come may consist, virtually entirely, of the poor. Some Joint Forest Management committees, for example, are composed of people who go into government-owned wooded areas to gather forest products for fuel or consumption, to feed their animals, or to sell for a small profit. Such people are usually almost all poor. Second, a user committee may be created in a locality where virtually the entire population is poor, so that – no matter what sort of committee is established – more or less all of its members will necessarily be impoverished. That is true, for example, of many of the local education committees created by the government in the Indian state of Madhya Pradesh (often in 'tribal' areas) to oversee new primary schools that have been created in villages that never previously had access to schools.[11]

b) User Committees whose Members are Appointed from Above

In some cases, the members of user committees are largely or entirely nominated from above, usually by low-level civil servants from line ministries[12] – the very people with whom they are to interact once the committees are formed, and over whom the committees are supposed to exercise oversight and influence. For example, a health committee at or near the local level might consist of a small number of medical personnel working there plus a larger number of residents selected by local health professionals and/or a bureaucrat from the health ministry who works at a somewhat higher level. There is often a danger that low-level bureaucrats and service providers (in this case, health professionals) may collude in the selection of members and the subsequent functioning of such committees to minimise the influence of local residents and thus to maintain practices that lead to poor service delivery.[13]

User committees constituted by appointment do not always fail to be relatively autonomous and representative,[14] but there is a serious danger that they will. Bureaucrats often prefer to give most of the seats on such committees to co-operative individuals, which weakens the capacity of committees to assert community interests. Bureaucrats also tend to select prominent local figures (usually, of course, the non-poor). These may include a few people from poorer groups, but these people rarely have much influence in such exalted company. This device might still benefit poorer groups if the power of appointment were used to ensure that poor people and their allies dominated or strongly influenced these institutions. However, while this practice is not unknown, it appears to be highly unusual.

Appointment from above leaves members beholden to bureaucrats for their places on committees. Even where this device is not intended – as it sometimes is – to co-opt prominent locals (a topic discussed later in this contribution), committee members who lack an independent mandate find it hard to take issue with higher authority.

c) User Committees Selected by 'Democratic' Methods

We badly need a careful, systematic survey of the methods used to select user committee members in various LDCs. At present, estimates are merely that – approximate reckonings. Yet it appears that in most cases, some sort of democratic or semi-democratic process is used, at least in part, to choose members. Consider, for example, a distinctly non-scientific survey, conducted by this writer, of specialists in decentralisation and natural resource management from a diversity of LDCs at a conference in early 2002 (the countries involved were Brazil, Cameroon, India, Indonesia, Mexico, Mongolia, Nepal, South Africa, Thailand, Vietnam and Zimbabwe). Respondents were asked to identify the methods employed to select members of user committees known to them. The three methods under discussion were considered: a) including all members of a particular category (or persons chosen by them); b) nomination by bureaucrats and/or politicians; and c) some sort of 'democratic' process. When two of these methods were employed simultaneously, the resultant mixed systems were placed *between* categories (a), (b) and (c). The total number of cases was 23. Of these, two did not fit within or between any of the three categories – cases in which 'traditional authorities' (African chiefs) and/or their designees provided the members of user committees.

The results of this exercise suggested that some sort of election from below is important most of the time. Ten of the remaining 21 cases fit entirely within category (c) ('democratic' processes). Three other cases entailed a mixture of category (c) and category (b) (external nomination), and two others entailed a mixture of category (c) and category (a) (membership for all within a particular group, or their chosen representatives).

At first glance, this evidence encourages the conclusion that user committees promote bottom-up input into development programmes and projects, but discussions in some depth with people who are closely involved in such processes raise doubts about this. Two questions are especially important here. First, how free and fair are such elections? Second, how much power do elected members of user committees have once they are in place? The second question is addressed in the next section of this contribution; we will now consider the first.

To examine the character of these 'elections', a colleague and I conducted discussions with members of user committees, other local residents and observers from civil society organisations who are closely involved in two Indian states – Madhya Pradesh and Karnataka.[15] Both states offer unusually promising conditions for genuine bottom-up involvement in decisions. By LDC standards, both have decidedly liberal governments. The chief ministers of both, unlike many of their counterparts in India and elsewhere, are largely uninterested in exercising top-down political control of events at the local level and genuinely enthusiastic about bottom-up participation in development projects. My interviews with both leaders elicited forceful comments about how such participation yielded better developmental outcomes than top-down approaches, and about how this was more politically advantageous for incumbent governments than attempts to control matters from on high.[16]

Interviews with leading civil servants in those state governments indicated that the chief ministers' views were widely shared in the upper reaches of both administrations.

And yet, despite these promising conditions and an extremely strong tradition in both states of free and fair elections to local councils and higher-level bodies, people at the grass roots expressed serious reservations about the character of 'elections' to user committees of all kinds. The main complaint was that 'elections' were conducted in a rather informal, cursory manner by low-level bureaucrats from the line ministries that deal with the subject to be addressed by user committees – the forest guard in the Joint Forest Management programme, the schoolteacher in the primary education sector, etc. Such 'elections' did not entail the rigorously secret ballots and independent counting of votes common in other elections in India.

It is very common – although, on present evidence, we cannot say *precisely* how common – for members to be named after a consultation of some description with those residents of a locality who happen to attend a public meeting. The names of certain persons are suggested by those attending the meeting and/or by outsiders such as low-level bureaucrats from a concerned ministry who attend and often conduct the meeting. The decisions on who is to be included in the user committee then tend to be taken by acclamation, or what is sometimes called 'consensus'.

These processes are not secret. Voters' preferences are visible to all – including powerful local figures on whom some voters are dependent and/or whom some voters have reason to fear. This can easily inhibit voters from poor and vulnerable groups from expressing their genuine preferences. Moreover, people from such groups often tend to avoid attending public meetings in the first place.[17] Where secret votes are cast, the counting tends to be done by low-level officials from the line ministries – the very people over whom the user committees are expected to exercise oversight and influence. The worry about all of this is that such processes tend to provide over-representation on user committees for elite and pliable individuals within local arenas.

In many localities, then, the result was seen to be highly dubious, with user committees being filled by persons whom low-level officials deemed preferable and amenable. Many local residents therefore believed that user committee members owed their places on committees to these officials. Even where this perception was inaccurate (as was apparently the case in some localities), the suspicion lived on and affected the working of the user committees.

Note once again that this pattern emerged in two places with a strong democratic tradition, and with senior politicians and bureaucrats – but *not* lower-level bureaucrats – firmly committed to genuine bottom-up development. In most other LDC settings, where one or both of these conditions are either absent or present in far less strength, we can surely expect similar scepticism. Where such scepticism exists, we can in turn expect user committee members to be less assertive in their dealings with low-level officials than full-blooded bottom-up development processes require.

Those in charge of constituting user committee members could of course save themselves the trouble of conducting separate 'democratic' exercises and turn to the existing (and, usually, more reliably elected) decentralised council, or a subcommittee of it, but this appears to be very unusual across the LDCs. That naturally inspires suspicions among analysts of decentralisation, and among local residents, about whether those constituting user committees are actually interested in seeing that these bodies are genuinely representative. It appears that in many cases they are not.

This is a concern that donors should take more seriously than at present. It is seldom the donors who decide to employ these inadequate methods to select members. That decision is usually taken by higher-level politicians who may be interested in packing user committees with loyalists, and/or by higher-level bureaucrats who prefer to see the committees peopled by tractable local notables. Donors are too often content with assurances from those in LDC governments that the processes are 'participatory' and 'transparent'. In reality, the participation is often seriously constrained, and the main thing that is transparent is the vote of a poor person – which goes a long way towards negating his or her freedom of choice.

It may be unrealistic to expect user committee members to be elected through processes that are as elaborate as those used to choose members of local councils, with (often) careful, elaborate and expensive provisions to ensure the secrecy of ballots and the impartiality of vote-counting. Yet there is an easy way to mitigate the damage to participatory development that follows from this. User committees could be placed under the influence or control of local councils that have been elected by more reliable methods (a topic discussed in detail in the final section below). This would ensure that properly elected representatives have significant leverage over decisions by user committees, and thereby erode the heavy influence or dominance that line ministry officials often retain (see the next section of this contribution).

However, LDC governments, and indeed donors, are reluctant to go down this road. In a few places, local councils enjoy some influence over user committees and the low-level line ministry officials with whom they work. Occasionally, subject-specific subcommittees of local councils (dealing with education, health, forestry, sanitation, etc.) have simply become the user committee for that subject. This is particularly useful when some seats on the local council have been reserved for members of socially excluded groups, such as women and perhaps members of other disadvantaged groups. In most cases, though, such arrangements have not been adopted (and such reservations on user committees are, as noted above, unusual). Line ministry officials, who usually operate separately from officials overseeing local government systems and are usually relatively or wholly free of influence by local councils, prefer user committees that stand at one level removed from elected, multi-purpose local councils. This creates a discontinuity between general-purpose local councils and single-purpose user committees. And despite some overlap in membership between the two bodies in many cases, this gives rise to the serious problems identified in the last section of this contribution.

III. THE POWERS OF NON-OFFICIAL MEMBERS OF USER COMMITTEES

Let us now turn to the question of how much influence non-officials who become members of user committees can exercise once they are selected. We should first note that the powers supposedly bestowed on such committees vary from case to case. Some of them are not granted any significant powers even in theory; others are assigned the task of selecting beneficiaries of programmes or projects – a rather limited role. In other cases, however, user committees are explicitly given powers to influence the implementation of policies or (most generously of all) both design and implementation. Yet even where that occurs, the formal 'remit of these committees generally remains confined to ensuring the efficiency of delivery rather than to give citizens more of a voice in determining the kinds of services they want or need' [*Cornwall and Gaventa, 2001: 10*]. At present, we have little evidence on the number of committees that fall into these various categories (research is urgently needed here).

There is, however, a good deal of scattered evidence to indicate that powers granted in theory often fail to materialise in practice. We saw above that when elections are heavily managed by line ministry bureaucrats – in full view of large numbers of local residents – it encourages the (often accurate) impression that user committee members owe their posts to the people whom they are meant to oversee and influence. This makes it very difficult for these members to play a critical, questioning, assertive role in user committees.

In some cases (it is impossible to say how many on present, fragmentary evidence), bureaucrats who are pressed hard by governments to form large numbers of user committees 'form' some of them on paper but not in reality. This has occurred in Andhra Pradesh state in India [*see also Baviskar, this volume*].[18]

When user committees are real, as is usually the case, government officials often extend only limited powers to their members. Evidence from Africa and India indicates that user committees often lack the power to set or amend agendas for meetings. They are also frequently denied much in the way of discretionary power. It appears to be quite unusual for them to have any influence over the *design* of programmes and even small projects, and many also lack the power to alter the *implementation* of projects so that they conform to distinctive local conditions and thus yield better developmental outcomes.[19] Indeed, sometimes user committees are not even briefed on what their powers and functions supposedly are [*Poffenberger and McGean, 1996*]. The frustration that all of this provokes among committee members sometimes causes attendance at meetings to decline [*see, for example, Veerashekharappa, 2000*].

The result of all of these restrictions is user committees that are often 'simply cosmetic, and tokenistic'; 'By denying people the agency to make choices outside the frame of reference afforded by their role in these programmes and by overlooking the complexity of relations of power between service providers and community members ... they operate with a very limited conception of "participation"' [*Cornwall and Gaventa, 2001: 11–12*].

We need to consider one other important factor in determining the varied degree to which governments in general and the low-level government employees with whom user committees must deal tend to pursue top-down control: the specific sector or sub-field with which the committee deals. There are at least three strands to this.

The first is less important than the latter two, but it still makes some impact. The traditional roles played by low-level government employees vary from sector to sector. For example, schoolteachers and health professionals have long been trained to act as sympathetic servants of citizens. This does not prevent many of them in LDCs from shirking their duties, but it is part of their self-image nonetheless. By contrast, low-level employees of forest services have traditionally been cast in a role akin to policemen or gamekeepers. Their relationship with local residents has been adversarial: they have been given the task of preventing citizens from intruding upon forests and making off with forest products to use as fuel, fodder, etc. In recent times, all of these varied types of government employees have been pressed to develop partnerships with local residents that at least theoretically enable the latter to participate in decision-making – often through user committees. It is far easier for teachers and health professionals to make this transition than for people like forest guards, since the traditional relationships of the former with citizens are much less adversarial than those of the latter.[20]

Second, and more importantly, governments and their employees tend to be more inclined to sustain top-down approaches when the sectors in which they work yield significant financial resources to governments, government actors and/or powerful private interests. Here again, the forest sector is a prime example. Governments often gain substantial revenues from taxation on logging or from the sale of forest products, including timber. It is, of course, well known that private interests frequently profit massively from logging – often pursued illegally in concert with corrupt governments or their employees. In such circumstances, governments and individuals are exceedingly reluctant to see forest user committees curtail their traditional incomes, and top-down approaches tend to survive as a result. In the primary education sector, by contrast, governments and their employees derive little or no financial benefit, so when top-down approaches persist in that sector, as they sometimes do, considerations of revenue and profit seldom loom large.

Third, top-down approaches tend to survive more often in technologically and technocratically complex sectors than in sectors that are simpler to manage. This point, and, to a degree, the second point noted above, is illustrated by a comparison of various sub-fields of the natural resource management sector.[21] The participants at the 2002 Bellagio Conference on 'Decentralisation and the Environment', most of whom are environmental specialists, generated the outline of various sub-fields and the practices that often develop within them displayed in Table 1.[22]

One last mitigating comment is in order here. Even when non-official members of user committees (or the committees themselves) have little power, they can still perform one useful function. Committee members who develop an understanding of government programmes are usually able to explain them more effectively to local people (their neighbours) in local arenas than can bureaucrats. This sometimes yields positive results. Committee members can,

TABLE 1

SUB-FIELDS OF DECENTRALISATION AND ASSOCIATED PRACTICES

Sub-field	Likely degree of top-down intervention
Watershed management (including soil erosion control)	High, because of technological complexity.
Irrigation systems (large)	Usually high, because of a perceived need for strong central control or at least co-ordination.
Irrigation systems (small, medium to low)	More bottom-up collaboration possible.
Wildlife	Medium, because governments nearly always organise or run a protection agency.
Forest management	Variations, but usually high when forest products yield (a) major profits for private interests and/or government actors, and/or (b) major government revenues.
Grasslands	Low (with some variations), owing to the comparative simplicity of the management of the sub-field.

for example, explain how pre- and post-natal care will benefit mothers and children in language that local people can grasp – so that the uptake on such programmes increases. This helps both the poor and the non-poor, but it fails to compensate fully for the problems identified above.

User Committees as a Means to Catalyse but also to Co-opt Civil Society

User committees, like other forms of decentralisation, catalyse civil society at the grass roots. When fresh powers and funds are injected into lower-level arenas, as is usually the case with user committees, residents within those arenas discern this and respond by becoming more active in order to influence the use of those powers and resources. Members of existing voluntary associations become more active, those associations acquire new members, and new associations emerge.

Some LDC leaders and many donors recognise this and see it as a welcome by-product of the change in policy because they see a more vibrant civil society as desirable in itself and as a means to deepen democracy and generate better developmental outcomes. Yet even when high-level leaders in LDCs take this view, their enthusiasm tends not be shared by officials in line ministries, especially at *lower* levels in bureaucratic hierarchies. Low-level bureaucrats see a more assertive civil society as a threat to their autonomy. They therefore often seek to curtail the influence of voluntary associations and user committees by employing methods that co-opt these committees so that their control of development processes survives.

In many cases, senior leaders (politicians and civil servants) in LDCs share this desire with bureaucrats at lower levels. This is especially true (as noted above) when the activities with which user committees deal yield profits to private and/or government actors, when they yield significant revenues to governments, or when the subjects are technocratically complex – but not only then. Such senior figures know that they must create user committees in order to obtain donor funds, but they also know that there are ways to manipulate these processes so that the co-optation, containment and even substantial control of committees and of civil society organisations result. On the present limited evidence, they appear quite capable of succeeding in their efforts.

This poses a serious danger to the legitimacy and popularity of governments in LDCs. When decentralisation stimulates increased efforts at participation by citizens (because it appears to offer fresh opportunities to influence matters that affect their well-being), and they then discover that those opportunities are largely illusory, they react with renewed exasperation and cynicism about government (see for example, the case of Ghana in Crook and Manor [*1999: Ch.5*]). Such cynicism can deepen when user committees are required to levy user fees for public services. Senior leaders (and, more often, low-level bureaucrats) pursue this approach at their peril.

IV. THE MYTH THAT USER COMMITTEES CAN INSULATE DEVELOPMENT FROM POLITICS

When user committees are discussed, we sometimes hear it said that it is important to ensure that they are insulated from 'politics'. This view is often expressed by senior and junior civil servants in LDCs (this writer has encountered it in Zambia, South Africa, Bangladesh and numerous Indian states), and less often by politicians. It is also found within some international development agencies, especially among economists. It is also not unknown in academic circles (where economists again stand out) and in some international non-governmental associations (where non-economists appear to provide the main body of believers).

This notion is a myth – and a dangerous myth at that. 'Politics', that is, the interplay of interests and forces in pursuit of power, resources, status, etc., is pervasive. A user committee may be thoroughly sealed off from interest groups in a society, and from other arenas and institutions in a political system. Yet the pursuit of power and resources will still occur among those with some leverage within it, and among individuals and groups outside it who seek some influence over it. If bureaucrats arrange things so that they exercise all or most of the leverage within a user committee, they are not excluding 'politics' from it. Rather, they are ensuring that they dominate the 'politics' within it.

The choice facing governments and societies is not between including or excluding 'politics' from certain arenas, but between different types of 'politics' that inevitably pervade all arenas. It entails in part a choice between top-down, 'commandist' 'politics' and bottom-up, participatory 'politics' – a central issue in the case of user committees and of decentralised systems more generally. When middle- and low-level bureaucrats and/or politicians sustain predominantly top-down approaches, they sometimes do so in collaboration with prosperous groups at the local level for mutual gain. When that is true, they do not insulate the administration from grass-roots 'politics'; rather, they intrude into local 'politics' and reinforce the influence of powerful interests there in order to benefit themselves.

Yet many people continue to cling to the myth. Some do so out of naivety, while others do so out of cynicism. These two things are in many ways opposites, but they produce very similar results.

The evidence currently available suggests that cynicism is a good deal more common than naivety. When cynical officials speak of insulating user committees from 'politics', they are dignifying efforts to sustain or extend commandism. What they really mean is that they are insulating them from participation from below, or indeed from democracy. That was, for example, clearly the view of the head of an important Zambian line ministry, speaking in 2001 to a conclave of his colleagues from other ministries (attended by this writer). He said that he favoured nominating user committee members from above because this would ensure that they consisted of sophisticated and co-operative people who would not create trouble. He characterised this as insulating the committees from the 'politics' of Zambia's largely powerless elected local councils. His colleagues voiced their agreement, even though the purpose of the conference was to strengthen local democracy.[23] Very similar views were expressed on this subject in the Indian state of Andhra Pradesh by the civil servant who oversees that state's system of elected local councils.[24] These are by no means isolated cases.

V. RELATIONS BETWEEN USER COMMITTEES AND ELECTED DECENTRALISED COUNCILS

The proliferation of user committees, most of which are single-purpose bodies, has (it appears) often had a damaging impact on elected multi-purpose bodies created in the first wave of decentralisation. This need not have happened and, as we shall see presently, the trend might still be reversed, but the ways in which many LDC governments have managed user committees – at times with donor encouragement – have caused it to happen. Where that is true, user committees may have had some beneficial effects, but their overall impact on democratic decentralisation has been negative.

The damage takes several forms. User committees often produce *confusion* and *dislocation*. This occurs in part simply because in a particular place, a user committee operates at a different *level* from an elected local council – it might cover a cluster of villages while a local council exists for each individual village, or vice versa. There is also often confusion about overlapping *jurisdictions* of the two types of bodies if, as often happens, both are given responsibility for a particular subject like sanitation, primary education, forests, etc.

Much more damage is done when user committees *usurp roles* and *functions* that had previously been *assigned* to elected multi-purpose councils. On occasion (it is not clear how often), they also *deprive them of revenues*, even though user committees are usually well-funded while local councils are strapped for resources.

Readers might wonder why LDC governments that have created local councils should disempower them in this way. There are two main answers. First, in virtually every country, some politicians at higher levels – typically legislators – resent the loss of powers and resources to decentralised bodies and urge national leaders to claw them back. They sometimes get results. Second, lower-level bureaucrats seize the opportunity provided by the creation of user committees to erode the power of elected members of multi-purpose councils whom they regard as unlettered rustics with too much influence – whether or not higher-level leaders wish this to occur.

Evidence on usurpation emerges mainly from field research by this writer in South Asia and Southern and Central Africa, and from numerous interviews with social scientists and development agency officials who have knowledge of other cases. There are also, though, studies by one of the few organisations to examine relations between user committees and multi-purpose councils – the Indian NGO Participatory Research in Asia (PRIA). It found that water user groups in the huge state of Uttar Pradesh had usurped local councils' role as overseers of water projects [*PRIA, 2001b: 7*].[25] In Gujarat state, Joint Forest Management user committees had deprived village councils of their legally mandated supervision of forest products – and of the not insubstantial income from their sale [*PRIA, 2001b: 7*], something that appears to have happened in a great many Indian states. And in the state of Haryana, bodies very like user committees that dealt with local construction projects have taken over functions that (again by law) had been given to multi-purpose local councils [*PRIA, 2001a: 9, 13*]. PRIA's [*2001a*] research, together with interviews in other Indian states by this writer, indicate that such displacement of multi-purpose decentralised councils has occurred in several other sectors.

We have noted that user committees usually have more, often far more, money than do multi-purpose councils [*see, for example, PRIA, 2001b, 7, 12–13; Mohanty, n.d.: 13*]. In some (and, apparently, many) cases, this produces a *destructive paradox*. Local councils are expected to perform tasks for which they lack adequate funds – so that they are crippled by *unfunded* or *badly underfunded* mandates. And yet in the same localities, user committees have such an over-abundance of funds that they cannot manage them effectively – they face *excessively funded* mandates. This situation of feast and famine, side by side in the same place creates huge problems, not only for relations between the two types of bodies but also for constructive development outcomes.

All of these problems tend to create destructive conflicts between the two types of bodies even where senior politicians do not set user committees against multi-purpose councils, as they sometimes do. To say this is *not* to argue that increased conflict within local arenas is always a bad thing. Certain kinds of conflict are essential if pre-existing hierarchies, inequalities and patterns of social exclusion are to be challenged – as they should be. But the kinds of conflicts that often arise between user committees and elected multi-purpose bodies tend strongly *not* to lend themselves to such challenges. Indeed, they undermine them, often by reinforcing the exclusion, especially of women and also of other disadvantaged groups – a point on which there is abundant evidence [*Agarwal, 1998; Cleaver, 1997; Mehra and Esim, 1997; Meinzen-Dick and Zwarteveen, 1997; Mehta, 1997; Mosse, 1997; Poffenberger and McGean 1998; Vettivel, 1992; World Bank, 1998: Ch.4*].

This raises questions about an important and for the most part valid argument long advanced by Norman Uphoff. He has repeatedly stressed the utility of providing local residents (not least the poor) with multiple channels through which to engage with governments. User committees, which are placed alongside elected, multi-purpose local bodies and pre-existing bureaucratic structures, clearly constitute new channels for people at the grass roots. This may at times produce benefits for local residents, but the dislocation and conflicts noted above often appear to outweigh any such benefits.

Indeed, in addition to all of the problems identified above, the creation of user committees often *fragments* popular participation, making it less coherent and effective (this point is suggested by Mohanty [*n.d.: 15*]). Part of the problem is that people are often drawn into user committees that lack real power, and their time and energy is sapped in vain attempts to make an impact, often in single sectors, so that their capacity to engage in other, more promising, areas of governance is undermined. The fragmentation of popular participation sometimes (and perhaps often) occurs in ways that undermines the influence of poorer, low-status groups [*see, for example, Jairath, 2001: 15*]. That is surely not what donors intended when they pressed for user committees.

Integration

These problems could have been greatly eased if the two waves of decentralisation had been *integrated*. User committees could have been linked to and placed under the control or strong influence of multi-purpose elected councils, or made organic parts of those councils.[26] Indeed, this remains an option. Donors are quite capable of seeing the utility of integration. For example, a World Bank report stressed precisely this, and noted correctly that subject-specific subcommittees of multi-purpose local councils (a common feature) already amount to user committees [*World Bank, 1999*]. Unfortunately, many (and probably most) donor loans – especially, but not only, for sectoral programmes – make it more, not less difficult for integration to take place.[27]

To recommend integration is not to claim that members and leaders of elected multi-purpose councils always behave in exemplary ways. They plainly do not. If they do err, though, their constituents have the option of registering their displeasure at (and indeed before) the next election. The frequency with which incumbents have been voted out in a great many LDCs indicates that this check on misbehaviour has substance.[28]

The integration of user committees and elected multi-purpose councils is patently feasible. We have clear evidence of this from the Indian state of Madhya Pradesh. The government there has turned user committees that deal with single sectors into single-subject subcommittees of village governments (which in that state means village councils plus mass meetings that deliberate on decisions). In so doing, it has simplified matters and streamlined the local decision-making process. Instead of having two different local institutions that are likely to come into conflict because they duplicate labour (for example, a parent–teacher user committee with plenty of funds alongside a penniless education subcommittee of the village council making decisions with no practical effect), the two are fused. There is thus no confusion about what body is responsible for decisions in any given sector and no risk that conflict between the two bodies will occur, or that the weaker of the two will lose legitimacy and credibility.

It should be stressed that one device sometimes used under the name of integration does more harm than good. In some places, Uganda for example, separate parallel bodies for women (and occasionally, young people) are created alongside multi-purpose councils – and function very like user committees for these groups. The clear danger here is that such a policy 'hives off women's concerns into a political cul-de-sac' [*Brock et al., 2002: 43*]. The reservation of a percentage of seats on multi-purpose councils for women does not always guarantee that they will have significant influence. They are often wilfully excluded from influence (and occasionally even from the councils[29]) by males. Yet there is also evidence from several countries – not least India – that, over time, women members develop the confidence and skills needed to assert themselves at least somewhat effectively [*Crook and Manor, 1999: 40–42, 78*].

If such approaches are avoided, the integration of user committees and elected, multi-purpose councils would reduce or eradicate most of the problems listed above and several difficulties that have recently caused concern at the World Bank.[30] Let us consider these in a little detail.

- Integrating user committees with multi-purpose councils would ease worries about dubious 'elections' to user committees, since council elections are usually conducted in more reliable ways. They are by no means perfect, but they are usually far more satisfactory than the methods employed with user committees. More reliable elections enhance the likelihood of a transition to a system in which accountability upwards (to bureaucrats) is matched by accountability downwards (to voters). User committees are often manipulated and dominated by bureaucrats, and, when that happens, it reinforces the predominance of upward accountability.
- Integration would ease one of the most crippling problems faced by multi-purpose councils in most countries – their inadequate funds; user committees tend to be generously resourced.

- It would help overcome the isolation of local communities both from each other and from higher levels in the political system. User committees on their own usually do little to tackle this problem because they are themselves cut off from similar bodies elsewhere. Integrating them with multi-purpose councils could help in two ways. 1) Local councils are usually linked into national systems of such councils (often including councils at higher levels) – systems through which information about problems and successes in specific local arenas often flows readily to other localities and upward. (Most user committees have to rely on low-level bureaucrats to transmit such information, and such bureaucrats are frequently hostile and manipulative and do not co-operate.) 2) Local council leaders often belong to relatively independent national or regional associations of council chairpersons, which enhance their confidence, collective influence and the flow of information among them. (There are seldom counterpart associations for user group leaders.)
- Within a single local arena, user committees also tend to be somewhat cut off from one another. This tends to fragment both the local community and various local development initiatives. If they were integrated with multi-purpose local councils, their isolated pursuit of development projects would be more effectively co-ordinated by leaders of those councils – indeed, co-ordination is one area where such councils excel. Even when multi-purpose councils function imperfectly, they tend to draw government employees from several different line ministries together to discuss projects in a single sector – so that the outcomes from such projects improve. (A plan for a fish pond profits from consultations with not only the fisheries specialist, but also the irrigation specialist, the sanitation specialist and the government engineer; see, for evidence from Bangladesh, Crook and Manor [*1999: Ch.3*].) Single-sector user committees often impede such co-ordination.
- Integration can also ease the problem of accountability to various donor agencies being Balkanised. This tends to occur when each donor supports a programme in a different sector and insists on the creation of a separate user committee to oversee its programme in each locality. Here, again, the tendency for multi-purpose councils to achieve greater inter-sectoral co-ordination produces benefits.
- Integration can also reduce the danger that narrow interests in a locality may keep important information to themselves, decide on projects that benefit them more than the whole community, and exclude some sections of the community from the implementation and monitoring of projects. When they operate in isolation, some user committees make these problems worse because they represent a limited subset of the whole community.

- Integrating user committees with multi-purpose councils can also ease the difficulties that low-level bureaucrats and community representatives have in working together. Bureaucrats and members of multi-purpose councils that have existed for several years have often begun – uneasily but substantially – to establish working relationships in which each side accommodates a little.

Despite all of this, few LDC governments are inclined to adopt a policy of integration. Their reluctance owes something to donors' naive enthusiasm for a discrete set of user committees for each developmental sector. Yet it also suggests that LDC governments are either unaware of the damage that is being done to democratic decentralisation or content (and in some cases eager) to see it occur.

NOTES

1. We need to recognise that some user committees existed prior to the 'first wave' of democratic decentralisation. The point here is that their *proliferation* has mainly occurred *since* the 'first wave' became well established.
2. For example, the government in the Indian state of West Bengal was active on this front in the late 1970s.
3. Later notes in this contribution refer to some of the often-valuable work that is currently available, but there is clearly a need for a great deal more. Consider, for example, accessible World Bank documents, identified by searching the World Bank website using the terms 'user committees' and 'stakeholder committees'. Roughly half of the documents that emerge deal with such committees located wholly or mainly at *higher* levels in political systems, often in connection with consultations about Poverty Reduction Strategy Papers. The rest deal with lower-level committees, the concern of this contribution (which, in some cases, are an aspiration and not yet a reality), in a diversity of countries – India, Bangladesh, Nepal, Malawi, Tuvalu, etc. Most simply state that user committees have been or ought to be established. The repetition of the same phrases about such committees in World Bank documents on diverse topics – they 'meet periodically, elect functionaries, assign tasks ...' etc. – indicates the incorporation of these institutions into Bank orthodoxy. But only limited analysis is available at present. Ruth Alsop at the World Bank is doing research on such committees in India, but her final findings are not yet available.
4. During the first wave, some exercises in decentralisation lacked democratic content. The discussion of the first wave here focuses on those *with* some sort of democratic content – which is to say, the large majority of cases.
5. Some bodies – most notably self-help groups, but also watershed committees – are intended to have an impact in multiple sectors. I am grateful to P. Sundaram for stressing this point.
6. It should also be said, however, that some donors *expect* people to make contributions, especially of funds. I am grateful to Andrea Cornwall for stressing this point.
7. For countervailing evidence to some of the points made in this contribution, see for example, Kumar *et al.* [*2000a, b*].
8. I am grateful to Elizabeth McColl of UNDP for this information.
9. I am grateful to Christopher Colclough for stressing this point.
10. This comment is based in part on discussions with social scientists and donor agency officials who focus on Africa and Latin America [*on India, see PRIA, 2001a: 1; 2001b: 11*].
11. These comments are based on this writer's interviews with knowledgeable people in that state in 2000, 2002 and 2003.

12. Politicians and civil servants at higher levels also occasionally play a role in the nominating process.
13. I am grateful to Andrea Cornwall for this point.
14. There is, for example, evidence from Malawi of appointed committees being 'relatively autonomous and relatively representative'. I am grateful to Joyce Stanley of the United Nations Capital Development Fund for this information.
15. I am grateful to Anand Inbanathan for input on Karnataka, and to the New Delhi office of SIDA for enabling us to pursue this investigation in 2002. In Madhya Pradesh, the non-governmental organisations (NGOs) Samarthan and Participatory Research in Asia (PRIA) provided crucial assistance.
16. Interviews with S.M. Krishna, Bangalore, 14 October, 2001, and Digvijay Singh, Bhopal, 28 April, 2002.
17. This has been documented in a study of this process in another Indian state – Uttaranchal [*Mohanty, n.d.: 9*].
18. I am grateful to Benjamin Powis for this information.
19. These comments are based on interviews with decentralisation specialists from five African countries, and on research in five Indian states by Anand Inbanathan, Benjamin Powis and myself, all in 2001–3 [see also *Farrington, Turton and James, 1999; Poffenberger and McGean, 1996; Saxena, 2000*].
20. Despite this, specialists in the study of primary education tend to regard parent–teacher associations in LDCs as largely 'regressive' – that is, they tend to benefit prosperous groups more than the poor. This occurs because prosperous parents often make greater voluntary contributions to local schools, which gives them greater leverage than poorer parents – especially as prosperous parents have the confidence, skills and connections to assert themselves more effectively. Moreover, where fees are charged, some poorer parents cannot afford to send children to school. I am grateful to Christopher Colclough for stressing this point.
21. I am grateful to Robin Mearns for initially stressing this point.
22. I owe this to the team of specialists who gathered at Bellagio, Italy in January 2002 to discuss decentralisation and natural resource management.
23. The conference took place just outside Lusaka on 7 March 2001.
24. These remarks were made in an interview with Benjamin Powis in Hyderabad in early 2002.
25. The authors were drawing upon research by a partner NGO, SKK in Lucknow.
26. We have evidence of the success of this sort of arrangement from some African countries. In these cases a user committee has handled tasks 'delegated to it by the local council' – and operated as an entity 'dominated by community interests, to plan, supervise the implementation of and eventually run, the community assets being created'. Clear benefits followed. I am grateful to Ronald McGill of the United Nations Capital Development Fund for this information.
27. I am grateful to P. Sundaram for stressing this point.
28. Communications from two different field representatives of the United Nations Capital Development Fund illustrate this point. Joyce Stanley rightly expressed concern about members and leaders of elected local councils behaving constructively, but Ronald McGill noted that when user committees were made subordinate to local councils the arrangement worked very well.
29. Joyce Stanley informs me that this has occurred, for example, in parts of Uganda.
30. I draw here on recent work by Hans Binswanger and Swaminathan Aiyar.

REFERENCES

Agarwal, B., 1998, 'Environmental Management, Equity and Ecofeminism: Debating India's Experience', *Journal of Peasant Studies*, Vol.25, No.4.

Brock, K., R. McGee and R. Ssewakiryanga, 2002, *Poverty Knowledge and Public Processes: A Case Study of Ugandan National Poverty Reduction Policy*, Brighton: Institute of Development Studies.

Cleaver, F., 1997, 'Gendered Incentives and Informal Institutions: Women, Men, and the Management of Water', in 'Gender Analysis and Reform of Irrigation Management: Concepts,

Cases and Gaps in Knowledge, Proceedings of the Workshop on Gender and Water', 15–19 Sept., Harbana, Sri Lanka.

Cornwall, A. and J. Gaventa, 2001, *From Users and Choosers to Makers and Shakers: Repositioning Participation in Social Policy*, Brighton: IDS Working Paper No.127.

Crook, R. and J. Manor, 1999, *Democratisation and Decentralisation in South Asia and West Africa: Participation, Accountability and Performance*, Cambridge: Cambridge University Press.

Farrington, J., C. Turton and A.J. James (eds.), 1999, *Participatory Watershed Development: Challenges for the Twenty-First Century*, Delhi: Oxford University Press.

Jairath, J., 2001, *Water User Associations in Andhra Pradesh – Initial Feedback*, New Delhi: Centre for Economic and Social Studies/Concept Publishing.

Kumar, M.D., V. Ballabh and J. Talati, 2000a, 'Augmenting or Dividing? Surface Water Management in the Water Scarce River Basin of Sabarmati', Working Paper No.147, Anand, Gujarat: Institute of Rural Management.

Kumar, M.D., V. Ballabh, R. Pandey and J. Talati, 2000b, 'Sustainable Development and Use of Water Resources: Sadguru's Macro-Initiatives in Local Water Harnessing and Management', Working Paper No.150, Anand, Gujarat: Institute of Rural Management.

Manor, J., 1999, *The Political Economy of Democratic Decentralization*, Washington, DC: The World Bank.

Mehra, R. and S. Esim, 1997, 'What Gender Analysis Can Contribute to Irrigation Research and Practice in Developing Countries: Some Issues', in 'Gender Analysis and Reform of Irrigation Management: Concepts, Cases and Gaps in Knowledge. Proceedings of the Workshop on Gender and Water', 15–19 Sept., Harbana, Sri Lanka.

Mehta, L., 1997, 'Social Difference and Water Resource Management: Insights from Kutch, India', *IDS Bulletin*, Vol.28, No.4.

Meinzen-Dick, R. and M. Zwarteveen, 1997, 'Gender Participation in Water Management: Issues and Illustrations from Water Users' Associations in South Asia', in 'Gender Analysis and Reform of Irrigation Management: Concepts, Cases and Gaps in Knowledge. Proceedings of the Workshop on Gender and Water', 15–19 Sept., Harbana, Sri Lanka.

Mohanty, R., n.d., 'Village Level Institution as Forum for Community Participation in Development: Experiences from Doon Valley Integrated Watershed Management Project', New Delhi: PRIA.

Mosse, D., 1997, 'The Symbolic Making of a Common Property Resource: History, Ecology, and Locality in a Tank-irrigated Landscape in South India', *Development and Change*, Vol.28, No.3.

Poffenberger, M., and B. McGean (eds.), 1996, *Village Voices Forest Choices: Joint Forest Management in India*, Delhi: Oxford University Press.

PRIA (Participatory Research in Asia), 2001a, *Participation and Governance*, New Delhi: PRIA, July.

PRIA, 2001b, *Parallel Bodies and Panchayati Raj Institutions (Experiences from the States)*, New Delhi: PRIA.

Saxena, R., 2000, 'Joint Forest Management in Gujarat: Policy and Managerial Issues', Working Paper No.149, Anand, Gujarat: Institute of Rural Management, Aug.

Veerashekharappa, 2000, 'Reforms in Rural Drinking Water Supply', *Economic and Political Weekly*, 12–18 Feb.

Vettivel, S.K., 1992, *Community Participation: Empowering the Poorest – Roles of* NGOs, New Delhi: Vetri Publishers.

World Bank, 1999, *Rural Water Supply and Sanitation*, New Delhi: Allied Publishers, South Asia Rural Development Series.

World Bank, 1998, *The World Bank Participation Sourcebook*, Washington, DC: The World Bank, Ch.4.

Decentralising Water Resource Management in Brazil

CHRISTIAN BRANNSTROM

I. INTRODUCTION

Decentralisation 'has quietly become a fashion of our time' because it is seen as a means to trim power from corrupt central governments, encourage use of local knowledge, deepen democracy and make government less costly [*Manor, 1999: 1*]. Multilateral organisations such as the World Bank often encourage or require decentralised governance of healthcare, education and natural-resource management in developing countries. The belief that 'greater participation in public decision-making is a positive good in itself or that it can improve efficiency, equity, development, and resource management' supports decentralised governance [*Agrawal and Ribot, 1999: 475*]. Decentralised governance has become extremely popular for forests, wildlife and water in several developing countries [*Alexander and McGregor, 2000; Gray, 2002; Guerrero, 2000; Kaimowitz et al., 1998; Kull, 2002; Larson, 2002; Logan and Mosley, 2002; Ribot, 2002; Sekhar, 2000*].

In Brazil, the state pursues decentralisation by transferring powers of management and decision-making over defined policy areas to lower levels of government, such as municipal councils, or to stakeholder committees. To whom are these decentralised groups accountable? On the issue of accountability, the literature has distinguished between decentralised groups accountable to local populations and to higher levels of government.

Christian Brannstrom is Assistant Professor in the Department of Geography, Texas A&M University. Research for this contribution was done for the Watermark Project, which received funding from the Hewlett Foundation and the MacArthur Foundation; grants from the Hewlett Foundation and Central Research Fund of the University of London to the Institute of Latin American Studies (University of London) also supported field research. Margaret Keck, Rebecca Abers, Hugo de Souza Dias, Jussara Lima de Carvalho, José Augusto Leandro, James Clarke and Mariana Newport assisted in various stages of research. The author is also grateful to Jesse Ribot's invitation to the 'Workshop on Decentralisation and the Environment' held at the Bellagio Conference Centre, Italy, in February 2002, and Anne Larson, Wendy Jepson and an anonymous reviewer for comments on earlier versions of this essay.

European Journal of Development Research, Vol.16, No.1, Spring 2004, pp.214–234
ISSN 0957-8811 print
DOI:10.1080/09578810410001688815

In democratic decentralisation, mechanisms exist for citizens, grass-roots movements, the media and the judiciary to hold decentralised groups accountable. Active participation of municipal governments is thought to be one of the best ways to increase downward accountability and encourage democratic decentralisation, thus producing superior equity and efficiency. By contrast, administrative decentralisation (or deconcentration) makes committees or councils upwardly accountable to higher levels of government. Thus, decentralised groups may remain disconnected from local populations and elected local governments. The state may only establish regional offices staffed by appointed officials who are accountable to headquarters rather than to local populations [*Agrawal and Ribot, 1999; Ribot, 2002*].

Since the mid-1990s 'single-issue user groups' have dominated a 'second wave' of decentralisation, taking over from a 'first' wave of multiple-issue groups. Single-issue groups focus on one concern, such as water, while multi-purpose groups take on several policy areas. Single-issue user groups may work in parallel with or in contradiction to multi-purpose groups. In addition, single-issue groups may be formed by appointments rather than democratic elections, becoming less downwardly accountable to local populations than multi-purpose groups. Watershed committees formed by water users are especially susceptible to top-down intervention through highly technical jargon and debates. For these reasons, single-issue groups are 'potentially damaging' to decentralisation and thus should be subordinated to multi-purpose councils [*Manor, this volume*].

In this contribution I examine how the participation of municipalities in single-issue user groups affects outcomes of decentralisation. Does participation of municipalities create downward accountability as expected? Will the predicted negative consequences of single-issue user groups override the expected positive benefits of downward accountability? Using three cases of decentralised water resource governance in Brazil (Figure 1),[1] I argue that claims stressing both the importance of municipalities in democratic decentralisation and the negative effects of single-issue groups may be overstated. Downward accountability mechanisms depend more on the characteristics of existing social and business groups and established rules encouraging (or discouraging) participation in decentralised groups. Civil society groups have responded positively to the new territories created by single-issue decentralisation, encouraging downward accountability.

Brazil makes for an illustrative case study of decentralisation using municipalities within single-issue groups for water management. Not only do Brazilian municipalities have significant fiscal and political power but they also have formed powerful inter-municipal consortia considered the strongest in Latin America [*Nickson, 1995: 120–30*]. Municipalities are also significant

FIGURE 1
STUDY CATCHMENTS (GRANDE, SOROCABA-MÉDIO TIETÊ AND TIBAGI VALLEYS) IN BRAZIL

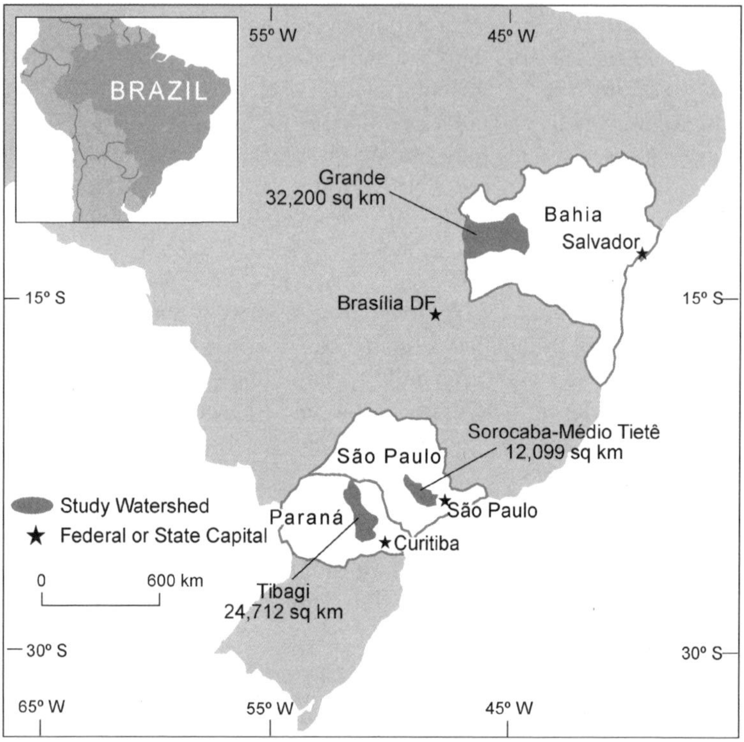

'users' of water through their municipal water–sewage autarchies; state-owned enterprises are powerful but by no means ubiquitous.[2]

Significant differences in decentralisation may be observed amongst individual Brazilian states, which have important legislative and administrative responsibilities in the environmental sector but vastly differing political cultures [*Ames and Keck, 1997*]. Since 1990 several Brazilian states have reformed water management along the following principles: water is a public and finite good with economic value; drinking water has the highest priority among multiple uses; the watershed is the basic spatial unit for planning and management; social actors should participate actively in decentralised management [*Porto, 1998; Tortajada, 2001*]. Reform-minded states have put these ideals into practice by creating watershed territories in which committees and agencies have received powers of deliberation, oversight, planning and establishment of a water tariff scheme.[3] Although goals of decentralisation may include better environmental management and more responsive government, the ultimate objective of reforms is to implement water tariff schemes to fund water-related investments at the watershed scale. Collection of water tariffs, however, is still a rather distant prospect.[4]

This essay explores issues of accountability and territories in cases of single-issue decentralisation in which municipalities play different roles. First, I outline three models of policy reform in the Brazilian states of Bahia, São Paulo and Paraná. Each state has defined decentralisation differently. Bahia has opted for a deconcentration policy, but São Paulo mandated equal participation of municipalities, civil society and state technicians. In Paraná, the state empowered firms and municipalities as water users at the exclusion of civil society. In each case, I introduce a study region that will focus the discussion. Evidence from study regions forms the basis for a subsequent analysis of accountability and territorial aspects.

II. THREE MODELS OF DECENTRALISATION IN BRAZIL

Deconcentration and Top-Down Influence: Bahia

Bahia's water management reforms, enacted by legislation passed in 1995 and implemented in 1997, merely shifted minor responsibilities from the state bureaucracy to 13 regional water districts [*Bahia, 2001*].[5] The Bahian water resources bureaucracy received funding from a World Bank-supported US$85 million water resources management project intended to 'strengthen the institutional structure' and 'carry out integrated water resources management'.[6] When project funds expire, the water resources bureaucracy will rely on water tariffs.

Under the slogan 'decentralise to optimise', the Bahian water resources bureaucracy has tried to identify, license and charge water users such as industries (including the petrochemical sector near Salvador) and irrigated agriculture. For this purpose, the bureaucracy gives little importance to fomenting stakeholder committees, opting instead to use a geographical information system (GIS) as its management tool for locating water users and calculating available surface water for licensing. The bureaucracy's director has stated that 'low cultural' and 'educational' levels amongst small-scale water users make stakeholder committees impractical; rather, the director has argued for the spontaneous formation of water user associations, for which water use licences are 'identity cards' that legitimise water users' participation [*Newport, 2002: 18, 28*].

Democratic decentralisation is a distant prospect in Bahia. Regional water districts have very little power and are upwardly accountable to the water resources bureaucracy based in Salvador. State law instructs regional water district offices to 'stimulate' the creation of stakeholder committees or associations, which would be downwardly accountable. However, this aspect of the water reform law has never been implemented. For example, in the Grande Valley (32,200 square kilometres), the main tributary of the Middle São Francisco River in the state's far west, the regional water office, established in August 2001, has not encouraged a catchment-wide committee. In practice, the Grande's water district merely assists water users prepare licence applications. Eventually, staff may process applications and update the state's water use GIS.

Mandatory Civil Society Participation: São Paulo

São Paulo's water management decentralisation began in the early 1990s [*São Paulo, 1994*]. The state required its 20 watershed territories to create stakeholder committees with the participation of municipalities, state agencies and civil society in equal thirds. Committees, which are legally part of the state, were granted deliberative (non-executive) powers to prioritise water investments, develop planning documents, resolve conflicts between water users and supervise the catchment's eventual water tariff scheme. The state required elections every two years to establish membership, officers (president, vice-president and executive secretary) and technical subcommittees. Elections for the one-third civil society membership usually ratify representatives of defined groups (trades unions, industrial associations, universities and environmental non-governmental organisations [NGOs]) indicated in a separate caucus. State representatives are appointed from within their bureaucracy; how municipalities vie for their third of committee seats is less clear. In most committees, an elected mayor holds the presidency, whilst civil society representatives usually hold the vice-presidency and state technicians serve as executive secretaries.[7]

The primary function of São Paulo's committees is to develop a water tariffs scheme, which would be implemented by a watershed executive agency subordinated to the committee. At present, many of São Paulo's river basin territories are in the process of establishing water agencies, but receipt of water tariffs is still distant. Instead, committees have overseen river-basin diagnostics and, at present, are carrying out river basin plans that will guide future investments and establish baselines for water tariffs. Until receipts from water tariffs become available, committees must rely on meagre grants from a state-wide pool that support projects for urban run-off control, environmental education and research, planning for sewage treatment facilities and planting riparian forest.

The river basin selected to analyse São Paulo's decentralisation was the Sorocaba-Tietê Valley (12,099 square kilometres) near the city of São Paulo, where state officials, municipalities and civil society representatives established a watershed committee in 1995. Elected mayors claimed the presidency, civil society representatives held the vice-presidency and the state's environmental quality agency claimed the executive secretary position. This routine, present in nearly all of São Paulo's watershed committees, is usually justified by the following argument: elected mayors use their high political visibility to hold meetings and persuade other mayors to participate in the committee. Civil society representatives are seen as a 'check' on the mayor's actions, but they lack necessary political clout to negotiate with municipalities. The staffs of water or environmental bureaucracies are well suited to daily management of the committee's work and prefer not to have a 'political' role. This justification is encouraged by the usual practice of conducting most debate in the sub-committees and working groups, rather than in public meetings.

Prioritising Water Users: Paraná

In the late 1990s the state of Paraná adopted a hybrid decentralisation policy for water management, somewhere between São Paulo's mandatory civil society participation in committees and Bahia's top-down deconcentration [*Paraná, 1999*]. The state first focused on setting guidelines for watershed-scale executive agencies, which will run the water tariff scheme. Later, officials encouraged the formation of stakeholder committees, which have deliberative powers and are formed by civil society representatives, municipalities and water users. The state water resources bureaucracy intends to sign contracts with catchment agencies. These contracts will authorise water agencies to implement water tariffs, carry out water investment projects and create planning documents. Officials in the state's water resources bureaucracy argue that large water users – businesses and municipalities (see note 2) – should manage Paraná's 16 watershed territories, because fees collected from industrial water users will support the future investments.

Who will control the decentralised water agencies? The state strongly favoured water users rather than civil society representatives. Rules specified that a consortium or association of municipalities must represent specified percentages of all municipalities and total population of the catchment. Alternatively, water user groups empowered as water agencies must include at least three water-using sectors (the sectors are: water supply and sewerage; drainage and solid waste; hydroelectricity; industrial use and waste; agro-pastoral uses; navigation; leisure and recreation) and members must include varying degrees of all licensed water users and total water use in the catchment [*Paraná, 2000*].

The Tibagi Valley (24,712 square kilometres) was chosen in order to evaluate Paraná's decentralisation policies. Formed in 1989, the Consortium for Environmental Protection of the Tibagi (*Consórcio para Proteção Ambiental do Tibagi* – COPATI), became the watershed's water agency in December 2002. COPATI originated as a consortium of municipalities that received approximately US$1 million from a large paper manufacturer in the Tibagi Valley to carry out environmental studies of fish populations. In the early 1990s COPATI's leadership changed its support base from municipalities to the catchment's large water users, such as breweries, coffee roasters and dairies. Taking advantage of Paraná's water management reforms, COPATI made necessary changes to become the Tibagi's executive agency and was forced to return to municipalities for support. It presently maintains a delicate balance of power between elected mayors steering the organisation's visible political front whilst industries provide financial and technical support. Encouraged by state officials, COPATI set up the Tibagi's provisional committee, which is the deliberative group required by state law. Notably, most members of the committee are also influential in COPATI. In June 2002 the full Tibagi committee was elected from caucuses in which water-using sectors, as defined by state law, met to select their representatives. Amongst the committees' 40 members, 13 were municipalities represented through their mayors or water–sewage autarchies and 10 were representatives of state bureaucracies or state-owned firms for water or electricity supply.

Comparing the states of Bahia, São Paulo and Paraná, three models of decentralisation may be observed: 1) Bahia has pursued deconcentration (administrative decentralisation) of state offices, ignoring municipalities and avoiding stakeholder committees; 2) São Paulo's reforms have mandated equal participation of representatives from civil society, municipal governments and state bureaucracies in stakeholder committees; 3) Paraná has empowered municipalities and businesses as water users in stakeholder committees and agencies (Table 1). Below, I explore how these three policy models have influenced the ability of municipalities and other actors to exercise downward accountability.

III. DOWNWARD ACCOUNTABILITY: MECHANISMS AND OBSTACLES

Downward accountability is essential to decentralisation because it may 'broaden the participation of local populations and enhances the responsiveness of empowered actors'. The 'greater participation and responsiveness' resulting from downward accountability may generate 'the many lauded benefits of decentralization' [*Agrawal and Ribot, 1999: 479*]. Apart from elections, mechanisms encouraging downward accountability include access to an independent judicial system, independent monitoring by NGOs and unimpeded media coverage. The participation of elected municipal

TABLE 1

SUMMARY OF KEY ISSUES IN WATER RESOURCE DECENTRALISATION

Initial Reform Date	Bahia (Grande Valley) 1995	São Paulo (Sorocaba-Médio Tietê Valley) 1991	Paraná (Tibagi Valley) 1999
Type of Decentralisation [Agrawal and Ribot, 1999]	Deconcentration	Democratic Decentralisation	Elements of democratic decentralisation and deconcentration
Objectives of decentralisation	Create catchment territories Empower state water agency (SRH) Identify and license water users Collect water tariffs	Create catchment territories Participatory watershed committees to manage water tariff system	Create catchment territories Large private and public water users to manage water tariff system
Decentralised Institutions	Regional office	Watershed committee Watershed agency	Watershed committee Watershed agency (COPATI)
Powers not Transferred	Water licensing Decision-making Establishment of investment priorities	Water licensing Small project funding	Water licensing Selection of watershed agency
Influence of Municipalities on Downward Accountability	None	'Technical' issues become 'political' (sewage) One powerful municipality (Sorocaba) dominates other municipalities	Shifting relationship with COPATI before and after decentralisation Tensions with private firms
Influence of Civil Society on Downward Accountability	Conflict and co-operation between water bureaucracy (SRH) and farmers' organisation (AIBA) Grass-roots activists petition public attorney (Ministério Público)	Civil society representatives are one-third of committee Environmental NGOs lobby watershed committee, not municipalities Environmental NGOs have set agendas and helped produce baseline study	Print media is influential in environmental reporting COPATI is isolated from activist campaign against dam construction Activist university staff works independently from COPATI

governments is critical to encouraging downward accountability and achieving the theorised positive benefits of decentralisation [*Ribot, 2002*].

How important are municipalities in São Paulo's decentralisation? A case in which a technical issue (sewage treatment) became a political issue is instructive. The Sorocaba municipality is headed by a dominant political figure amongst the catchment's much smaller and economically weaker municipalities. During two terms as president of the committee, Sorocaba's mayor obtained federal funding for construction of a municipal sewage treatment system. The watershed committee strongly endorsed the mayor's sewage policy, even claiming publicly that the Sorocaba River would be South America's first 'de-polluted' river. Such hyperbole conferred substantial environmental credentials to Sorocaba's mayor, a politician with ambition to higher elected office. In return, Sorocaba's mayor leveraged the participation of small municipalities in the committee by siding with technicians, who encouraged municipalities to apply for small grants to develop sewage treatment plans. If not for participation of the river basin's small municipalities, the committee would not have met the required minimum of one-third municipal representation in meetings and would have failed to generate political legitimacy.

Hyperbole aside, treatment of Sorocaba's sewage (432,000 people of a total 1.4 million population in the basin) would contribute significantly to the basin's water quality. The political result of Sorocaba's actions is encouragement of the idea that 'sewage gains votes' amongst other municipalities. However, municipalities represent only one source of downward accountability. The region's proximity to the metropolitan São Paulo region has encouraged formation of a strong network of NGOs responding to high levels of untreated sewage and pollution introduced from upstream São Paulo [*CBH-SMT, 1997*]. The same NGOs and activists who denounced river pollution helped establish and maintain the river basin committee by serving as officers or leading working groups, thus fulfilling part of the mandatory one-third civil society membership. NGOs lobbied for public hearings on an upstream dredging project, which had neglected to study downstream impacts, secured small grants for environmental education projects on water quality and encouraged debate leading to land use policies for the source catchment for Sorocaba's water supply.

Certainly, the civil society representatives active in the Sorocaba-Tietê committee encourage downward accountability in that they foster debate on issues that municipalities or state officials might ignore, thus influencing the committee's agenda. Yet to whom are civil-society representatives accountable? NGOs on the committee range from a highly sophisticated group, with thousands of supporters and dozens of ongoing projects in several Brazilian states, to very small groups focusing on one issue in a single municipality. University professors sit on the committee because they 'represent' their public or private universities. The committee has never included an NGO representing shantytown dwellers or water consumers. The absence of the basin's industries is especially important; São Paulo's legislation required that regional associations would represent individual industries, thus preventing a single water-using business from sitting on the committee. The committee's leaders have 'organised' small-scale irrigation farmers into associations that can nominate a representative; whether this is paternalism or necessary encouragement remains to be seen.

Municipalities have had a different relationship with decentralisation in the Tibagi Valley. In 1989 municipalities in the Tibagi (especially its lower reaches) created COPATI as a consortium with two purposes: to manage a US$1 million fish population study and to deliver short-term visible returns. Accountable only to municipalities that paid monthly fees, COPATI apprehended illegal fishing nets, planted small areas of riparian forest and provided environmental education to primary schools. Mayors also wanted the Tibagi to be restocked with native fish species in response to citizen complaints; this project was never carried out on the advice of university biologists. Overall, municipalities used COPATI as a means to produce tangible political returns that could not be obtained from state institutions.[8] Indeed, COPATI thrived as long as it could generate clear political returns on a short-term basis for its benefactors.

However, by the mid-1990s COPATI's support base had eroded. Cash-strapped municipalities, led by new mayors with four-year mandates, did not confront water shortages or conflicts. As new mayors entered office, they stopped paying monthly fees to COPATI. After a period of crisis, COPATI's leadership looked to the Tibagi's industrial water users, for which water quality and environmental performance were serious matters. During the 1990s, industries such as breweries and paper pulp firms were beginning to install pollution-reducing technologies to lower costs or promote a 'green' marketing image. COPATI collected monthly fees, based on the number of employees, in exchange for organising courses and providing various services to environmental managers. By February 2003, COPATI had 27 fee-paying firms, including breweries, paper pulp firms, hydroelectricity generation, coffee roasters, packaging and municipal water–sewage autarchies, and 35 municipalities amongst its associates. When Paraná established its decentralisation policies in 1999, COPATI's leadership began necessary reforms to become the Tibagi's water executive, a goal it achieved in December 2002. The strongest challenge came from municipalities that demanded more attention to projects with short-term political returns, such as environmental education, and less attention to expensive courses on water management for industries.

How downwardly accountable is COPATI? The consortium's responsiveness to its subscribers is strong. Paraná's requirement for COPATI to represent the Tibagi's water users has consolidated this trend. However, COPATI's search for financial support – from municipalities to industries – has blinded it to issues important to the catchment's environmental well-being. Grass-roots activists in several of the Tibagi's water-related conflicts have not tapped COPATI, but rather have sought other organisations or bureaucracies. For example, in the case of a proposed hydroelectric project that would partially flood indigenous lands, COPATI has maintained distanced neutrality. One of COPATI's strongest financial supporters is Paraná's state electricity enterprise, which would operate the hydroelectric plant; several municipalities supporting COPATI are strongly opposed. The debate over a hydroelectricity project has been dominated by a new network of activists that finds COPATI irrelevant [*Clarke, 2002*]. Actively involved in resolving industrial and domestic pollution in the Tibagi's main city, Londrina (population 421,000), are a local university's biology professors in collaboration with the public attorney's office and grass-roots activists. The biology professors generally consider COPATI to be biased toward water-using industries or municipalities that want immediate results for political gain. Similarly, COPATI is not directly involved in a dispute involving contamination of public water supply in the Tibagi's second-largest city, although it has assisted a nearby brewery in resolving a water quality issue. In the lower Tibagi, a separate consortium of municipalities formed to collect and manage funds arising from a successful lawsuit regarding compensation for flooded lands during the 1970s and early 1980s.[9]

Do the interests of large water users in the Tibagi impede the type of downward accountability that civil society representatives have created in the Sorocaba-Tietê? Decentralisation reforms arrived later in Paraná and empowered industrial water users rather than grass-roots activists. COPATI's origins created the expectation amongst municipalities that it was a source for short-term and visible political returns. Municipalities want short-term returns, but are these compatible with significant environmental benefits? An optimistic interpretation is that COPATI helped some industries reduce pollution and encouraged some municipalities to adopt environmental education, but it avoided a more radical agenda that would have antagonised industries or municipalities. Nevertheless, using the state's key objective (water tariffs) as a criterion for evaluation, COPATI is the most advanced actor in Paraná in terms of developing a water tariff scheme – primarily because it has already generated trust amongst industries that would pay into the system. These same industries exert considerable influence over COPATI, thus limiting the accountability that municipalities might exercise. It remains to be seen whether COPATI and its water user membership will be held accountable to the stakeholder committee, and whether the municipal and state actors will be accountable to local populations.

The question of downward accountability must be understood differently in the case of Bahia, where municipalities have had a negligible role in decentralisation. Power remains concentrated in the water resources bureaucracy, which is led by an outspoken opponent of downward accountability and stakeholder committees. In the Grande Valley, challenges to this top-down policy represent a sort of downward accountability. These challenges have emerged from three sources: a private water user group; grass-roots activists lobbying of the state's public attorney's office; and decentralisation of the environmental bureaucracy.

The most direct challenge to top-down deconcentration has come from a powerful farmers' association with a recently established support base.[10] Commercial agriculture in the Grande Valley was established only after 1979, when farmers from southern Brazil migrated to the region because of cheap land, abundant credit and suitable soybean cultivars [*Haesbaert, 1997; SRH, 1993*]. Farmers rapidly converted the natural *Cerrado* (savanna) to annual crops, especially in the Grande headwater reaches – where mean annual rainfall is highest in the catchment. After 1990, farmers began to irrigate fruit and coffee fields near the Grande's tributaries; irrigation, however, has conflicted with hydroelectricity generation by reducing stream flow during the dry season. Some rivers have been banned for irrigation, but, in response, farmers are drilling wells to reach groundwater.

In early 2002 the farmers' association criticised Bahia's water resources bureaucracy as contradictory to federal mandates because it had not established a stakeholder committee in the Grande. The association argued that the state's top-down policy was unconstitutional because it excluded water users from participating in management committees. Water tariffs would become 'another tax on irrigated agriculture' [*personal interview, Barreiras, July 2001*] that eventually would fund sewage treatment in the state capital, rather than attend to the Grande's needs. The farmers' association was participating simultaneously in the formation of a stakeholder committee for the multi-state São Francisco River (640,000 square kilometres) [*Romano and Garcia, 1998*] and in a national water policy forum for water tariffs as the representative of the irrigation sector. In this context, its exclusion from state-level debates was particularly insulting. Ironically, the farmers' association used the same discourse for increased 'participation' – meaning influence – of NGO activists elsewhere in Brazil who are also demanding an increased presence in decentralised water management.

The public attorney's office, which has responded to allegations filed by environmental activists, is a second important mechanism for downward accountability in the Grande Valley. Under Brazilian law, citizens may file allegations of environmental crimes with the public attorney's office, which is obliged to open an inquiry. In practice, the public attorney's offices in the Grande lack infrastructure and staff to conduct inquiries, although the public attorney may pursue some allegations more vigorously than others. Reports of illegal irrigation and construction along stream banks have provoked inquiries revealing gross omissions by federal and state environmental offices. Inquiries also have shown that the state's water resources bureaucracy licensed too much water volume and failed to regulate licensed users. Notably, activists and the public attorney have not found legal mechanisms for addressing frequent leaks of raw sewage in the Grande's main city, Barreiras (114,000 residents in a total catchment population of 194,000), which relies almost exclusively on rudimentary septic pits.

In contrast to the farmers' association and the public attorney, municipalities have a relatively small role in encouraging downward accountability. Commercial farmers pursue their claims through the farmers' association, and grass-roots activists use the public attorney's office. Favourable political contacts with the state government have created a modest role for municipalities in carrying out a micro-catchment soil conservation project. In 2002 the Barreiras municipality received authorisation to licence irrigation and construction projects in their territories as an initiative of the state's environmental bureaucracy. Municipal staff will evaluate projects, issue licences and collect fees. Thus, Barreiras will license irrigation projects on environmental criteria, even though they have no role in licensing and regulating the use of water on the same site.[11]

As these cases indicate, downward accountability depends not only on whether municipalities participate in decentralisation but also on the characteristics of civil society and business interests. Significantly, state governments have determined the extent to which civil society organisations may participate in decentralised groups. In São Paulo, municipalities and civil society representatives encourage different types of downward accountability in stakeholder committees – with state-enforced rules and criteria mandating participation of three sectors. NGOs exert downward accountability, but it is unclear what interests – beyond 'the environment' – NGOs represent. In Paraná, classification of municipalities as water users may isolate catchment committees and agencies from polemic water issues reaching a broad public. COPATI remains accountable to its members – municipalities and industries as large water users – but not to local populations. The case of the Grande Valley in Bahia reveals how business groups and grass-roots activists exert downward accountability, independently from municipalities, to confront deconcentration.

There are important reasons to support the inclusion of municipalities in decentralised groups. Elected municipal governments are the smallest unit of government and, in some cases, the most responsive to local populations.

Municipalities may also reduce the prospect of elite domination of decentralised groups. However, there are other means to encourage downward accountability. The Brazilian examples indicate benefits of dividing stakeholder committees amongst different sectors or groups, including (but not limited to) municipalities, state bureaucracies, grass-roots activists and water users. The precise formula adopted depends on the ultimate objective of decentralised groups: collection of water tariffs, environmental education, watershed planning or responsiveness to the concerns of citizens. Observed differences in downward accountability in Bahia, São Paulo and Paraná may derive from the different objectives of policy-makers, but they are also derived from the different nature of interactions between civil society and the state – which, in turn, are influenced by territorial-scale changes resulting from some single-issue decentralisations.

IV. SINGLE-ISSUE GROUPS AND NEW TERRITORIES: FURTHERING DEMOCRATIC DECENTRALISATION?

Single-issue or stakeholder groups formed under decentralisation policies have spread rapidly since the mid-1990s. Manor [*this volume*] termed this a 'second wave' of decentralisation because states previously encouraged the formation of multi-purpose councils with broad remits encompassing education, health, infrastructure, sanitation and welfare. According to Manor, single-issue groups may undermine the benefits of decentralisation. International donors, rather than governments, have been the main supporters of single-issue groups. Governments generally have been sceptical about such groups and have attempted to exert greater control over them. However, single-issue groups usually are better funded than multiple-issue groups. In addition, single-issue groups are often appointed or elected by non-democratic means, and thus are not downwardly accountable to local populations. Single-issue groups may have shorter life spans than multiple-issue groups because they were often created to implement development projects and 'avoid politics' [*Manor, this volume; see also Baviskar, this volume*].

Evidence from the cases outlined above makes for a relevant test of Manor's critique.[12] To begin, Bahia represents the case most intimately related to international donors, as a World Bank-supported US$85 million project has modernised its water resources bureaucracy. Although the World Bank required stakeholder committees in the region of the main project as a 'pilot' for the state, the water resources bureaucracy used several techniques to severely curtail stakeholder committees [*Newport, 2002*]. Technocrats, moreover, have successfully implemented policies in opposition to international donors. In Paraná and São Paulo, however, international donors have had little direct or indirect influence on water resources decentralisation.[13]

Territorial aspects of single-issue groups may be more relevant than relationships to international donors. Although forest decentralisation frequently relies on existing municipal territories [*Kaimowitz et al., 1998; Larson, 2002*], new territories for water management are more likely to be drainage basins that include several municipalities. In most instances of Brazilian water management decentralisation, governments have defined watersheds as territories for which stakeholder committees have received specified powers.

What are the implications of new territories for downward accountability and democratic decentralisation? Although the strong environmental arguments for managing water resources in drainage basins are well known [*Barrow, 1998*], the establishment of new territories, under certain circumstances, may have positive implications for democratic decentralisation. Potentially, new territories are novel political spaces that encourage interactions between grass-roots activists or business interests and state technicians. They are also are new organisational spaces that encourage intervention and management at scales beyond municipalities.

Evidence of how civil society networks lobby stakeholder committees supports the case that new territories are political spaces that potentially encourage democratic decentralisation. In the case of São Paulo, where the powers of committees include funding of small projects and setting of agendas for water investment, the committee has become a focal point for grass-roots activists who previously would have lobbied individual municipal governments or bureaucratic headquarters. NGOs, as they engage in committee-wide discussions, have established not only a network with other civil society groups but also strong relations with local technicians. Activists have identified state technicians they consider to be open to dialogue with civil society and on whom they can rely for support. These technicians, in turn, have begun to rely on grass-roots activists as sources of information and checks on the power of municipalities in order to set the priorities of watershed management, claiming that 'they [civil society leaders] let us see new issues' and 'allow us to do our jobs better' [*personal interview, Sorocaba July 2001*].

These relations between state officials and grass-roots activists lie behind the public front of the committee, which municipalities dominate. One of the most tangible products of collaboration between civil society and state technicians is the committee's mandatory baseline study [*CBH-SMT, 1997*], which established a strong basis for future co-operation. Such positive interactions between civil society and state bureaucrats in Brazil have been reported previously [*Lemos, 1998*]; in the case of São Paulo's decentralisation, the state–society relationships developed around watershed committees would have been very difficult to form within the confines of the municipality. The political and environmental legitimacy of the watershed territory – which resulted from the strong role of the state in establishing clear rules – encouraged civil society and state technicians to forge a stronger alliance than would have been possible in the confines of individual municipal territories.

New territories have yet to inspire strong relationships between civil society and bureaucrats in the Tibagi Valley of Paraná, mainly because decentralisation has empowered large water users and excluded grass-roots activists. Instead, COPATI has used the state's legitimisation of the Tibagi as a new territory to create the stakeholder committee in its own image by packing the provisional committee with its own supporters. In the Grande, the new watershed territory does not yet have a stakeholder committee; nevertheless, the idea of stakeholder committees, in the absence of state initiative, has influenced two phenomena. First, the farmers' association believes in the inevitable establishment of a stakeholder committee in the Grande. The association has demanded greater participation in Bahia's top-down water resources bureaucracy, publicly criticising the state's plans for managing future water-tariff revenues. By contrast, the rather weak civil society in the Grande Valley has chosen the public attorney's office, rather than the idea of a committee, as the means to raise legal challenges. Competition between Bahia's water resources bureaucracy and the farmers' association may quickly dominate a future stakeholder committee. If the state establishes clear rules for mandatory participation of municipalities and grass-roots activists, then issues falling outside arguments on water tariffs for irrigation, such as sanitation and water costs for consumers, might find space for debate in the committee.

When empowered by the state with clear powers and responsibilities, new territories may also develop into organisational spaces, which in turn may encourage democratic decentralisation. New catchment territories expand the potential area for policy interventions beyond individual municipalities. The change in scale from municipality to drainage basin means that grass-roots actors may lobby committees, rather than municipalities, on issues affecting water quality, quantity or distribution – which often lay outside municipal boundaries. Although not all activists will be successful, an important mechanism for downward accountability will have been established.

Returning to the Grande River in Bahia, the absence of a stakeholder committee has not prevented grass-roots activists from using the idea of the catchment in asserting that the main water problem is found in headwater reaches (in a municipality west of Barreiras) where extensive large-scale commercial farms replaced nearly all native vegetation. Agriculture allegedly has reduced soil permeability, which has decreased dry-season river levels and increased peak wet-season run-off; irrigation has reduced low-season river volume even further. Although farmers admit that agriculture has affected the catchment's rivers, they assert that housing and leisure construction along stream banks in Barreiras, not upstream agriculture, is the Grande's main water-related problem. The eventual creation of a stakeholder committee may at least provide a public forum for advancing this debate with empirical evidence. If the state requires civil society participation, the concerns of grass-roots activists may be legitimised.

In the case of the Socoraba-Tietê basin, the grass-roots actors and technicians have exploited the catchment as an organisational space in order to address issues long neglected by municipalities. For example, grass-roots activists demanded that the committee hold meetings on the downstream environmental impacts of a dredging project in the upstream Tietê River. As a result, the committee issued a public statement calling on project managers to address a list of issues. Second, state technicians, long concerned about untreated sewage in the basin, established alliances with grass-roots activists to make sewage the top priority. With access to funding for municipalities to prepare proposals for sewage-treatment infrastructure, the committee attracted interest from municipalities to build treatment centres. Third, grass-roots activists and state technicians allied to prioritise the issue of Sorocaba's water supply region, which lacked land-use policy controls to limit mining and urbanisation. In these three cases, water-related issues were distributed spatially amongst several municipalities within a newly empowered territory.

The function of river basins as organisational spaces is somewhat different in the Tibagi, largely because COPATI preceded the state's decentralisation reforms. During COPATI's business-oriented phase of the mid-1990s, the Tibagi 'brand', removed from municipal politics, attracted public and private firms. COPATI's legitimacy in lobbying businesses derived from its claims to represent water-related issues in the Tibagi basin, rather than the interests of municipalities. Although pollution control was not a novel idea amongst the basin's industries, COPATI argued that pollution reduction was in the interest of a watershed territory, rather than a firm's image or bottom line. The exclusion of civil society representatives is partially a result, as the Tibagi 'brand' encouraged participation of firms willing to subscribe to the idea. In the absence of state-established rules for civil society participation, the 'branding' strategy led COPATI to avoid the current controversy surrounding the hydroelectricity dam project.

Decentralisation's new territories are political spaces for interactions between grass-roots actors, business interests and state technicians. They are also organisational spaces for interventions beyond individual municipalities. However, examples indicate that the state must take a strong role in defining the participation of social actors and transfer clearly defined powers to decentralised groups for the territorial effects to be realised [*Agrawal and Ribot, 1999*]. In the case of São Paulo, with the most promising democratic decentralisation, the state-imposed committee structure eliminates powerful local business interests from participating, unless they take the unlikely step of forming regional associations. Nevertheless, alliances amongst members of the committee have resulted in tangible gains towards reducing untreated domestic sewage and setting the agenda beyond the narrow remit of water tariffs.

V. CONCLUSION

Water management decentralisation in Brazil relies on somewhat different models. Although it is beyond the scope of this essay to elaborate on the different political cultures in each state, the ultimate objective of decentralisation policies is straightforward: collection of water tariffs. In Paraná and Bahia, policies appear limited to water tariffs, although each state is pursuing this goal with different instruments. Paraná has empowered public and private water users, whilst Bahia has empowered its water resources bureaucracy. In São Paulo, policies have encouraged discussion of a broader range of water issues beyond a narrow focus on tariffs, including environmental education, sewage treatment and watershed protection. In a clever manoeuvre, São Paulo obtained the commitment of grass-roots activists to a project that included eventual water tariffs; the policy, however, has marginalised the firms that eventually would pay tariffs.

Varying mechanisms for accountability and participation of municipalities, firms, grass-roots activists and state technicians may be observed. Mechanisms for downward accountability are not limited to municipalities but are also present in the independent judiciary and grass-roots activist networks. Nevertheless, it is unclear exactly what or whom NGOs represent. Furthermore, the capacity of public attorney's offices is highly variable. Positive steps encouraging downward accountability appear in cases where the state has defined participation broadly amongst municipalities, state technicians and civil society representatives, but also specifically in that stakeholder committees are equally divided. Successful decentralisation may rely not on a transfer of power from central to local government or civil society but on a vigorous and precise state presence that changes the way state, locality and civil society relate to each other [*Tendler, 1997: 142–57*]. The participation of municipalities is no guarantee of downward accountability, nor does exclusion of municipalities eliminate downward accountability – especially in the presence of grass-roots activists and business interests. Rather, the state's ability to encourage a three-way dynamic among central authorities, local government and civil society, as Tendler [*1997*] argued, may do more to advance the positive benefits of decentralisation than reliance solely on municipal governments.

Finally, the debate on decentralisation seems to have overlooked its spatial implications. Decentralisation policies often create new territories, which may have unintended effects on downward accountability. Territories encompassing several municipalities may become new political and organisational spaces that encourage new relationships between grass-roots activists and state technicians. Again, examples indicate that positive territorial effects of decentralisation may result when the state clearly defines the participation of social actors and transfers meaningful powers to decentralised groups. How new territories develop as political and organisational spaces, and whether environmental management improves as a result of this, are subjects of ongoing research.

NOTES

1. The author carried out qualitative, semi-structured interviews with key actors during April 2001, June–August 2001 and July–August 2002. Interview framework and reports on each of the three watersheds studied are available in Portuguese from the author.
2. As Manor argues, 'water users' are usually large industrial or agricultural consumers of water, rather than groups of household consumers or 'water drinkers' [*Manor, this volume*]. Municipalities fall into the former category, although they are accountable to citizens through elections and municipal councils. For example, in the case of São Paulo's Sorocaba-Tietê Valley, a state enterprise (Companhia de Saneamento Básico do Estado de São Paulo – SABESP) provides water and sewage service to 68 per cent of the municipalities, whilst municalities service 67 per cent of the catchment's population [*CBH-SMT, 1997: 51*].
3. An overall assessment of these recent reforms is unavailable at present, but this issue is the subject of ongoing multidisciplinary research by the Watermark (Marca d'Água) project that facilitated the author's research.
4. At the time of writing, in January 2003, in the Paraíba do Sul River of Minas Gerais, São Paulo and Rio de Janeiro states, water tariffs are scheduled to begin in March 2003. By late January 2003, approximately 4.5 per cent of known water-using industries were signed up to pay R$0.02 per thousand litres of water used and returned without treatment, or R$0.008 per thousand litres of water used and returned treated. Officials hope to generate R$11 million annually, approximately US$3.1 million [*Menocchi, 2003*].
5. These districts are known as RAAs (Regiões Administrativas de Água).
6. Most funding was devoted to the Ponto Novo dam (US$15.8 million) and resettlement (US$9.6 million). Overall, the World Bank is to fund 60 per cent of the project [*Newport, 2002*].
7. Officials from the state's water and electricity department (*Departamento de Águas e Energia Elétrica* – DAEE) control most executive secretary positions in the state's committees.
8. For example, mayors paid diesel fuel for COPATI's 400 fishing regulation expeditions; in return, mayors would take political credit for the apprehended nets and gear that would be burned in front of the waiting local media.
9. In the first two cases, university staff have participated as 'neutral' information gatherers in settlements reached between the public attorney (*Ministério Público*) and polluting industries.
10. The farmers' association is the *Associação de Agricultores e Irrigantes do Oeste da Bahia*, which has approximately 1,000 dues-paying members. In western Bahia, 1.2 million hectares of farmland – of which 67,000 hectares are irrigated – was devoted to soybeans (800,000 hectares), maize (100,000 hectares), cotton (60,000 hectares) and irrigated coffee (12,300 hectares).
11. In January 2003 Bahia established a new Water and Environment Secretariat under its newly inaugurated governor. However, it is unlikely that water fees and licensing will be targeted for 'horizontal' decentralisation in which a bureaucracy divides responsibilities amongst several agencies, as was the case for the Bahian environment bureaucracy for the creation of protected areas [*Oliveira, 2002*].
12. Limitations of space prevent a full discussion of Manor's analysis, such as his points on

democratic elections of stakeholder committees; however, the Watermark (Marca d'Água) project is collecting and analysing data on elections of stakeholder committees.

13. In São Paulo, technicians adapted the French water management model; Paraná copied aspects of São Paulo's legislation and federal water reforms passed in 1997. The political culture of these states is the subject of ongoing research by the Watermark project.

REFERENCES

Agrawal, A. and J. Ribot, 1999, 'Accountability in Decentralization: A Framework with South Asian and West African Cases', *Journal of Developing Areas*, Vol.33, No.4, pp.473–502.

Alexander, J. and J. McGregor, 2000, 'Wildlife and Politics: CAMPFIRE in Zimbabwe', *Development and Change*, Vol.31, No.3, pp.605–27.

Ames, B. and M.E. Keck, 1997, 'The Politics of Sustainable Development: Environmental Policy Making in four Brazilian States', *Journal of Interamerican Studies and World Affairs*, Vol.39, No.4, pp.1–40.

Bahia (State), 2001, *Recursos Hídricos: Legislação Básico do Estado da Bahia*, Salvador: Superintendência de Recursos Hídricos.

Barrow, C.J., 1998, 'River Basin Development Planning and Management: A Critical Review', *World Development*, Vol.26, No.1, pp.171–86.

Clarke, J., 2002, 'An Analysis of State-Society Relations in the Context of an Anti-Dam Mobilisation in Southern Brazil', Master's dissertation, Institute of Latin American Studies, University of London.

CBH-SMT (Comitê da Bacia Hidrográfica Sorocaba-Médio Tietê), 1997, *Relatório de Situação dos Recursos Hídricos 1995: UGRHI-10 Sorocaba-Médio Tietê*, Sorocaba: CETESB, Universidade de Sorocaba.

Gray, L.C., 2002, 'Environmental Policy, Land Rights, and Conflict: Rethinking Community Natural Resource Management Programs in Burkina Faso', *Environment and Planning D: Society and Space*, Vol.20, No.6, pp.167–82.

Guerrero R., L.A.E.V., 2000, 'Towards a New Water Management Practice: Experiences and Proposals from Guanajuato State for a Participatory and Decentralized Water Management Structure in Mexico', *International Journal of Water Resources Development*, Vol.16, No.4, pp.571–88.

Haesbaert, R., 1997, *Des-Territorialização e Identidade: A Rede "Gaúcha" no Nordeste*, Niterói, RJ: Editora da Universidade Federal Fluminense.

Kaimowitz, D., C. Vallejos, P.B. Pacheco and R. Lopez, 1998, 'Municipal Governments and Forest Management in Lowland Bolivia', *Journal of Environment and Development*, Vol.7, No.1, pp.45–59.

Kull, C.A., 2002, 'Empowering Pyromaniacs in Madagascar: Ideology and Legitimacy in Community-based Natural Resource Management', *Development and Change*, Vol.33, No.1, pp.57–78.

Larson, A.M., 2002, 'Natural Resources and Decentralization in Nicaragua: Are Local Governments Up to the Job?' *World Development*, Vol.30, No.1, pp.17–31.

Lemos, M.C. de M., 1998, 'The Politics of Pollution Control in Brazil: State Actors and Social Movements Cleaning up Cubatão', *World Development*, Vol.26, No.1, pp.75–87.

Logan, B.I. and W.G. Mosley, 2002, 'The Political Ecology of Poverty Alleviation in Zimbabwe's Communal Area Management Programme for Indigenous Resources (CAMPFIRE)', *Geoforum*, Vol.33, No.1, pp.1–14.

Manor, J., 1999, *The Political Economy of Democratic Decentralization*, Washington, DC: The World Bank.

Menocchi, S., 2003, 'Água do Paraíba Começa a Ser Cobrada em Março', *Agência Estado* (São Paulo), 29 Jan.

Newport, M., 2002, 'Making Decentralisation and Participation in Water Resource Management Work for Rural Women: The Case of the Itapicuru Basin', Master's dissertation, Institute of Latin American Studies, University of London.

Nickson, R., 1995, *Local Government in Latin America*, Boulder, CO: Lynne Reinner.

Oliveira, J.A.P. de, 2002, 'Implementing Environmental Policies in Developing Countries through Decentralization: The Case of Protected Areas in Bahia, Brazil', *World Development*, Vol.30, No.10, pp.1713–36.

Paraná (State), 2000, 'Decreto No.2.316', *Diário Oficial*, 18 July.

Paraná (State), 1999, 'Lei No.12.726/99', *Diário Oficial*, 26 Nov.

Porto, Monica, 1998, 'The Brazilian Water Law: A New Level of Participation and Decision Making', *International Journal of Water Resources Development*, Vol.14, No.2, pp.175–82.

Ribot, J.C., 2002, *Democratic Decentralization of Natural Resources: Institutionalizing Popular Participation*, Washington, DC: World Resources Institute.

Romano, P.A. and E.A.C. Garcia, 1998, 'Policies for Water-Resources Planning and Management of the São Francisco River Basin', in A.K. Biswas, N.V. Cordeiro, B.P. F. Braga and C. Tortajada (eds.), *Management of Latin American River Basins: Amazon, Plata, and São Francisco*, Tokyo: United Nations University Press, pp.245–71.

São Paulo (State), 1994, *Legislação sobre Recursos Hídricos*, São Paulo: Departamento de Aguas e Energia Elétrica.

Sekhar, N.U., 2000, 'Decentralized Natural Resource Management: From State to Co-Management in India', *Journal of Environmental Planning and Management*, Vol.43, No.1, pp.123–38.

SRH (Superintendência de Recursos Hídricos), 1993, *Plano Diretor de Recursos Hídricos: Bacia do Rio Grande*, Salvador: HIGESA.

Tendler, J., 1997, *Good Government in the Tropics*, Baltimore, MD: Johns Hopkins University Press.

Tortajada, C., 2001, 'Institutions for Integrated River Basin Management in Latin America', *International Journal of Water Resources Development*, Vol.17, No.3, pp.289–301.

Decentralising Natural Resource Management: A Recipe for Sustainability and Equity?

WICKY MEYNEN and MARTIN DOORNBOS

I. INTRODUCTION

In recent years, there has been a considerable restructuring of the institutional arrangements governing natural resource management (NRM). This restructuring has taken place in the context of ongoing efforts at economic reform and decentralisation in various countries. Deliberate policy interventions by the state and donor agencies, initiatives by voluntary agencies and local groups, and the impact of market forces on local economic structures have all contributed to this restructuring. Initially, market deregulation and privatisation were the guiding principles in these endeavours, while more recently decentralisation of governance and local participation have been emphasised. These institutional changes amount to a redefinition of the role of the state and have stimulated further exploration and experimentation regarding a variety of local government and non-state forms of management and co-management. Restructuring efforts of this kind often involve local communities and user groups, joint environmental management schemes, non-governmental organisation (NGO)-based initiatives, co-operative bodies and other actors at the micro and meso level. Such altered institutional arrangements have been done, it is often argued, to bring about more sustainable and equitable forms of NRM through the enhancement of local participation. It remains to be seen, however, whether these institutional changes – particularly decentralisation in its various forms – can promote more sustainable NRM practices. In order to achieve this outcome, new practices

Wicky Meynen and Martin Doornbos are at the Institute of Social Studies, The Hague. The authors thank K.N. Nair of the Centre for Development Studies, Trivandrum, for his contributions to a provisional collaborative project outline which served as a point of departure for the present essay. Thanks for constructive criticisms are also due to colleagues at the Centre for Development Research, Copenhagen, where Wicky Meynen worked on a preliminary draft of the essay. An earlier version of this essay was presented at the international symposium 'Governance and Adjustment in an Era of "Globalization"', University of Manitoba, Winnipeg, 8–9 Nov. 2002 and has appeared in the *Indian Journal of Political Science*, Vol.63, No.4 (2002).

European Journal of Development Research, Vol.16, No.1, Spring 2004, pp.235–254
ISSN 0957-8811 print
DOI:10.1080/0957881041000168824

must be capable of transcending past institutional rigidities. They must be capable of containing environmental degradation, promoting sustainable and equitable natural resource use, allowing more effective handling of resource conflicts and facilitating joint environmental resource development – all of which indicate the need to identify and rectify pre-existing problems in the field of policy. At the same time, though, there are potential policy tensions between the equity of access that sustainable NRM practices demand and the process of decentralisation that is used to facilitate more sustainable NRM practices. Moreover, many of the arrangements concerned seem to have made an already competitive situation around scarce natural resource utilisation all the more complex.

Thus, while appreciating the potentially positive effects of decentralisation and participation in opening or enlarging spaces for peoples' movements and other forms of collective action from below, it nonetheless appears appropriate to take a critical look at current modes of thinking and practices regarding decentralisation and participation in NRM. Therefore, this contribution attempts an exploration of the terrain, which will be undertaken on the basis of a non-exhaustive review of recent trends and literature – with a particular interest in the political dimensions of the issues. Specifically, the essay seeks to draw attention to the ways in which different, at times even contradictory, policy models and directives, together with political and economic dynamics, shape the mixture of institutional arrangements for NRM as well as their limitations. In pursuing this discussion, we will be particularly interested in problems found with regard to access to and sustainable use and development of resources, the handling of resource conflicts and the relative empowerment of different user categories.

The next section of the essay will review several theoretical and policy debates on the issue of decentralised institutional arrangements for sustainable and equitable environmental resource management. Although our discussion on decentralisation and NRM is closely related to participation, we will not specifically address this dimension [*see Leeuwis, 2000; Mayoux, 1995; Nelson and Wright, 1995; Utting, 2001*]. Following this, the essay will consider more closely some of the issues and arguments that have arisen in connection with decentralising NRM. This discussion will be informed by recent experiences of decentralised NRM in India and various African countries, which include local government as well as non-state forms, and will be followed by our concluding observations.

II. THEORETICAL AND POLICY DEBATES

The changes in institutional arrangements that we are concerned with have given rise to several theoretical and policy debates. Within the realm of theory,

Hardin's 'the tragedy of the commons' thesis set in motion, at an early stage, an intense discussion among social scientists on the role of property rights regimes and related institutional arrangements in the management of natural resources [*Hardin, 1968*]. In particular, the merits and demerits of private, state and community-based resource management systems became a hotly debated issue. Among economists this debate initially focused on the question of whether decentralised collective action could be effective [*White and Runge, 1995: 1683*].

In contrast to this, anthropological perspectives tended to highlight the historically well-adapted, flexible and potentially renewable roles of 'traditional' local communities and institutions in NRM [*Klooster, 2000: 2*]. The correlates of the relative success of such resource management systems, in terms of ecological and social sustainability, also came under debate [*see, for example, Bromley et al., 1992; McCay and Acheson, 1987; Ostrom, 1990; Runge, 1986; Wade, 1988*]. These debates have centred on the conditions that facilitate or hamper the emergence, maintenance and sustainability of such institutional arrangements [*Klooster, 2000; White and Runge, 1995*].

Despite these different perspectives, there is broad consensus among researchers and policy-makers on the pivotal role of institutional arrangements in shaping peoples' interactions with their natural environments and negotiation processes in NRM. These arrangements determine who has what kind of access to which kind of natural resources and what use they can make of such resources. While institutional choice theorists like Ostrom [*1990, 1992*] are particularly interested in grasping processes of institutional crafting and consolidation, reflexive, explanatory approaches have highlighted serious limitations of many design-oriented perspectives. It has been argued that, by adhering to rational choice-based models, design-oriented approaches negate the complex nature of institutions and run the risk of imposing formal institutional forms on previously existing informal, but often invisible, ones [*Cleaver, 2000; Klooster, 2000; Leach et al., 1997, 1999*]. According to these critics, the inherent tendencies towards functionalism in design-oriented approaches and the view of institutions as simply 'rules-in-use' that progress from weak to robust forms and to steady states given adequate support, are oversimplified, static and evolutionistic.

In these critical perspectives, institutions encompass not only sets of formal and informal rules, regulations and norms but also social meaning – namely, shared values, understandings and perceptions of 'the right way of doing things' [*Cleaver, 2000: 368*]. Thus, institutions are intrinsically permeated and shaped by notions and ideologies of gender, class and other social divisions in societies; related 'deeply-sedimented social practices' may also be considered as institutions, or as part of institutions [*Giddens, 1979: 80*]. In much of the literature an even broader concept of institutions – encompassing organisations – is used.

However, such a conception must be handled with caution, even though the idea of viewing institutions simply as rules – and thus sharply distinguishing rule from practice – has been dismissed. As noted by Leach *et al.*, only some institutions that are of critical importance to resource access and control have organisational forms. Many have 'no single or direct organisational manifestations, including money, markets, marriage, and the law' [*Leach et al., 1999: 237*].

These critical views emphasise the diversity, multiplicity and interrelatedness of the institutions involved in NRM – among which there are many informal ones – as well as their dynamic and often conflict-ridden nature. Institutions are 'subject to multiple interpretations and frequent redefinition in the course of daily practice' and 'often operate as arenas of negotiation and struggle', as Berry [*1993: 4, 20*] states. In other words, they constitute contested terrain in which different interests are played out, subject to the power dynamics of human agency. Institutions thus have to be analysed not only in relation to material resources but also in relation to culture and to power and authority relations, including gender relations. Due attention should be given to the contested dimensions of institutions and to their potential for change under the influence of human agency [*Berry, 1993, 1997; Cleaver, 2000; Klooster, 2000; Leach et al., 1997, 1999; Mosse, 1995, 1997*].

Public Choice, Good Governance and Populist Advocacy at the Policy Level

The embracing of decentralised and participatory NRM approaches in many countries since the 1980s has entailed extensive discussions and debates concerning the merits of such organisational and institutional interventions. Among policy-makers as well as academics there appears to exist a widespread consensus at one level about the desirability of decentralisation, derived from the commonly held idea that devolving powers from the centre to lower political and administrative levels may facilitate people's participation in development and resource management. Beyond this, however, the meanings attached to the term 'decentralisation', the views about the extent and forms of participation to be realised, the institutional changes needed regarding the role and structure of the state and the way in which the restructuring process should be achieved, tend to diverge. Not surprisingly, these differences, and the respective debates about them, reflect the theoretical, ideological and political interests of the advocates concerned [*Carney and Farrington, 1998; Mohan and Stokke, 2000; Webster, 1995*].

The most influential actors in the decentralisation arena are, first, neo-liberal public choice advocates, who begin from a market-focused agenda designed to 'roll back the state' and achieve service delivery efficiency through privatisation or delegation – with a preference for such delegation being outside the public sector. Within this perspective, 'participation' implies market transactions, with 'the people' in the role of consumers and possibly providers. Accordingly, in the field of NRM the idea of contracting out services for local natural resource management to NGOs or developing joint delivery systems in NGO and private sector partnerships is increasingly articulated. For example, since the late 1980s a range of Indian policy documents concerning forest and watershed development have been making recommendations in this vein [*Baumann, 2000: 16–17*]. The state is basically seen as a constraint on efficient management. Nevertheless, under 'the enabling state' discourse, neo-liberals have argued more recently that it should provide the kind of administrative and political institutional context necessary to facilitate efficient and effective service delivery [*Mohan and Stokke, 2000: 248*].

In operational terms, the latter perspective has strengthened the overlap of the public choice agenda with a second stream of thought shaping the ideas and practices of decentralisation, namely the 'good governance' agenda. The good governance agenda has clear neo-liberal overtones even as it advocates institutional reforms that should 'bring the state closer to the people' and increase its accountability and transparency [*Baumann, 2000: 17*]. This is to be achieved by administrative and political decentralisation, in combination with a strengthening of local government capacities and efforts to involve the participation of local communities and other local 'stakeholders' in development and NRM activities. Both public choice advocates and good governance protagonists start from a top-down institutional restructuring process in which the state itself is expected to play a central role, with NGOs as key allies. However, the possibility of resistance to such restructuring occurring within the state apparatus, as opportunities for clientelism are lost and power and resources are relinquished to local actors in the periphery, tends to be overlooked. Local structural inequalities and related external and internal patronage and power relations also tend to be neglected. This omission is not necessarily due to the technocratic perspectives of neo-liberals and donor bureaucracies, however; it may also result from populist influence over the design of decentralisation policies, particularly in the field of NRM.

Populist advocates of decentralised NRM, who particularly are favouring community-based approaches, tend to turn a blind eye to local social inequalities and related intra- and inter-community resource controversies and struggles. This allows them to uphold a highly romanticised vision of 'traditional communities' as homogeneous and harmonious entities, inherently capable and inclined to maintain socially and ecologically sustainable NRM systems [*Agrawal and Gibson, 1999; Li, 1996*]. The use of such idealised representations of community in the policy arena can produce 'strategic gains' in 'ongoing processes of negotiation', according to Li [*1996: 502, 509*]. But she cautions against the translation of these images at the operational level because of their misleading generalising and exclusionary tendencies.

Operational Debates

At the operational level, the adoption of decentralised and participatory NRM approaches has frequently taken place within the context of particular programmes or projects for sustainable development that utilise sectoral approaches [*Leach et al., 1997*]. As a consequence, the different forms of institutional arrangements available in given sectoral contexts such as forestry, watershed management, fisheries and the like – as well as the appropriateness of each for the management of the various types of local resources concerned, are now frequently debated issues. One branch of this literature focuses on apparently successful NRM undertakings and contemplates the insights they provide [*for example, Bromley et al., 1992; White and Runge, 1995; Veit et al., 1995*]. A more critical discussion questions the appropriateness of presently prevailing decentralised NRM efforts on various grounds, often related to their technocratic, ahistorical and apolitical features [*see, for example, Mosse, 1997; Steins et al., 2000*]. In particular, the conceptual and operational approaches commonly adopted with respect to 'community', 'participation' and 'jointness' have been repeatedly criticised [*Mosse, 1997; Agrawal and Gibson, 1999; Nelson and Wright, 1995; Sundar, 2000; Utting, 2001*]. It has also been advanced that the question of uncertainty that surrounds the socio-political, economic and ecological conditions shaping people's livelihoods and natural resource use should be seriously considered in decentralised NRM efforts [*Mehta et al., 2001*].

A related discussion concerning forms of NRM decentralisation has narrowly focused upon the question of the extent to which the state should devolve management authority and property rights to local-level communities and groups [*Agrawal and Ribot, 2000; Poffenberger and McGean, 1996*]. The prevalence of the sectoral approach in project operations and in many discussions concerning NRM has narrowed the perspective further. Together, these factors may help explain why many proponents appear to favour the maximum devolution of governance to local-level user groups. However, in embracing this position it appears that the limitations and pitfalls of 'going local', as Mohan and Stokke [*2000: 254*] refer to it, have received insufficient attention.

III. DECENTRALISING NRM: MIXED OBJECTIVES, MIXED RESULTS

It will be clear from the above discussion that operational strategies for decentralisation and participation tend to be informed by a mix of policy objectives, some of which may be inconsistent or even contradictory. As noted, their sources of inspiration are often markedly heterogeneous. On the one hand, national and international agencies are engaged in the promotion of market liberalisation, which is designed to mobilise capital internally and facilitate economic globalisation by opening up local economies to international capital. This requires attuning institutional and organisational arrangements. As a result, the promotion of local participation is often focused on providing support to local private enterprise in the commercial exploitation of natural resources. On the other hand, decentralisation strategies are expected to promote local participation in NRM 'from below', with the goal of defending the subsistence and resource interests of poor communities and user groups dependent on a particular natural resource base for their survival. These opposite demands give rise to various political, economic and administrative contradictions in the moves towards decentralisation.

The lack of compatible objectives, arising from different conceptual and policy approaches to decentralisation, may be reflected in inconsistencies in national legislative and policy frameworks. Contrasted and opposed policy goals from different state agencies can conceivably create new or fuel existing resource conflicts and power struggles at various levels. These may occur within the state and local government apparatus, between state agencies and local communities, and within local communities. For example, in Bangladesh the ministry in charge of the development of fisheries resources has been hampered in developing and implementing an ecologically adequate fisheries policy due to the overlapping involvement of competing ministries in the floodplains concerned [*Rashed, 1998*]. The priorities of the competing ministries are in commercial or revenue-raising resource management activities rather than resource conservation. This situation has not only led to power struggles among different ministries and departments but also to local-level resource conflicts between farming and fishing communities, and within fishing communities between fish traders and artisan or small-scale fishermen [*Rashed, 1998*].

The tendency for different interests to find support in separate branches of the state, such as the conflicting claims of natural resource conservation versus agricultural intensification, has also been reinforced by global institutional factors. Different international donor agencies have often advocated distinct and conflicting strategies for rural and environmental resource management and development [*Lélé, 1991; Utting, 1993: Ch.12*]. The implications of such policy inconsistencies and institutional fragmentation for resource conservation efforts at the local level can be considerable, as will be discussed further below.

The question of conceptual and policy inconsistencies can also be looked at from yet another angle. In constitutional terms, decentralisation has often been based on a principle of 'subsidiarity', which involves the premise that higher state bodies should not be doing what lower organs can do better [*Martinussen, 1997: 215*]. In theory, this remains a useful point of departure to determine which decision-making powers may best be placed at which level.

The test for meaningful decentralisation then becomes the extent to which lower organs are in a position to set their own priorities within the parameters established for their jurisdiction. Further preconditions for decentralisation to become successful are that the lower-level organs should enjoy legitimate authority and adequate capacity, and have sufficient autonomous financial capability – from taxes and revenues and/or central grants – to execute what they have been authorised to do. Nor should such arrangements absolve higher-level bodies from their informational, supervisory, co-ordinating and possible conflict-resolving roles with respect to the execution of decentralised NRM functions, or from ultimate authority over the field of activities concerned.

However, a number of recent examples indicate that decentralisation policies may primarily amount to a selective deconcentration of state functions under the continuing control of the central government. In respect of West Africa, for example, it has been argued that 'the reality of decentralisation so far is that local decision-makers have very little discretion in decision-making, and few skills for effective implementation and monitoring of decisions taken' [*Moore et al., 2000: 1*]. Such policies have often been adopted, it appears, as a way of freeing governments or higher-level organs from financial and administrative responsibility for the activities concerned. Such cost-saving devices have been part of the general drive to push back the role of central government under the aegis of structural adjustment programmes. With reference to certain Sahel country governments, for example, Toulmin [*1991: 35*] suggests that:

> the only 'responsibilisation' that will take place ... is likely to concern cases where the state can divest itself from certain costly obligations, for example by transferring responsibility for maintenance of bore-holes to pastoral associations, and by handing over the role of maintaining irrigation schemes to water user groups.

Decentralisation, which in this and other instances may be closely linked to privatisation, may thus be introduced as a device to generate fiscal savings. In such circumstances the decentralised entities concerned, which may be districts or lower tiers of government, are actively encouraged to find their own resources for the activities they wish to undertake. However, different regions and localities start out with unequal endowments, and are unlikely to find that their respective governments are prepared to come forward with significant redistributive measures [*De Bruijne, 2001: 24, 29*]. This implies that poor districts and local communities will be less able than better endowed ones to make use of the new 'opportunities'. Moreover, environmental protection and equitable participation in NRM may not rank very high on the list of priorities to which modest resources are allocated. What remains then, at best, is the possibility of a foreign donor being prepared to step in and fund the initiation of environmental projects thought to be of longer-term relevance, even though such an intervention is in principle temporary and will generate the need for sustainable follow-up.

Closely related to the subsidiarity rationale for decentralisation is the argument that decentralisation can build on the efforts of local groups and communities, thereby engaging local knowledge to resolve local problems. However, within the local context, broader, more comprehensive perspectives on the interlocking problems of a particular natural resource base may not always be articulated. Indeed, different stakeholders may be inclined to act on matters in line with their own specific interests and horizons. In many situations no mechanisms exist to juxtapose these different interests. Where such institutional gaps occur, it is important to try to overcome them through the creation of channels for informed dialogue among stakeholders. This may raise awareness of the implications of each group's actions on the interests and welfare of others, and of the legitimate claims of other users to access the resource base concerned. Attempts to do this have been advocated, and tentatively pursued, with regard to resource conflicts involving various pastoralist groups and farming communities in the Horn of Africa [*Doornbos, 2001*]. It remains to be seen, however, whether they will be sufficient to meet the demands of equity.

An important related question concerns the determination of 'stakeholders'. If decision-making on such issues is based on prevailing institutional patterns in respect of property rights or identities, most often women will not be defined as stakeholders. The likelihood of such a course of affairs is particularly great if existing networks of local leaders and 'knowledgeable' state and NGO representatives play a key role in the process of establishing contacts and gathering information, as is frequently the case. Local leadership institutions as well as state and NGO agencies working in the fields of agriculture, forestry and water resource management are in general 'male spaces' that lack gender sensitivity. In short, 'stakeholder consultations, if not handled properly, may serve the ends of (continued) social exclusion – most especially that of edging women out of the process' [*Pantana et al., n.d.: 17*].

The Indian Experience: Contradictory Decentralisation Dynamics

The Indian experience may be used to further illustrate the extent of unfulfilled expectations regarding decentralisation. There has been considerable pressure in India from below – exerted by various people's movements and NGOs – for both the decentralised management of natural resources and increased people's participation in such management [*Dwivedi, 2001; Poffenberger and McGean, 1996; Sinha et al., 1997*]. At the same time, consistent with worldwide trends stimulated by international financial institutions, the central Indian government has, in recent years, initiated decentralisation of NRM along sectoral lines by establishing guidelines for devolving decision-making powers and central government funds to lower administrative levels. Decentralisation further down to the community level is also being encouraged, facilitating participatory resource management that focuses on local, community-based user groups. However, as economic globalisation has increasingly demanded the opening up of local economies, local NRM in many parts of the country has become geared towards commercialisation without adequate attention to the subsistence needs of the poor, or indeed protection of natural resources.

These contradictory decentralisation dynamics have been compounded by a complex set of political, economic and administrative problems. First, the central government of India has issued not only specific guidelines for the sectoral decentralisation of NRM but also legislation and guidelines that stipulate decentralisation of government itself, with the latter, not surprisingly, having implications for NRM. However, the ways in which these two forms of decentralisation should interface in practice has remained an unresolved question. This is partly because it has been largely up to the state governments, and in the case of specific natural resources to the line departments within states, to implement the various sets of decentralisation guidelines in ways that they see fit. Thus, the forms and political and legal contents of decentralisation depend largely on the particular constellations of political forces within the various state polities and administrations. In many states, it appears that politicians, bureaucrats or members of legislative bodies have thwarted the devolution of adequate resources, powers and authority to elected local government (*panchayati raj*) institutions and to user groups. Local politicians and power-holders have in fact often hijacked decentralisation of NRM initiatives for electoral and related purposes. Only in five or six states have serious attempts been made to carry through democratic or political – as distinct from merely administrative – decentralisation by devolving powers and resources to representative bodies that are accountable to local populations [*Manor, n.d.; Webster, 1995*]. When noting this, though, we should also remember that this record still contrasts favourably to that of many other countries.

Aside from intra-state obstacles, constructive implementation of both the *panchayati raj* and sectoral NRM forms of decentralisation has been frustrated by political strife between the central and state governments. The principal arena of contention – functions, powers and authority within the policy field of development planning and implementation – happens to be central for both the *panchayati raj* and sectoral NRM decentralisation activities [*Baumann, 1998*]. The multilayered administrative and political competition and conflicts accompanying decentralisation in India are also fuelled by the problems surrounding the relationship between the system of *panchayati raj* and newly evolved sectoral NRM institutions at the local level. The same is true for the relationship between different sectoral NRM institutions established within the same geographical area. Concerns noted in this respect include a lack of complementarity in the functioning of the different institutions and a lack of constructive interlinking between different institutions [*Kant and Cooke, 1998*]. Instead, there is often a tendency to subsume local user groups into local government bodies, which may erode their effectiveness [*Poffenberger and Singh, 1996*]. The reverse may also occur – namely, sectoral NRM institutions taking on the functions assigned to *panchayati raj* institutions [*Baumann, 1998*]. Evidently, therefore, where the democratic functioning of local bodies is impaired and internal political deadlocks occur, weaker user groups tend to be disadvantaged in conflicts regarding resource allocation. In such circumstances, decentralisation may mean further empowerment of the powerful and the progressive weakening of the poor. At a range of different institutional levels, new NRM policies and arrangements may thus constitute fresh targets for political gain and competition. Such anomalies may occur particularly in the context of transitions towards decentralisation, though there is a danger that they may turn into more permanent features.

In its attempts to create a more market-friendly economic framework, the Indian government has also been encouraging a greater role for the private sector – thus allowing resource management regimes in various areas to become oriented towards, if not governed by, specific user categories of particular environmental resources. For example, in several parts of India poor owners of small ruminants, as well as other resource users, have been losing their customary access to village commons as these areas have been given to commercial dairy farming co-operatives for pasture cultivation [*Doornbos and Gertsch, 1994*]. Similar selective group privatisation tendencies have been noted in favour of other commercial farming activities and of commercial woodland exploitation [*Agarwal, 1992; Blair, 1996*]. Resource use clashes not only pertain to land-based resources but have also increasingly occurred with regard to maritime resources, over which artisan fishermen have been competing with the mechanised fishing sector for their livelihood [*Meynen, 1989*]. As in the case of forests, this process has resulted in the formation of various social and political movements for the protection of the rights of the artisanal sector and the conservation of the resource base.

Clearly, potentially conflicting pressures arise from the opening up of local markets in response to globalisation and liberalisation on the one hand, and the demand to ensure equitable access to environmental resources to the weaker sections of local populations on the other. First, market forces may influence incentives for collective action positively as well as negatively. Hobley and Shah, for example, note the potentially positive role of market incentives in inducing local group-based NRM efforts. They also warn, however, that 'markets are difficult to predict and products that have a high value today may equally have a low value tomorrow, possibly endangering the viability of resource management organisations' [*Hobley and Shah, 1996: 5*]. Moreover, differences in market access among users of a particular resource are a crucial source of conflicting demands, which may also constrain or jeopardise co-operation in NRM [*Kurian, 2001; Meynen, 1989*]. The more heterogeneous the resource use interests and household endowments of a community, the more susceptible they may be to such conflicting pressures. Out of fear of the squabbles that might ensue, some Indian *panchayats* even appeared to be reluctant to engage in community-based forest management endeavours [*Blair, 1996: 489*]. The influence of heterogeneity on the scope for community-based or collective NRM is not always negative, however. According to Hobley and Shah [*1996*], this will largely depend on the representativeness and effectiveness of management and decision-making structures.

Technocratic Paradigms and Boundary Setting

Several authors stress that technocratic paradigms in and of themselves may leave a strong imprint on the currently prevailing approaches towards decentralised and participatory NRM [*Cleaver, 2000; Gauld, 2000; Gronow, 1995; Utting, 2000*]. One of the implications is a selective targeting and mode of implementation of environmental and sustainable development concerns. This can have far-reaching consequences, including the adoption of a divisible and fragmented perspective on 'nature'. Decentralised interventions in NRM tend to focus on specific natural resources, like forests, wildlife or water. Which resource is targeted is strongly influenced by environmental and economic fads and fashions. Such a perspective treats specific natural resources as isolated systems. It negates the 'nested' and interdependent nature of ecosystems, and thus the need for an integrated and holistic approach to ecosystem regeneration [*Agarwal and Narain, 2000; Uphoff, 1998*]. Bureaucratic reification also occurs by placing communities and user groups, conceptualised as spatially and socially bounded entities, centre stage in conservation and resource management, to the neglect of broader identities and wider relationships and their fluid and ambiguous institutional boundaries. This tendency prevents adequate recognition of how newly established or reconstituted and formalised institutional spaces are being used politically for the sake of reshaping social, economic and political relationships between genders, ethnic groups and the like in the interest of dominant parties [*Mosse, 1997; Rashed, 1998*]. It also negates the possibility that decentralising resource management and use rights to relatively small, spatially bounded, permanent units may be counter-effective in terms of sustainability if considered from a wider perspective [*Agrawal and Gibson, 1999; Uphoff, 1998*].

Various case studies of newly established community forest and watershed management systems in India demonstrate the ways in which the aforementioned problems are a real threat to both ecological and social sustainability. They reveal inter-village as well as intra-village conflicts over boundaries, the barring of access to enclosed commons and the overriding of the rights of weaker communities or subgroups – like tribals, landless, herdsmen, women and migrants – by more powerful ones [*Ahluwalia, 1997; Poffenberger, 1996; Sarin, 1996*]. For example, a forest regeneration programme studied by Shah and Shah [*1995*] resulted in fierce confrontations between the different villages involved. This was because its decentralised village-based approach to NRM led the most forest-dependent members of such villages to raid the forest areas of adjoining villages in order to allow for the regeneration of their own forest. The extent to which this situation threatened to disrupt the widespread network of social relationships on which the sustainability of the village communities depended is very well portrayed by the following lament by one of the village leaders:

> I am wondering what we [Pingot people] are gaining from protecting our forests so religiously? … If it continues like this, every village around Pingot will be our enemy. Then their relatives in other villages will become our enemies as well. At this rate our daughters in Pingot will never be able to get married. Who will want to marry an enemy's daughter? [*Shah and Shah, 1995: 81*].

It is not only with regard to community groups that sensitivity to the possible negative consequences of place-based boundary setting for sustainable and equitable natural resource use and development has been frequently lacking. The same is true for districts and local government units. As Veit notes with respect to the African context, 'too often, local administrative boundaries are not conducive to or supportive of local-level socio-economic development or environmental management'. Instead, he recommends boundary setting, or 'redistricting' as he calls it, 'more sensitive to ecosystems and natural resource endowments' [*Veit, 1996: 1–2*].

This discrepancy between the boundaries of specific ecosystems and those of respective local government units that should manage them has also been observed elsewhere. In India, boundary questions are complicated by the failure to reconcile the roles of different institutions with formal or customary mandates to manage natural resources in a certain region. In some areas, then, competition and conflicts arising from the overlap of roles and/or jurisdictions exist between *panchayats* and newly established watershed committees, and between the latter committees and the new forest protection committees. Competition and conflicts are also evident between these formal institutions and informal institutions operative in the same area [*Baumann, 1998; Kant and Cooke, 1998*].

Decentralised sectoral approaches to 'nature' and to 'people' thus present a danger of producing fragmented and disjointed approaches to resource policy and governance. It is possible to end up with situations in which no institution has sufficient authority and scope to coordinate and accommodate the diversity of resource interests and/or the aggregate of formal and informal institutions with a resource management role.

Institutionalised Exclusion

Cumulatively, the above factors tend to accentuate rather than diminish resource conflicts, the unsustainable use of certain natural resources and social inequality. This danger is aggravated by the exclusion of insufficiently represented or indeed non-represented interests from access to NRM endeavours, and by their likely reaction. These interests include female community members, mobile and/or transitory user groups, non-residential stakeholders or villages located elsewhere within the geographical spread of the resource concerned. Women in particular are frequently excluded through representative systems of community institutions and organisations. Such institutions tend to accept only one member per household – usually the formal head, the formal titleholder or the 'owner' of certain resources such as land, trees or forest resources: these are positions largely occupied by men. Moreover, even without formal exclusion, women are often unable or unwilling to participate in formal mixed gender meetings, or, even if they do participate, they may be unable or unwilling to voice their views and concerns. This can be due to numerous factors, such as restrictions on women's mobility, skills, time, access and control of resources, and authority and constraints in the discursive interactions between men and women [*Mayoux, 1995: 246–7; Zwarteveen 2001: 3–5; Jackson, 1997*].

With such problems in mind, Meinzen-Dick and Zwarteveen, writing on south Asia but with wider relevance, conclude that attempts at improvement 'cannot be left to local communities' but will need 'external pressure, guidance and intervention' [*Meinzen-Dick and Zwarteveen, 1997: 4*]. Yet it is not only local communities that need this kind of external pressure and support to improve gender equity. The same is true for local governments, and for many state agencies and NGOs engaged in NRM in agriculture, forestry and water resources. Preferably, local women's movements and organisations with sufficient gender expertise in the areas concerned should take the lead in this, as they already do in various instances.

Another related and frequently reported source of exclusion, with harmful implications extending beyond gender relations, are systems of representation in NRM that rely on constructs of property or usufruct that neglect the multidimensional nature of overlapping and nested rights to and uses of natural resources [*Rocheleau and Edmunds, 1997*]. As may be easily recognised, this is a long-standing problem. For example, Sundar observes that in northern India in the early and mid-nineteenth century, village commons were established by enclosures that annihilated existing communal relationships between highland and lowland cultivators [*Sundar, 2000: 253*]. The same practice occurred during the Peruvian agrarian reform of the 1970s, when collectives were created in valleys of the Sierra with boundaries that negated the user rights of and exchange relationships with agro-pastoralists of the Altiplano. Again, recent 'community'-based NRM approaches exhibit similar tendencies of exclusion, especially impinging on mobile and non-residential user-groups like pastoralists, shifting cultivators, seasonal gatherers and migrants. An important reason for this is, as suggested earlier, that the enclosure of commons is frequently linked conceptually to a notion of 'local community', conceived in terms of 'permanent, year-round residency' [*McLain and Jones, 1998: 1*]. This community is thought to have a clear-cut, 'identifiable relationship to an identifiable resource', to use the words of Sundar [*2000: 254*]. Other characteristics commonly attributed to 'the community' are that it 'consists of stable married households' and 'privileges the male links of property as against the multiple other links that individual households share with their affines' [*Sundar, 2000*]. It will be clear from the above discussion that these assumptions tend particularly to harm the resource use interests of women.

Thus, the analytical, empirical and policy prioritisation of 'going local' through decentralisation and participation may fail to place the institutional issues concerned within a wider complex of interactions, making it difficult to capture the combined effects of various kinds of institutional interventions. Questions about the interrelations, interactions and possible contradictions between different institutional arrangements for resource management certainly appear to have received less attention than they deserve. The same is true with respect to the question as to whether or not there are sufficiently meaningful mechanisms in place for overall resource use co-ordination, including the handling of changing resource claims, resource conflicts and instances of unwarranted exclusion.

IV. CONCLUDING REMARKS

One of the basic problems encountered in NRM decentralisation efforts concerns the contradictory dynamics arising from the policy inconsistencies discussed in this essay. The pressures exerted by global economic forces and processes and the policy prescriptions of international financial agencies have led many states to adopt liberalisation, privatisation and market deregulation. The weaker the resource base of national economies and the more they suffer from debt burdens and political instability the less manoeuvring room they will have *vis-à-vis* these international pressures and demands. Moreover, sometimes the same international agencies that prescribe economic policies favouring opportunities for private capital to lay claims on and exploit valuable natural resources also advocate local government- and/or community-based NRM approaches presumed to strengthen the resource base and livelihood options of poor people. Thus, policy inconsistencies at national levels – and the kind of economic reforms and institutional restructuring processes they have given rise to – reflect and are strongly conditioned by interactions with international actors and factors. Only strong states, that is to say ones that over time have managed to maintain a 'relative autonomy' and capacity to govern, are able to manoeuvre in international and national arenas in ways that would allow national policy reforms to be consistent with the requirements of democratic decentralisation. This, of course, also assumes that they have the political will and determination to do so.

An equally fundamental problem hindering democratic NRM decentralisation concerns structural inequalities that prevent politically and economically marginalised classes and groups from effectively voicing and defending their resource interests and claims *vis-à-vis* powerful competitors and in broader decision-making processes. In many countries, redressing such inequalities would require interventions in production and property systems in ways that run counter to the dominant forces and processes at work. With respect to presently favoured property systems, it should be noted, for example, that even those rural people who are involved in NRM activities under community-based or co-management programmes often do not have secure long-term property or usufruct rights to the natural resources they are expected to manage.

If the gains from decentralised decision-making and community participation are to materialise, a further requirement is that decentralising state organs should not be allowed to abandon their ultimate responsibility for natural resource policy. Instead, they should ensure that the decentralised organs command sufficient powers, including financial and judicial powers, to be able to adequately execute their responsibilities. Moreover, given the many different institutional initiatives for resource management at the local or micro levels, adequate mechanisms at a common or central level are needed that can handle potentially conflicting or even exclusionary NRM initiatives. For such mechanisms to be meaningful, however, the kinds of interests that tend to dominate policy processes must be taken into account. Interest in the promotion of grass-roots participation in NRM should not be allowed to degenerate into a smokescreen for powerful local interests to capture and exploit particular resources.

Adding to the complexity, it is important to anticipate that, beyond broad structural similarities, different situations may present different kinds of contradictions. Rather than allowing for the application of uniform NRM models, there is a need for solutions sensitive to the situations in question. For example, in some resource conflict situations state agencies representing a particular interest may themselves figure as one of the key parties in conflict over access to environmental resources. Thus, forest departments have been known to try to prevent forest dwellers from encroaching upon the forest so that they can harvest its products [*Pathak, 1994; Matose, 1997*]. In other situations the state may find itself called upon to protect the interests of weaker resource-dependent communities *vis-à-vis* more powerful private agents. While the shaping or reshaping of political arenas, through decentralisation or otherwise, will give rise to changing opportunity structures, the precise alignment of 'weak' and 'strong' may vary from case to case – calling for differentiated responses.

In short, if decentralisation of NRM is to stand any chance of success, a variety of demands must be made on the process. Yet these can hardly be realised without well-organised local bodies and civil society groups capable of articulating and effectively pursuing the diversity of local interests, particularly those of politically marginalised categories. This alone is difficult enough, but the other condition for meaningful decentralisation is even more problematic: powerful countervailing forces must be built at the global level in order to achieve a more enabling global environment that can sustain if not promote effective NRM strategies at different levels. The latter would require a fundamental reversal of the way policy priorities are presently established – a process that will take time and perseverance. In the interim, the most one could expect is no more than piecemeal gains within a framework of continuing contradictions and contestations between and among global, local and intermediate interests.

REFERENCES

Agarwal, A. and S. Narain, 2000, 'Community and Household Water Management: The Key to Environmental Regeneration and Poverty Alleviation', http://www.undp.org/seed/pei/publication/water.pdf, accessed 14 Jan. 2002.

Agarwal, B., 1992, 'The Gender and Environment Debate: Lessons from India', *Feminist Studies*, Vol.18, No.1, pp.119–58.

Agrawal, A. and C. Gibson, 1999, 'Enchantment and Disenchantment: The Role of Community in Natural Resource Conservation', *World Development*, Vol.27, No.4, pp.629–49.

Agrawal, A. and J. Ribot, 2000, 'Analyzing Decentralization: A Framework with South Asian and West African Environmental Cases', Digital Library of the Commons Working Paper, http://dlc.dlib.indiana.edu/documents/dir0/00/00/04/40/dlc-00000440-01/agrawalribot440.pdf, accessed 25 Jan. 2002.

Ahluwalia, M., 1997, 'Representing Communities: The Case of a Community-Based Watershed Management Project in Rajasthan, India', *IDS Bulletin*, Vol.28, No.4, pp.23–34.

Baumann, P., 2000, 'Sustainable Livelihoods and Political Capital: Arguments and Evidence from Decentralisation and Natural Resource Management in India', *ODI Working Paper No.136*, London: Overseas Development Institute.

Baumann, P., 1998, '*Panchayati Raj* and Watershed Management in India: Constraints and Opportunities', *ODI Working Paper No.114*, London: Overseas Development Institute.

Berry, S., 1997, 'Tomatoes, Land and Hearsay: Property and History in Asante in the Time of Structural Adjustment', *World Development*, Vol.25, No.8, pp.1225–41.

Berry, S., 1993, *No Condition is Permanent: The Social Dynamics of Agrarian Change in Sub-Saharan Africa*, Madison, WI and London: The University of Wisconsin Press.

Blair, H.W., 1996 'Democracy, Equity and Common Property Resource Management in the Indian Subcontinent', *Development and Change*, Vol.27, No.3, pp.475–99.

Bromley, D.W., et al. (eds.), 1992, *Making the Commons Work: Theory, Practice and Policy*, San Francisco, CA: Institute for Contemporary Studies Press.

Carney, D. and J. Farrington, 1998, *Natural Resource Management and Institutional Change*, London and New York: Routledge.

Cleaver, F., 2000, 'Moral Ecological Rationality, Institutions and the Management of Common Property Resources', *Development and Change*, Vol.31, No.2, pp.361–83.

De Bruijne, A., 2001, 'Globe, Oikoumene en Oikos: Reflecties over *Human Geography*', Valedictory address, 30 Nov., University of Amsterdam, Amsterdam: Vossiuspers.

Doornbos, M., 2001, 'Research-Led Policy Deliberation in Eritrea and Somalia: Searching to Overcome Institutional Gaps', in M.A. Mohamed Salih, T. Dietz and A.G.M. Ahmed (eds.), *African Pastoralism: Conflict, Institutions and Government*, pp.278–92, London: Pluto Press.

Doornbos, M. and L. Gertsch, 1994, 'Sustainability, Technology and Corporate Interest: Resource Strategies in India's Modern Dairy Sector', *Journal of Development Studies*, Vol.30, No.3, pp.916–50.

Dwivedi, R., 2001, 'Environmental Movements in the Global South', *International Sociology*, Vol.16, No.1, pp.11–31.

Gauld, R., 2000, 'Maintaining Centralized Control in Community-Based Forestry: Policy Construction in the Philippines', in M. Doornbos, A. Saith and B. White (eds.), *Forests: Nature, People, Power*, Oxford: Blackwell, pp.223–48.

Giddens, A., 1979, *Central Problems in Social Theory*, London: Macmillan.

Gronow, C.J.V., 1995, 'Shifting Power, Sharing Power: Issues from User-Group Forestry in Nepal', in N. Nelson and S. Wright (eds.), *Power and Participatory Development*, London: Intermediate Technology, pp.125–32.

Hardin, G., 1968, 'The Tragedy of the Commons', *Science*, Vol.162, pp.1243–8.

Hobley, M. and K. Shah, 1996 'What Makes a Local Organisation Robust? Evidence from India and Nepal', *ODI Natural Resource Perspectives*, No.11, http://www.oneworld.org/odi/nrp/11.html, accessed on 2 May 2000.

Jackson, C., 1997, 'Actor Orientation and Gender Relations at a Participatory Project Interface' in A. Goetz (ed.), *Getting Institutions Right for Women in Development*, London and New York: Zed Books, pp.161–75.

Kant, S. and R. Cooke, 1998, 'Complementarity of Institutions: A Prerequisite for the Success of Joint Forest Management. A Comparative Case of four Villages from India', International Workshop on Community-Based Natural Resource Management, Washington, DC, http://www.worldbank.org/wbi/conatrem/India-01-Paper.htm, accessed 2 May 2000.

Klooster, D., 2000, 'Institutional Choice, Community, and Struggle: A Case Study of Forest Co-Management in Mexico', *World Development*, Vol.28, No.1, pp.1–20.

Kurian, M., 2001, 'Farmer Managed Irrigation and Governance of Irrigation Service Delivery: Analysis of Experience and Best Practice', *ISS Working Paper No.351*, The Hague: Institute of Social Studies.

Leach, M., R. Mearns and I. Scoones, 1999, 'Environmental Entitlements: Dynamics and Institutions in Community-Based Natural Resource Management', *World Development*, Vol.27, No.2, pp.225–47.

Leach, M., R. Mearns and I. Scoones, 1997, 'Institutions, Consensus and Conflict: Implications for Policy and Practice', *IDS Bulletin*, Vol.28, No.4, pp.90–95.

Leeuwis, C., 2000, 'Reconceptualizing Participation for Sustainable Rural Development: Towards a Negotiation Approach', *Development and Change*, Vol. 31, No.5, pp.931–60.

Lélé, S.M., 1991, 'Sustainable Development: A Critical Review', *World Development*, Vol.19, No.6, pp.607–21.

Li, T.M., 1996, 'Images of Community: Discourse and Strategy in Property Relations', *Development and Change*, Vol.27, No.3, pp.501–27.

Manor, J., n.d., 'Democratic Decentralisation in two Indian States: Past and Present', Draft paper, http://www.livelihoodoptions.info/papers/htm, accessed 23 Sept. 2002.

Martinussen, J., 1997, *Society, State and Market: A Guide to Competing Theories of Development*, London and New York: Zed Books.

Matose, F., 1997, 'Conflicts around Forest Reserves in Zimbabwe: What Prospects for Community Management?' *IDS Bulletin*, Vol.28, No.4, pp.69–78.

Mayoux, L., 1995, 'Beyond Naivety: Women, Gender Inequality and Participatory Development', *Development and Change*, Vol.26, No.2, pp.235–58.

McCay, B.J. and J.M. Acheson, 1987, 'Human Ecology of the Commons', in B.J. McCay and J.M. Acheson (eds.), *The Question of the Commons: The Culture and Ecology of Communal Resources*, Tucson, AZ: The University of Arizona Press, pp.1–34.

McLain, R. and E. Jones, 1998, 'Whose Mushrooms? Dealing "Outsiders" into Communal Management of Common Natural Resources', http://www.id21.org, accessed 5 May 2000.

Mehta, L., M. Leach and I. Scoones, 2001, 'Editorial: Environmental Governance in an Uncertain World', *IDS Bulletin*, Vol.32, No.4, pp.1–9.

Meinzen-Dick, R. and M. Zwarteveen, 1997, 'Gendered Participation in Water Management: Issues and Illustrations from Water Users' Associations in South Asia', http://www.iar.ubc.ca/centres/cisar/MEINZEN-DICK/MD1.html, accessed 9 Oct. 2001.

Meynen, W., 1989, 'Fisheries Development, Resource Depletion and Political Mobilization in Kerala: The Problem of Alternatives', *Development and Change*, Vol.20, No.4, pp.735–70.

Mohan, G. and K. Stokke, 2000, 'Participatory Development and Empowerment: The Dangers of Localism', *Third World Quarterly*, Vol.21, No.2, pp.247–68.

Moore, K.M., M.K. Bertelsen, L. Diarra, A. Kodio, S. Cissé and P. Wyeth, 2000, 'Natural Resource Management Institution Building in the Decentralized Context of West Africa: The SANREM CPRS Approach', Paper prepared for the IFSA Symposium in Santiago, Chile, Nov., http://www.oird.vt.edu/sanremcrsp/workpapers/0102.pdf, accessed 9 Oct. 2001.

Mosse, D., 1997, 'The Symbolic Making of a Common Property Resource: History, Ecology and Locality in a Tank-Irrigated Landscape in South India', *Development and Change*, Vol.28, No.3, pp.467–504.

Mosse, D., 1995, 'Local Institutions and Power: The History and Practice of Community Management of Tank-Irrigation Systems in South India', in N. Nelson and S. Weight (eds.), *Power and Participatory Development*, London: Intermediate Technology, pp.144–56.

Nelson, N. and S. Wright (eds.), 1995, *Power and Participatory Development*, London: Intermediate Technology.

Ostrom, E., 1992, *Crafting Institutions for Self-Governing Irrigation Systems*, San Francisco, CA: Institute for Contemporary Studies Press.

Ostrom, E., 1990, *Governing the Commons: The Evolution of Institutions for Collective Action*, New York: Cambridge University Press.

Pantana, P., M. Real and B. Resurreccion, n.d., 'Officializing Strategies: Participatory Processes and Gender in ADB's Capacity Building in Thailand's Water Resources Sector', Bangkok, Mekong Regional Environmental Governance Perspective Paper, REPSI-WRI, 2000–1.

Pathak, A., 1994, *Contested Domains: The State, Peasants and Forests in Contemporary India*, London: Sage.

Poffenberger, M., 1996, 'The Struggle for Forest Control in the Jungle *Mahals* of West Bengal, 1750–1990', in M. Poffenberger and B. McGean (eds.), *Village Voices, Forest Choices: Joint Forest Management in India*, Delhi: Oxford University Press, pp.133–59.

Poffenberger, M. and B. McGean (eds.), 1996, *Village Voices, Forest Choices: Joint Forest Management in India*, Delhi: Oxford University Press.

Poffenberger, M. and C. Singh, 1996, 'Communities and the State: Re-establishing the Balance in Indian Forest Policy', in M. Poffenberger and B. McGean (eds.), *Village Voices, Forest Choices: Joint Forest Management in India*, Delhi: Oxford University Press, pp.57–81.

Rashed un Nabi, 1998, 'The Inland Capture Fisheries in Bangladesh: Institutions and Endowments', Unpublished MA Research Paper, The Hague: Institute of Social Studies.

Rocheleau, D. and D. Edmunds, 1997, 'Women, Men and Trees: Gender, Power and Property in Forest and Agrarian Landscapes', *World Development*, Vol.25, No.8, pp.1351–71.

Runge, C.F., 1986, 'Common Property and Collective Action in Economic Development', *World Development*, Vol.14, No.5, pp.623–35.

Sarin, M., 1996, 'From Conflict to Collaboration: Institutional Issues in Community Management', in M. Poffenberger and B. McGean (eds.), *Village Voices, Forest Choices: Joint Forest Management in India*, Delhi: Oxford University Press, pp.165–203.

Shah, M.K. and P. Shah, 1995, 'Gender, Environment and Livelihood Security: An Alternative Viewpoint from India', *IDS Bulletin*, Vol.26, No.1, pp.75–82.

Sinha, S., S. Gururani and B. Greenberg, 1997, 'The "New Traditionalist" Discourse of Indian Environmentalism', *Journal of Peasant Studies*, Vol.24, No.3, pp.65–99.

Steins, N.A., V.M. Edwards and N. Röling, 2000, 'Redesigned Principles for CPR Theory', *The Common Property Digest*, No.53, June.

Sundar, N., 2000, 'Unpacking the "Joint" in Joint Forest Management', in M. Doornbos, A. Saith and B. White (eds.), *Forests: Nature, People, Power*, Oxford: Blackwell, pp.249–73.

Toulmin, C., 1991, 'Bridging the Gap between Top-Down and Bottom-Up in Natural Resource Management', in P.T.W. Baxter (ed.), *When The Grass Is Gone*, Uppsala: The Scandinavian Institute of African Studies, pp.27–36.

Uphoff, N., 1998, 'Community-based Natural Resource Management: Connecting Micro and Macro Processes, and People within their Environments', International Workshop on 'Community-Based Natural Resource Management', Washington, DC, http://www.frameweb.org/pdf/CBNRM_micro_macro_processes.pdf.

Utting, P., 2001, 'An Overview of the Potential and Pitfalls of Participatory Conservation', in P. Utting (ed.), *Forest Policy and Politics in the Philippines: The Dynamics of Participatory Conservation*, Honolulu: University of Hawaii Press.

Utting, P., 1993, *Trees, People and Power. Social Dimensions of Deforestation and Forest Protection in Central America*, London: Earthscan._

Veit, P.G., 1996, 'Place-based Environmental Management: The Role of Local Gvernment', http://www.melissa.org/English/publications/Proceedings1996/role96.htm, accessed 9 Oct. 2001.

Veit, P.G, A. Mascarenhas and O. Ampadu-Agyei, 1995, *Lessons from the Ground Up: African Development that Works*, Washington, DC: World Resources Institute.

Wade, R., 1988, *Village Republics: Economic Conditions for Collective Action in South India*, Cambridge: Cambridge University Press.

Webster, N., 1995, 'Democracy, Decentralized Government, and NGOs in Indian Rural Development', *Journal für Entwicklungspolitik*, Vol.11, No.2, pp.187–212.

White, T.A. and C.F. Runge, 1995, 'The Emergence and Evolution of Collective Action: Lessons from Watershed Management in Haiti', *World Development*, Vol.23, No.10, pp.1683–98.

Zwarteveen, M., 2001, 'Thinking about User based Irrigation Organisations from a Feminist Perspective: Access, Participatory Parity and Democracy', Paper presented at Institute of Social Studies Rural Development Seminar, The Hague, 29 Jan.

Abstracts

Between Micro-Politics and Administrative Imperatives: Decentralisation and the Watershed Mission in Madhya Pradesh, India
AMITA BAVISKAR

This essay examines the Watershed Development Mission in Madhya Pradesh, India, where the pressure to show tangible 'success', combined with the bureaucratic imperative to retain control, subverts the decentralised structure of participatory resource management. Project and funding imperatives have helped to undermine the very processes that they purport to support. Yet decentralised management is not simply empty rhetoric, but rather its success or subversion depends on the active collaboration of the state government and villagers. Villagers and lower-level bureaucrats bring diverse agendas and perspectives to development projects, co-opting new institutions and assimilating them into ongoing individual and collective projects of social survival and gain. In conclusion, ways to improve accountability in resource management are suggested.

Decentralisation when Land and Resource Rights are Deeply Contested: A Case Study of the Mkambati Eco-Tourism Project on the Wild Coast of South Africa
BEN COUSINS and THEMBELA KEPE

A failed eco-tourism project in South Africa illustrates the weakness of decentralisations that place insufficient emphasis on democracy. The project promoted 'empowerment' of local communities (and entrepreneurs) and government facilitation of community 'partnerships' with private-sector investors. However, the devolution of effective powers and the accountability of local bodies to community were both neglected. Project planning failed to promote local participation, which would have allowed a clear understanding of local livelihoods and deep-seated land and resource tensions. An entrepreneurial elite attempted to capture project benefits, ordinary community members resisted. Severe conflicts erupted, stalling the project. To overcome such dynamics, democratic decentralisation requires a strong central state to provide resources for land-tenure reform and to promote the devolution of powers and the accountability of local bodies.

European Journal of Development Research, Vol.16, No.1, Spring 2004, pp.255–260
ISSN 0957-8811 print
DOI:10.1080/0957881041000168883

Formal Decentralisation and the Imperative of Decentralisation 'from Below': A Case Study of Natural Resource Management in Nicaragua
ANNE M. LARSON

This essay argues that decentralisation of natural resource management is a political process resisted by central government due to the feared loss of power and/or economic resources to local governments. In Nicaragua, although the formal process of power transfers largely stagnated from 1997 to 2003, decentralisation 'from below' continued to advance thanks to political pressure from civil society and municipal governments and the increasing legitimacy of local authority. At the same time, many municipal governments have little interest in resource management where there are few apparent economic benefits. Local governments, however, respond among other pressures to pressure from constituents and non-governmental organisations to take on resource-management initiatives. At both levels of government, local and grass-roots processes are necessary conditions to make formal decentralisation democratic and responsible.

Democratic Decentralisation and Traditional Authority: Dilemmas of Land Administration in Rural South Africa
LUNGISILE NTSEBEZA

Post-apartheid South Africa embarked on an important democratisation process that included reforms in local government and land administration in the former Bantustans. A new conception of 'developmental local government' introduced the notion of elected local leadership and an emphasis on improving the quality of life of previously disadvantaged sectors. Nevertheless, this democratisation process risks serious compromise due to the concessions being made to traditional rural authorities – the same autocratic local authorities who enjoyed significant powers under apartheid. In particular, the legal transfer of land administration to elected officials has not occurred, leaving this important power under the authority of unaccountable local chiefs and headmen. Is democratic decentralisation compatible with the traditional authorities (chiefs of various ranks) who inherit their posts? While some chiefs and headmen may choose to promote local participation, the freedom to choose one's leaders is automatically excluded – seriously limiting downward accountability. This contribution argues that the central government must recognise this incompatibility and support the rights of rural residents to full citizenship.

What Lies behind Decentralisation? Forest, Powers and Actors in Lowland Bolivia
PABLO PACHECO

Bolivia has undertaken important policy reforms since the mid-1990s aimed at institutionalising popular participation and promoting democratic decentralisation. In the forestry sector, municipal governments have received responsibilities and various mechanisms have been established to hold these governments accountable to local populations. In spite of being among the most advanced forestry sector decentralisations in the region, the democratisation of decision-making is limited – with local governments being primarily responsible for monitoring forest management and illegal activities and promoting forest management by local users. The national government has retained the right to define standards and allocate forest resources. Still, the decentralisation has created conditions for local forest users and municipal governments to become stronger players in natural resources governance. Outcomes of decentralisation are mixed, mainly due to municipal resources and capacity, local power relationships and the degree to which local economies depend on forest resources.

Closer to People and Trees: Will Decentralisation Work for the People and the Forests of Indonesia?
IDA AJU PRADNJA RESOSUDARMO

For over 30 years Indonesia's central government controlled its forests – the third largest area of tropical forests in the world. Driven by serious political, administrative and economic demands for reforms, the central government has begun to decentralise, transferring new powers to the district and municipal levels. Decentralisation in the forestry sector has included transferring income from permits, logging and reforestation fees, as well as the right for these lower levels of government to issue logging permits. This sudden, new access to Indonesia's lucrative timber market has led local peoples and governments to rush to take advantage of a resource to which they previously had little right. The result has included the proliferation of permits with little regard for the effect on forest resources. Large areas, including some protected areas, are being destroyed and threatened with conversion to other uses. Local peoples, however, appear not to have been the ones receiving the primary benefits; they have been taken instead by those who have the required capital for permits and logging.

Decentralisation, Rural Livelihoods and Pasture-Land Management in Post-Socialist Mongolia
ROBIN MEARNS

Mongolia's post-socialist transition since 1990 has included, among other changes, reforms toward democratic decentralisation. For natural resource governance, and pasture-land management in particular, decentralisation has been at best incomplete and at worst 'empty'. It has created an institutional vacuum that herders and others have sought to fill with recourse to formal and informal, new and old arrangements. Herding households are also rapidly increasing against a background of economic hardship and vulnerability. The effects include an altered distribution of grazing pressure, with discernibly adverse impacts on the pastoral environment, and the acceleration of already rising inequality. Democratic decentralisation could help to restore environmental and social justice.

Decentralisation and Accountability in Forest Management: A Case from Yunnan, Southwest China
JIANCHU XU and JESSE C. RIBOT

Over the last two decades, China has introduced forest resources management reforms aiming to protect forests and enhance rural livelihoods. As part of these reforms, some powers over forestry management have been decentralised to village-level institutions. However, this decentralisation has so far failed to give local communities adequate control over forest resources, especially in areas like Yunnan where the ethnic minority population is heavily dependent on these resources for its livelihood. Insufficient powers have been decentralised, the village-level institutions are not sufficiently accountable to the public and some of the reforms designed to protect forest resources have had a negative impact on rural livelihoods.

The Social and Organisational Roots of Ecological Uncertainties in Cameroon's Forest Management Decentralisation Model
PHIL RENÉ OYONO

Decentralisation in Cameroon's forestry sector has opened opportunities for peripheral actors to participate in forest management. Yet local governance structures created to represent local communities are not grounded in local realities. Instead, these committees obey instrumental and administrative priorities, resulting in weak structures that are not supported by sound institutional arrangements or local collective action. This weak organisational infrastructure has generated inefficiency in the local management of forests and related benefits, a new social stratification and the hijacking of committees by a self-interested elite connected to state authorities. The process has also led to ecological uncertainty, due to local opportunistic behaviour.

User Committees: A Potentially Damaging Second Wave of Decentralisation?
JAMES MANOR

Decentralisations in the 1980s transferred powers to multi-purpose local governments. In recent years, international donors and central governments are increasingly turning towards single-purpose user committees. Although these committees appear to be less democratically accountable and less representative than local government, donors view user committees as a mechanism to give local peoples greater say over the development decisions that affect them. Central government officials establish user committees at the insistence of donors but then manipulate them by selecting committee members and by reigning in their powers. This contribution explores how these proliferating single-purpose committees are undermining the democratic processes that were presumably institutionalised with the creation and strengthening of elected local governments in Third World countries. This new approach fragments local participation, reducing its coherence and effectiveness; the poor may even be worse off than before. These committees appear to usurp local government functions and deprive local governments of revenues. These myriad problems result in destructive conflicts and the undermining of local government authority.

Decentralising Water Resource Management in Brazil
CHRISTIAN BRANNSTROM

Recent studies of decentralisation of natural-resource management have advanced two related claims: participation of municipalities encourages downward accountability to local populations and single-issue decentralisation encourages upward accountability to higher levels of government. This contribution examines a case at the intersection of these arguments: participation of municipalities in single-issue decentralisation. Evidence from Brazil's water-resource decentralisation indicates that participation of municipalities is not the best indicator of downward accountability; rather, the nature of social and business groups, and mechanisms that encourage their participation, better predict downward accountability. New territories of single-issue decentralisation may have unintended positive effects on downward accountability.

Decentralising Natural Resource Management: A Recipe for Sustainability and Equity?
WICKY MEYNEN and MARTIN DOORNBOS

This contribution draws attention to the ways in which different, at times contradictory, policy models and directives, together with political and economic dynamics, shape the mixture of institutional arrangements for natural resource management (NRM) as well as their limitations. The essay concludes that if decentralisation of NRM is to stand any chance of success, several demands must be made on the process. Yet these can hardly be realised without well-organised local bodies and civil society groups, particularly those of politically marginalised categories, whilst powerful countervailing forces must be built at the global level to achieve a more enabling environment for effective NRM strategies.

Book Reviews

Imagining the Congo: The International Relations of Identity by Kevin C. Dunn. New York: Palgrave Macmillan, 2003. Pp.xii + 221. £16.99 (paperback). ISBN 1 4039 6160 3

This is an important and engaging book. Kevin Dunn has combined a sophisticated discussion of the dominant representations of the 'Congo' with careful attention to wider 'international' trends as well as processes on the ground in Africa. A key theme of the book is the way in which 'Western understandings of the Congo, even in the twenty-first century, rely heavily upon earlier representations generated by Westerners' (p.ii). This results, he argues, in the 'interesting paradox' that although 'Westerners are generally uninformed about Congolese history and politics, they feel they know it well because of the powerful images' of the Congo that they regularly encounter (p.4). For example, in January 2002 the ABC network broadcast a weeklong series of news reports (described as 'in-depth' coverage) on the Congo under the umbrella title of 'Heart of Darkness'. This, and numerous other examples, argues Dunn, highlight the way in which long-standing imagery continues to be used by the international media 'to make the events in central Africa comprehensible to their viewers by drawing on a tradition that frames that part of the world through the lens of primitivism, backwardness, and irrationality' (p.5).

The central theme of Dunn's book, however, is that such 'representations have political consequences'. He argues that: 'representing the Congo as a primitive, chaotic "heart of darkness" has made certain things happen in the political world' (p.5). For example, in the case of the journalist-cum-explorer Henry Morton Stanley, who spearheaded the conquest and colonisation of the Congo on behalf of King Leopold II of Belgium, the constant use of 'images of the Congo as chaotic, backward, and uncivilized/uncivilizable' facilitated the forcible displacement of 'existing socio-political practices and systems of knowledge with Western-scripted notions of sovereignty, modernity and development' (p.6). In relation to contemporary developments in the Congo, Dunn emphasises that 'the state in which the people of the Congo now find their country can be directly traced back to historical constructions of their identity' insofar as 'those past imaginings have cumulatively helped make the current situation possible' (p.141).

Another key concern of Dunn's book is to interrogate a range of concepts that are routinely deployed to discuss foreign affairs. He demonstrates, with considerable efficacy, that 'the reified concepts and categories that traditional international relations theorists often accept as solid structures – such as identity, interest, state, and sovereignty – are shown to be constructed through repeated patterns of human practice' (pp.176–7). As a result his approach emphasises the need to examine international relations in terms of 'identity-making, interest-making, state-making, sovereignty-making and so forth' (p.180). All these questions are explored in relation to the Congo via the examination of what Dunn characterises as four 'pivotal historical periods of identity production'. These are the 'invention' of the Congo as a Belgian colony in the late nineteenth century; decolonisation and independence in 1960; the reinvention of the Congo as 'Zaire' in the 1970s; and the re-establishment of the 'Congo' at the very end of the 1990s (p.7).

I can find very little to disagree with in this book. One quibble might be Dunn's reliance on the notion of 'Western' and the 'West'. While his book develops a powerful

European Journal of Development Research, Vol.16, No.1, Spring 2004, pp.261–278
ISSN 0957-8811 print
DOI:10.1080/0957881041000168842

critique of the shortcomings of a range of homogenising international narratives on the 'Congo', his use of a unitary notion of 'Western' conjures up more spatial and temporal coherence in these representations than might be warranted. Furthermore, Dunn assumes a high degree of continuity rather than addressing the importance of the rupture between colonial ideas of racial uplift and the civilising mission on the one hand and post-colonial notions of an anti-Communist modernising mission on the other hand (p.97). While there is insufficient space to address this latter issue properly, a case can certainly be made for seeing international ideas about development and modernisation that were consolidated at the time of decolonisation and the universalisation of the nation-state as representing an important departure from the earlier more explicitly racial and religious notions of a civilising mission that were characteristic of the formal colonial era in Africa.

Dunn's analysis raises important questions about the theorisation of international relations generally and Africa's position in the changing global order more specifically. His book is part of a still small, but growing, tendency in the study of international relations (sometimes characterised collectively as 'constructivist') to go beyond Marxist, neo-liberal and realist approaches to international relations and international political economy by drawing attention to the important role of cultural representations and the need to avoid the naturalisation of nation-states and related concepts. Anyone interested in ways of rethinking established international relations paradigms would want to read this book, as will anyone looking for a fresh and persuasive approach to understanding the ongoing crisis in the Congo. In fact, Dunn has brought admirable clarity to bear on both a highly contested and sometimes murky set of debates in international relations theory and on a part of the world that has regularly been explained by recourse to the argument that events there are inexplicable.

MARK T. BERGER
International Studies Programme,
The University of New South Wales

Currents of Change: Globalization, Democratization and Institutional Reform in Latin America edited by Jaime Behar, Ulf Jonsson and Mats Lundahl. Stockholm: Institute of Latin American Studies, 2002. Pp.x + 394. £15.99 (paperback). ISBN 91 85894 59 1

This book covers issues that are very much on the cutting edge of academic and wider public debate throughout Latin America. Divided into four parts, the first covers globalisation, the second democratisation and the third and fourth parts institutional reform, divided into Part 3 on current developments and Part 4 on historical and theoretical perspectives. Its origins lie in a conference held in 2001 to mark the fiftieth anniversary of the Institute of Latin American Studies, Stockholm University. Written mostly by leading Latin American and Swedish scholars, the topics covered range from very broad overviews of democratisation, or the state in the Latin American social sciences, through specific treatments of such issues as transnational agro-food companies in Latin America, the relationship of political parties to civil society, especially in Bolivia, women and democratisation in the Anglophone Caribbean and agrarian policy in Peru from 1960 to 2000, to very detailed examinations of the structural reform of social security in the region or Brazil's Amazon development policy. The book is therefore very broad in the range of topics covered and in the lenses used to cover them.

In their Introduction, the editors highlight briefly where the debate stands on the book's three principal themes. On globalisation, they state that the concerns about the unprecedented deepening integration of Latin American and Caribbean (LAC) countries into the world economy relate not to the importance of trade and capital flows for the region, but rather to 'the ability of LAC countries to shape national strategies according to their own interests and needs' (p.2). On democratisation, they highlight three principal weaknesses of the present approaches to analysing the issue: treating it as a succession of stages each predetermined by the previous one, the difficulties of linking the actions of political actors to outcomes that threaten democracy and the adoption of a limited definition of democracy. Finally, they see that the polarised views of institutional reform in the 1980s and 1990s have now given way to more nuanced approaches, with reformers admitting dubious social consequences and opponents taking a more pragmatic view that no longer defends old institutions as sacrosanct. On the latter issue, the authors write: 'Their problem is to integrate all these perspectives into a coherent body of thought that can be accepted by their domestic constituency' (p.7). In this way, the book provides a sharp, succinct and valuable overview of where the debates have got to on these important topics.

This also, of course, provides a yardstick against which to evaluate the book's contribution to these debates. By and large, with some notable exceptions, the book's contribution is to provide a useful descriptive overview of some subjects; only a few contributors engage more analytically offering important empirical or theoretical advances. On globalisation, the chapter by Bajraj and Bustillo on regional relations between Latin America and the United States on the one hand, and Europe on the other, provides a detailed descriptive overview but is notably lacking in any critical interrogation. By contrast, the chapter by Jonsson on transnational agro-food companies in the Latin American market provides an excellent critical survey of ways in which a small cluster of global companies is gaining more control over the production and distribution of food in Latin America to the detriment of local states, the local environment and small farmers. Importantly, he focuses attention on the need for states to provide 'strong institutional support' (p.65) to domestic producers, particularly small farmers, if they are to benefit from this situation. Finally, the chapter by Behar on shifts in relative wages provides a somewhat inconclusive examination of the reasons why the growing gap in the wages of skilled and unskilled workers in Latin America contradicts neo-classical economic theory that would predict a narrowing of the gap under the conditions of market liberalisation. He concludes that, in the context of liberalisation, market forces 'are raising additional obstacles to Latin American and Caribbean countries' current policy efforts to reduce inequality' (p.82).

Part 2, on democratisation, contains the book's most original contributions. The lengthy chapter by Brachet-Márquez that, as an alternative to transition studies, analyses the long-term gestation of democracy in Latin America since independence maps very impressively a whole research programme of immense promise. In doing this, she establishes analytical categories distinguishing the respective roles and interrelationships of citizenship, government and state that have the potential to provide important breakthroughs in our understanding of processes of democratisation in the region. Uggla's more empirical chapter, based largely on the recent Bolivian experience, highlights what is one of the great puzzles of contemporary politics in the region, namely that, as political parties are more strongly consolidated in their states, their standing in society is growing weaker. In this 'two-track polity', he writes, not much indicates that parties will be able to stabilise and strengthen their roots in society. Finally, Rhoda Reddock offers a very descriptive overview of the participation of women in electoral politics in the Anglophone Caribbean.

Parts 3 and 4 on institutional reform, while containing informative chapters, offer a much more partial and fragmented treatment of this important subject than do the contents of the previous two parts of their respective subjects. Mesa-Lago's lengthy examination of the structural reform of social security in ten countries of the region is the most comprehensive, offering useful detailed lessons about pension reforms, healthcare reforms and reforms of unemployment insurance and social assistance. Other chapters, such as those by Márquez on public training policies and Sabatini and Smolka on the access of the poor to urban land, cover much more specific aspects of institutional reform, while the chapters by Pedrone on economic and political reforms in Brazil and Carvalho *et al.* on Brazil's Amazon development policy are limited to one country. What is lacking is any attempt to integrate the insights derived from these specific studies into a wider treatment of the logic and course of institutional reform in the region, something notably lacking in general scholarship on the issue. This book therefore reflects the problem that it itself identifies in the literature on this subject and which is quoted above.

Finally, the chapters in Part 4, while very interesting in themselves, contribute almost nothing to the book's overall theme. Lundahl examines the history of economic development of Haiti, noting the conflict between factor endowments and ruling-class objectives on the one hand and rulers and ruled on the other. Alberts and Genberg review Peruvian agrarian policy over the period 1960–2000 tracing the far-reaching transformations that agrarian structures went through in the two decades following the reform of 1969. Their preliminary findings suggest that at an aggregate level equity improved and agricultural growth increased, but they emphasise that these contradict most analysts' conclusions and therefore a deeper examination is necessary. Borón's chapter on the role played by the state in Latin American social science has the potential to draw together the main themes in the book, but neither attempts to do this nor moves beyond a very general treatment of its subject. While containing many fascinating and informative chapters, this book is somewhat uneven in is treatment of its key subjects.

PEADAR KIRBY
School of Law and Government,
Dublin City University

Globalization, the Third World State and Poverty-Alleviation in the Twenty-First Century edited by B. Ikubolajeh Logan. Aldershot: Ashgate, 2002. Pp.viii + 204, £39.95 (hardback). ISBN 0 7546 0923 5

This book is a very worthy addition to the growing but still rather limited literature on the impact of globalisation on the South. In particular, its examination of the respective roles of state, market and civil society in poverty alleviation provide it with a focus that is both broad and yet well-defined in addressing what is arguably the greatest challenge facing the processes we label globalisation and the agents furthering them, namely reducing global poverty. By and large, the book's 14 chapters succeed well in contributing to its central theme, with the five chapters following the Introduction addressing general topics about the impact of globalisation on Africa and the next seven taking more particular themes, mostly related to one country. These include science parks in metropolitan Shanghai, Taiwan's policy of importing foreign labour, the developmental impact of trade liberalisation in Mexico, the conversion of the ANC to neoliberalism in South Africa, the changing roles of the state, donors and non-governmental organisations (NGOs) in Mali between 1960 and 1999 and the political ecology of cotton production, again in Mali. The only topic of a wider nature among these chapters is Timothy M. Shaw's fascinating treatment of new forms of regionalism among state and non-state actors in Africa (such as development corridors, transnational informal trade in diamonds, private security networks) as responses to globalisation. The brief concluding chapter is more philosophical, arguing that to be sustainable globalisation must become more universal in showing it can provide global common goods.

A major strength of this book lies in its crosscutting treatment of subjects. For example, it links the neoliberalisation of the state with issues concerning democracy, and in particular the participation of the poor in decision-making. It links the market freedoms offered by neoliberalism to the political freedoms offered by democratisation, treating how they affect the potential for poverty alleviation and how they interact with one another. It adopts a critical focus on the role of civil society (both globalised civil society in the form of international NGOs and local civil society), examining whether it is a conduit for neoliberal globalisation or an agent for resisting it. In these ways, it offers a fresh optic on familiar subjects. Furthermore, its combination of chapters with a regional focus and ones with a national focus offers a fruitful mixture of deductive and inductive approaches towards the issues being examined, though the only focus of regional attention is Africa whereas two Asian cases and a Latin American case are included among the inductive chapters. As a result, the book provides a multifaceted treatment of its central themes.

The topic receiving the fullest treatment is the changing role of the state. In his chapter on what has been happening to the African state under the conditions of globalisation, Carmody tellingly shows the effects of economic liberalisation on the African state and argues that the extensive focus on state failure in Africa has absolved the market from blame for the present crisis. He writes:

> As global deregulation has made certain types of capital more footloose, state functions have been cut backing order to pay back debt and attract international capital through low tax rates. In Africa, the cutbacks are sometimes so large as to leave the state a virtual entity [p.54].

Mengisteab's analysis of what he calls 'market democracy' complements Carmody, showing how market actors are achieving more power, shifting power from collective actors like trade unions and creating an evermore powerful economic elite which undercuts both the economic and political authority of the state. Yet, as Nyango'ro argues, a strong state is needed if African countries are to industrialise and find a more beneficial niche in the international division of labour. While arguing for a middle road between Afro pessimists and Afro optimists, he draws quite pessimistic conclusions that much of the features that make for competitive and comparative advantage are not possessed by African states. An important contribution he makes is to add a focus on regional level, arguing that weak states provide a weak basis for strong regional organisations. Examining the role of South Africa in the Southern African Development Community (SADC), he asks whether most countries will 'be reduced to the status of a periphery of and a market for a much more powerful RSA' (p.85) within this form of regional integration.

In this context, Walcott's chapter on science parks in metropolitan Shanghai and Walker's chapter on the active labour market policies of Taiwan, while interesting examples of state responses to the pressures of globalisation, seem light years away from the challenges facing the African state. If anything, they highlight even further the extent of the challenges facing Africa as both cases clearly rest on a state capacity and flexibility built up over decades. Rozo's chapter on the impact of economic liberalisation on development in Mexico fits far better with the discussion of Africa since it shows how economic liberalisation exacerbates structural dependencies and undermines developmental capacity. Glenzer's chapter on state, donor and NGO configurations in Malian development and Shaw's chapter on new forms of 'trilateral relations among states-inter-state organizations, companies, and civil societies in a post-neoliberal era' (p.145) bring civil society into the picture. While Glenzer shows how the new development paradigm gives a key role to civil society, he tellingly analyses its weaknesses and incapacity to fulfil this role. He points out that many NGOs are aligned with local elites while civil society lacks capacity to address the larger, structural issues. Shaw's broad and novel focus allows him identify levels of civil society activism that can often be missed by analysts; however, much of this seems directed at capturing economic spoils, usually illegally, for specific groups in a context of economic and political turmoil, rather than reinforcing development for the majority.

A final and very valuable focus of this book is provided by Yapa's chapter critiquing the socially constructed nature of poverty discourse and Peet's chapter on neoliberalism in South Africa. In identifying that 'discourse creating' establishments 'form a dominant academic-institutional-media (AIM) complex' (p.134), Peet highlights the 'struggle for discursive power' in which 'development remains an area of contention between competing discourses of modernity based in different social and political imaginations' (p.136). Yapa's chapter is a very good example of a particularly influential construction of a discourse on the key subject of poverty. Together, these chapters illustrate how 'the myriad of sites over which global forces exert their will, are simultaneously sites of opportunity for organized resistance', as Yapa puts it (p.17).

Given the success of this book in maintaining a coherent focus on its central themes throughout the chapters, allowing different authors contribute in different ways, it is surprising that the conclusion does not draw together the many strands of the discussion. The book offers many valuable and largely pessimistic conclusions about the prospects for poverty alleviation in Africa under the conditions of globalisation; the lessons of these conclusions need urgently to be emphasised and, on the basis of them, dominant approaches more robustly contested. In this way, this book has the potential to contribute to 'the battle between alternative visions' that Peet calls for (p.136). It is an important addition to the literature and deserves a wide and attentive readership.

PEADAR KIRBY
School of Law and Government,
Dublin City University

Corruption Fighters' Tool Kit: Civil Society Experiences by Transparency International. Berlin: Transparency International, 2002. Pp.508. £19.99 (paperback). ISBN 3 935711 02 6

The Transparency International's corruption fighters' tool kit presents innovative anti-corruption tools developed and implemented by Transparency International national chapters (NCS) and other civil society organisations (CSOs) from around the World (Introduction, p.7). This compendium of global anti-corruption best practices comprises of seven strategies that evolved out of local experiences world-wide. These strategies are designed to meet the anti-corruption standards of today's international business and lending institutions, as well as provide a roadmap for those combating corruption.

Strategies that have proved effective in combating the scourge of corruption, and are highly recommended by Transparency International, commence with *awareness raising.* Three areas are highlighted: projects that make citizens become aware of the fact that corruption is a cancer in our society; the need to mobilise citizen support for necessary reforms; and the imperative to convince citizens that they can make a positive contribution towards combating corruption. This strategy was successfully employed through the anti-corruption radio spots broadcasts, and source book adaptation projects in Brazil, the Clean Korea 21' Fair, the national corruption observatory project in Morocco, the anti-corruption television sketches project in Niger, the public awareness campaign project in Slovakia and the national anti-corruption week project in Uganda.

Procurement transparency is the second strategy: The strategy makes public procurement of goods and services more transparent, removes discretionary powers from state bureaucrats, opens all procurement bidding and tenders to public scrutiny and widely publicises the database on public procurement. Ecuador, Serbia and Paraguay have implemented this strategy.

Election campaigns are recommended as the third strategy. Corruption during election campaigns can be combated by monitoring media election coverage and making public income and expenditure of political parties during election campaigns. The strategy was utilised in Chile and Costa Rica.

Access to information is the fourth strategy. Educating citizens on how they could gain free access to public information and obtain public services, such as passports, permits, etc., without having to bribe civil servants, is of vital importance. Countries that have applied this tool include Lebanon, Poland, Serbia and Romania.

The fifth strategy is the use of *public institutions*. This ensures that citizens gain access to the inner workings of public institutions, such as courts, parliaments and municipal legislatures, monitor their performances and hold them accountable. Argentina, Bangladesh, Bolivia, Kazakhstan and Mexico have successfully used this strategy.

A *business ethics* moral imperative is the sixth and penultimate strategy. Corruption is best combated by ensuring that the mission of every business enterprise includes the adoption of an ethical approach to business. Colombia has had success with this strategy.

The seventh and final strategy is the use of *diagnostics*. This tool is used in the form of a forensic audit of an institution, providing data on the level of good governance, transparency and bribery. The database then serves as a benchmark of integrity for the institution.

The intellectual content of the tool kit make it one of the finest reports to come from Transparency International. Its style and flavour are different from previous annual and special descriptive narratives and indexes of corruption cases around the world. Instead, this report departs from the previous familiar and predictable adversarial style; it delineates important solutions, which serve as guidelines in the fight against corruption world-wide.

Another important perspective of the tool kit is the global representation of its main architects and the involvement of civil society in the conceptualisation and implementation of the strategies. Yet another important aspect of the tool kit is the presentation style of the suggested instruments: while previous suggested solutions to corruption were often presented piecemeal, the *Corruption Fighters' Tool Kit* has perfected the system by taking a more holistic approach to the solution of the problem.

This new approach will make it easier for the guidelines to be enacted into national law by governments. In addition, the empirical approach of the tool kit makes it readable, practical and appear mundane to the ordinary citizen.

From a practical perspective, however, these strategies have discernible flaws. First, the over dependence, by local civil society, on the initiatives, organisation and resources of Transparency International presents a problem. Second, an unrealistic optimism exists throughout, conveying the impression that the seven tools, *ipso facto*, can provide a panacea for corruption ills; paying civil servants a living wage, for example, should be one of the tools to reduce bribery. Third, governments should be urged to make a firm commitment to the high ideals, norms, values and mission presented by the tool kit. This is necessary because many of the strategies require governments' support if they are to be successfully implemented. Fourth, no attempt is made to understand and solve the root causes of corruption. Finally, lessons of experience teach us that for such a novel programme to achieve its goals, a global partnership or compact, involving civil society, governments and the private sector, must be forged, strengthened and drive the process. Efforts should therefore be made to bring national governments into the alliance by emphasising damaging impact of corruption on economic and human development, as well as highlighting many benefits that could accrue to governments in a corruption free society, such as the fulfilment of donor corruption-free conditionalities.

Despite these shortcomings, the *Corruption Fighters' Tool Kit* succeeds in its main purpose of providing guidelines and good practices for curbing corruption. It should prove a useful survival kit for many governments determined to curb corruption for its pernicious consequences; donor nations willing to increase development aid for poverty reduction; law enforcement agents responsible for combating corruption in public institutions; the ordinary citizen who has been the unwilling victim of this iniquitous system; non-governmental organisations who have been fighting a lone battle against the eradication of this pervasive system; and democratic practitioners and academics whose vision is a world free of corruption.

SAM KONGWA
Department of Political Studies,
University of Transkei

African Identities: Contemporary Political and Social Challenges edited by Ahluwalia Pal and Zegeye Abebe. Aldershot: Ashgate, 2002. Pp.xiv + 175. £42.50 (hardback). ISBN 0 7546 1947 8

African Identities: Contemporary Political and Social Challenges is a collection of essays on various themes, such as boundaries of the African state, women and resistance, ethnicity, contemporary political systems, co-operatives and labour practices. The book seeks to 'evaluate the borders and boundaries, which have encapsulated post-colonial Africa' (p.x). It explores both formalised and less formalised borders and attempts to look at the interstitial spaces between the diverse areas of political, economic, social and cultural systems, which have predominated in defining not only Africa but also the African. It looks at how fluid African identities are, challenging colonial markers of difference by 'problematising borders and boundaries that are no longer relevant to the post-colonial world of the African' (p.x). Finally, 'it challenges the boundaries and borders, which the discipline of African studies has established and vigorously policed' (p.x). Unfortunately this ambitious agenda is only partially covered by the selection of very heterogeneous essays, which do not all explicitly refer to the main theme of the book.

However, some interesting sub-themes emerge around the main theme of the book. The first chapter, written by Bill Ashcroft, explores the linkages between the European representation of Africa and modernity. Ashcroft defines modernity as an epoch in which the world reality came to be formulated and regulated by Europe. This epoch is characterised by the construction of visible boundaries, which represent order and rationality of European civilisation and define the border between civilised self and primitive other. This idea of state boundaries as markers of national identity was transferred to the rest of the world. It is still determining the post-independent African state, which is 'territorially co-extensive' with colonial occupation. Therefore, he argues that social and political transformation of Africa will not occur at the level of state, but rather through African cultural production, which may give new meanings to the 'cross-border' spaces of people's daily life. He suggests new ways to 'inhabit' the boundaries, which draw upon a local cultural reality, while utilising the technology of global culture instead of simply rejecting it. Finally, if the idea of Africa is an invention of modernity, then can we conclude that a crisis of African state is in reality a crisis of modernity itself? Consequently, is the deconstruction of Africa necessary to disrupt the power of modernity to regulate our thoughts?

The subsequent chapters continue on the theme of boundaries and typologies defined by the modern European mind. In the second chapter, Roger Knight challenges the European typology, which distinguishes between settler colonialism (in the Cape) and the colony of exploitation (in Java). This artificial distinction explains the lack of historical comparisons between European colonial communities in Java and the Cape. In contrast, he argues that such comparisons may inform us about the construction of ethnicity in colonial peripheries and parallel evolution of metropolitan understandings. Finally, analysing the boundaries of ethnicity in the colonies tells us more about the markers of 'European' identity than about local realities in these colonies.

The third chapter, written by Elizabeth Rankin, reviews the European myth of continuous Khoisan history as 'hunter-gatherers pursuing an untrammelled lifestyle, unchanged from the beginning of time' (p.28). She shows how modern San artists in Southern Africa use both old philosophy *and* modern urban themes in their art, although Western tourists continue to look for romantic expressions of their 'primitive' existence. In reality, these artists have understood the concept of art making in market economy and are no longer willing to return to old lifestyles. The fourth chapter, written by Tanya Lyons and Mark Israel, also questions the heroic image and the illusion of 'equality' of women in the armed liberation struggles in Southern Africa. The authors analyse the contradictory representations of women as symbols of tradition ('mother of the nation') and as symbols of liberation/modernisation. They also suggest that one should look beyond the armed struggle and focus on more subtle forms of resistance through everyday activities and 'hidden transcripts', which illustrate a more complex involvement of women in resistance than previously believed.

Several chapters deal with 'politics' and 'democracy' in African states (Sierra Leone, Tanzania, Kenya, Uganda). The authors show how the state is viewed as a means of personal self-interest for authoritarian leaders and argue that the state has lost its meaning for the common man in Africa. 'Democracy' in Africa is thus seen as fragile, despite the emergence of electoral politics in the 1990s. The authors argue that the reality of African politics is characterised by 'ethnic enclaves' (Kenya), a 'movement system of government' seen as a 'camouflage' of a one-party state (Uganda) or interethnic rivalries (Zanzibar). These analyses reflect multiple local forms that a European state model has taken in Africa.

Two final chapters deal with the ideology and social practices of co-operatives in Zimbabwe and South Africa. In Chapter 11, Patrick McAllister analyses beer drinking in a co-operative in South Africa's Transkei as a part of a wider social entity, which links beer to labour within a system of reciprocal exchange. This analysis, together with articles in the beginning of the book, suggest the importance of contextualising social practices (that is, beer drinking, women's resistance, etc.) within a single local system, which often questions the accuracy of typologies and boundaries established by the modern European mind.

Interestingly, the authors of this collection of essays seem to focus more on dismantling the categories of European modernity than on analysing 'African identities' *as such*, as the name of the book suggests. However, the book provides interesting ideas on how to reflect on the crisis of modernity through analysing the reality of African states and the emerging (cross-border) social spaces, which define people's daily lives.

TERHI LEHTINEN
Department of Political Science,
University of Helsinki

From Kosovo to Kabul: Human Rights and International Intervention by David Chandler. London: Pluto Press, 2002. Pp.xv + 268. £14.99 (paperback). ISBN 0745318835

This is a brilliant book, which deserves the attention of all those interested in human rights, humanitarianism, Great Power foreign policy and contemporary multilateralism. The author covers a great deal of ground and makes a number of arguments, but his central point is that we appear to be living through a transition from foreign policy based on international law, regard for the UN Charter, and power-politics considerations, to a foreign policy which grants greater prominence to human rights and the intervention required to enforce them, particularly in weakened countries, especially in the Global South.

To do this, the author has written a book with six substantive chapters, in which he ranges broadly over the terrain of humanitarian intervention, ethical foreign policy, human rights theory, international law, 'Positive war' and sovereign (in)equality. He is particularly troubled by the neglected implications of the rise of the view that there are universal human rights, even in the absence of a global legislature to recognise and enforce them.

While Chandler makes reference to some common concerns, such as the selectivity of application of this new perspective, the book is most valuable for his articulation of some novel points. He argues that this new focus tends to present people as 'victims' or 'perpetrators', even if in some circumstances such distinctions are not so neat. It is based on a misanthropic view of the typical Southern state and a righteous view of 'Global Civil Society', which Chandler sees as dominated by the Western world. It is also accompanied by a transition *back to* sovereign inequality, in which double standards are accepted and even embraced, after an 80-year experiment in trying to build a rules-based global system, through the League of Nations, United Nations and the twentieth-century system of international law.

One strong stylistic aspect of this book is its sobriety. The author has produced a well-documented and serious work of scholarship that is not tendentious in the cause of either Realist power politics or Marxism or any other form of Critical Theory. Rather, this work will appeal to both groups, as against the liberal consensus that the author argues seems to be holding sway. The author on balance seems to hold 'progressive' views, but he is certainly not blind to the strengths of the cold war system of global relations, in which the existence of a counter-balancing Soviet Union restrained the *hubris* of the Western world, particularly the United States. The author also notes that the human-rights perspective takes the question of war and peace out of the realm of domestic debate, thus reducing governmental accountability to its population. On the last page of his book (p.236), Chandler argues that:

> the human rights discourse itself is deeply corrosive of the political process. There is little positive vision on offer, merely the distrust of governments and people in non-Western society and cynicism about the actions of governments and international institutions in the West.

On page 70 Chandler notes that the obligation to enforce human rights by-passes domestic accountability, but this reader could not help but notice that this has been happening at the same time as the 'Internationalisation of the state' more generally (a concept developed by Robert Cox), in which increasing numbers of public policies, such as fiscal, monetary, trade, investment and social policies are insulated from popular pressures.

Having said all this, there are a number of things that this reviewer would recommend to enhance the book. First, the author is clear in a number of places that he does not want to discuss the possibility that there is a 'hidden Great Power agenda'. Even briefly, it should be noted that there is a long tradition in which the most successful Great Power adventures are those in which people of varied and contradictory positions (such as Realism and Idealism) find reasons to support the policy. Further, is it a coincidence that so many of the regimes that the West has distaste for in fact owe their existence to past Western patronage?

Further, this reviewer would have welcomed some discussion of the origins of the human rights perspective. While Chandler does not discuss this, it is clear that what he calls the 'foreign policy of criticism' developed in the United States (particularly in Congress) after the Watergate scandal, at a time when the European countries resisted it. It would be useful to consider that with the end of the cold war this perspective has been projected to the global level, through a process like that described by Mark Rupert in *Producing Hegemony* (1995) on an earlier period in the twentieth century. This is clearly a very stimulating book, with valuable insights on virtually every page, which deserves to be widely discussed in a variety of disciplines.

GEOFF MARTIN
Department of Political Science,
Mount Allison University

The Economics of Poverty and Inequality edited by Frank A. Cowell. Cheltenham: Edward Elgar, 2003. Pp.xxxv + 1360. £340 (hardback). ISBN 1 84064 567 9

This book is number 158 in the International Library of Critical Writings in Economics series of thematically organised compilations. The two volumes contain 71 essays written by 84 authors, dating from 1896 to 2000. These include writings by famous economists such as Amartya Sen (with no less than four contributions), Francois Bourguignon, Joseph Stiglitz, A.C. Pigou and others, but of course also by a large number of less well known writers. The editor himself, Frank A. Cowell, has five contributions in addition to his introduction. The oldest article is Vilfredo Pareto's 1896 paper, 'On the Distribution of Wealth and Income', which is published in an English translation from 2001, and the most recent article is by Peter Vallentyne (2000), 'Equality, Efficiency, and the Priority of the Worse-off'. The collection only covers articles published in English, or where translations have already been published. This means that for instance Gini's 1914 article on inequality, where he introduces the Gini coefficient, 'Sulla misura della concentrazione e della variabilità dei caratteri', is not included; instead, an article in English where Gini draws attention to this work is taken in. The publisher should perhaps have put a little more resources into the finished layout, for instance by inserting a title page before each article. The articles reproduce their original layout and chapters taken from monographs frequently do not list the name of the author, thus making the book difficult to navigate.

This type of thematic compilation is of interest to readers for different reasons at different times. The first thing this reviewer did was to look up some of the rare original articles that are otherwise hard to come across, such as the original article by Lorenz from 1905 (Vol.1, pp.133–219) with hand-drawn Lorenz curves of the income distributions in Prussia in 1892 and 1901. However, of the 71 contributions, only ten were written before 1960, indicating that the aim of this anthology is not to provide a history of economic thought in the field of poverty and inequality, but rather to include the writings that today remain the defining contributions within this field.

Hence, after the rarities, the main interest lies in the compilation of seminal articles that makes this book a reference work for researchers working within the field. For example, Foster, Greer and Thorbecke's 1984 article, 'A Class of Decomposable Poverty Measures' (Vol.2, pp.165–70) or Sen's 1976 article, 'Poverty: An Ordinal Approach to Measurement' (Vol.2, pp.199–211) are widely quoted in essays on the topic of poverty measures and it is tremendously useful to have such contributions at hand, both when reading today's debates, and of course for one's own writing.

Furthermore, this type of collection allows the reader the possibility of following the debate among economists, as several of these articles reply to, elaborate on, or refute arguments made in other articles. For instance, Amiel and Cowell refer in a footnote of their 1992 article (Vol.1, p.100) to a text by Pigou from 1912. With these two articles in the same book, the interested reader can easily verify if Pigou actually said what Amiel and Cowell claim, which, incidentally, he did not.

The editor has organised the writings in 17 chapters, where the bulk of Volume 1 (first eight chapters) focus on inequality and the bulk of Volume 2 (last nine chapters) focus on poverty. The editor's introduction gives a succinct summary of the arguments put forward in each of these chapters, thereby also exposing the logical structure of the book. Unfortunately, Cowell's introduction does not give any account of the considerations behind the selection of writings, and this is a weak point in the book. Surely, some of the choices made have been subject to constraints (for example, type of publication, language), while others reflect the editor's judgement of the merits and importance of the various contributors to this field. As it is, the reader is unaware of these judgements.

The selected writings are almost all from economic journals, close to half are from the following four: *Econometrica* (14 articles), *Journal of Economic Theory* (eight articles), *Economic Journal* (five articles) and *Review of Economic Studies* (four articles). A few pieces are from non-economic journals and 11 are chapters from books. This indicates how the anthology concentrates on income- or consumption-based approaches to inequality and poverty that lend themselves to mathematical analysis. Sen's 1983 paper 'Poor, relatively speaking' introduces the alternative 'human capability approach' to poverty analysis, but this is typically one of the contributions that the editor does not mention in his introduction. The editor appears to select writings that are analysing poverty and inequality primarily with mathematical tools, leaving little room for contributions such as Sen's.

For a practitioner, the absence of World Bank publications is somewhat surprising, as this institution to a large extent shapes the debate on poverty in the global context. Many of the contributors are, or have been, affiliated with the World Bank (among them the current Chief Economist and one of his predecessors), but their contributions are not

World Bank publications. Without moving into other social sciences by referring to the 'Voices of the Poor', why not at least include some of the writings (for instance the World Development Report 1990) that introduced the $1/$2 poverty lines? These publications have had an enormous impact on both the practical and theoretical perspectives on poverty in the 1990s because of the World Banks ability to place the debate within its own analytical framework.

PÅL SLETTEN
Institute for Applied International Studies, Fafo

From the Local to the Global: Key Concepts in Development Issues edited by Gerard McCann and Stephen McClosky. London: Pluto Press, 2003. Pp.240. £13.99 (paperback). ISBN 0 7453 1812 6

The term 'development' can be endlessly unpacked and debated and students approaching the subject for the first time are often daunted by the seemingly innumerable interpretations and approaches. Likewise the term 'globalisation', which is open to contention and discussion, confuses students. Books that help in explaining what development is – or rather, what it can be – are hence of major importance and relevance. This is particularly so when the belief that there exists a sort of universally applicable set of economic laws that development must fit with. The book interrogates the ability of states to oversee the markets in a globalised, neoliberal world and seeks to ask how they might employ such processes to advance developmental goals and social needs. Those that (rightly) reject the hegemonic notion that there is no alternative often struggle to come up with alternatives and certainly seem to not succeed in informing and shaping development practice. The book under review is thus an important contribution to the debate and one that can – and without doubt will – be used in pushing the debate regarding development.

In the light of shifting definitions of what constitutes development, this very powerful term is evidently a historically contingent form of knowledge, closely tied to dominant structures and global power relations. It is not some sort of ahistorical set of universally applicable goals, as the book makes clear. Indeed, it is important that the book challenges the dominant neo-liberal discourse surrounding globalisation and development that seeks to represent as 'inevitable' the push to create a global free market. Thus the volume starts out with an enlightening chapter on what constitutes development in the globalisation era. The attempt to narrow down research on globalisation, which this book implicitly rejects, is significant not least because it has important normative implications for the direction of study, enabling the acceptance and rejection of 'appropriate' research agendas, such as the development implications of globalisation.

The book evaluates the tasks and characters of multilateral organisations. Focusing on the World Trade Organisation and the World Bank, the contributors seek to unpack the developmental implications of such bodies, as well as scrutinising other important developmental questions such as colonial legacy, global justice, aid, security, poverty, debt education, gender and the environment. All of these issues are contextualised within broader global political economy.

The book is a student-friendly and wide-ranging overview to the main debates and ideas associated with development. I can easily imagine using the book in class to help students work through the concepts they need in order to grasp the sources of poverty and unfairness in the world. The book has contributions mostly from Northern Ireland and the Republic of Ireland, but many of these are people with experience in the developing world. There are a couple of contributions from the global South. I think it is a very useful text and one that I will certainly be using. I warmly recommend it.

IAN TAYLOR
Department of Political and Administrative Studies,
University of Botswana

Publications Received

The following publications have been received by the journal. Appearance in this list does not preclude review in the *EJDR*.

Adeoti, John O., 2002, *Technology and the Environment in Sub-Saharan Africa: Emerging Trends in the Nigerian Manufacturing Industry*. Aldershot: Ashgate. Pp.xi + 275. £47.50 (hb). ISBN 0 7546 1990 7

Ahluwalia, Pal and Abebe Zegeye (eds.), 2002, *African Identities: Contemporary Political and Social Challenges*. Aldershot: Ashgate. Pp.xiv + 175. £42.50 (hb). ISBN 0 7546 1947 8

Ahmad, Mokbul Morshed, 2002, *NGO Field Workers in Bangladesh*. Aldershot: Ashgate. Pp.xiii + 220. £42.50 (hb). ISBN 0 7546 0970 7

Behar, Jaime, Ulf Jonson and Mats Lundahl (eds.), 2002, *Currents of Change: Globalization, Democratization and Institutional Reform in Latin America*. Edsbruk, Sweden: Akademitryck AB. Pp.xi + 394. £19.99 (hb). ISBN 9 1858 9459 1

Berg-Schlosser, Dirk and Norbert Kersting (eds.), 2003, *Poverty and Democracy: Self-Help and Political Participation in Third world Cities*. London: Zed Books. Pp.xiii + 237. £16.95 (pb). ISBN 1 8427 7205 8

Berns, Jessica (Project Manager), 2003, *Corruption Fighters' Tool Kit: Civil Society Experiences and Emerging Strategies*. Berlin: Transparency International. Pp.63. £19.99 (pb). ISBN 3 935711 02 6

Brainard, Lael, Carol Graham, Nigel Purvis, Steven Radlet and Gayle E. Smith, 2003, *The Other War: Global Poverty and the Millenium Challenge Account*. Washington, DC: Brookings Institution Press. Pp.x + 265. £13.50 (pb). ISBN 0 8157 1115 8

Bryceson, Deborah Fahy (ed.), 2002, *Alcohol in Africa: Mixing Business, Pleasure and Politics*. Oxford: Greenwood. Pp.viii + 305. ISBN 0 3250 7115 2

Cawthra, Gavin and Robin Luckham (eds.), 2003, *Governing Insecurity: Democratic Control of Military and Security Establishments in Transitional Democracies*. London: Zed Books. Pp.xii + 340. £45.00 (pb). ISBN 1 8527 7149 3

Chan, Raymond K.H., Kwan Kwok Leung and Raymond M.H. Ngan, 2002, *Development in Southeast Asia: Review and Prospects*. Aldershot: Ashgate. Pp.xx + 265. £45.00 (hb). ISBN 1 8401 4863 2

Chandler, David, 2002, *From Kosovo to Kabul: Human Rights and International Intervention*. London: Pluto Press. Pp.xv + 268. £14.99 (pb). ISBN 0 7453 1883 5

Cleaver, Francis (ed.), 2003, *Masculinities Matter! Men, Gender and Development*. London: Zed Books. Pp.xiv + 241. £15.95 (pb). ISBN 1 8427 7065 9

Coakley, John (ed.), 2003, *The Territorial Management of Ethnic Conflict*. London and Portland, OR: Frank Cass. Pp.xiii + 330. £17.50 (pb). ISBN 0 7146 8051 6

Cowell, Frank A., 2003, *The Economics of Poverty and Inequality Vols.I–II*. Cheltenham: Edward Elgar. Pp.1,350. £340.00 (hb). ISBN 1 8406 4567 9

Das, Bhagirath Lal, 2003, *WTO: The DOHA Agenda. The New Negotiations on World Trade*. New York: Zed Books. Pp.vii + 121. $17.50 (pb). ISBN 1 8427 7299 6

Degnbol-Martinussen, John and Poul Engberg-Pedersen, 2003, *Aid: Understanding International Development Cooperation*. London: Zed Books. Pp.xv + 350. £27.50 (pb). ISBN 1 8427 7039 X

Dunn, Kevin C., 2003, *Imagining the Congo: The International Relations of Identity*. Basingstoke: Palgrave MacMillan. Pp.x + 214. £16.99 (pb). ISBN 1 4039 6160 3

Dutt, Amitava Krishna and Jaime Ros (eds.), 2003, *Development Economics and Structuralist Macroeconomics*. Cheltenham: Edward Elgar. Pp. xi + 450. £85.00 (hb). ISBN 1 8406 4939 9

Ellis, Patricia, 2003, *Women, Gender and Development in the Caribbean: Reflections and Projections*. London: Zed Books. Pp.x + 181 (pb). ISBN 1 8564 9933 2

Fitzgerald, E.V.K., 2003, *Global Markets and the Developing Economy*. Basingstoke: Palgrave Macmillan. Pp.xxix + 224. £50.00 (hb). ISBN 1 4039 1538 5

Galal, Ahmed and Bernard Hoekman (eds.), 2003, *Arab Economic Integration: Between Hope and Reality*. Washington, DC: Brookings Institution Press. Pp.viii + 170. £15.00 (pb). ISBN 0 8157 3031 4

Gatzweiler, Franz W., Renate Judis and Konrad Hagedorn, 2002, *Sustainable Agriculture in Central and Eastern European Countries: The Environmental Effects of Transition and Needs of Change*. Berlin: Shaker Verlag. Pp.xvii + 378. n/g

Gore, Charles (team leader), 2002, *The Least Developed Countries Report 2002*. Geneva: UNCTAD. Pp.xiv + 285. ISBN 9 2111 2562 6

Gray, Clive S. (ed.), 2003, *Inside Independent Nigeria: Diaries of Wolfgang Stolper 1960–1962*. Aldershot: Ashgate. Pp.xxx + 321. £35.00 (hb). ISBN 0 7546 0995 2

Griffiths, Peter, 2003, *The Economist's Tale: A Consultant Encounters Hunger and the World Bank*. London: Zed Books. Pp.viii + 248. £15.95 (pb). ISBN 1 8427 7185 X

Hill, Tony, 2002, *Voluntary Approaches to Corporate Responsibility: Readings and a Resource Guide*. Geneva: United Nations. Pp.viii + 211. n/g

Inozemtsev, Vladislav L., 2001, *Les Leurres de l'Economie de Rattrapage: La fracture postindustrielle*. Paris: L'Harattan. Pp.vii + 379. n/g (pb). ISBN 2 7475 1651 2

Inozemtsev, Vladislav L., 1998, *The Constitution of the Post-economic State*. Aldershot: Ashgate. Pp.xviii + 435. n/g (pb). ISBN 1 184014 706 7

Inozemtsev, Vladislav L., 2001, *One World Divided: Existing Causes and Possible Results of the Coming Post-Economic Revolution*. Leeds: Wisdom House. Pp.xviii + 542. n/g (pb). ISBN 1 8429 0002 1

Kirby, Peadar, 2003, *Introduction to Latin America: Twenty-First Century Challenges*. London: Sage Publications. Pp.xv + 229. £ 18.99 (pb). ISBN 0 7619 7373 7

Laws, Sophie, Caroline Harper and Rachel Marcus, 2003, *Research for Development: A Practical Guide*. London: Sage. Pp.xiii + 475. £70.00 (pb). ISBN 0 7619 7327 3

Lloyd-Evans, Sally and Robert B. Potter, 2002, *Gender, Ethnicity and the Informal Sector in Trinidad*. Aldershot: Ashgate. Pp.xiii + 300. £45.00 (hb). ISBN 0 7546 1256 2

Logan, B. Ikubolajeh (ed.), 2002, *Globalization, the Third World State and Poverty-Alleviation in the Twenty-First Century*. Aldershot: Ashgate. Pp.vii + 203. £39.95 (hb). ISBN 0 7546 0923 5

Morrison, Christian, 2002, *Education and Health Expenditure, and Development: The Cases of Indonesia and Peru*. Paris: OECD. Pp.166. £18.00 (pb). ISBN 9 2641 8714 6

Mans, Minette, 2003, *Music as Instrument of Diversity and Unity*. Uppsala: Nordic Africa Institute. Pp.55. £7.95 (pb). ISBN 9 1710 6510 5

McCann, Gerard and Stephen McCloskey (eds.), 2003, *From the Local to the Global: Key Issues in Development Studies*. London: Sterling. Pp.xi + 260 £13.99 (pb). ISBN 0 7453 1812 6

McConnel, D.J., 2003, *The Forest Farms of Kandy and other Gardens of Complete Design*. Aldershot: Ashgate. Pp.vii + 535. £69.95 (hb). ISBN 0 7546 0958 8

McIntyre, Robert J. and Bruno Dallago (eds.), 2003, *Small and Medium Enterprises in Transitional Economies*. Basingstoke: Palgrave Macmillan. Pp.xv + 261. £50.00 (hb). ISBN 1 4039 0800 1

Mikhalev, Vladimir (ed.), 2003, *Inequality and Social Structure during the Transition*. Basingstoke: Palgrave Macmillan. Pp.xi + 313. £55.00 (hb). ISBN 1 4039 0801 X

Mukhija, Vinit, 2003, *Squatters as Developers? Slum Redevelopment in Mumbai*. Aldershot: Ashgate. Pp.xv + 190. £45.00 (hb). ISBN 0 7546 1910 9

Nitsch, Manfred, 2002, *Glaspalâste und Mikrofinanz*. Frankfurt am Main: Peter Lang. Pp.228. n/g (pb). ISBN 3 6313 8563 3

O'Brien, Karen and Coleen Vogel (eds.), 2003, *Coping with Climate Variability: The Use of Seasonal Climate Forecasts in Southern Africa*. Aldershot: Ashgate. Pp.xvi + 220. £55.00 (hb). ISBN 0 7546 1766 1

O'Hanlon, Michael, 2003, *Expanding Global Military Capacity for Humanitarian Intervention*. Washington, DC: Brookings Institution Press. Pp.x + 125. £13.95 (pb). ISBN 0 8157 6441 3

Pearce, David, Corin Pearce and Charles Palmer (eds.), 2002, *Valuing the Environment in Developing Countries: Case Studies*. Cheltenham: Edward Elgar. Pp.xii + 585. £ 95.00 (hb). ISBN 1 8406 4148 7

Pottier, Johan, Alan Bicker and Paul Sillitoe (eds.), 2003, *Negotiating Local Knowledge: Power and Identity in Development*. London: Pluto Press. Pp.vi + 332. £16.99 (pb). ISBN 0 7453 2006 6

Ray, Kalyan (ed.), 2003, *Water and Sanitation and the World's Cities: Local Actions for Global Goals*. London: Earthscan. Pp.xxv + 274. n/g (pb). ISBN 1 8440 0004 2

Robinson, Mary, 2003, *Duties sans Frontières: Human Rights and Global Social Justice*. Vernier: Atar Roto Press. Pp.iv + 94. n/g (pb). ISBN 2 9402 5933 X

Tomasevski, Katarina, 2003, *Education Denied: Costs and Remedies*. London: Zed Books. Pp.xiv + 203. £15.95 (pb). ISBN 1 8427 7251 1

Toye, John (ed.), 2003, *Trade and Development: Directions for the 21st Century*. Cheltenham: Edward Elgar. Pp.vi + 321. £69.95 (hb). ISBN 1 8437 6044 4

Zeller, Manfred and Richard L. Meyer (eds.), 2003, *The Triangle of Microfinance: Financial Sustainability, Outreach and Impact*. Baltimore, MD: The Johns Hopkins University Press. Pp.xxii + 399. $35.00 (pb). ISBN 0 8018 722

NOTES FOR CONTRIBUTORS

The European Journal of Development Research is a refereed journal. Articles submitted to *The European Journal of Development Research* should be original contributions and should **not** be under consideration for any other publication at the same time. If another version of the article is under consideration by another publication, or has been, or will be published elsewhere, authors should clearly indicate this at the time of submission. Articles may be submitted in English; French or Spanish.

Manuscripts should be submitted as email attachments to ejdr@eadi.org. Articles should be formatted as A4/letter documents, double spaced and with ample margins. All pages (including those containing only diagrams and tables) should be numbered consecutively.

There is no standard length for articles but 7,000 words (including notes and references) is a useful target. The article should begin with an indented and italicised summary of around 100 words, which should describe the main arguments and conclusions of the article.

Details of the author's institutional affiliation, full address and other contact information should be included on a separate coversheet. Any acknowledgements should be included on the coversheet, as should a note of the exact length of the article.

All diagrams, charts and graphs should be referred to as figures and consecutively numbered. Tables should be kept to a minimum and contain only essential data. Each figure and table must be given an Arabic numeral, followed by a heading, and be referred to in the text.

Following acceptance for publication, articles should be submitted on high density 3½ inch disks IBM PC or Macintosh compatible (Microsoft Word is preferred but files in WP 5.1 are also acceptable), together with a hard copy. To facilitate the typesetting process, notes should be grouped together at the end of the file. Tables should also be placed at the end of the file. Tables should be saved as text using the appropriate function within your word processor. If this function is not available then tables should be prepared using tabs. Any diagrams or maps should be copied to a separate disk in uncompressed .TIF or .EPS format in individual files. These should be prepared in black and white. If maps and diagrams cannot be prepared electronically, they should be presented on good quality white paper. If mathematics are included 1/2 is preferred over ½.

Each disk should be labelled with the journal's name, article title, lead author's name and software used. It is the author's responsibility to ensure that where copyright materials are included within an article the permission of the copyright holder has been obtained. Confirmation of this should be included on a separate sheet enclosed with the disk. Copyright in articles published in *The European Journal of Development Research* rests with the publisher.

Authors are entitled to a copy of the issue in which their article appears and either 50 offprints or a PDF file of their article.

STYLE

Authors are responsible for ensuring that their manuscripts conform to the journal style. The Editors will not undertake retyping of manuscripts before publication. A guide to style and presentation is obtainable from the Editors, or from the Publisher, Taylor & Francis Ltd., 4 Park Square, Milton Park, Abingdon, Oxfordshire OX14 4RN, UK; Tel.: +44 (0)1235 828600; Fax: +44 (0) 1235 82900; Email: enquiry@tandf.co.uk.

NOTES

(a) Simple references without accompanying comments: to be inserted at appropriate place in text, underlined and in squared brackets stating author's surname, publication date of work referred to, and relevant pages, e.g. [*Délano and Lehmann, 1993: 62–3*].

(b) References with comments: to appear as Notes, indicated consecutively through the article by raised numerals corresponding to the list of Notes placed at the end.

(c) Book titles and names of journals should be underlined; titles of articles should be in single inverted commas (see below).

REFERENCES

A reference list should appear after the list of Notes. It should contain all the works referred to, listed alphabetically by author's surname (or name of sponsoring body where there is no identifiable author).

(a) References to books should give the author's surname, forename and/or initials, date of publication, title of publication (underlined), place of publication, and publisher. Thus:

Deere, Carmen Diana and M. León (eds.), 1987, *Rural Women and State Policy*, Boulder, CO: Westview Press.

Schüssel, W., 1982, 'Zu den wirtschaftspolitischen Positionen der österreichischen Volkspartei', in H. Abele, E. Nowotny, S. Schleicher and G. Winckler (eds.), *Handbuch der österreichischen Wirtschaftspolitik*, Vienna: Manz, pp.143–85.

(b) References to articles in periodicals should give the author's surname, forename and/or initials, the date of publication, the title of the article in single quotation marks, title of periodical (underlined), the number of the volume and issue in arabic numerals, and the page numbers:

Délano, Priscilla and D. Lehmann, 1993, 'Women Workers in Labour-Intensive Factories: The Case of Chile's Fish Industry', *The European Journal of Development Research*, Vol.5, No.2, pp.43–67.